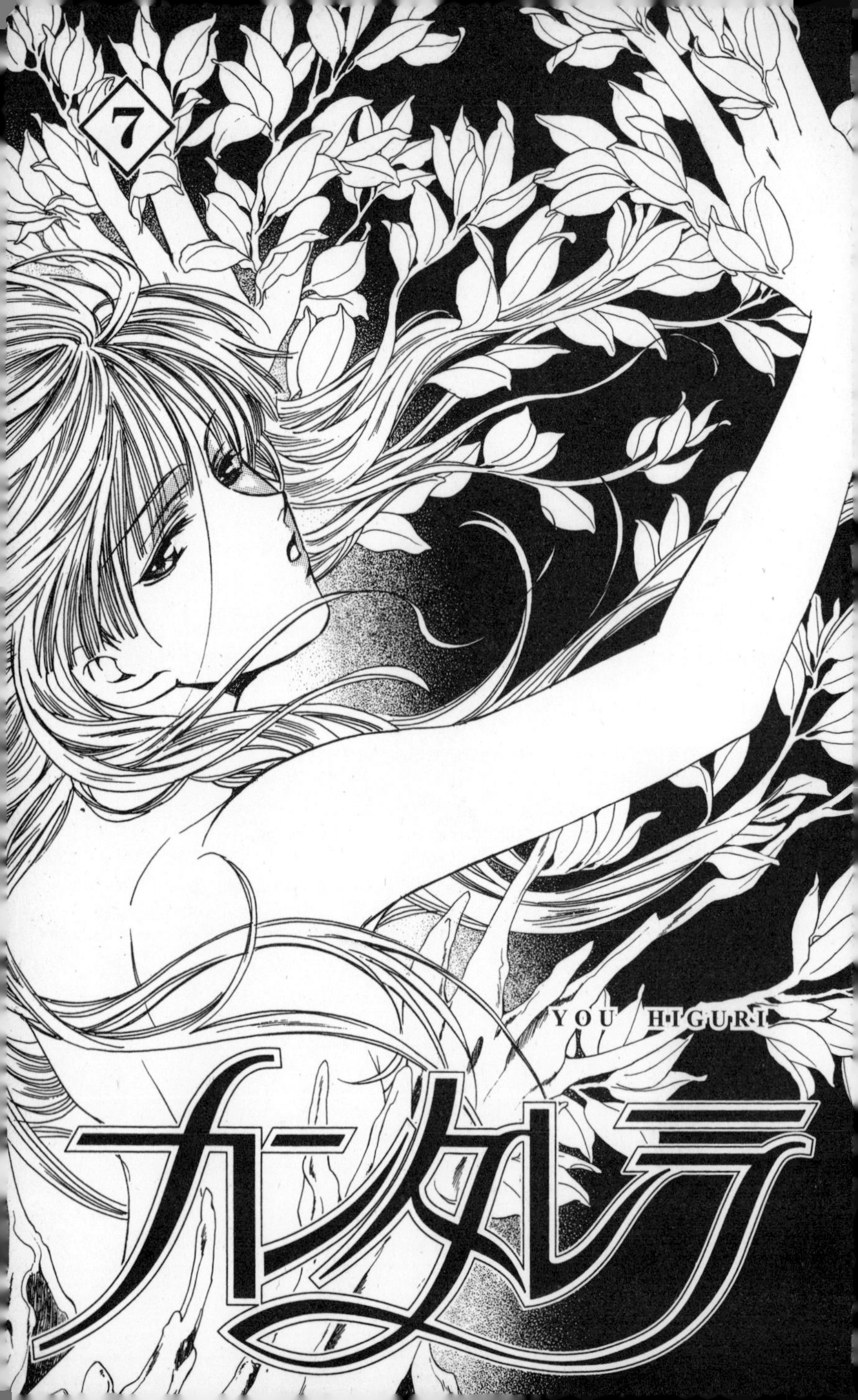
7
YOU HIGURI

Translation – Christine Schilling
Adaptation – Audry Taylor
Editorial Assistant – Mallory Reaves
Lettering & Design– Fawn Lau
Production Manager – James Dashiell
Editor – Brynne Chandler

A Go! Comi manga

Published by Go! Media Entertainment, LLC

Cantarella Volume 7
© YOU HIGURI 2004
Originally published in Japan in 2004 by Akita Publishing Co., Ltd., Tokyo.
English translation rights arranged with Akita Publishing Co., Ltd.
through TOHAN CORPORATION, Tokyo.

English Text © 2007 Go! Media Entertainment, LLC. All rights reserved.

Visit us online at www.gocomi.com
e-mail: info@gocomi.com

ISBN978-1-933617-26-8

First printed in June 2007

1   2   3   4   5   6   7   8   9

Manufactured in the United States of America

Cantarella

STORY AND ART BY
YOU HIGURI

VOLUME 7

go!comi

& Cast of Characters

Table of Contents

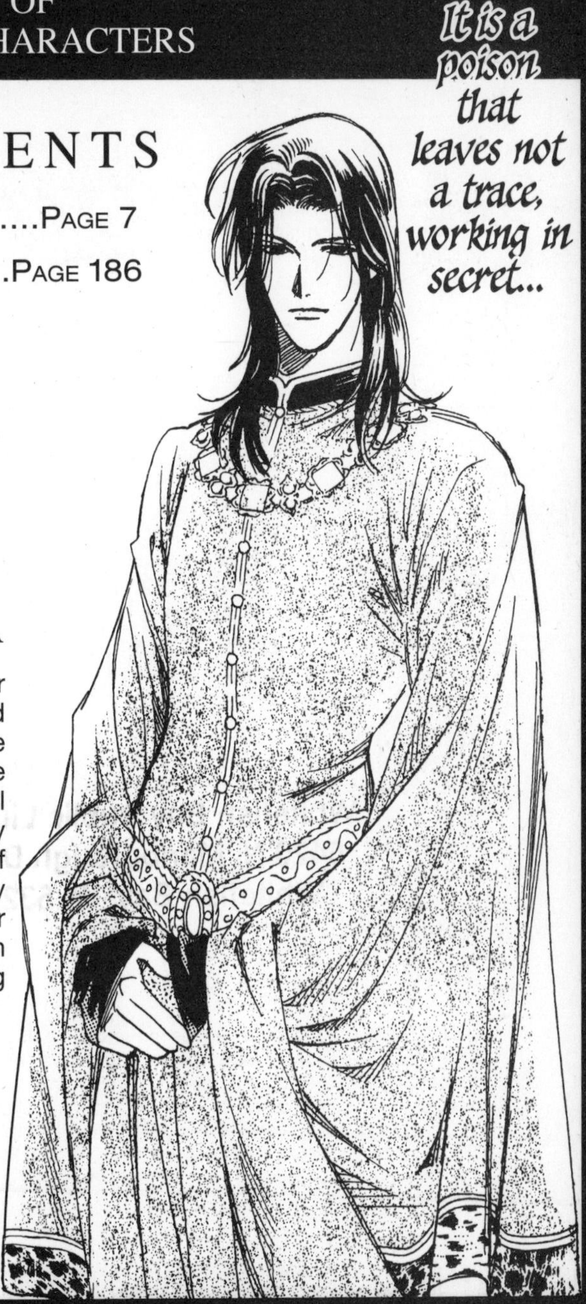
It is a poison that leaves not a trace, working in secret...

Cesare Borgia

The hero of our story. His father sold Cesare's soul to the devil in exchange for gaining the Papal throne. Constantly on the brink of being devoured by the demonic power within, he is driven by the all-consuming desire to unify Italy.

◆ POPE ALEXANDER VI ◆

An ambitious man who sold his own son's soul to the devil in exchange for the Papal throne. He has solidified his authority through nepotism.

◆ MICHELOTTO (CHIARO) ◆

A legendary assassin who wears the mask of "Michelotto." He holds the power to repel the evil spirits possessing Cesare.

◆ DELLA VOLPE ◆

Cesare's loyal retainer. He looks up to Cesare because of his tyrannical nature.

◆ LUCREZIA BORGIA ◆

A sweet girl who adores her older brother, Cesare. She was forced to wed the Lord of Pesaro but she has been called home and now resides in a monastery.

◆ IL PEROTTO ◆

A chamberlain of the Pope's.

◆ PANTACILIA ◆

Lucrezia's attendant. She would do anything to protect her precious charge.

STORY SO FAR

Separated by circumstances surrounding Juan's death, Cesare and Chiaro are forced to face their struggles alone. The demonic spirits possessing Cesare fight to take control of his body and without Chiaro around to suppress them, the mighty Cardinal finds himself rapidly falling under their power. While he presses himself to the very brink of madness, Chiaro heals his wounds in the arms of Lucrezia. But their romance may meet a bitter end when an envoy of the Pope uses the secret of their affair to blackmail Lucrezia...

Various cities and territories of Italy during *Cantarella* period
(end of the 15th century)

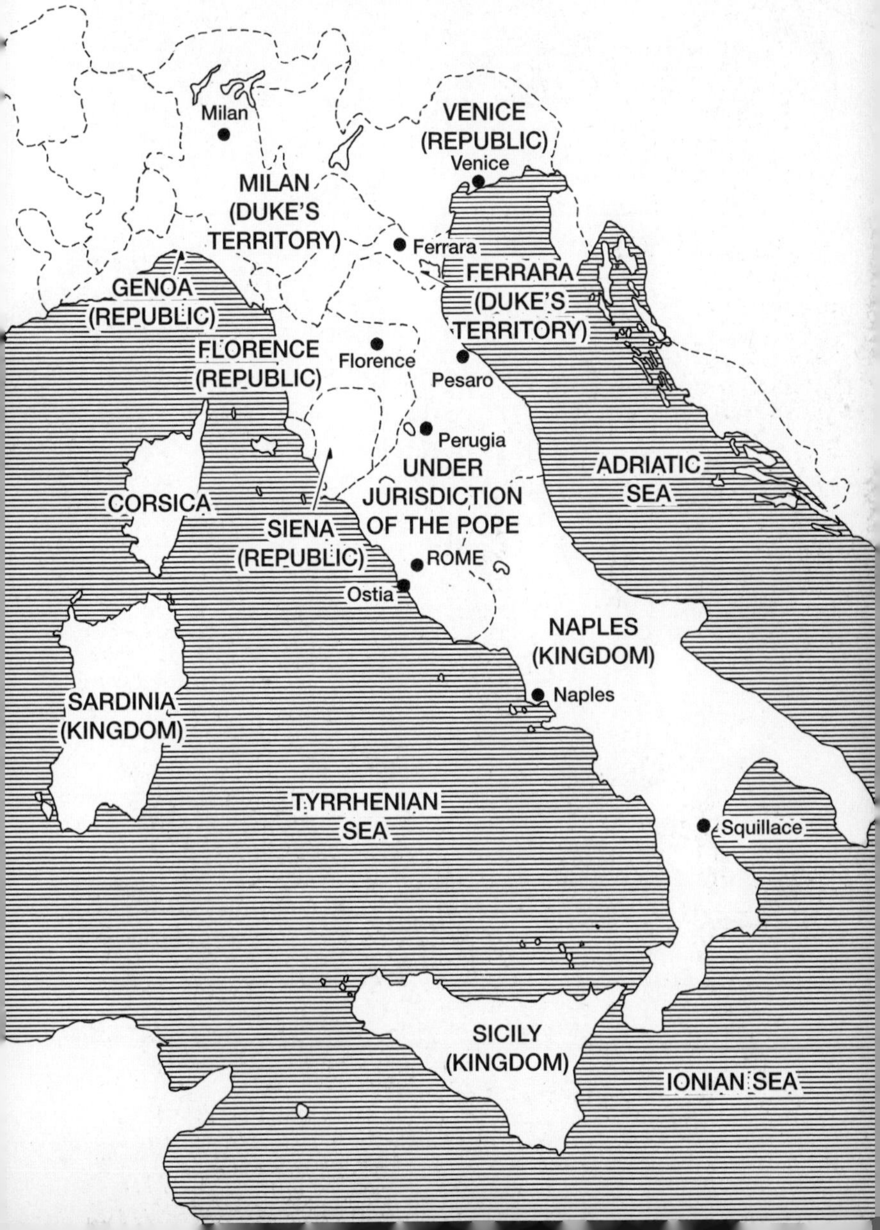

Milan
VENICE
(REPUBLIC)
Venice
MILAN
(DUKE'S
TERRITORY)
Ferrara
FERRARA
(DUKE'S
TERRITORY)
GENOA
(REPUBLIC)
FLORENCE
(REPUBLIC)
Florence
Pesaro
Perugia
UNDER
JURISDICTION
OF THE POPE
ADRIATIC
SEA
CORSICA
SIENA
(REPUBLIC)
ROME
Ostia
NAPLES
(KINGDOM)
Naples
SARDINIA
(KINGDOM)
TYRRHENIAN
SEA
Squillace
SICILY
(KINGDOM)
IONIAN SEA

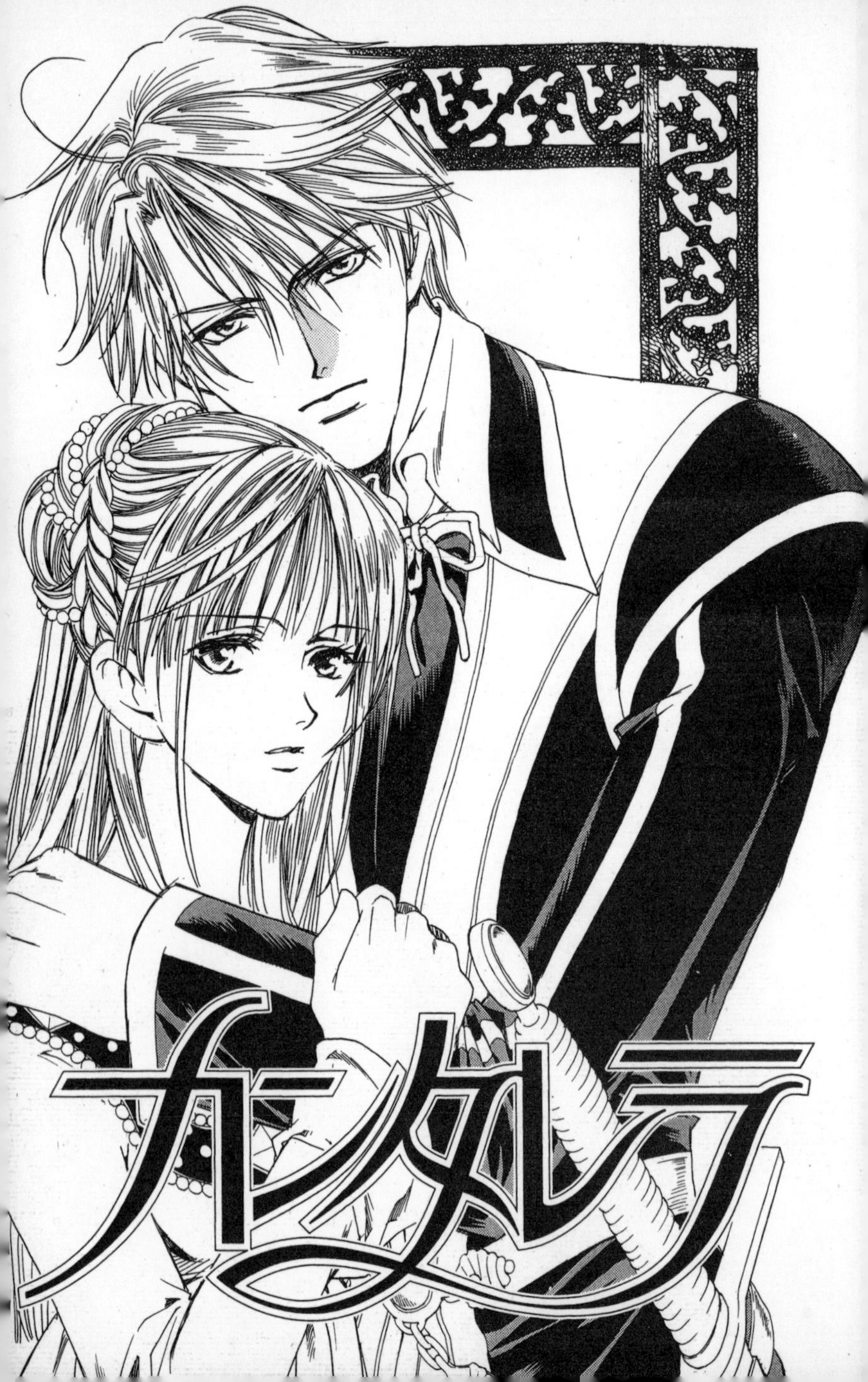

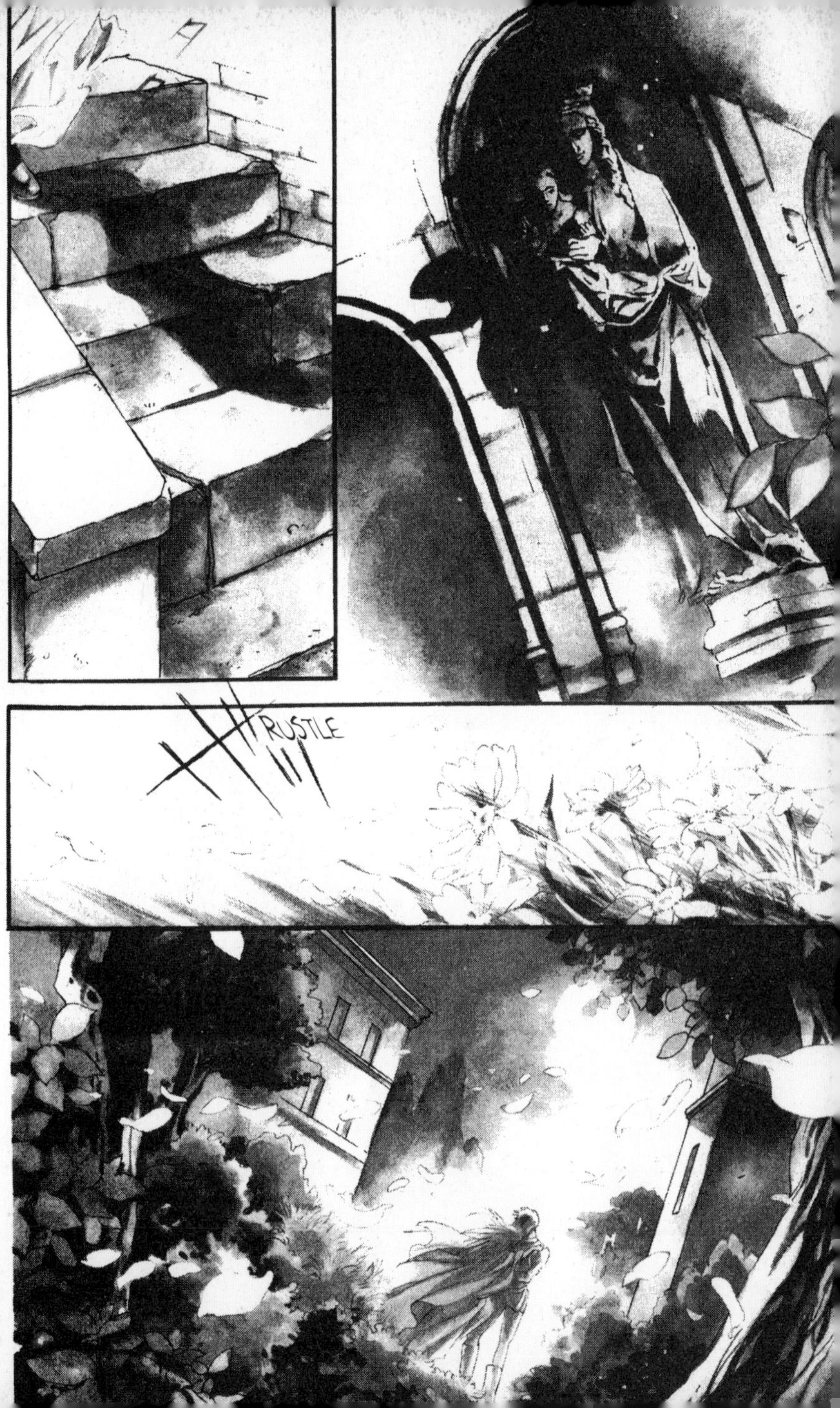
RUSTLE

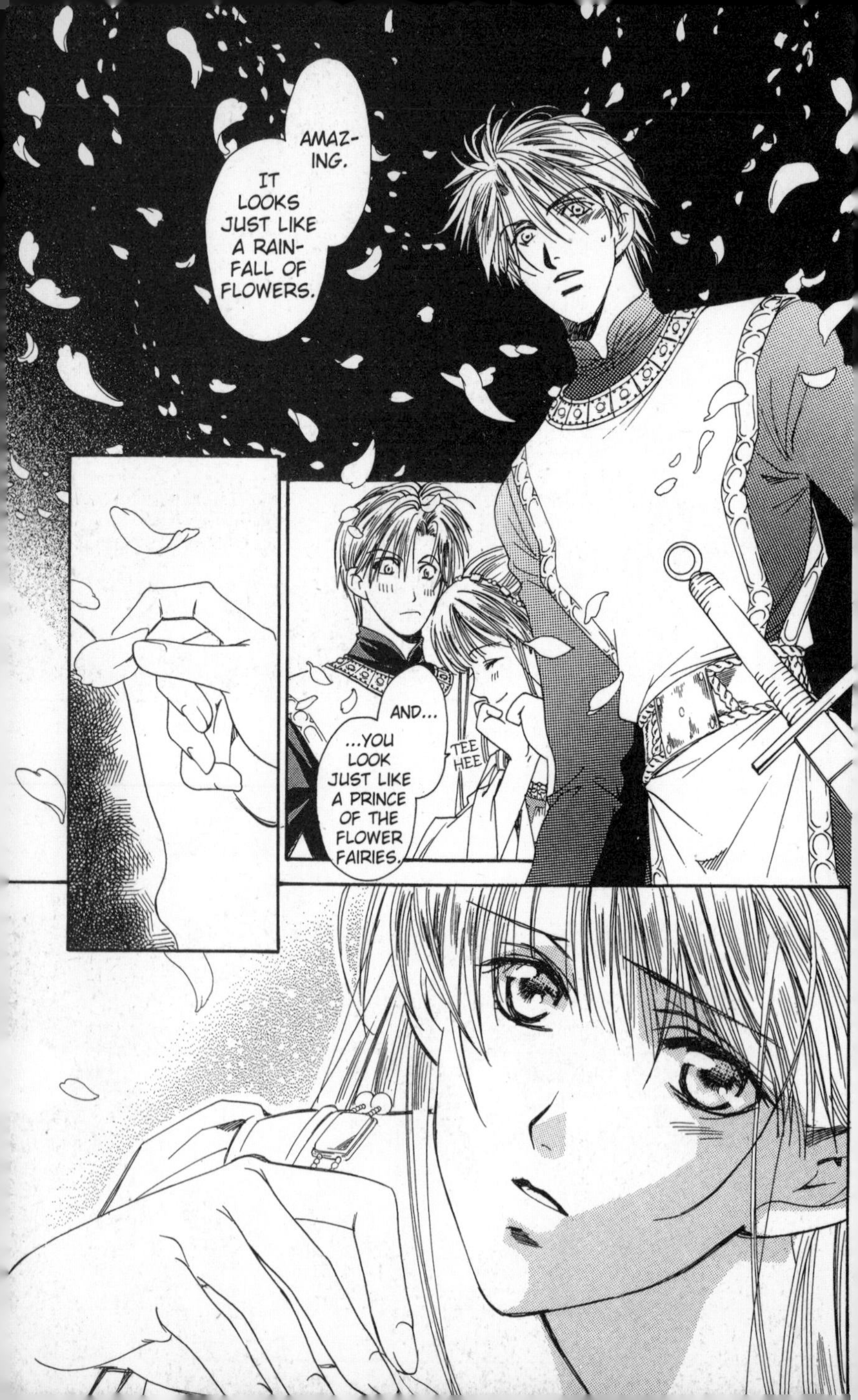
AMAZ-ING.
IT LOOKS JUST LIKE A RAIN-FALL OF FLOWERS.
AND...
...YOU LOOK JUST LIKE A PRINCE OF THE FLOWER FAIRIES.
TEE HEE

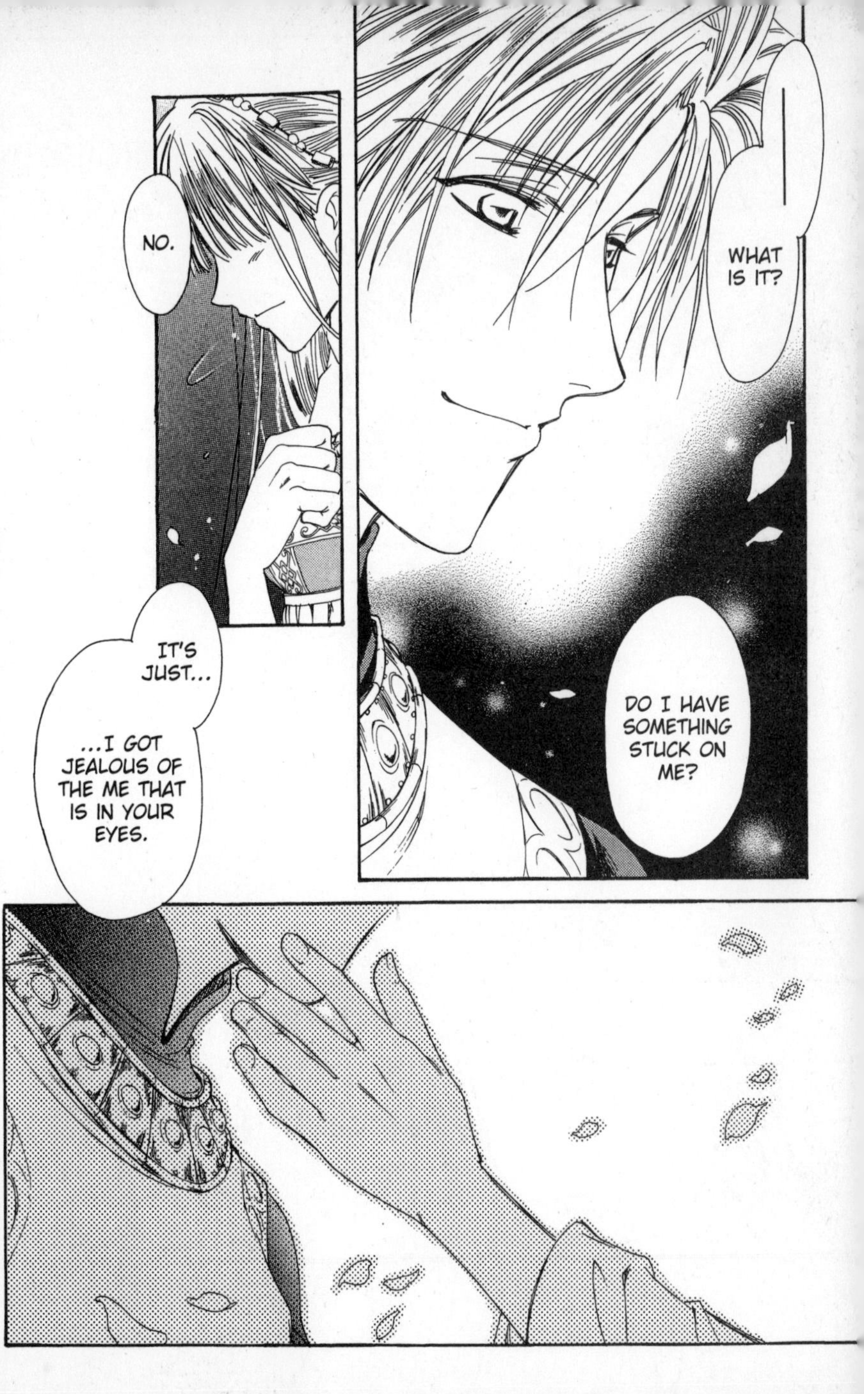
WHAT IS IT?
DO I HAVE SOMETHING STUCK ON ME?
NO.
IT'S JUST...
...I GOT JEALOUS OF THE ME THAT IS IN YOUR EYES.

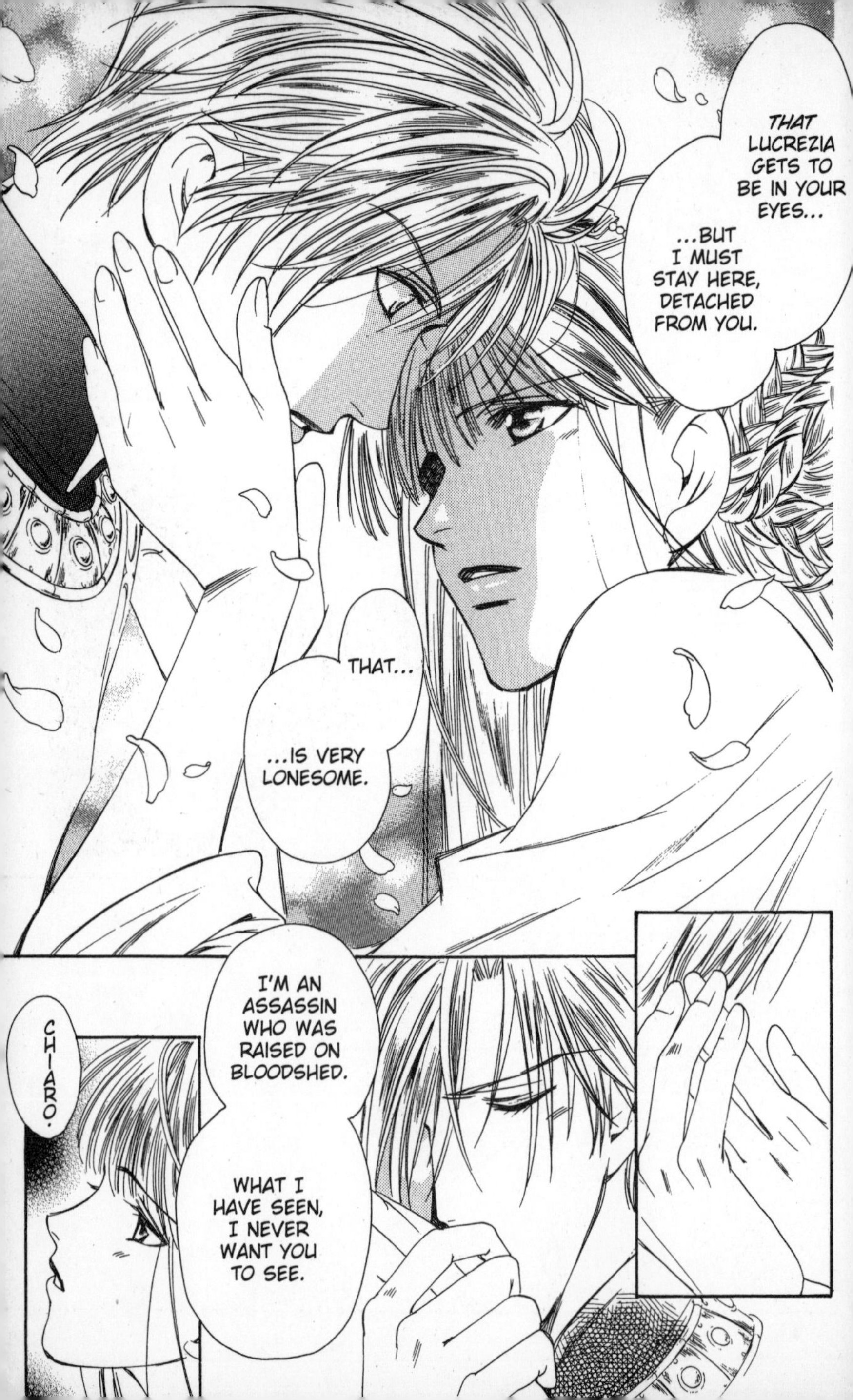
THAT LUCREZIA GETS TO BE IN YOUR EYES...
...BUT I MUST STAY HERE, DETACHED FROM YOU.
THAT...
...IS VERY LONESOME.
I'M AN ASSASSIN WHO WAS RAISED ON BLOODSHED.
WHAT I HAVE SEEN, I NEVER WANT YOU TO SEE.
CHIARO.

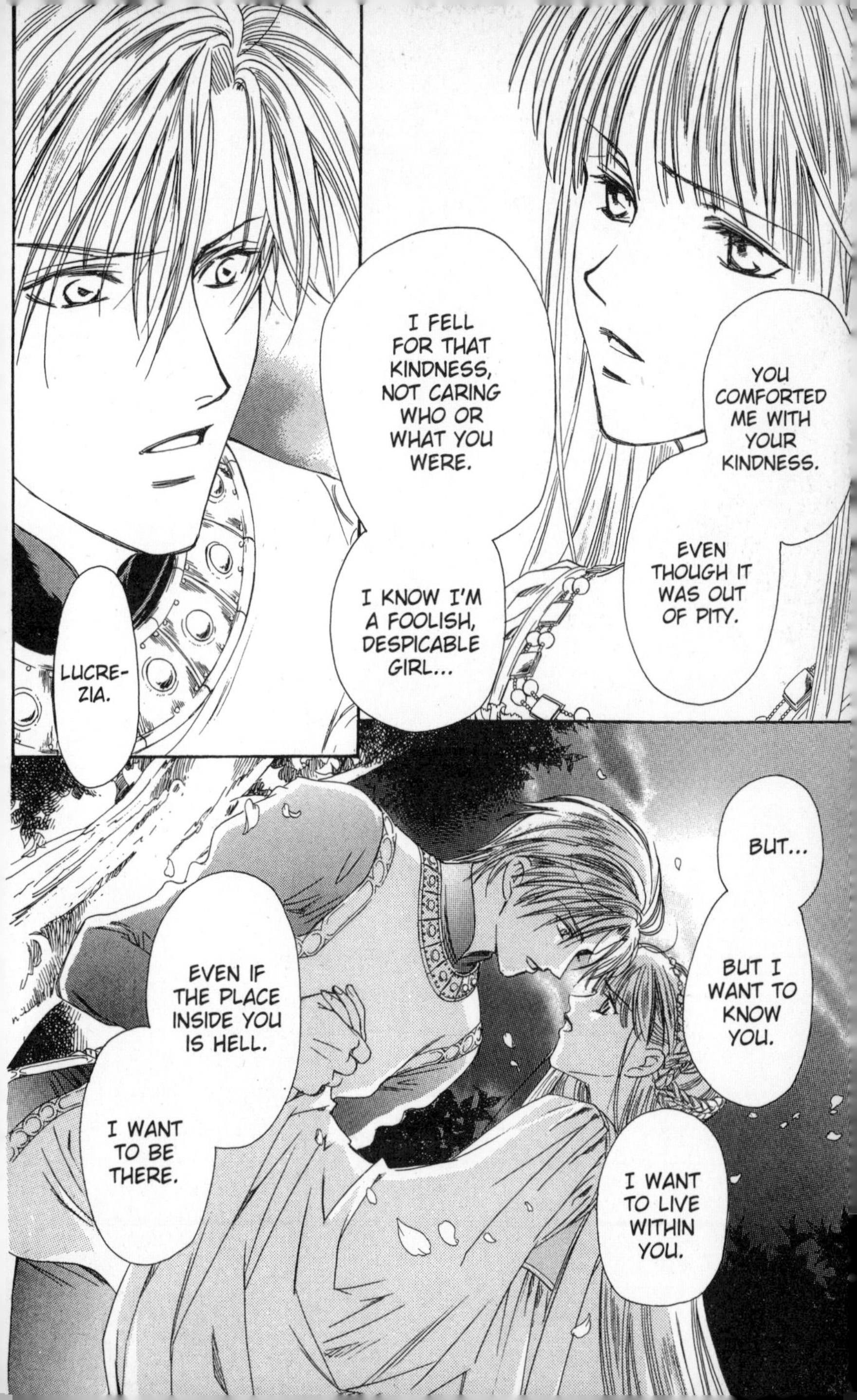
YOU COMFORTED ME WITH YOUR KINDNESS.
EVEN THOUGH IT WAS OUT OF PITY.
I FELL FOR THAT KINDNESS, NOT CARING WHO OR WHAT YOU WERE.
I KNOW I'M A FOOLISH, DESPICABLE GIRL...
LUCRE-ZIA.
BUT...
BUT I WANT TO KNOW YOU.
I WANT TO LIVE WITHIN YOU.
EVEN IF THE PLACE INSIDE YOU IS HELL.
I WANT TO BE THERE.

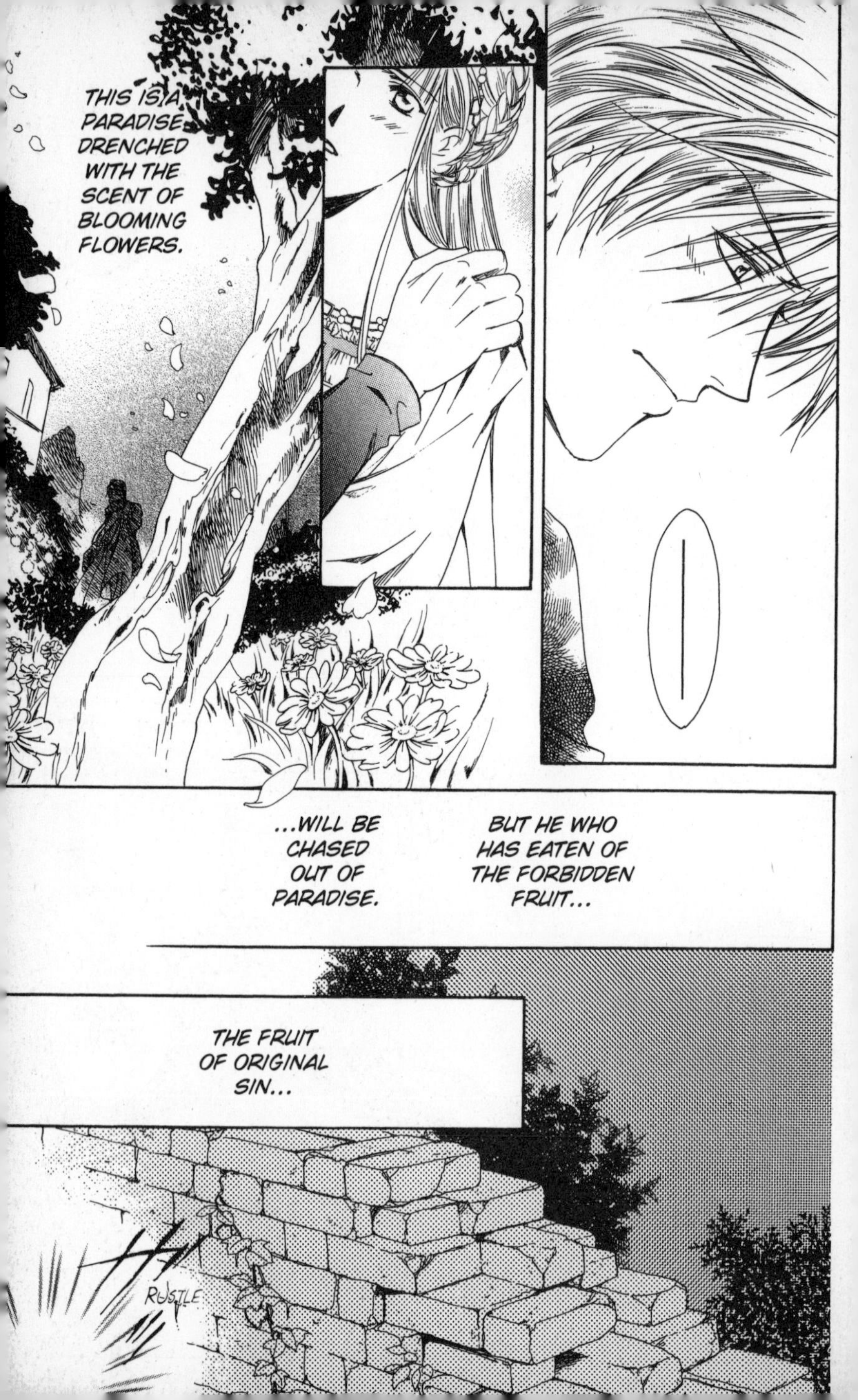
THIS IS A PARADISE DRENCHED WITH THE SCENT OF BLOOMING FLOWERS.
BUT HE WHO HAS EATEN OF THE FORBIDDEN FRUIT...
...WILL BE CHASED OUT OF PARADISE.
THE FRUIT OF ORIGINAL SIN...
RUSTLE

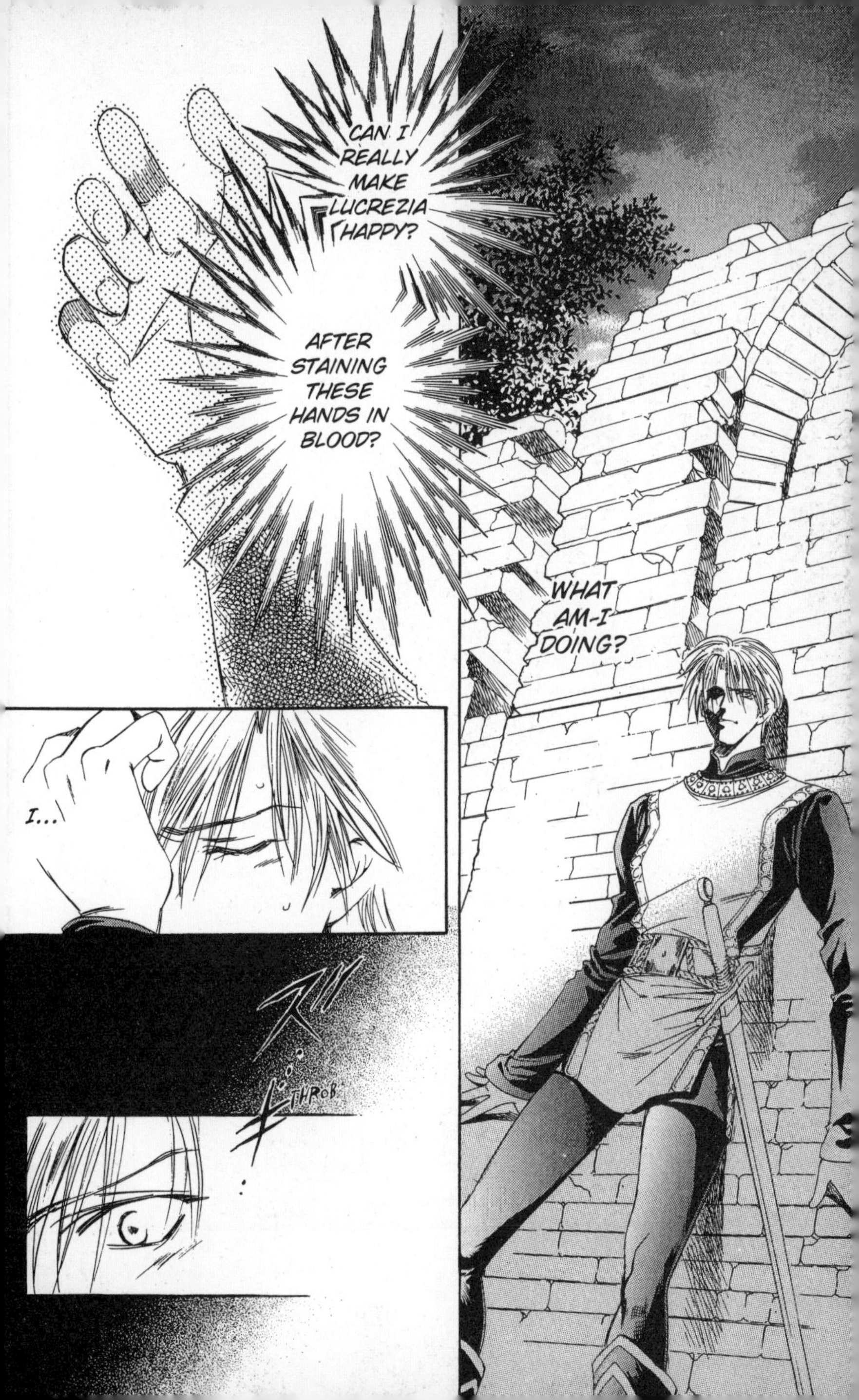
WHAT AM-I DOING?
CAN I REALLY MAKE LUCREZIA HAPPY?
AFTER STAINING THESE HANDS IN BLOOD?
I...
THROB

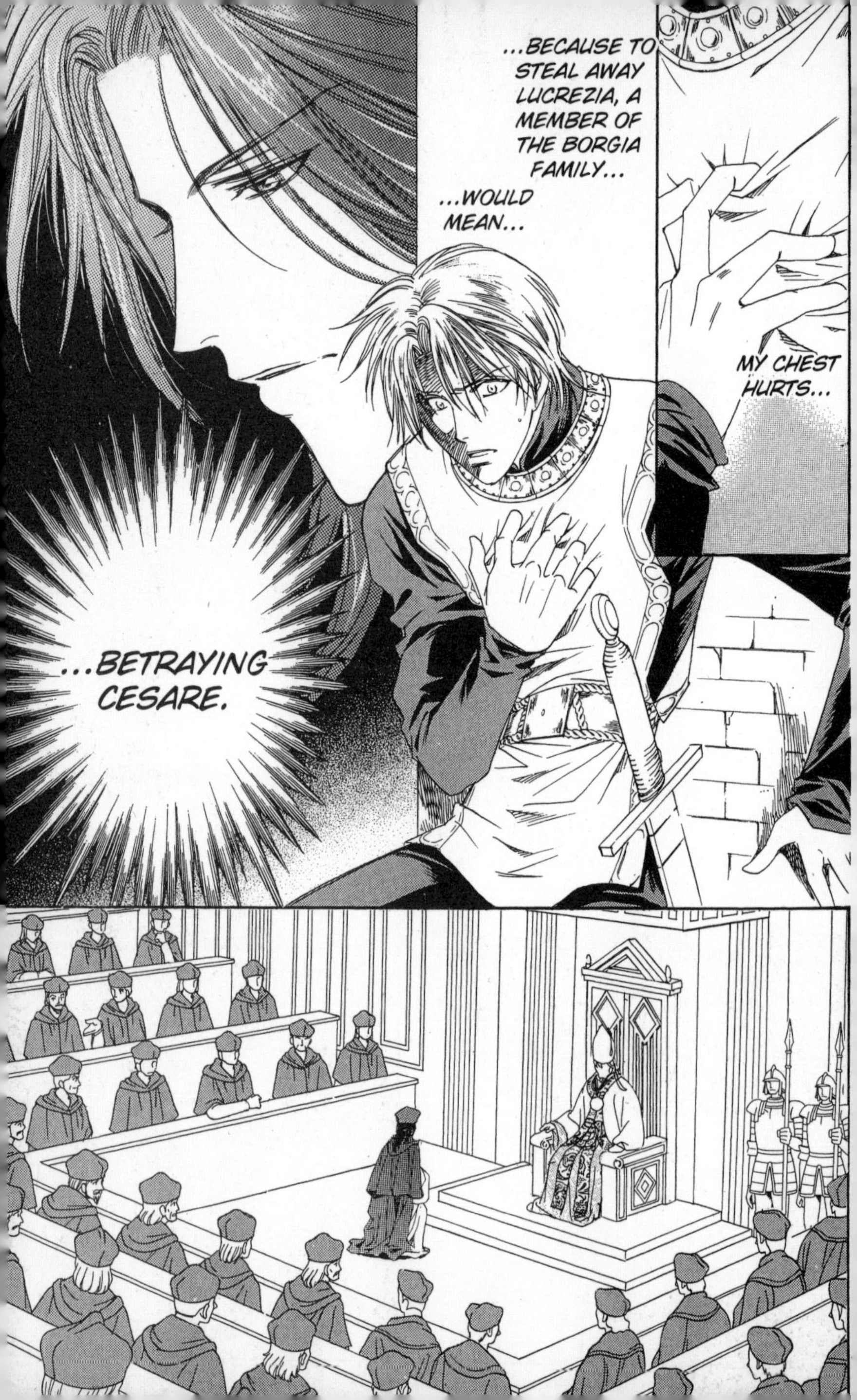
...BECAUSE TO STEAL AWAY LUCREZIA, A MEMBER OF THE BORGIA FAMILY...
...WOULD MEAN...
...BETRAYING CESARE.
MY CHEST HURTS...

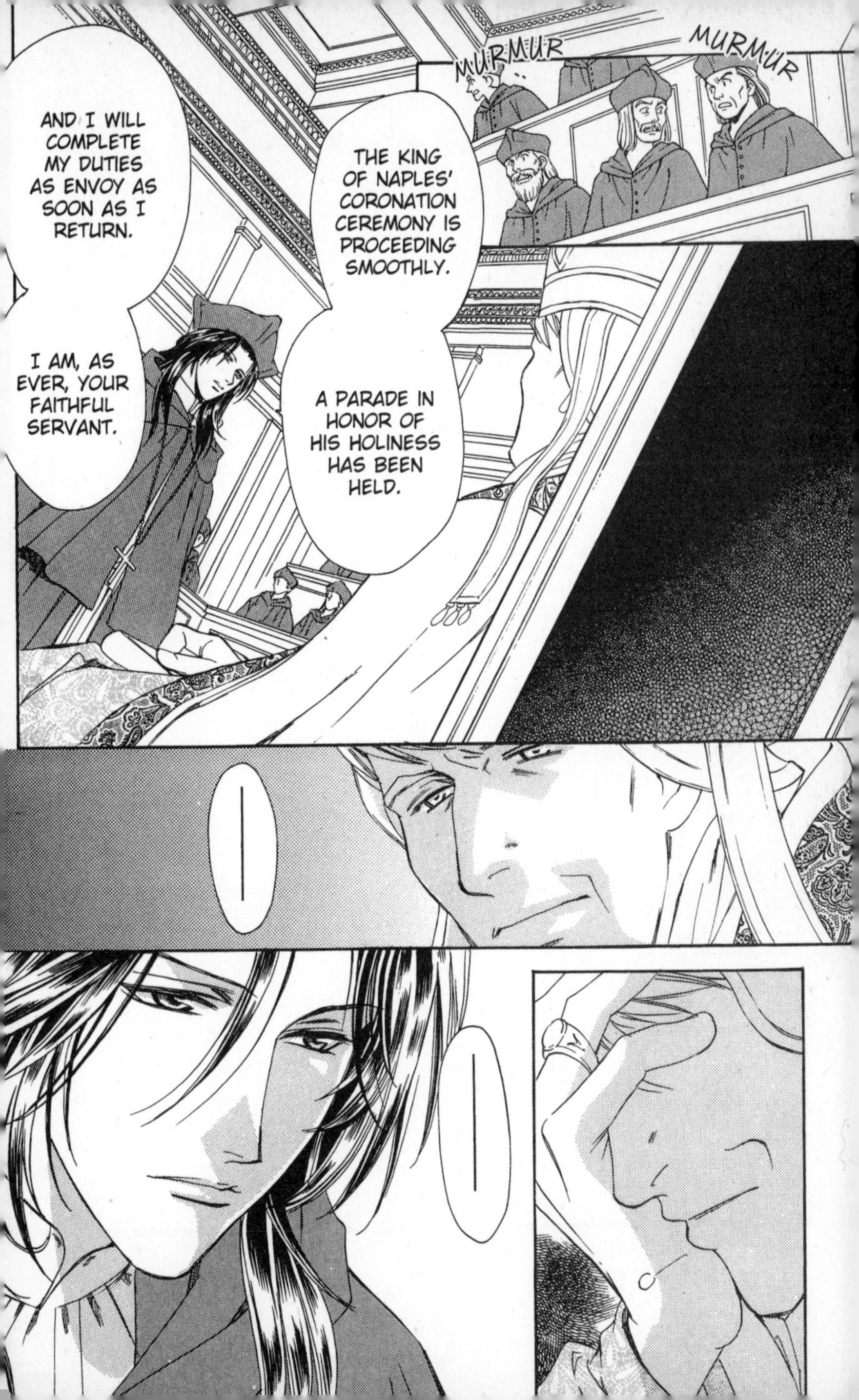
MURMUR
MURMUR
THE KING OF NAPLES' CORONATION CEREMONY IS PROCEEDING SMOOTHLY.
A PARADE IN HONOR OF HIS HOLINESS HAS BEEN HELD.
AND I WILL COMPLETE MY DUTIES AS ENVOY AS SOON AS I RETURN.
I AM, AS EVER, YOUR FAITHFUL SERVANT.
—
—

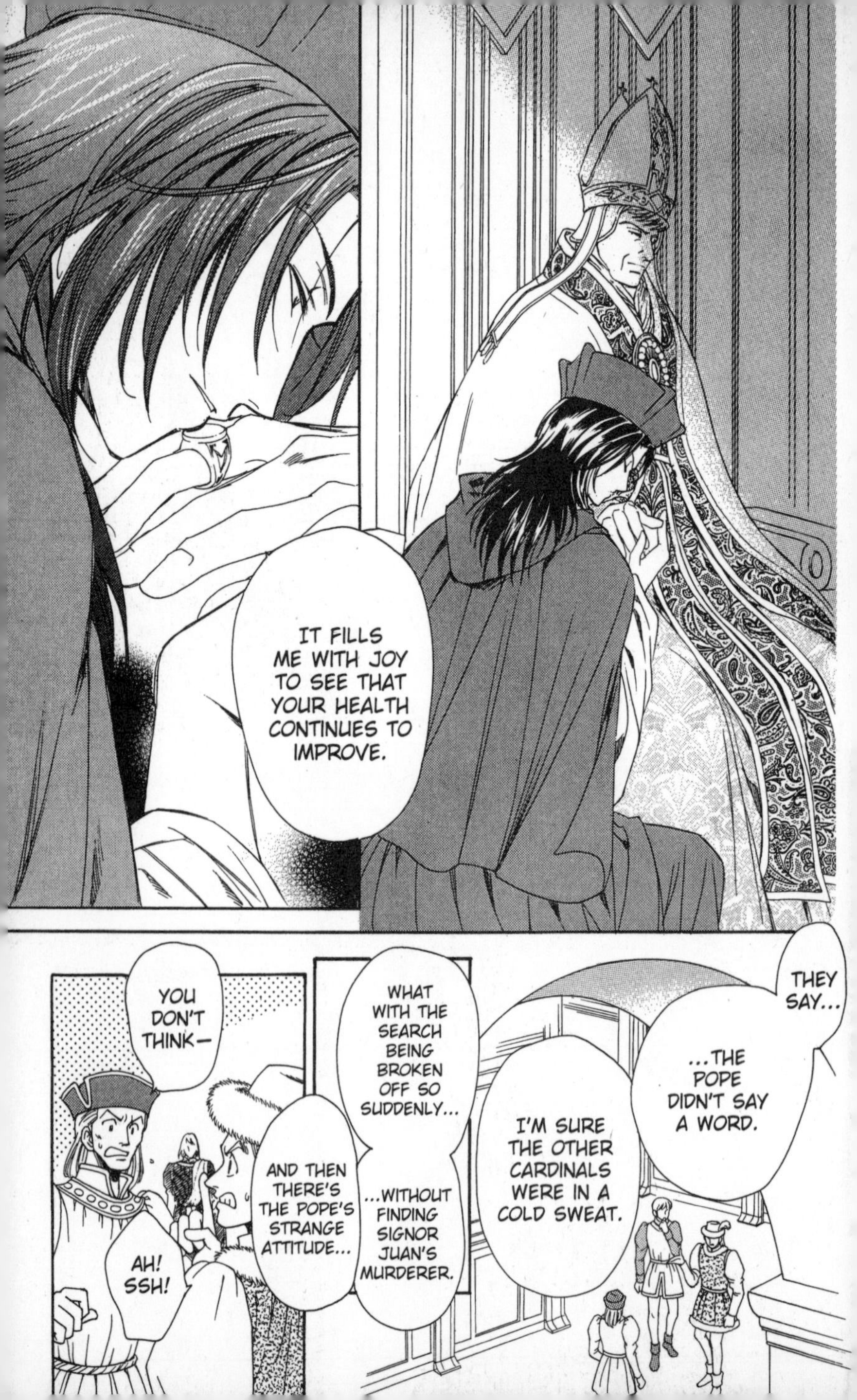
IT FILLS ME WITH JOY TO SEE THAT YOUR HEALTH CONTINUES TO IMPROVE.
THEY SAY...
...THE POPE DIDN'T SAY A WORD.
I'M SURE THE OTHER CARDINALS WERE IN A COLD SWEAT.
WHAT WITH THE SEARCH BEING BROKEN OFF SO SUDDENLY...
...WITHOUT FINDING SIGNOR JUAN'S MURDERER.
AND THEN THERE'S THE POPE'S STRANGE ATTITUDE...
YOU DON'T THINK—
AH! SSH!

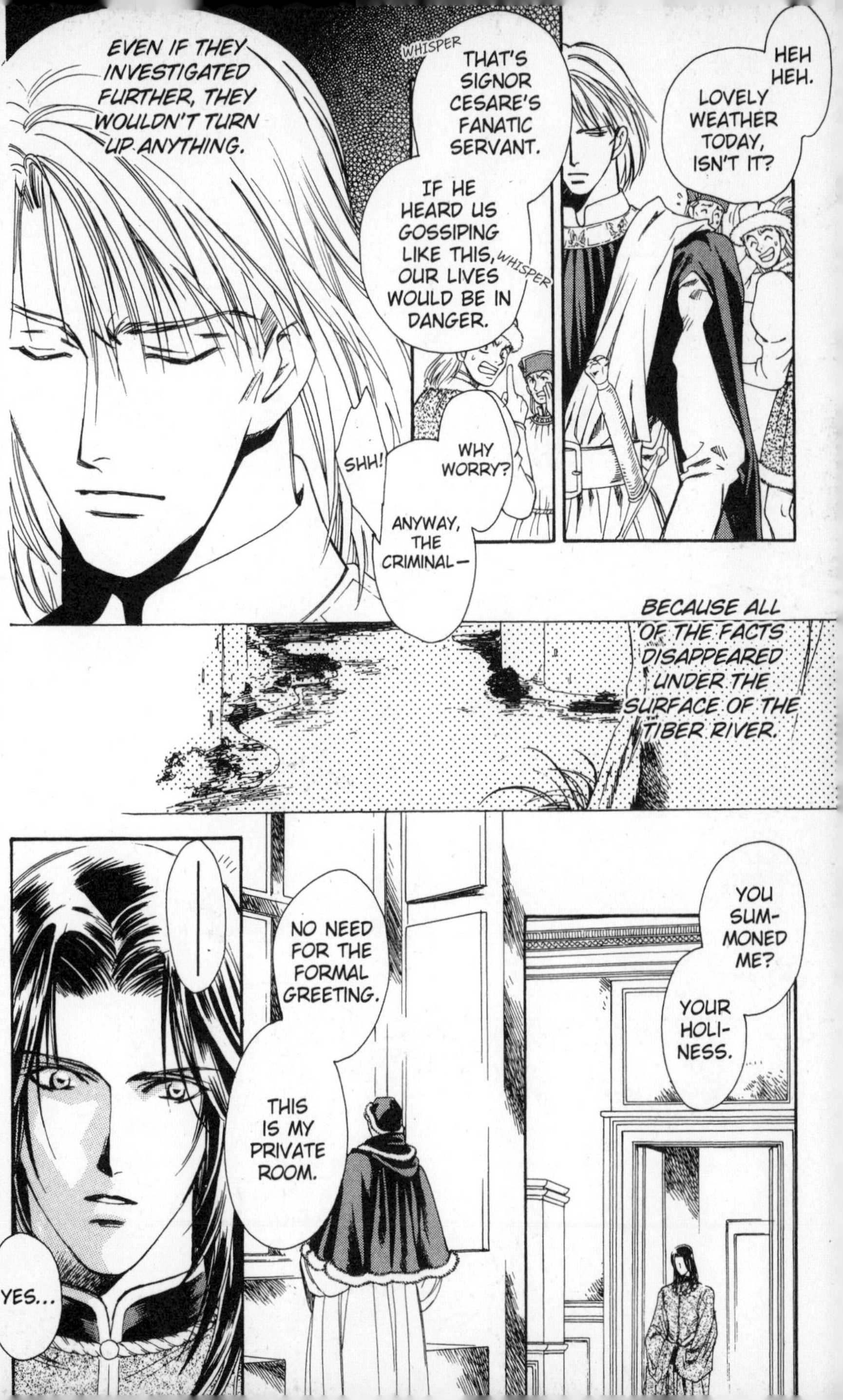

HEH HEH. LOVELY WEATHER TODAY, ISN'T IT?
WHISPER
THAT'S SIGNOR CESARE'S FANATIC SERVANT.
IF HE HEARD US GOSSIPING LIKE THIS, OUR LIVES WOULD BE IN DANGER.
WHISPER
WHY WORRY?
SHH!
ANYWAY, THE CRIMINAL—
EVEN IF THEY INVESTIGATED FURTHER, THEY WOULDN'T TURN UP ANYTHING.
BECAUSE ALL OF THE FACTS DISAPPEARED UNDER THE SURFACE OF THE TIBER RIVER.
YOU SUMMONED ME?
YOUR HOLINESS.
NO NEED FOR THE FORMAL GREETING.
THIS IS MY PRIVATE ROOM.
!
YES...

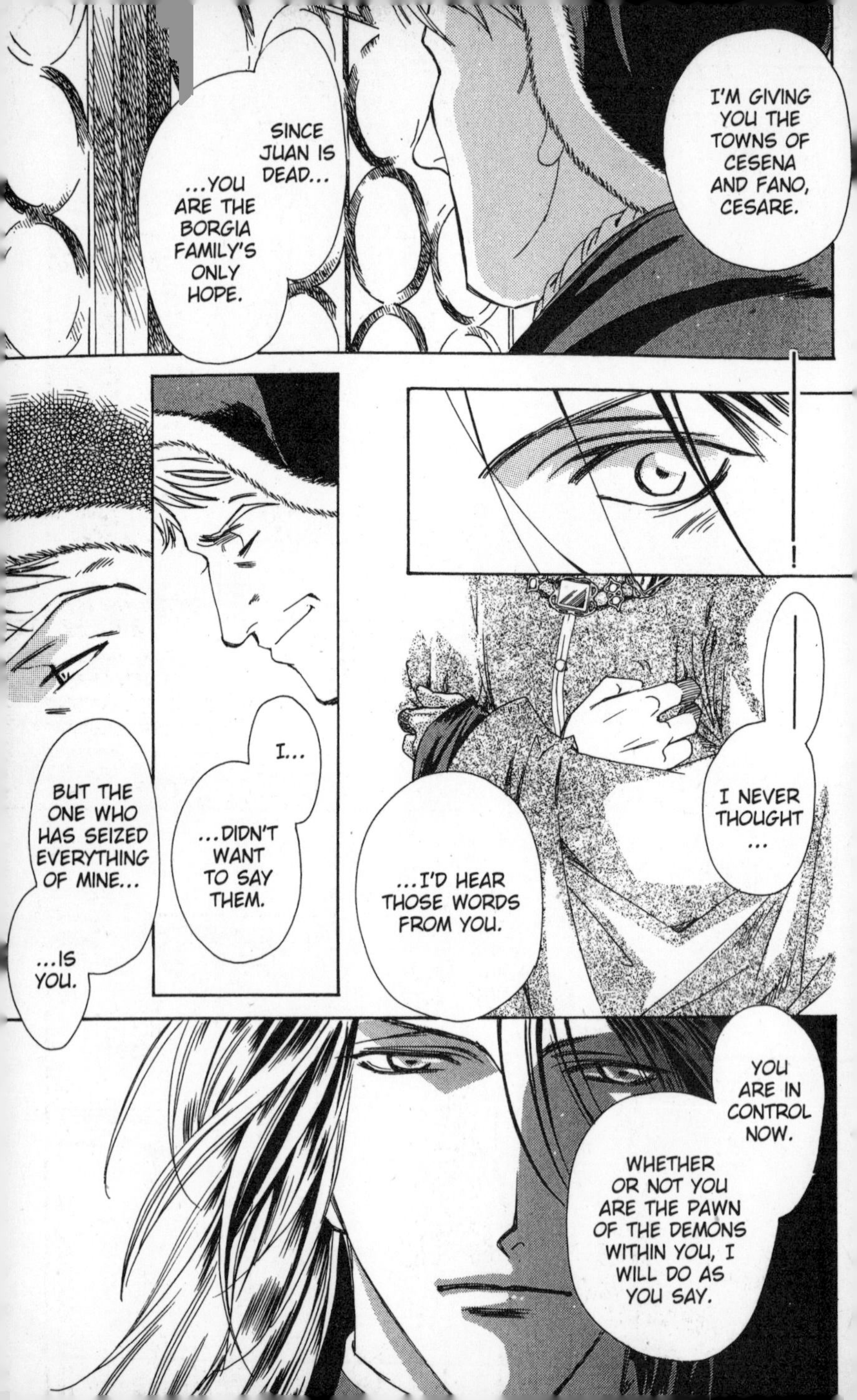

I'M GIVING YOU THE TOWNS OF CESENA AND FANO, CESARE.
SINCE JUAN IS DEAD...
...YOU ARE THE BORGIA FAMILY'S ONLY HOPE.
I NEVER THOUGHT ...
...I'D HEAR THOSE WORDS FROM YOU.
I...
...DIDN'T WANT TO SAY THEM.
BUT THE ONE WHO HAS SEIZED EVERYTHING OF MINE...
...IS YOU.
YOU ARE IN CONTROL NOW.
WHETHER OR NOT YOU ARE THE PAWN OF THE DEMONS WITHIN YOU, I WILL DO AS YOU SAY.

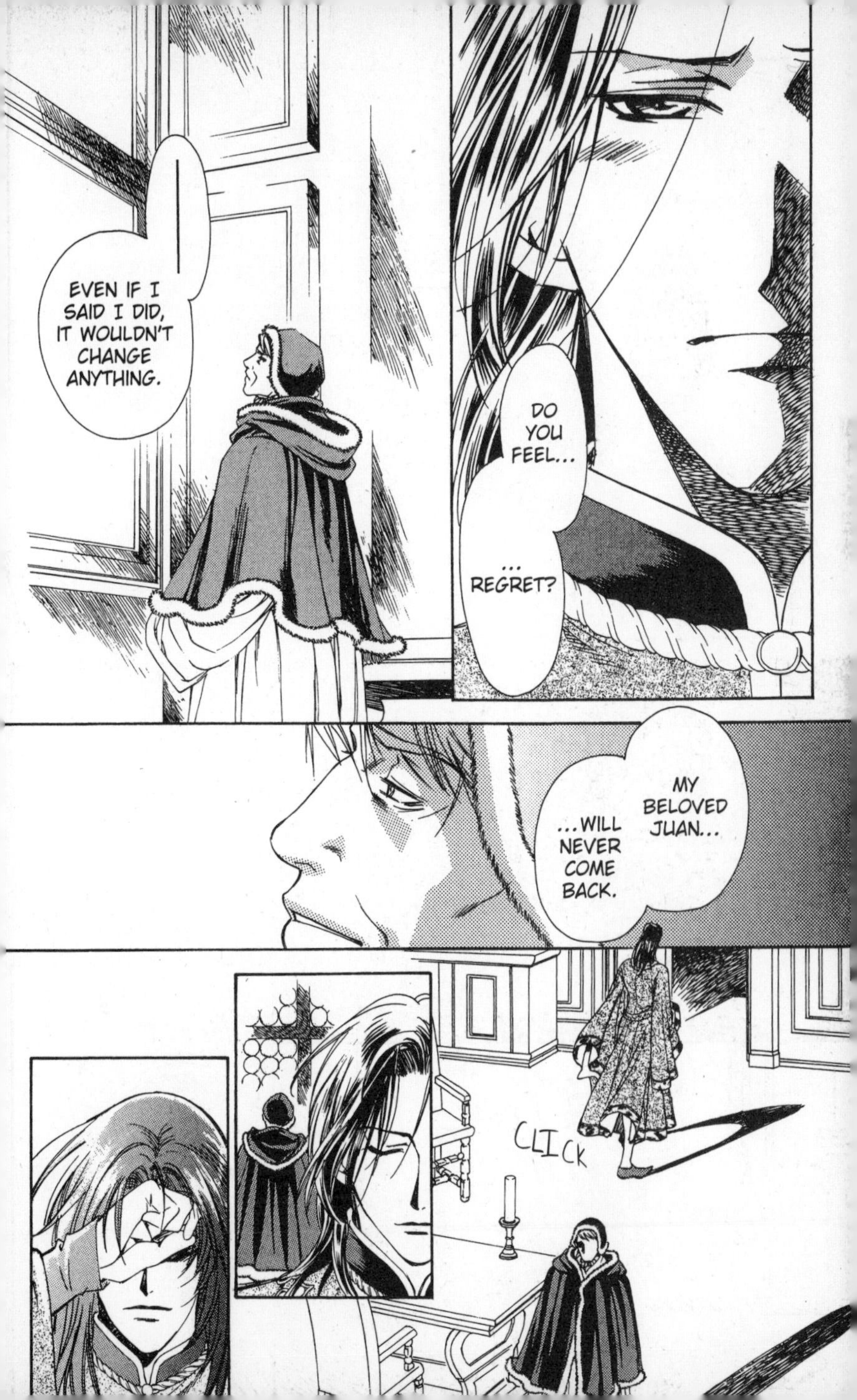
DO YOU FEEL...
...REGRET?
EVEN IF I SAID I DID, IT WOULDN'T CHANGE ANYTHING.
MY BELOVED JUAN...
...WILL NEVER COME BACK.
CLICK

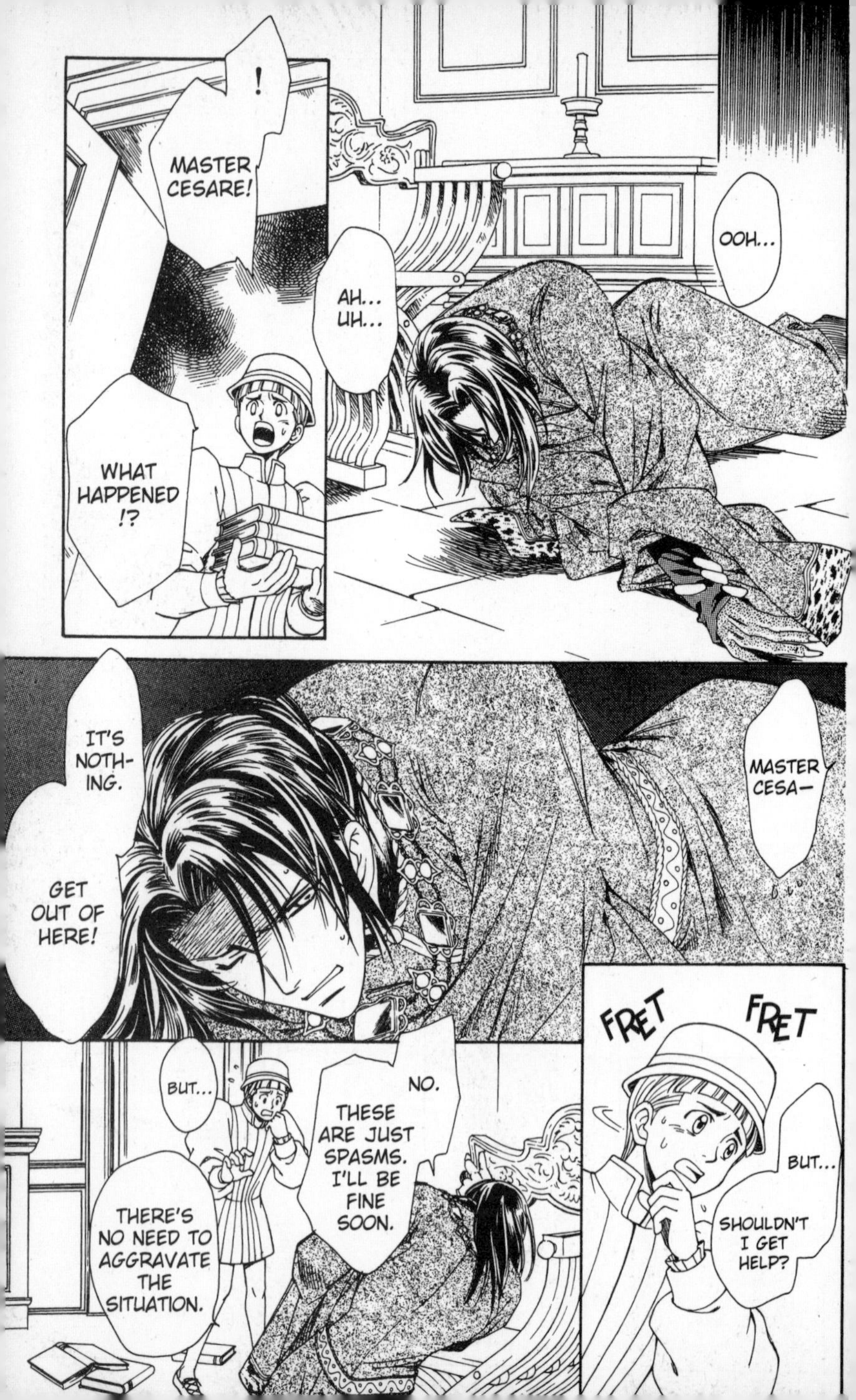
OOH...
!
MASTER CESARE!
AH... UH...
WHAT HAPPENED!?
MASTER CESA—
IT'S NOTHING.
GET OUT OF HERE!
FRET FRET
BUT...
SHOULDN'T I GET HELP?
NO.
THESE ARE JUST SPASMS. I'LL BE FINE SOON.
BUT...
THERE'S NO NEED TO AGGRAVATE THE SITUATION.

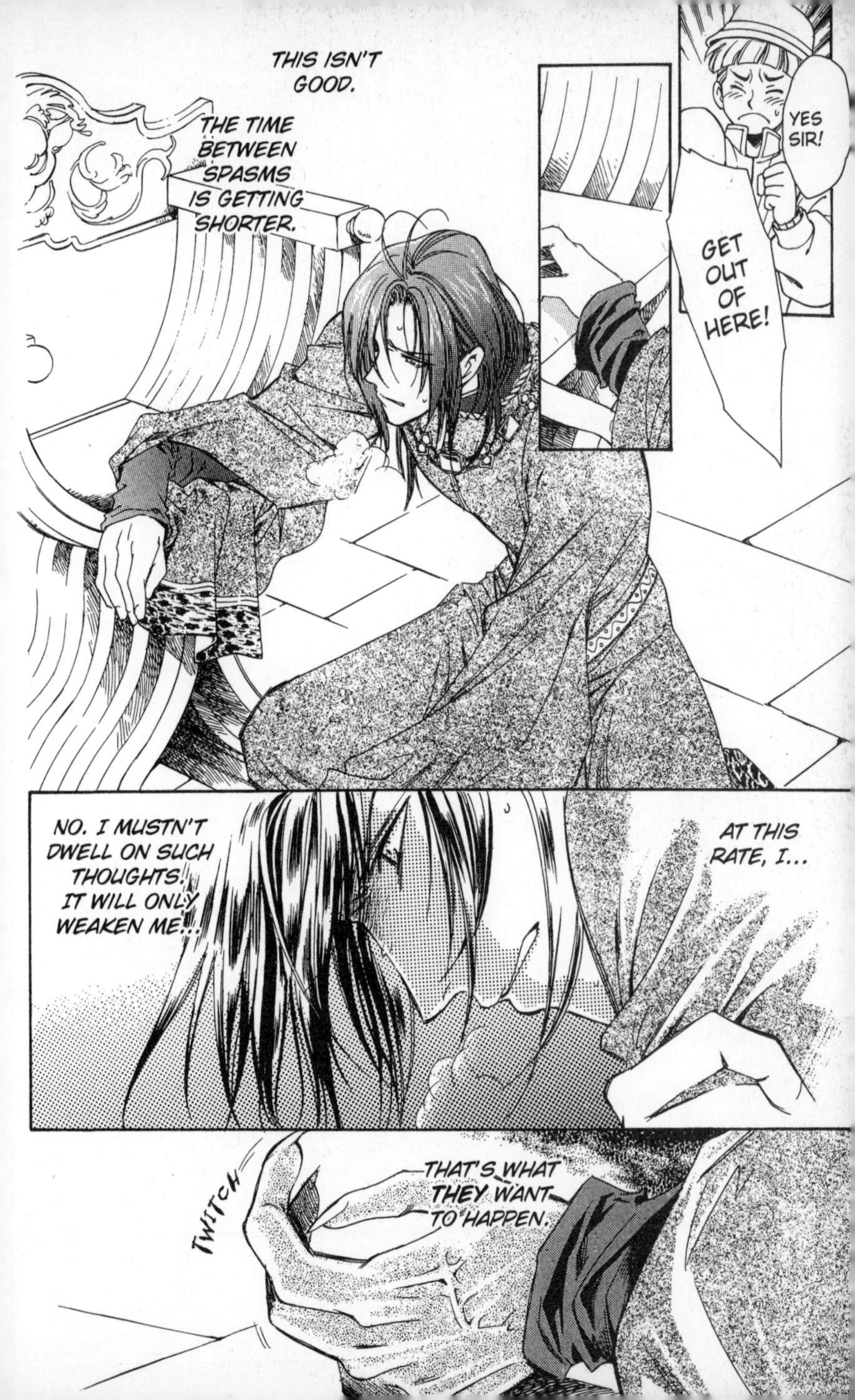
GET OUT OF HERE!
YES SIR!
THIS ISN'T GOOD.
THE TIME BETWEEN SPASMS IS GETTING SHORTER.
AT THIS RATE, I...
NO. I MUSTN'T DWELL ON SUCH THOUGHTS. IT WILL ONLY WEAKEN ME...
THAT'S WHAT THEY WANT TO HAPPEN.
TWITCH

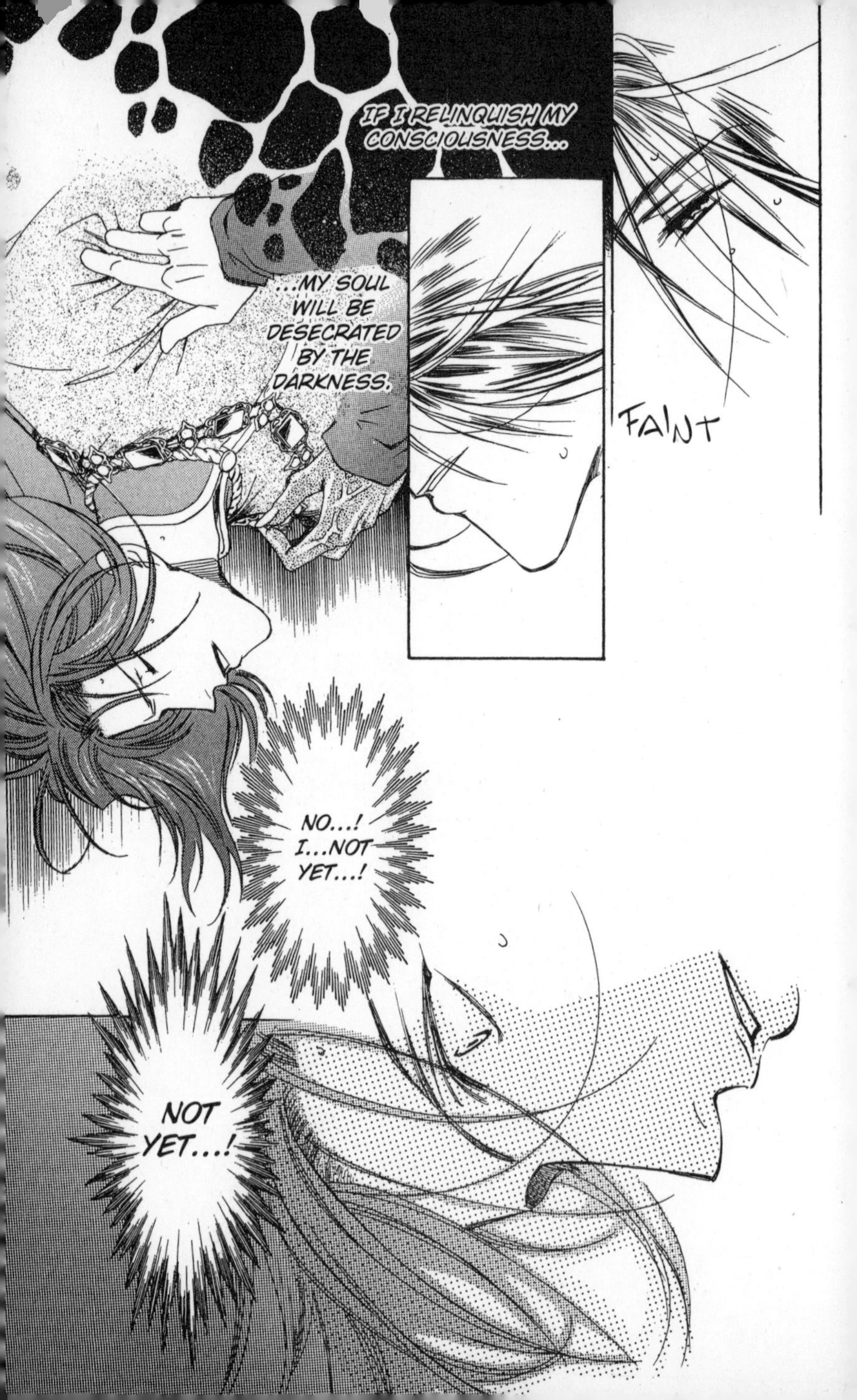
FAINT
IF I RELINQUISH MY CONSCIOUSNESS...
...MY SOUL WILL BE DESECRATED BY THE DARKNESS.
NO...! I...NOT YET...!
NOT YET...!

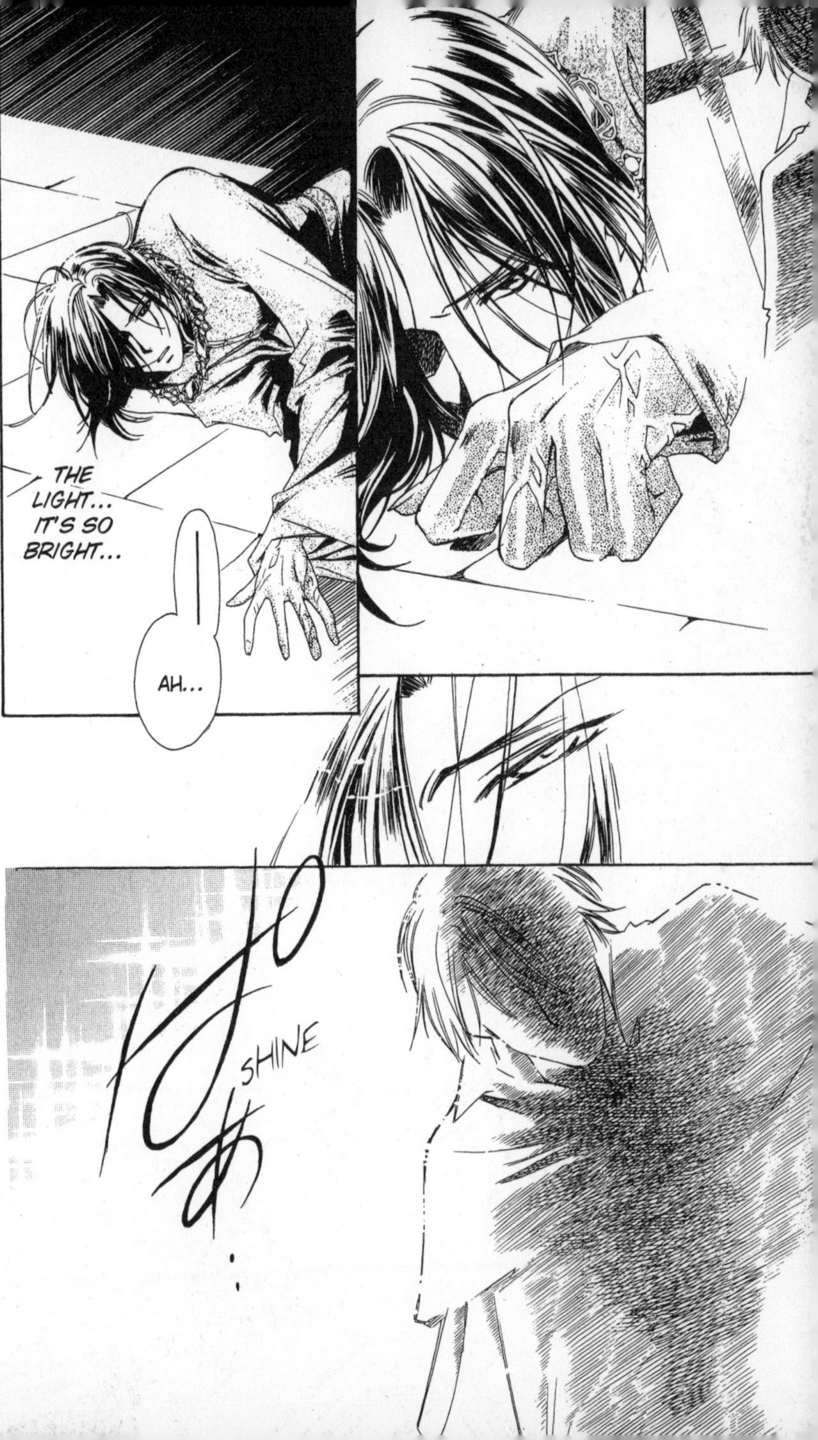
THE LIGHT... IT'S SO BRIGHT...
AH...
SHINE

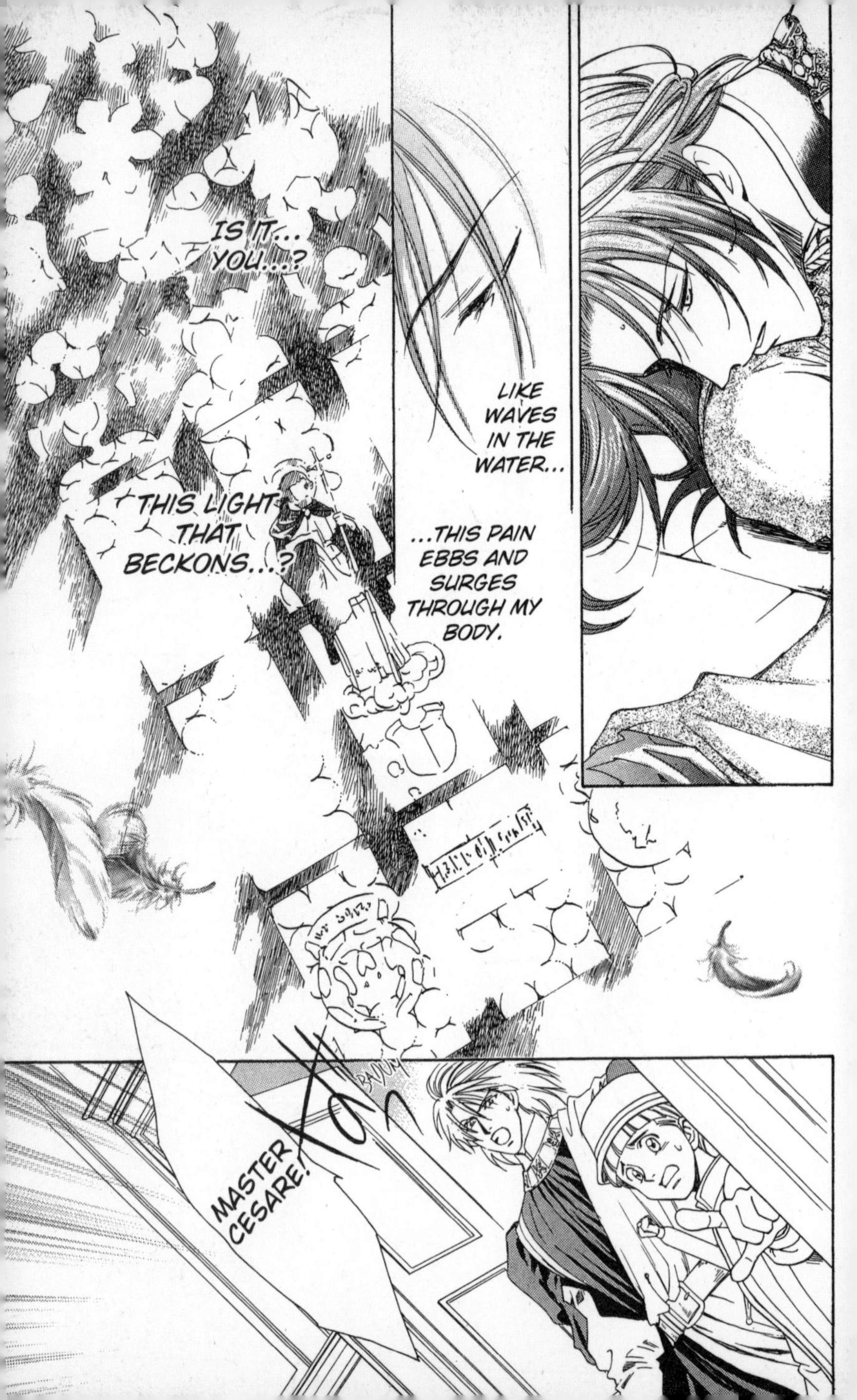
LIKE WAVES IN THE WATER...
...THIS PAIN EBBS AND SURGES THROUGH MY BODY.
IS IT... YOU...?
THIS LIGHT THAT BECKONS...?
BAJUM
MASTER CESARE!

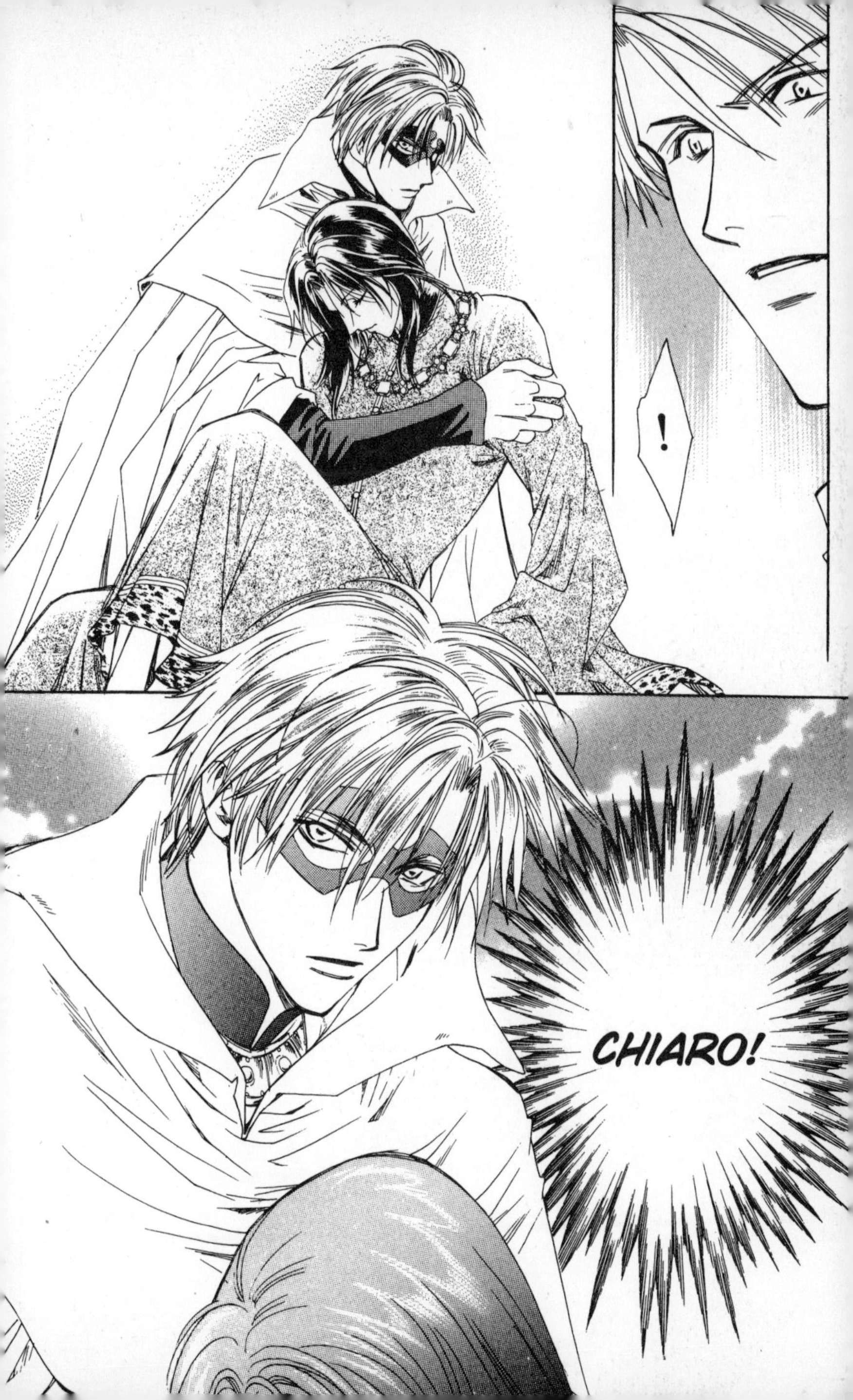
!
CHIARO!

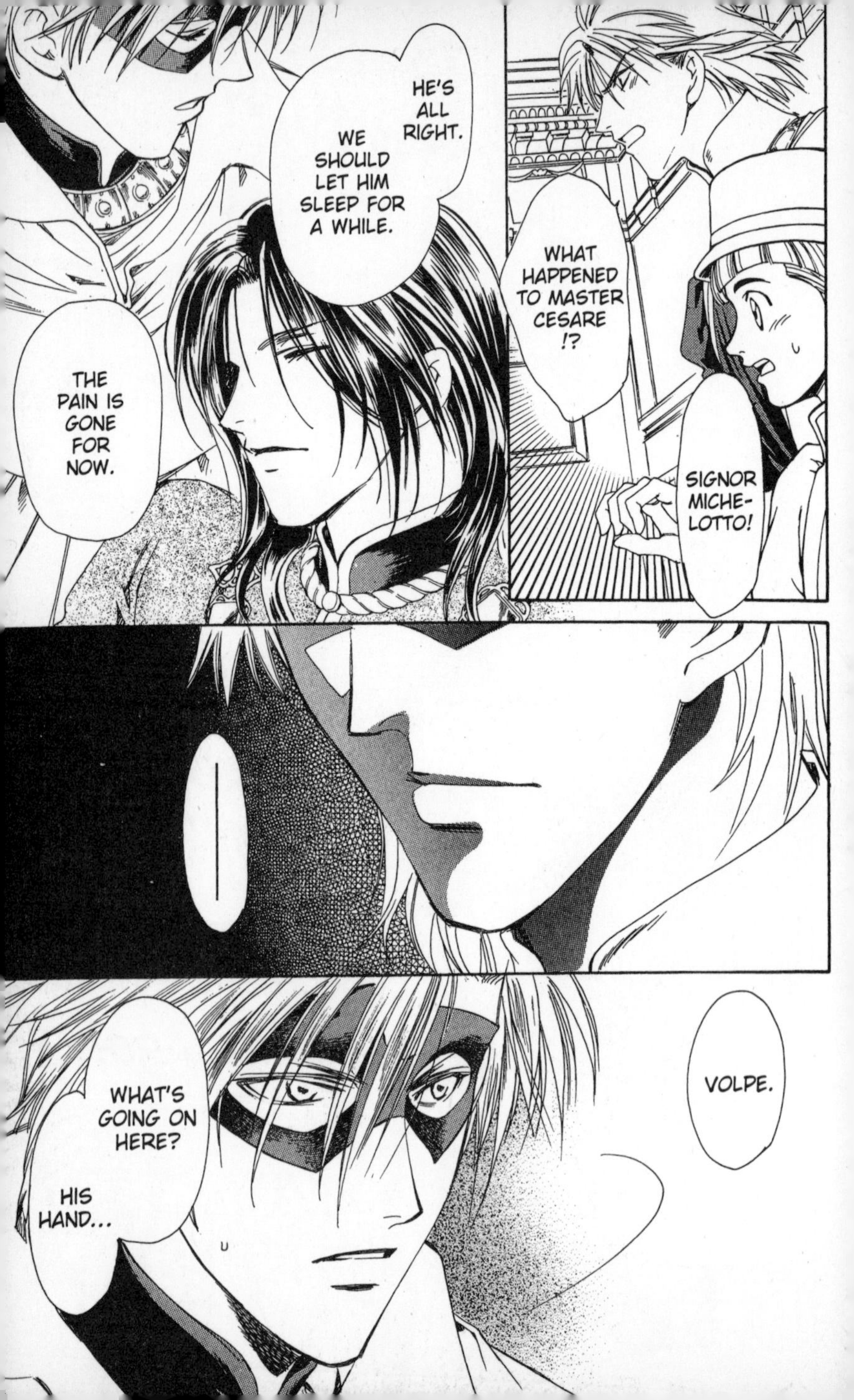
WHAT HAPPENED TO MASTER CESARE !?
SIGNOR MICHE-LOTTO!
HE'S ALL RIGHT. WE SHOULD LET HIM SLEEP FOR A WHILE.
THE PAIN IS GONE FOR NOW.
—
VOLPE.
WHAT'S GOING ON HERE? HIS HAND...

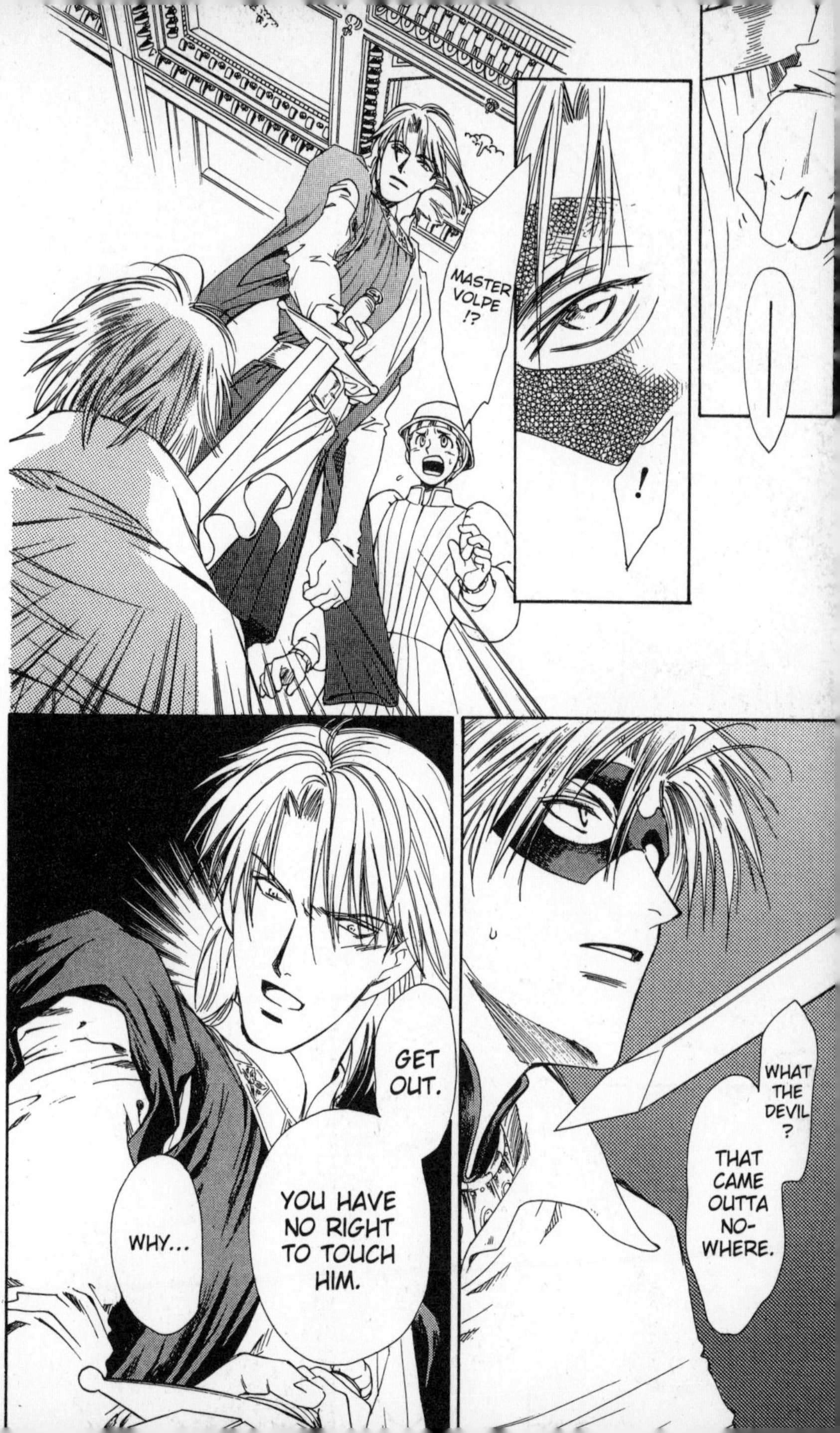
!
MASTER VOLPE !?
WHAT THE DEVIL?
THAT CAME OUTTA NO-WHERE.
GET OUT.
YOU HAVE NO RIGHT TO TOUCH HIM.
WHY...

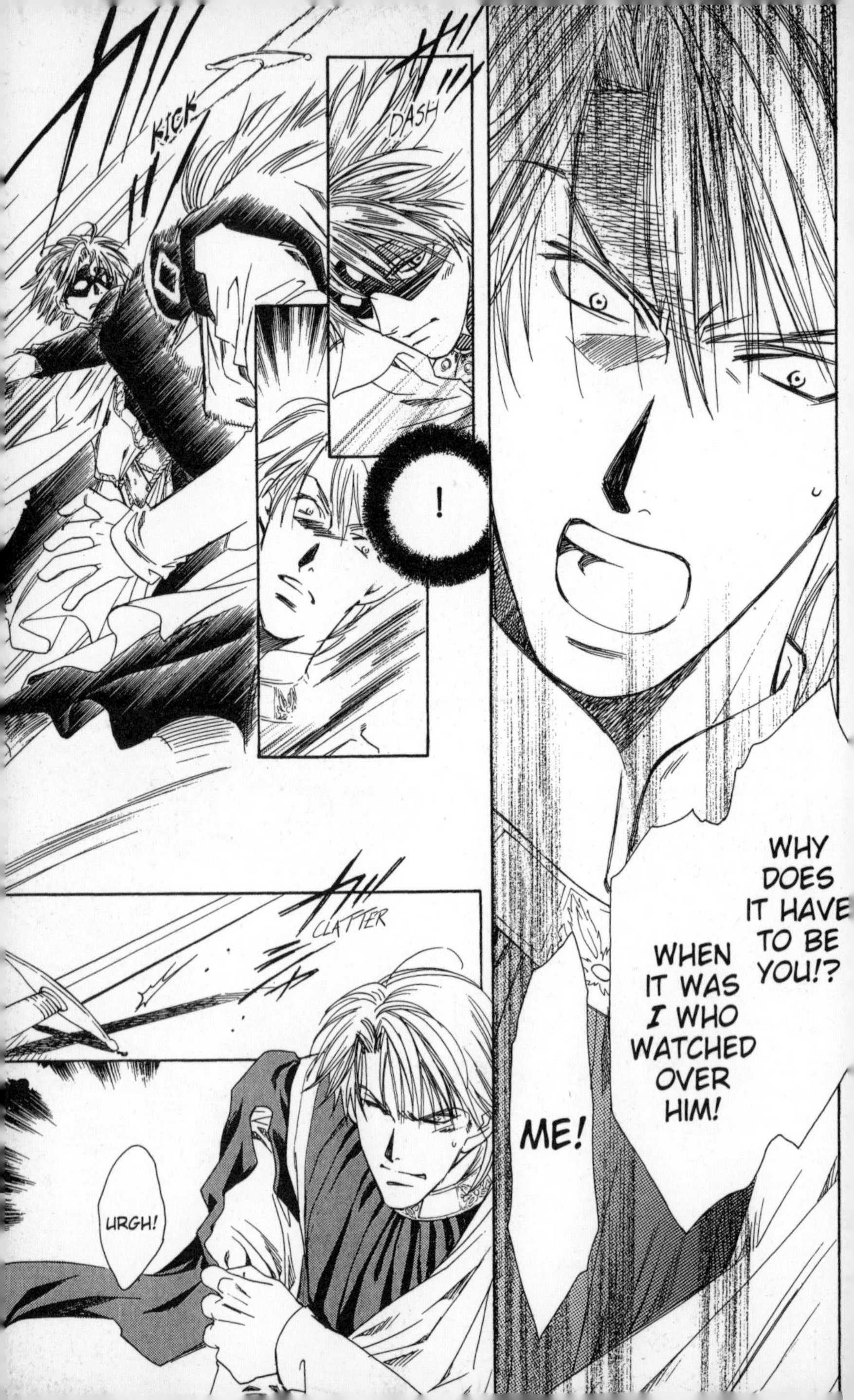
WHY DOES IT HAVE TO BE YOU!?
WHEN IT WAS *I* WHO WATCHED OVER HIM!
ME!
DASH
KICK
!
CLATTER
URGH!

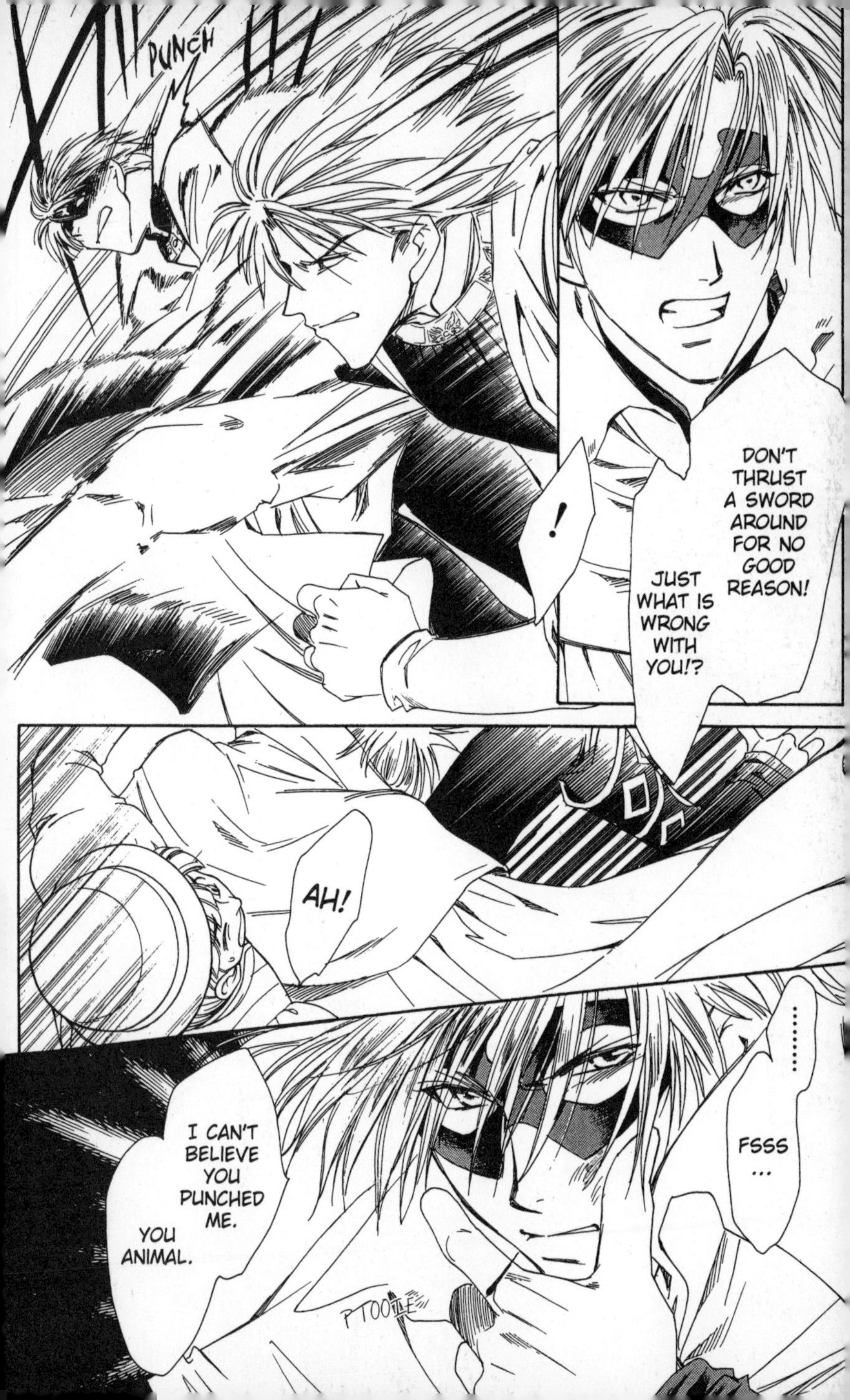
DON'T THRUST A SWORD AROUND FOR NO GOOD REASON!
JUST WHAT IS WRONG WITH YOU!?
PUNCH
!
AH!
......
FSSS ...
I CAN'T BELIEVE YOU PUNCHED ME.
YOU ANIMAL.
PTOOIE

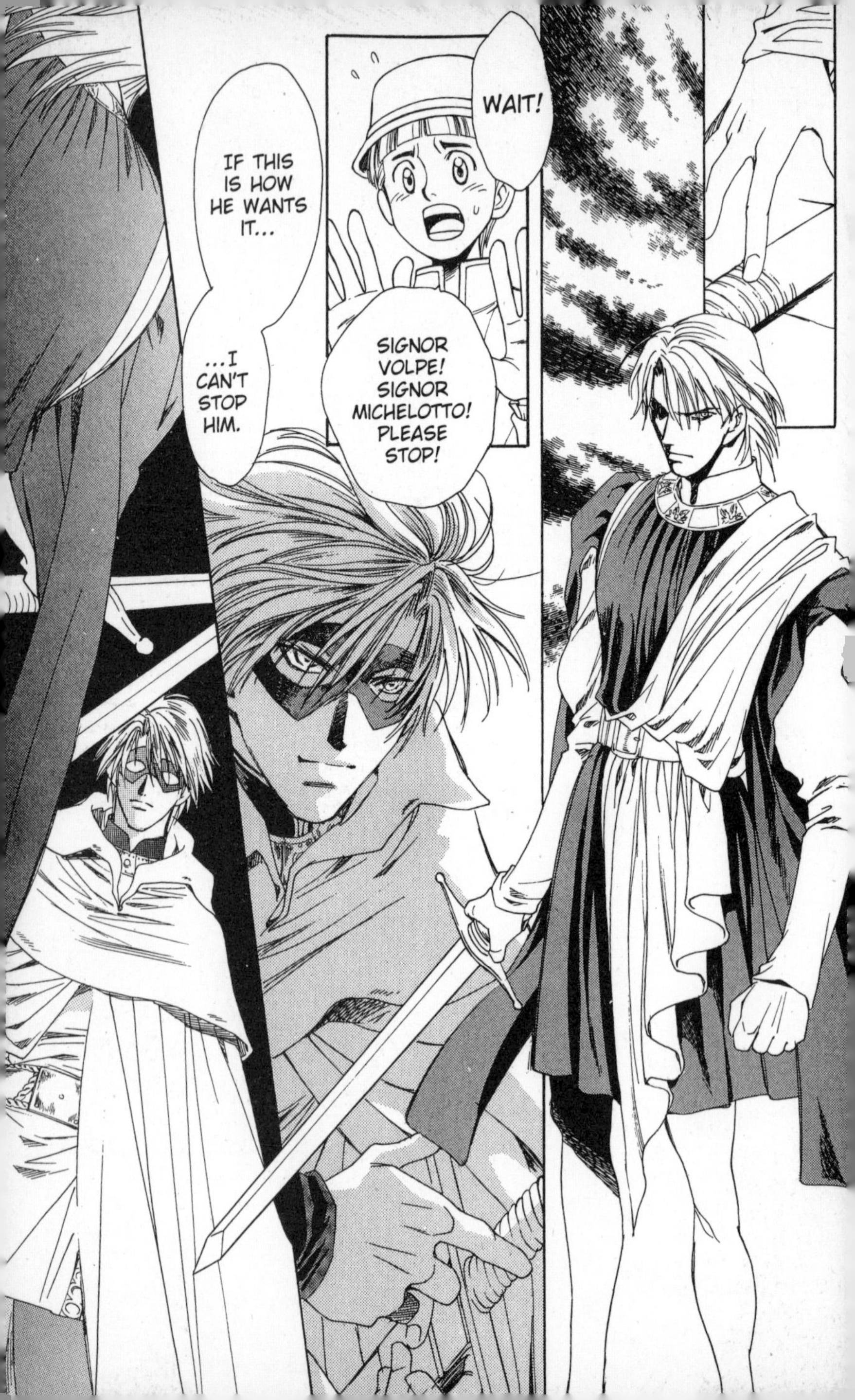
WAIT!
SIGNOR VOLPE! SIGNOR MICHELOTTO! PLEASE STOP!
IF THIS IS HOW HE WANTS IT...
...I CAN'T STOP HIM.

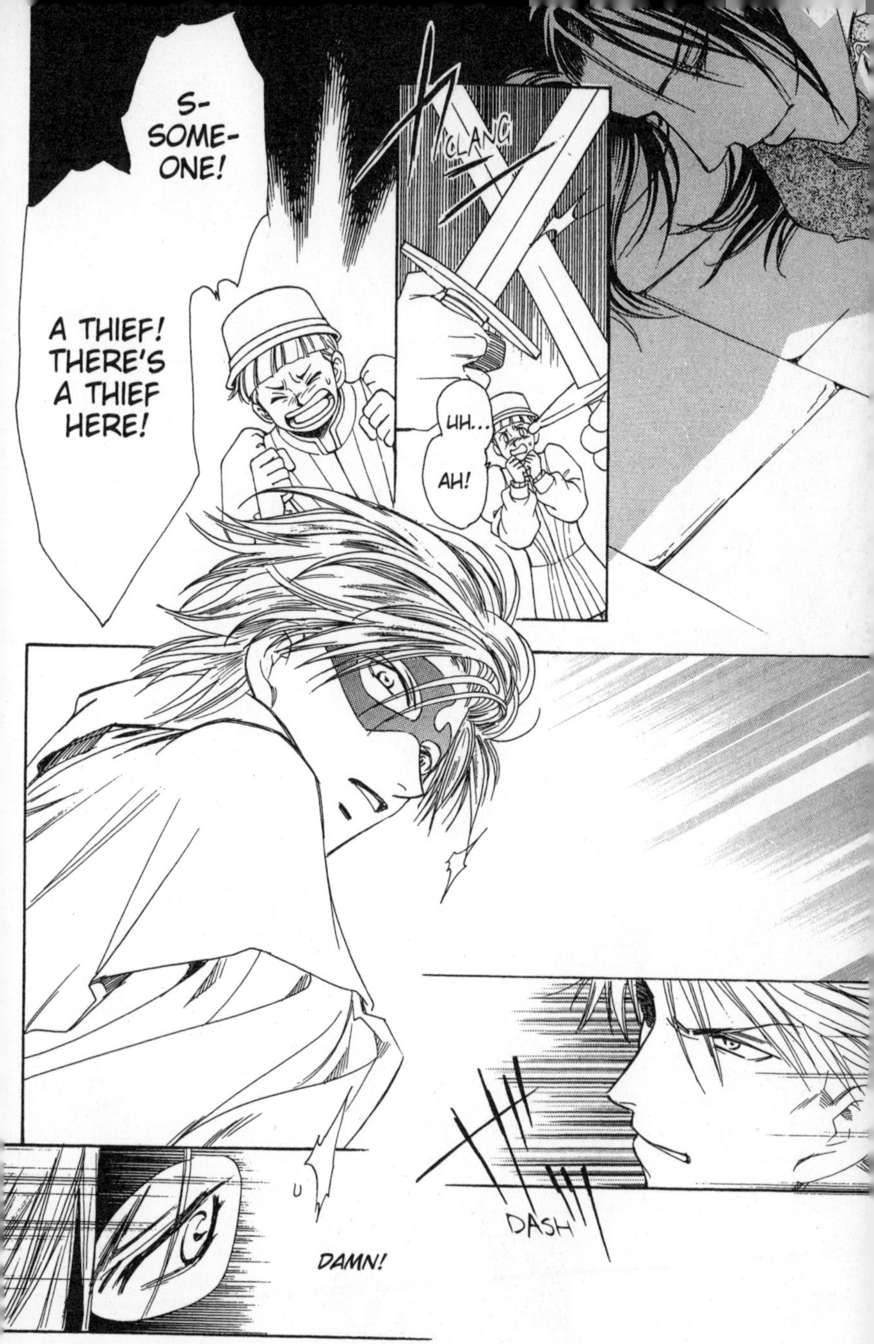
CLANG
UH...
AH!
S-SOME-ONE!
A THIEF! THERE'S A THIEF HERE!
DASH
U
DAMN!

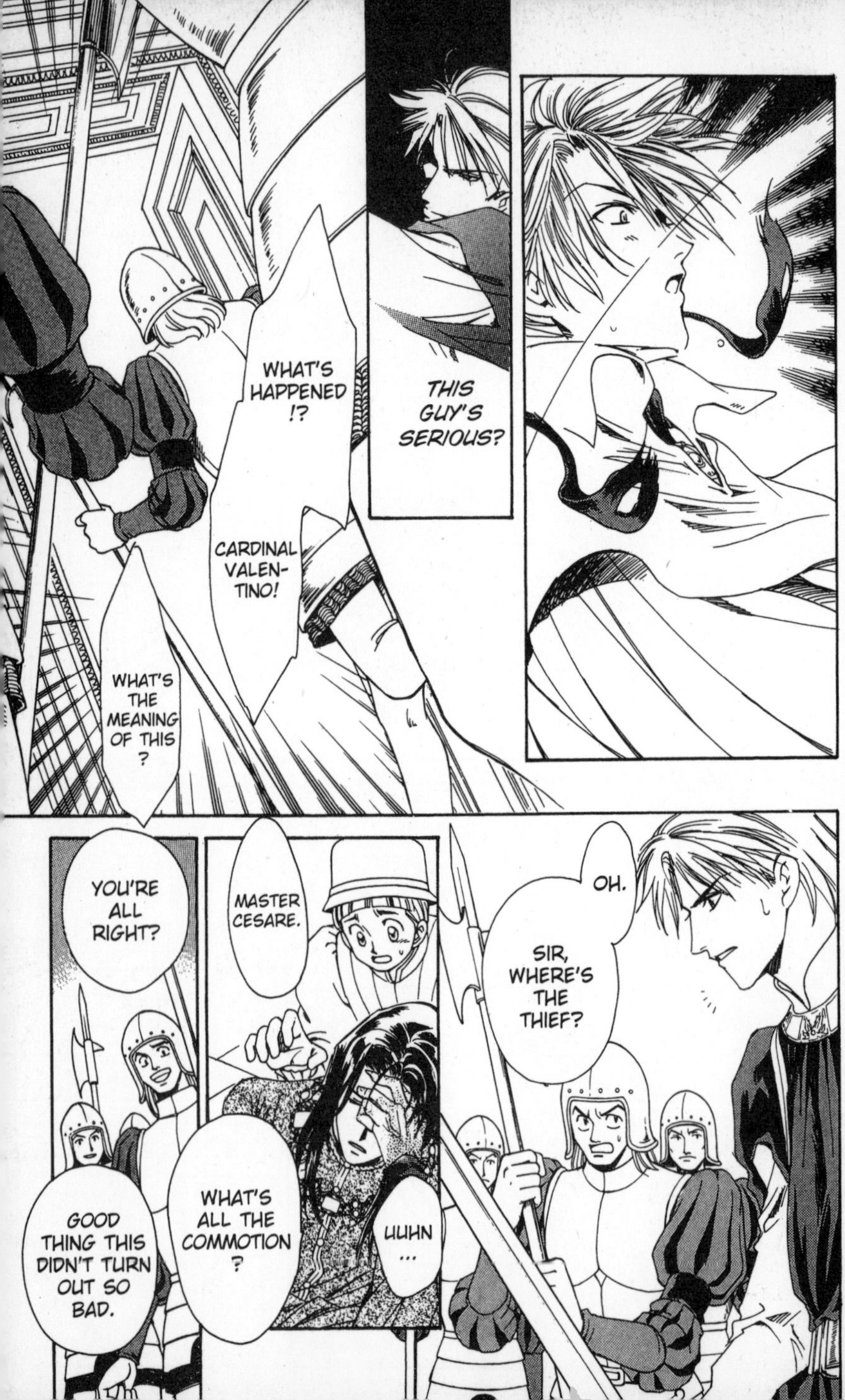
THIS GUY'S SERIOUS?
WHAT'S HAPPENED!?
CARDINAL VALENTINO!
WHAT'S THE MEANING OF THIS?
OH.
SIR, WHERE'S THE THIEF?
MASTER CESARE.
UUHN...
WHAT'S ALL THE COMMOTION?
YOU'RE ALL RIGHT?
GOOD THING THIS DIDN'T TURN OUT SO BAD.

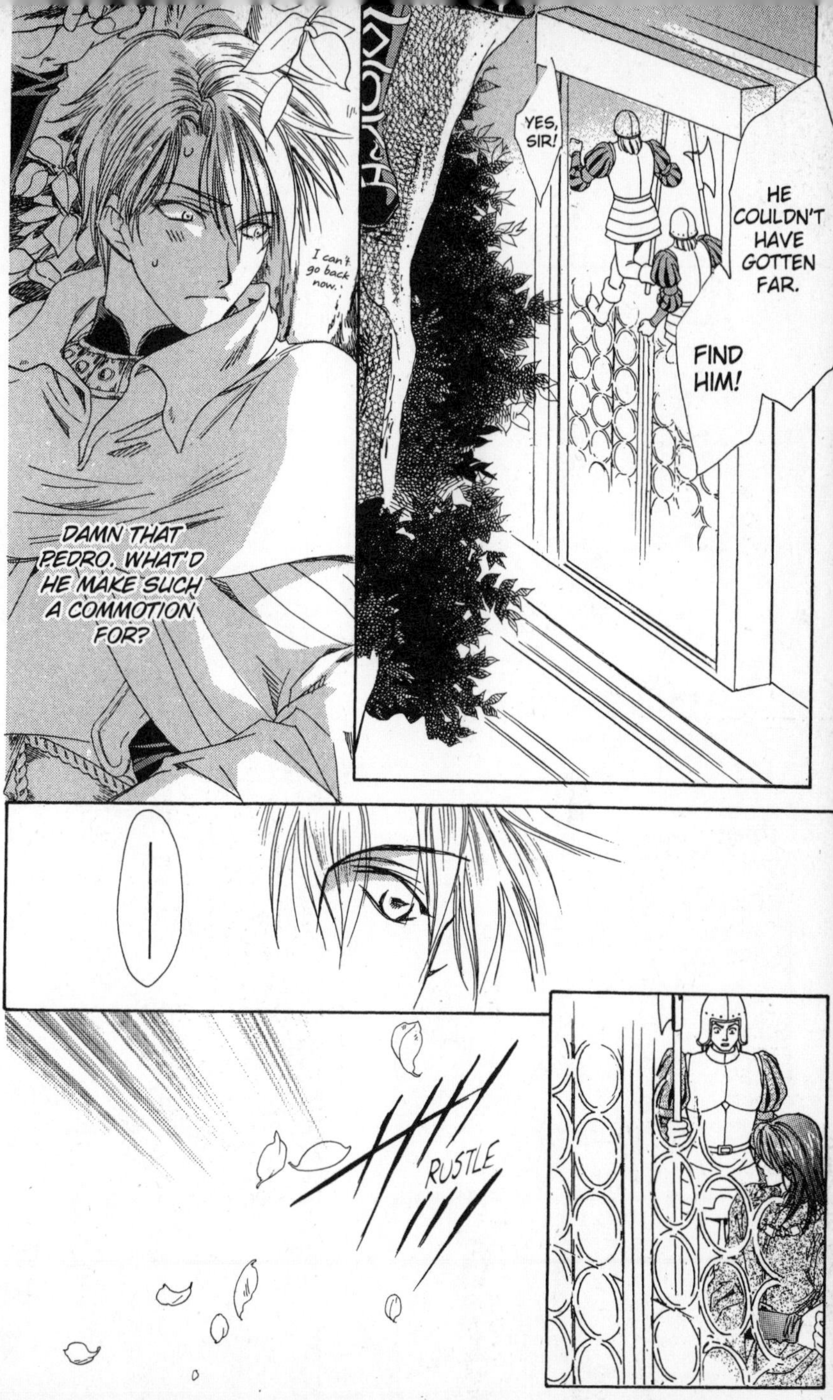
HE COULDN'T HAVE GOTTEN FAR.
FIND HIM!
YES, SIR!
I can't go back now.
DAMN THAT PEDRO. WHAT'D HE MAKE SUCH A COMMOTION FOR?
RUSTLE

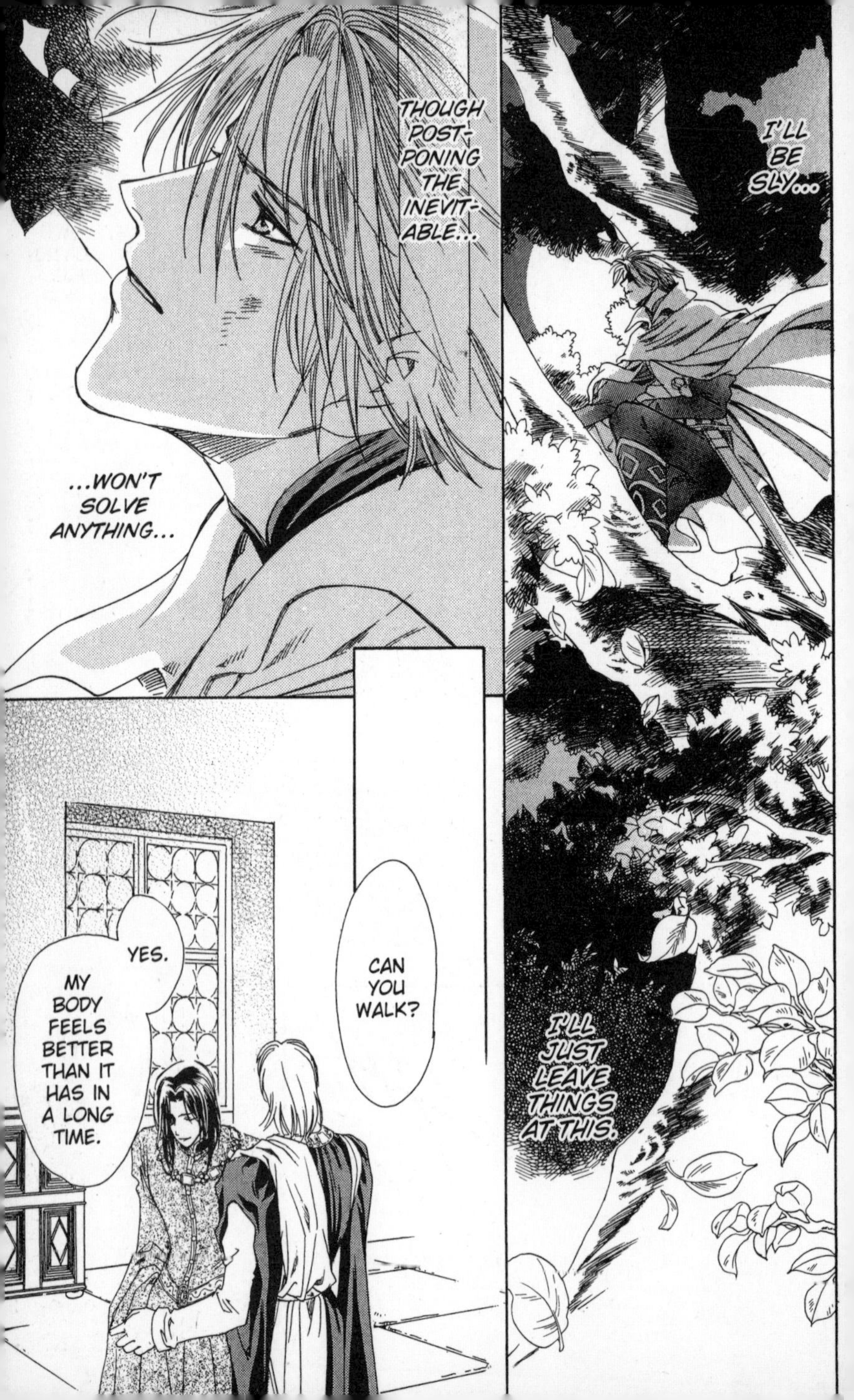
I'LL BE SLY...
I'LL JUST LEAVE THINGS AT THIS.
THOUGH POST-PONING THE INEVIT-ABLE...
...WON'T SOLVE ANYTHING...
CAN YOU WALK?
YES.
MY BODY FEELS BETTER THAN IT HAS IN A LONG TIME.

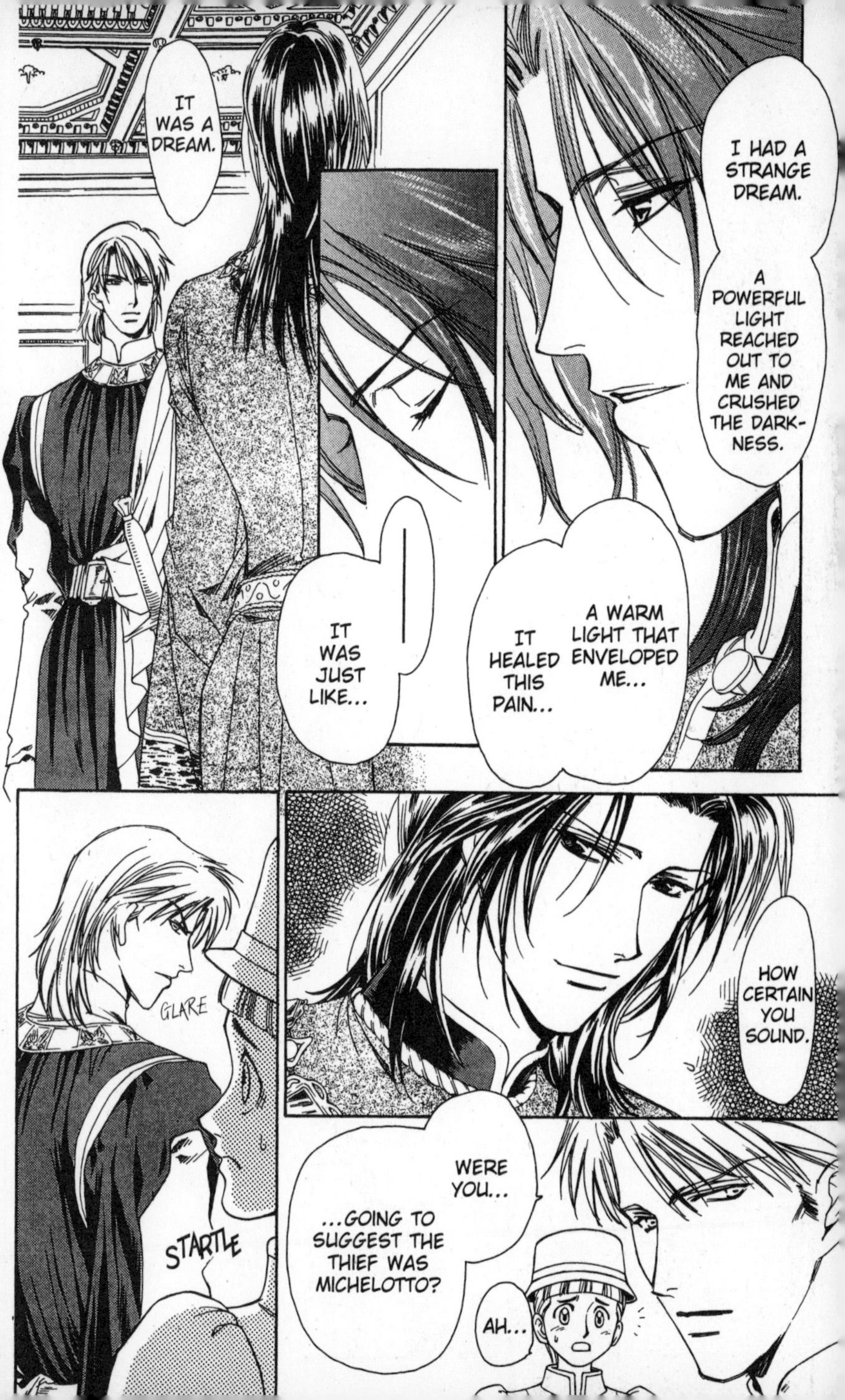
I HAD A STRANGE DREAM.
A POWERFUL LIGHT REACHED OUT TO ME AND CRUSHED THE DARK-NESS.
A WARM LIGHT THAT ENVELOPED ME...
IT HEALED THIS PAIN...
IT WAS JUST LIKE...
IT WAS A DREAM.
HOW CERTAIN YOU SOUND.
WERE YOU...
...GOING TO SUGGEST THE THIEF WAS MICHELOTTO?
AH...
GLARE
STARTLE

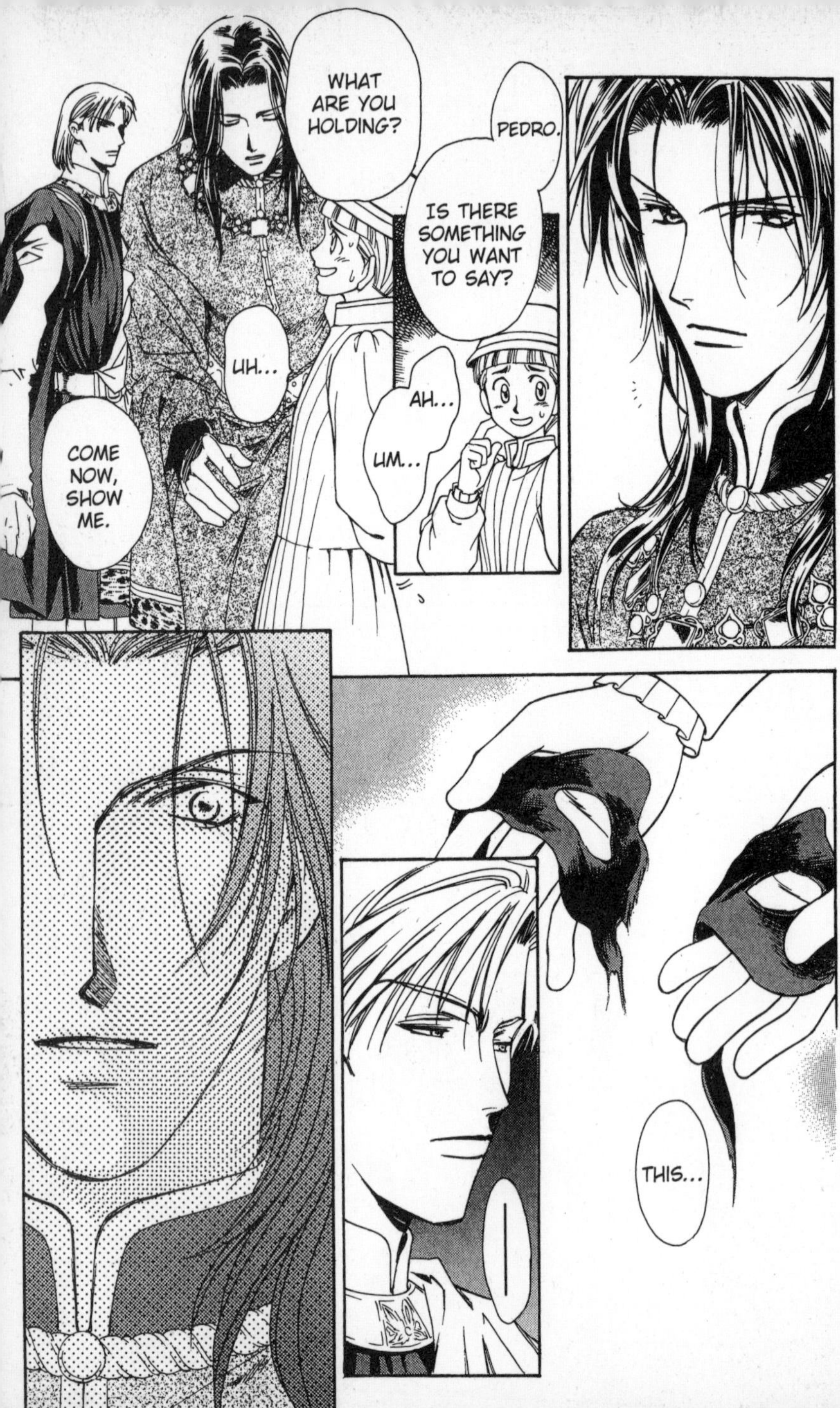
PEDRO.
IS THERE SOMETHING YOU WANT TO SAY?
AH...
UM...
WHAT ARE YOU HOLDING?
UH...
COME NOW, SHOW ME.
THIS...

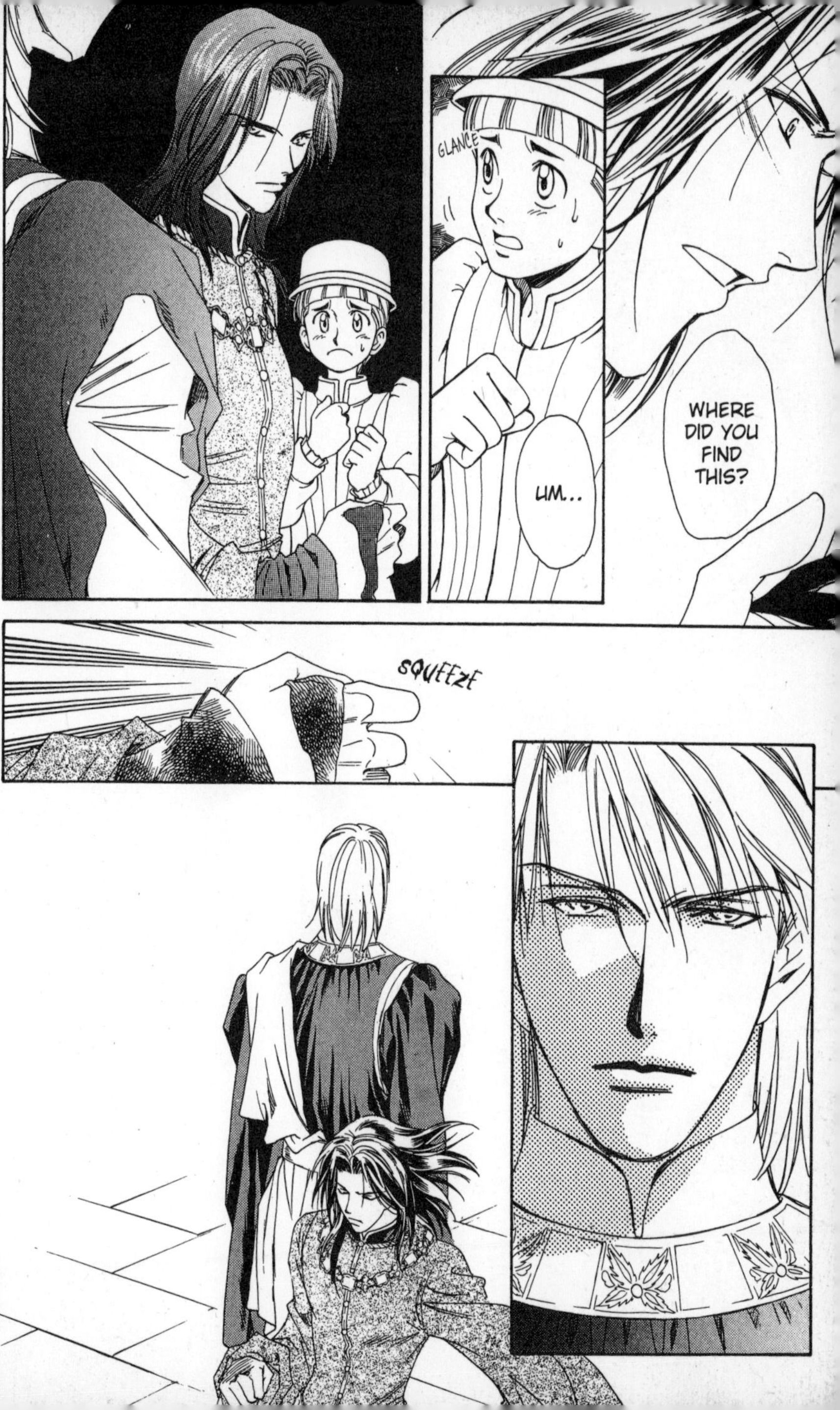
WHERE DID YOU FIND THIS?
GLANCE
UM...
SQUEEZE

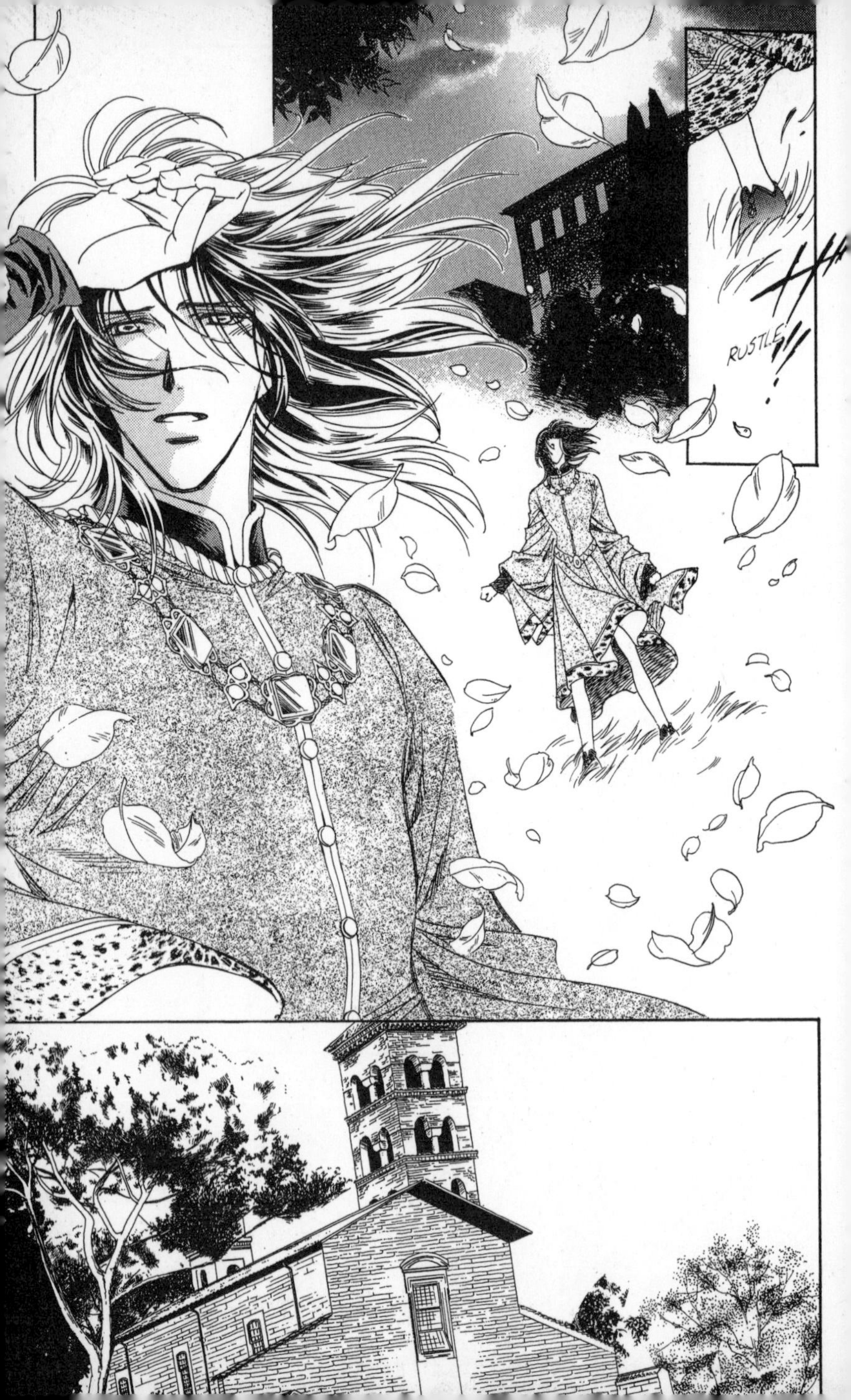
RUSTLE

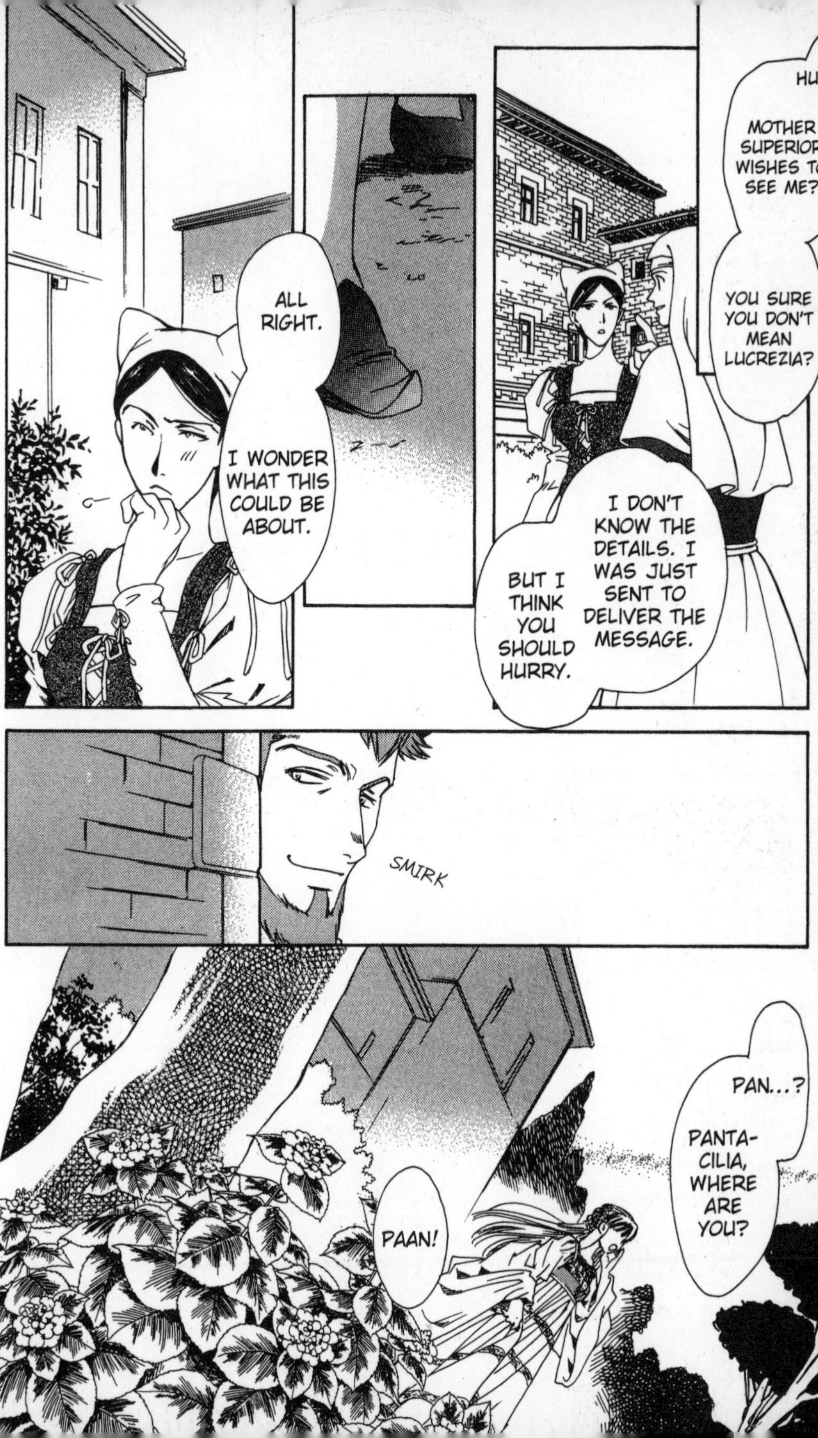
HUH?
MOTHER SUPERIOR WISHES TO SEE ME?
YOU SURE YOU DON'T MEAN LUCREZIA?
I DON'T KNOW THE DETAILS. I WAS JUST SENT TO DELIVER THE MESSAGE.
BUT I THINK YOU SHOULD HURRY.
ALL RIGHT.
I WONDER WHAT THIS COULD BE ABOUT.
SMIRK
PAN...?
PANTA-CILIA, WHERE ARE YOU?
PAAN!

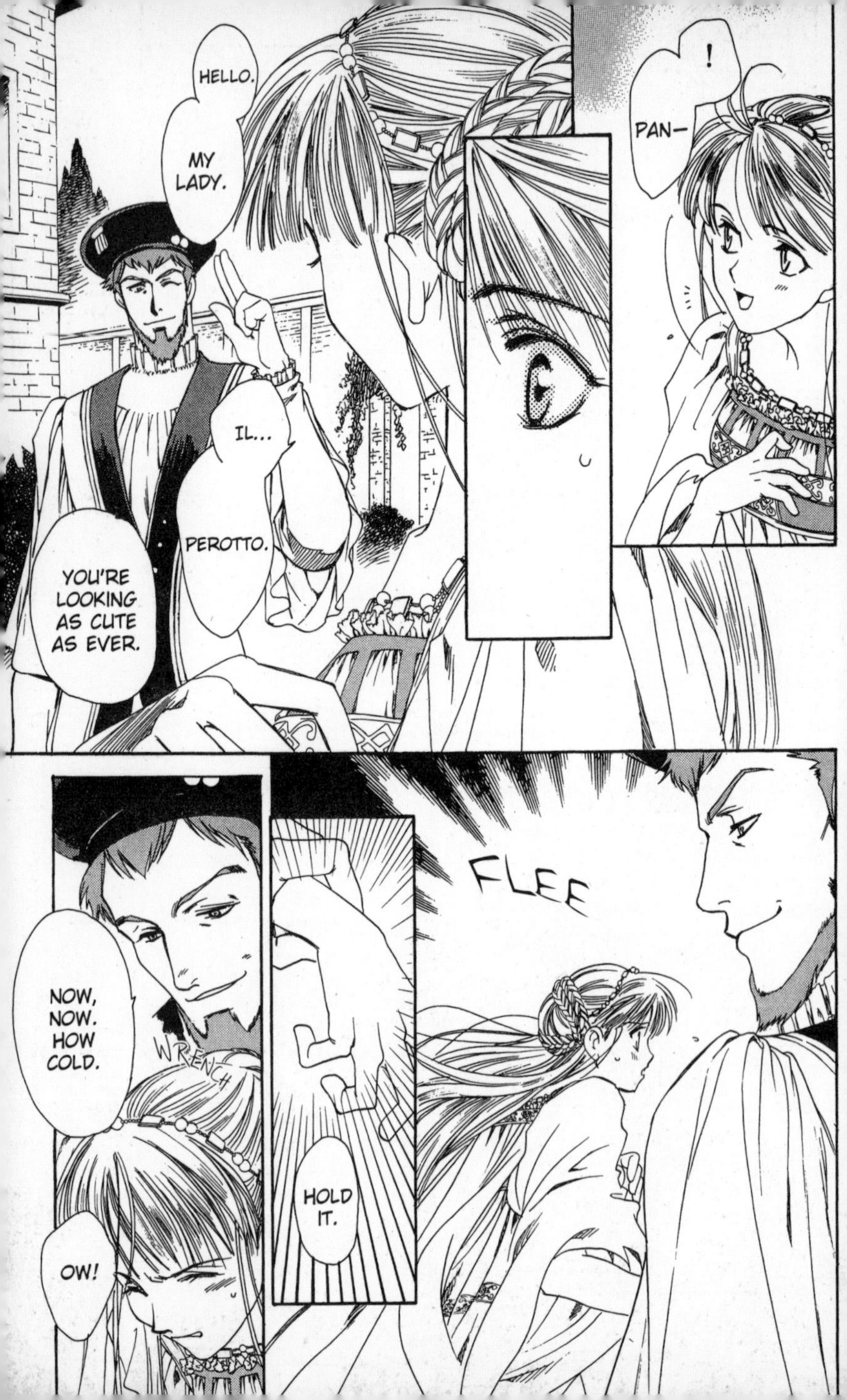
!
PAN—
HELLO.
MY LADY.
IL...
PEROTTO.
YOU'RE LOOKING AS CUTE AS EVER.
FLEE
HOLD IT.
NOW, NOW. HOW COLD.
WRENCH
OW!

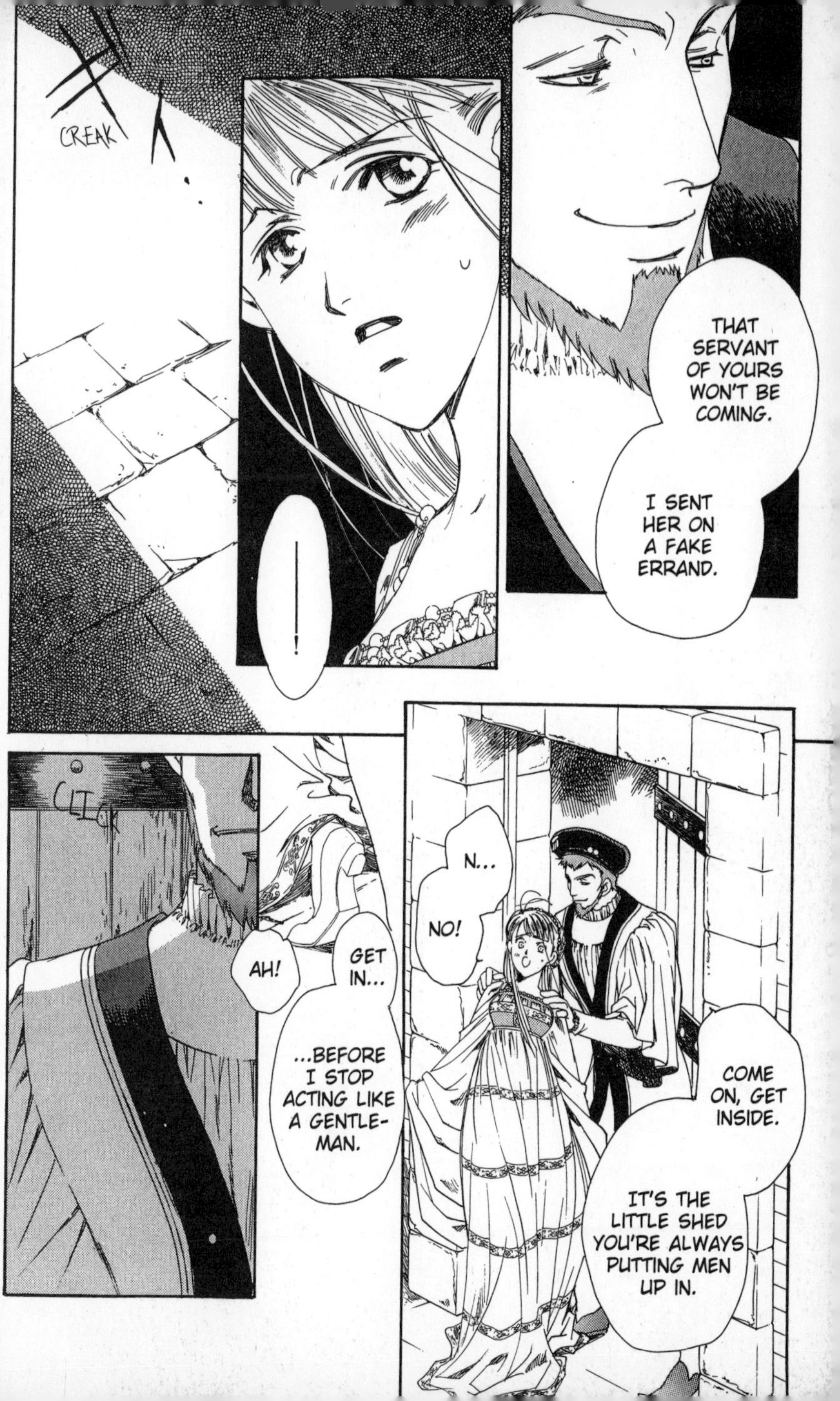
THAT SERVANT OF YOURS WON'T BE COMING.
I SENT HER ON A FAKE ERRAND.
!
CREAK
COME ON, GET INSIDE.
IT'S THE LITTLE SHED YOU'RE ALWAYS PUTTING MEN UP IN.
N...
NO!
GET IN...
...BEFORE I STOP ACTING LIKE A GENTLE-MAN.
AH!

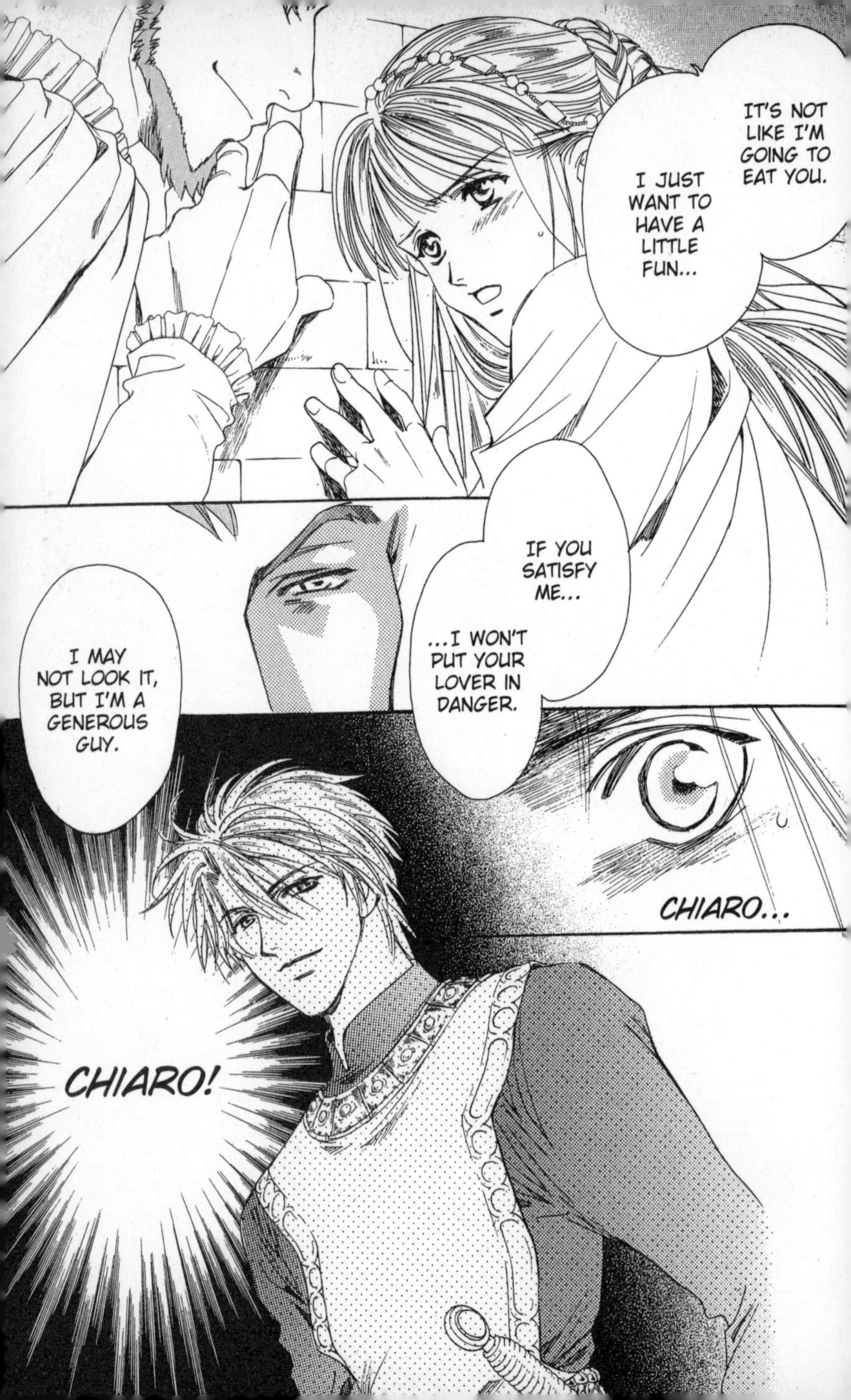
IT'S NOT LIKE I'M GOING TO EAT YOU.
I JUST WANT TO HAVE A LITTLE FUN...
IF YOU SATISFY ME...
...I WON'T PUT YOUR LOVER IN DANGER.
I MAY NOT LOOK IT, BUT I'M A GENEROUS GUY.
CHIARO...
CHIARO!

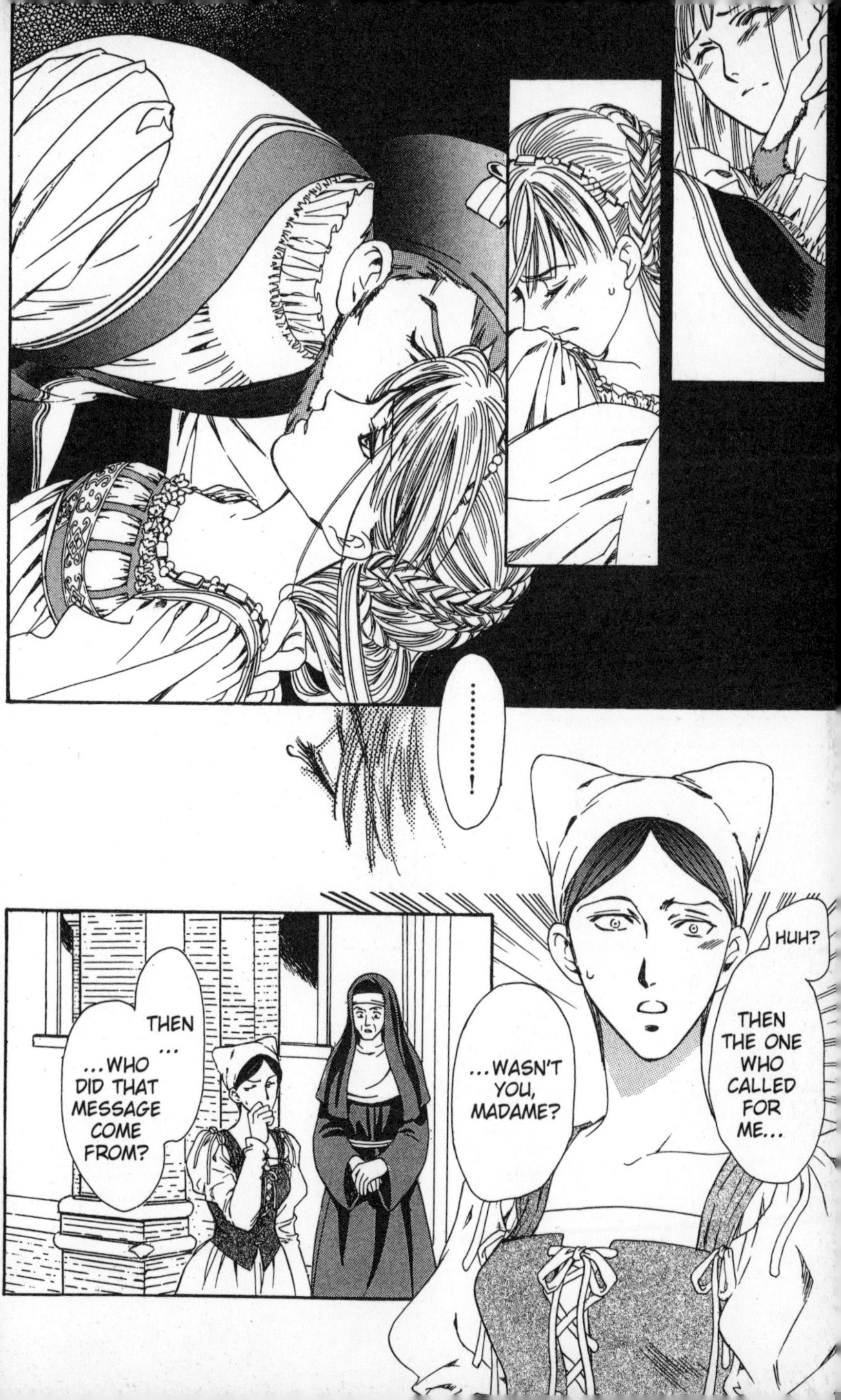
......!
HUH?
THEN THE ONE WHO CALLED FOR ME...
...WASN'T YOU, MADAME?
THEN ... ...WHO DID THAT MESSAGE COME FROM?

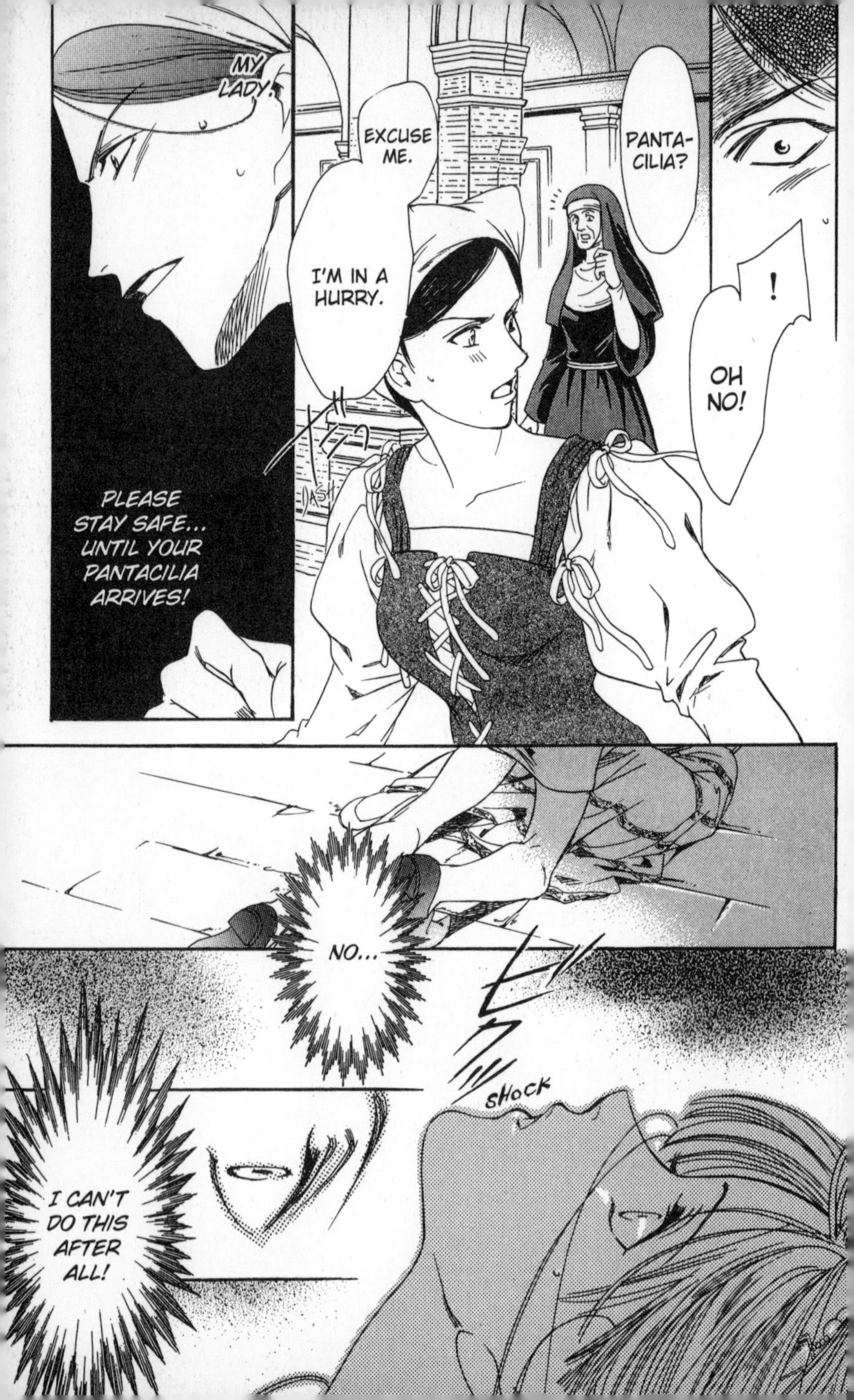
!
OH NO!
PANTA-CILIA?
EXCUSE ME.
I'M IN A HURRY.
DASH
MY LADY.
PLEASE STAY SAFE... UNTIL YOUR PANTACILIA ARRIVES!
NO...
SHOCK
I CAN'T DO THIS AFTER ALL!

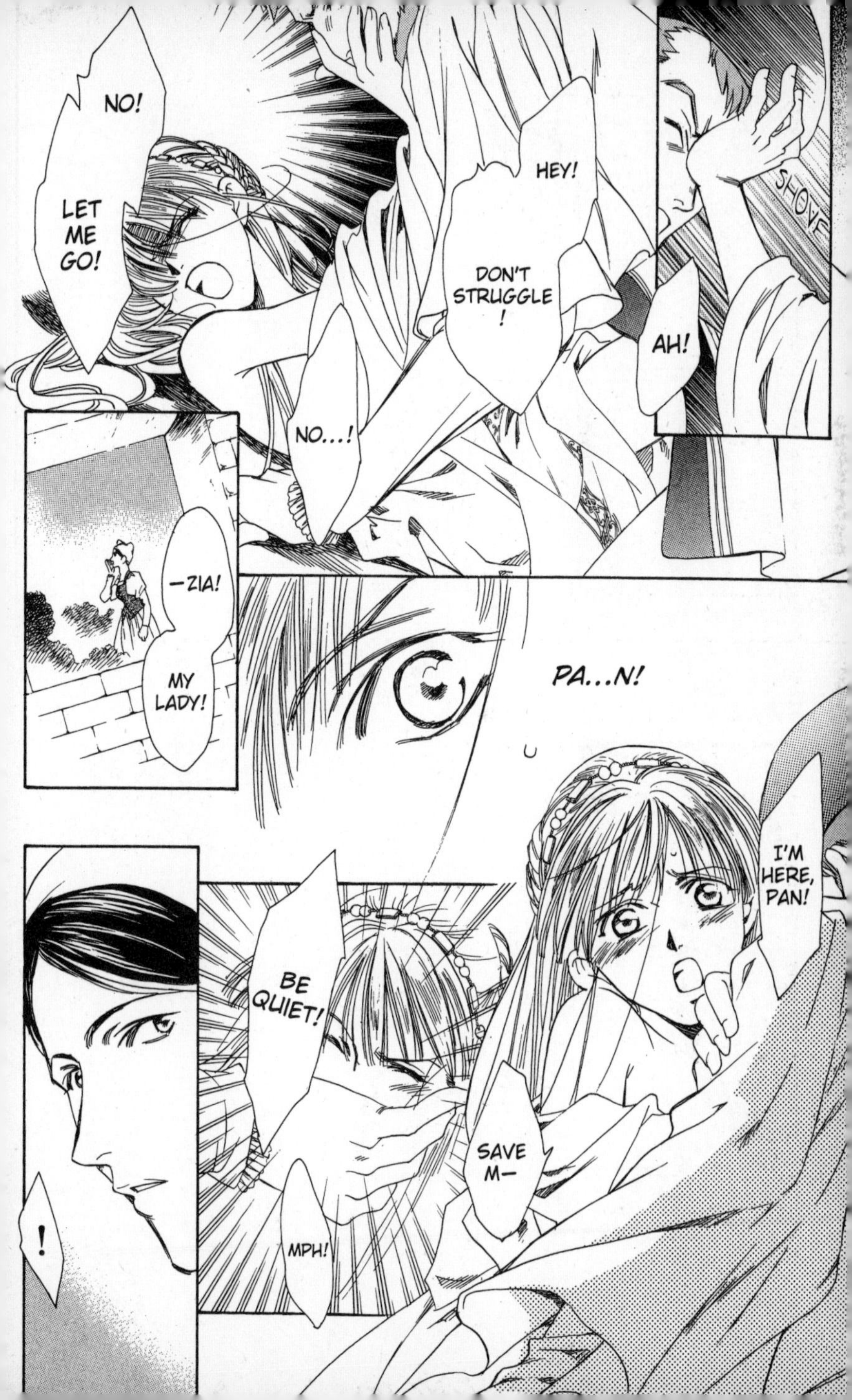
SHOVE
AH!
HEY!
DON'T STRUGGLE!
NO!
LET ME GO!
NO...!
PA...N!
—ZIA!
MY LADY!
I'M HERE, PAN!
BE QUIET!
SAVE M—
MPH!
!

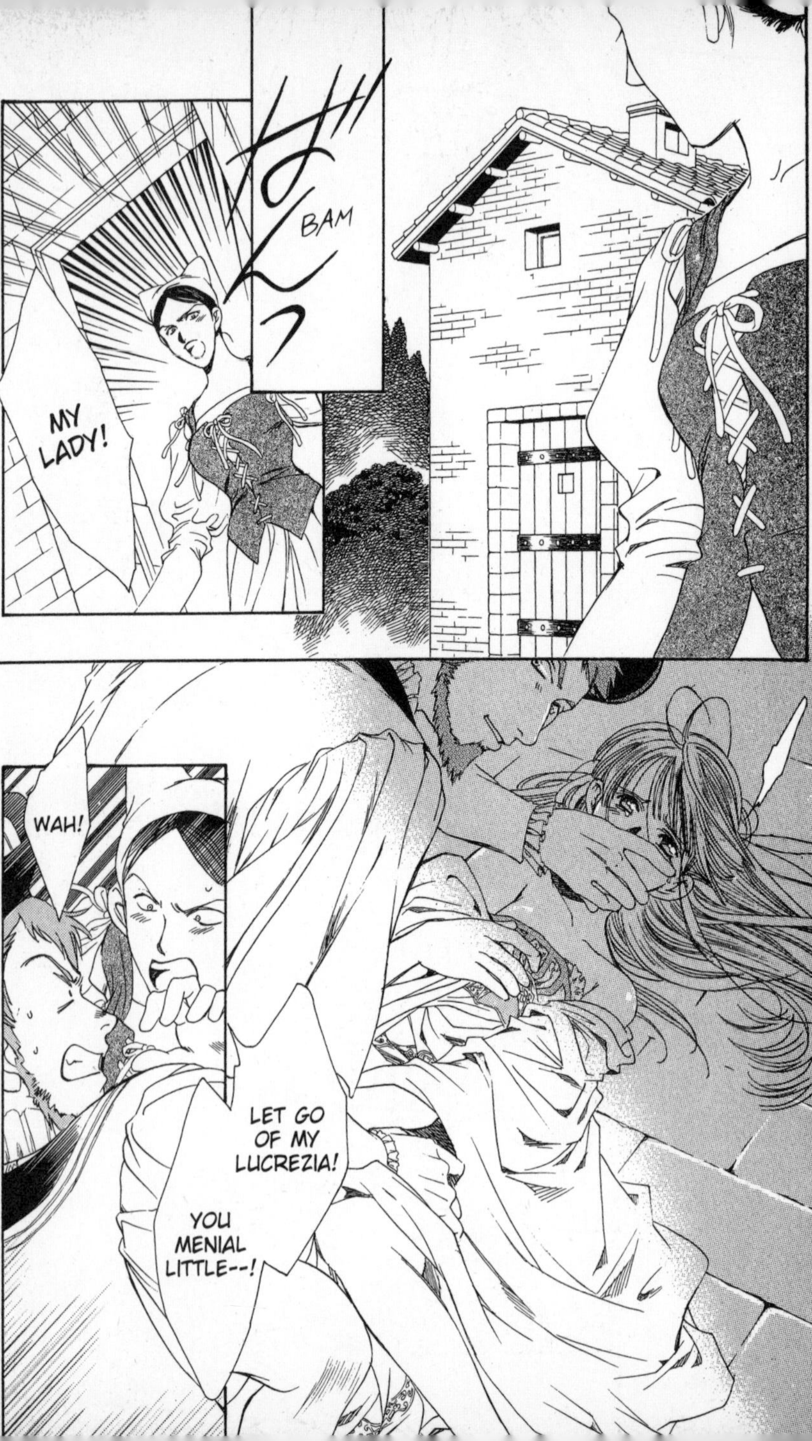
BAM
MY LADY!
WAH!
LET GO OF MY LUCREZIA!
YOU MENIAL LITTLE--!

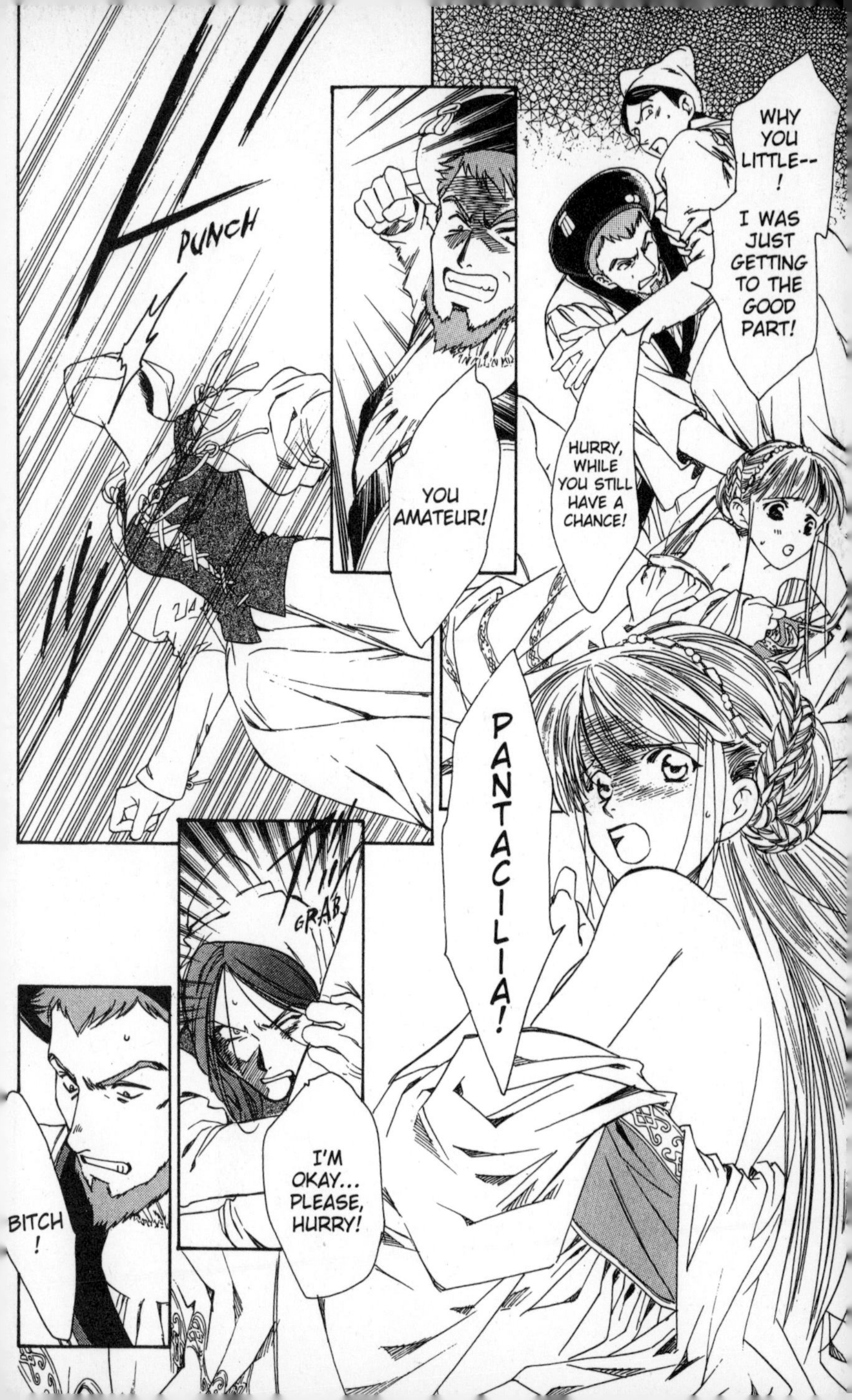
WHY YOU LITTLE--!
I WAS JUST GETTING TO THE GOOD PART!
HURRY, WHILE YOU STILL HAVE A CHANCE!
YOU AMATEUR!
PUNCH
PANTACILIA!
GRAB
I'M OKAY... PLEASE, HURRY!
BITCH!

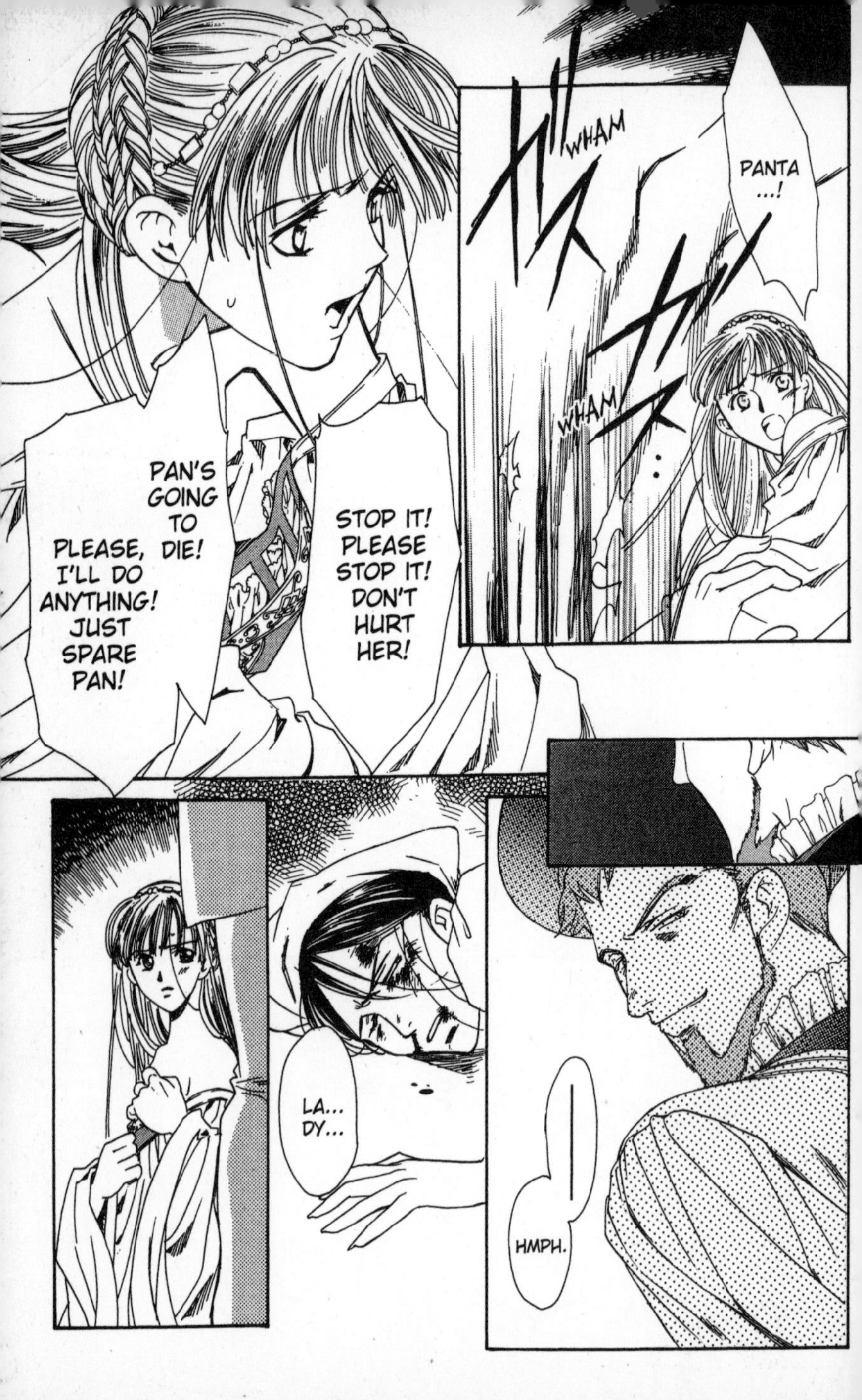
WHAM
PANTA ...!
WHAM
STOP IT! PLEASE STOP IT! DON'T HURT HER!
PAN'S GOING TO DIE!
PLEASE, I'LL DO ANYTHING! JUST SPARE PAN!
— HMPH.
LA... DY...

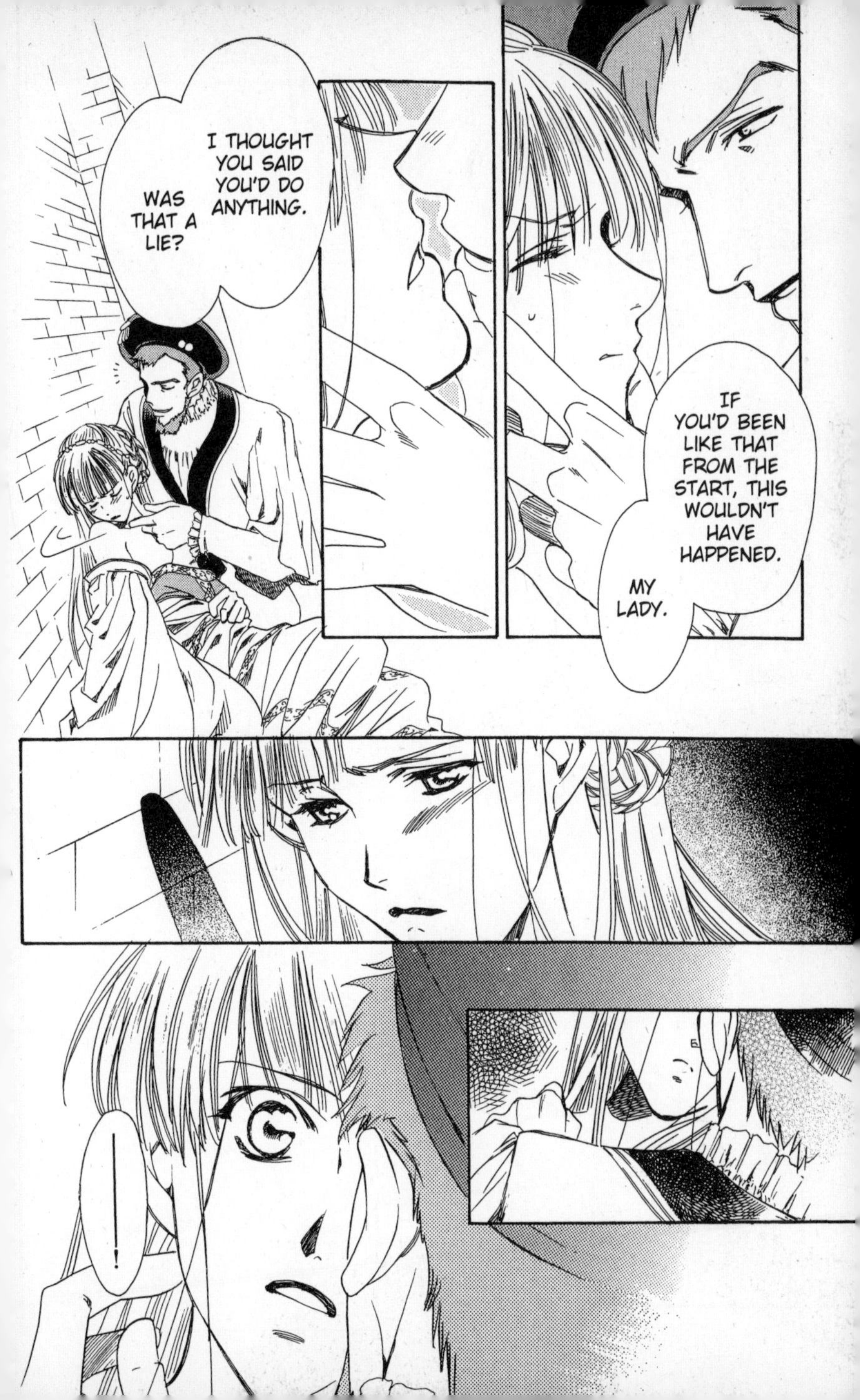
IF YOU'D BEEN LIKE THAT FROM THE START, THIS WOULDN'T HAVE HAPPENED.
MY LADY.
I THOUGHT YOU SAID YOU'D DO ANYTHING.
WAS THAT A LIE?
!

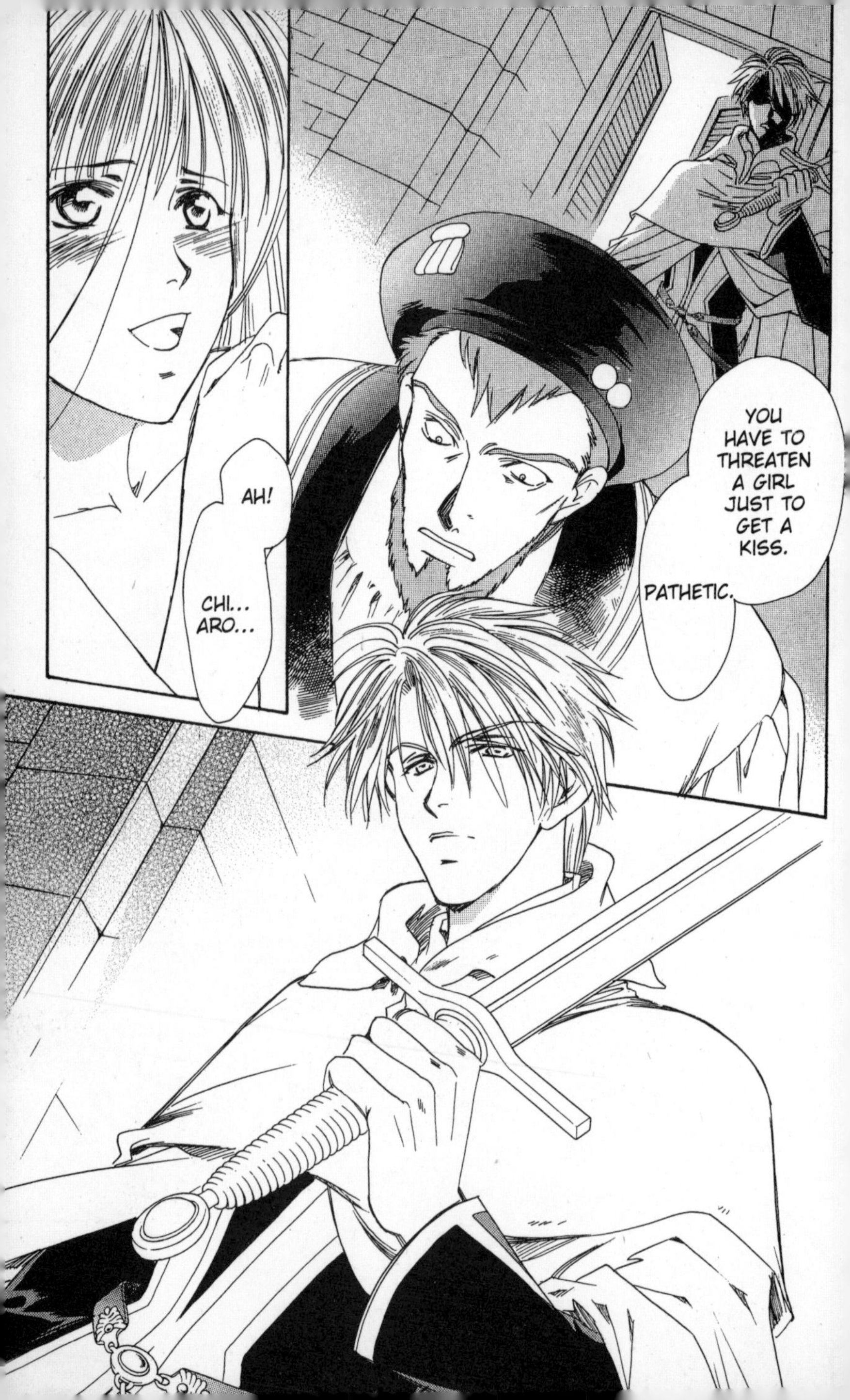
YOU HAVE TO THREATEN A GIRL JUST TO GET A KISS.
PATHETIC.
AH!
CHI... ARO...

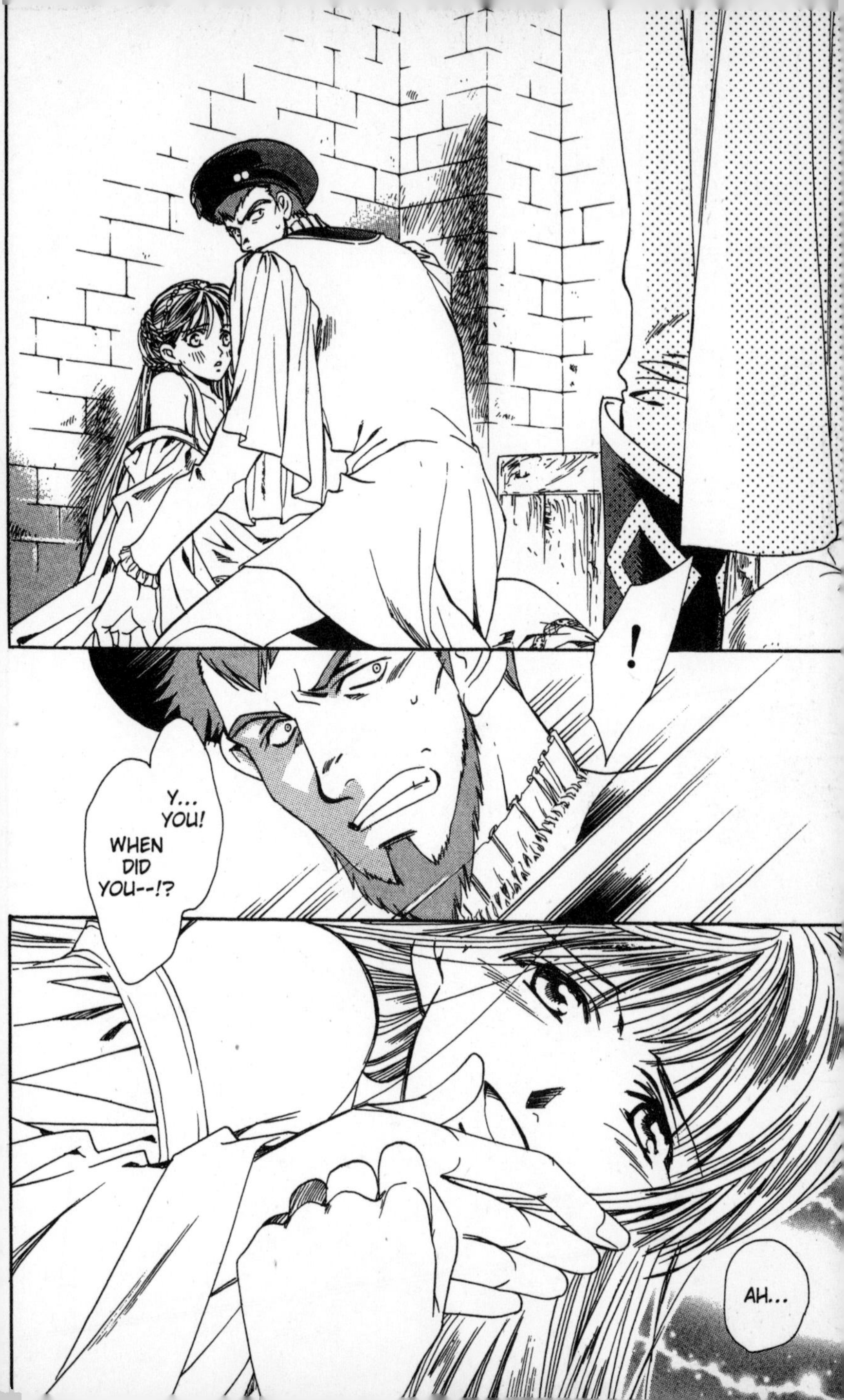
!
Y... YOU! WHEN DID YOU--!?
AH...

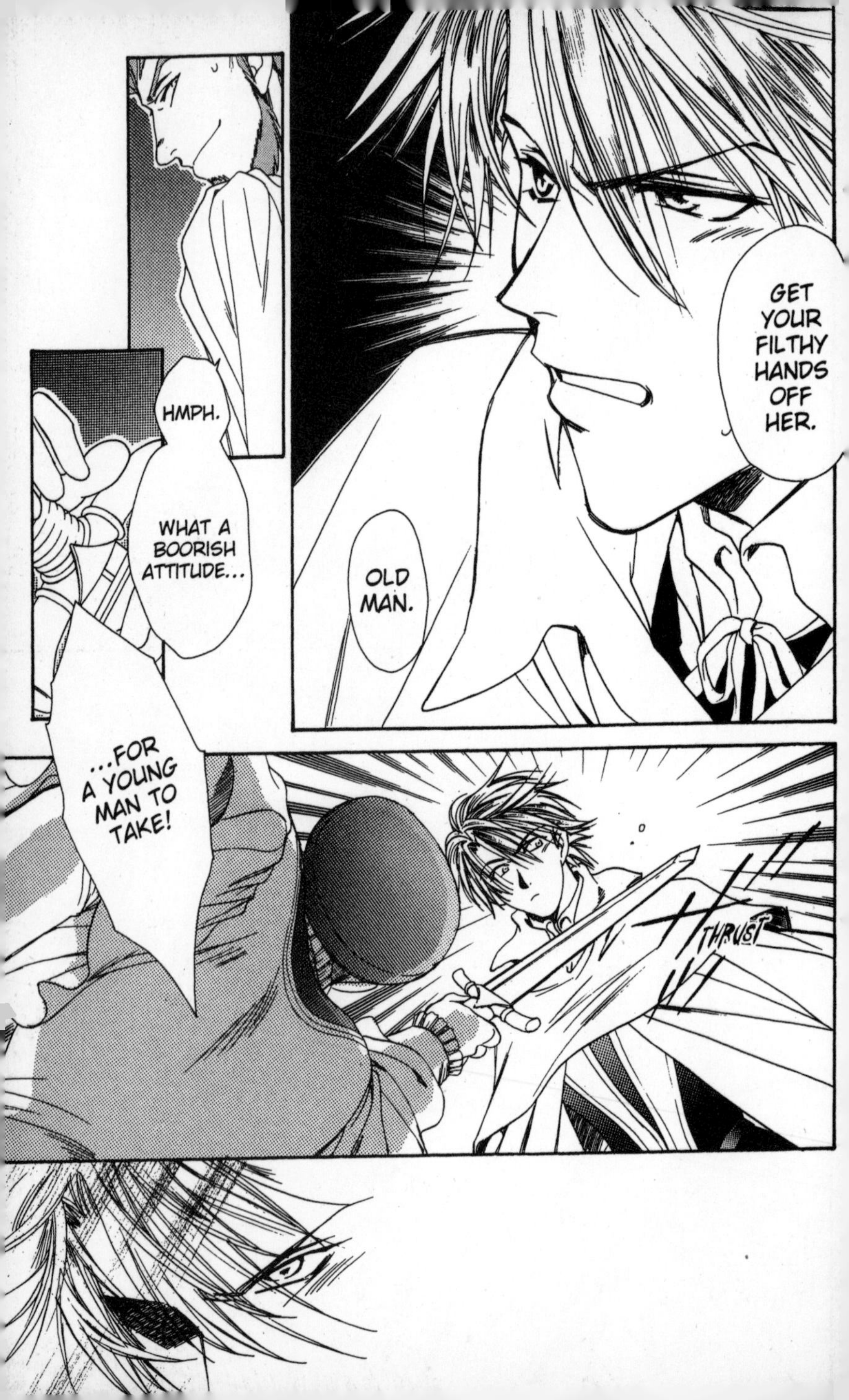
GET YOUR FILTHY HANDS OFF HER.
OLD MAN.
HMPH.
WHAT A BOORISH ATTITUDE...
...FOR A YOUNG MAN TO TAKE!
THRUST

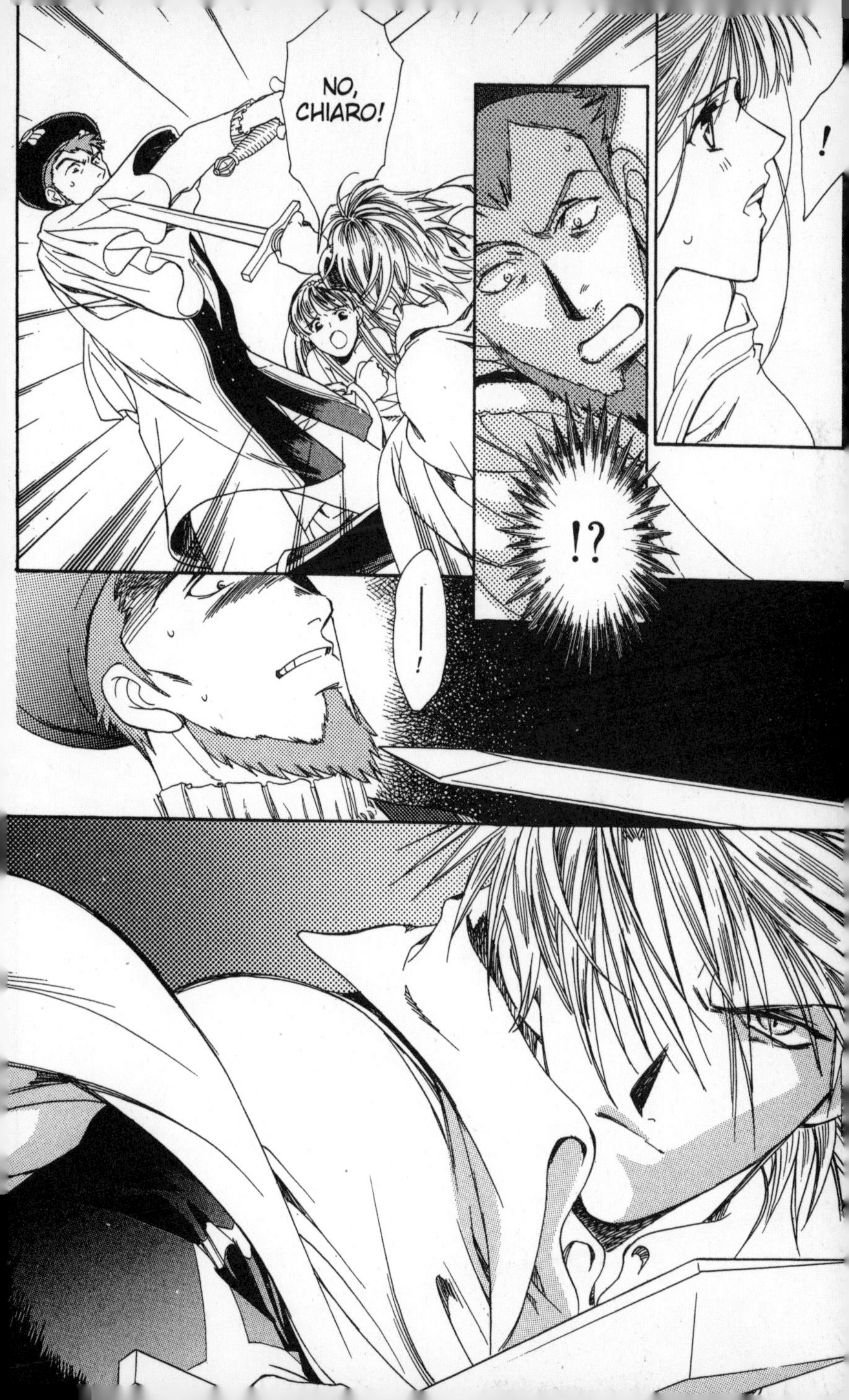
!
!?
NO, CHIARO!
!!

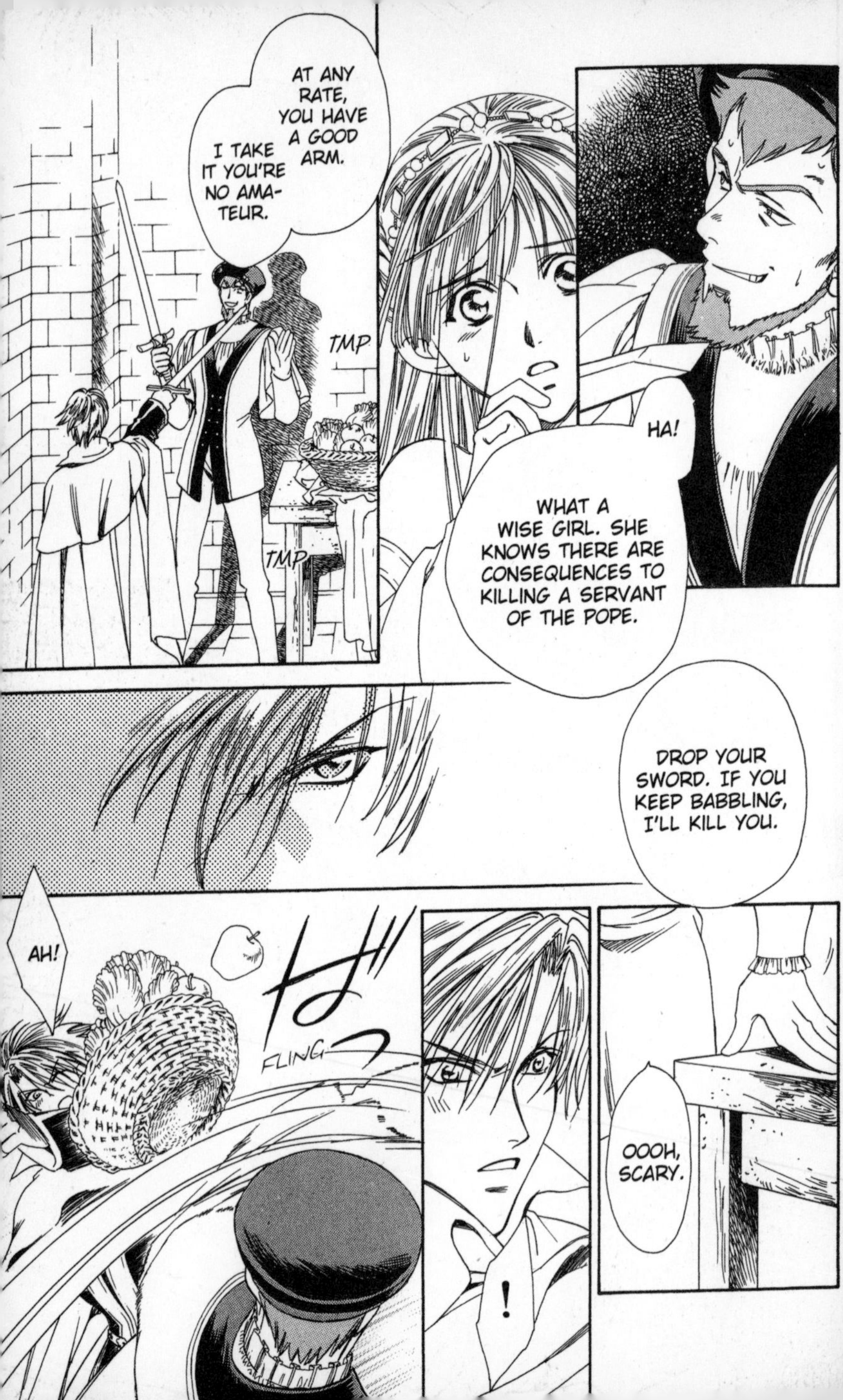
HA!
WHAT A WISE GIRL. SHE KNOWS THERE ARE CONSEQUENCES TO KILLING A SERVANT OF THE POPE.
AT ANY RATE, YOU HAVE A GOOD ARM.
I TAKE IT YOU'RE NO AMATEUR.
TMP
TMP
DROP YOUR SWORD. IF YOU KEEP BABBLING, I'LL KILL YOU.
OOOH, SCARY.
!
FLING
AH!

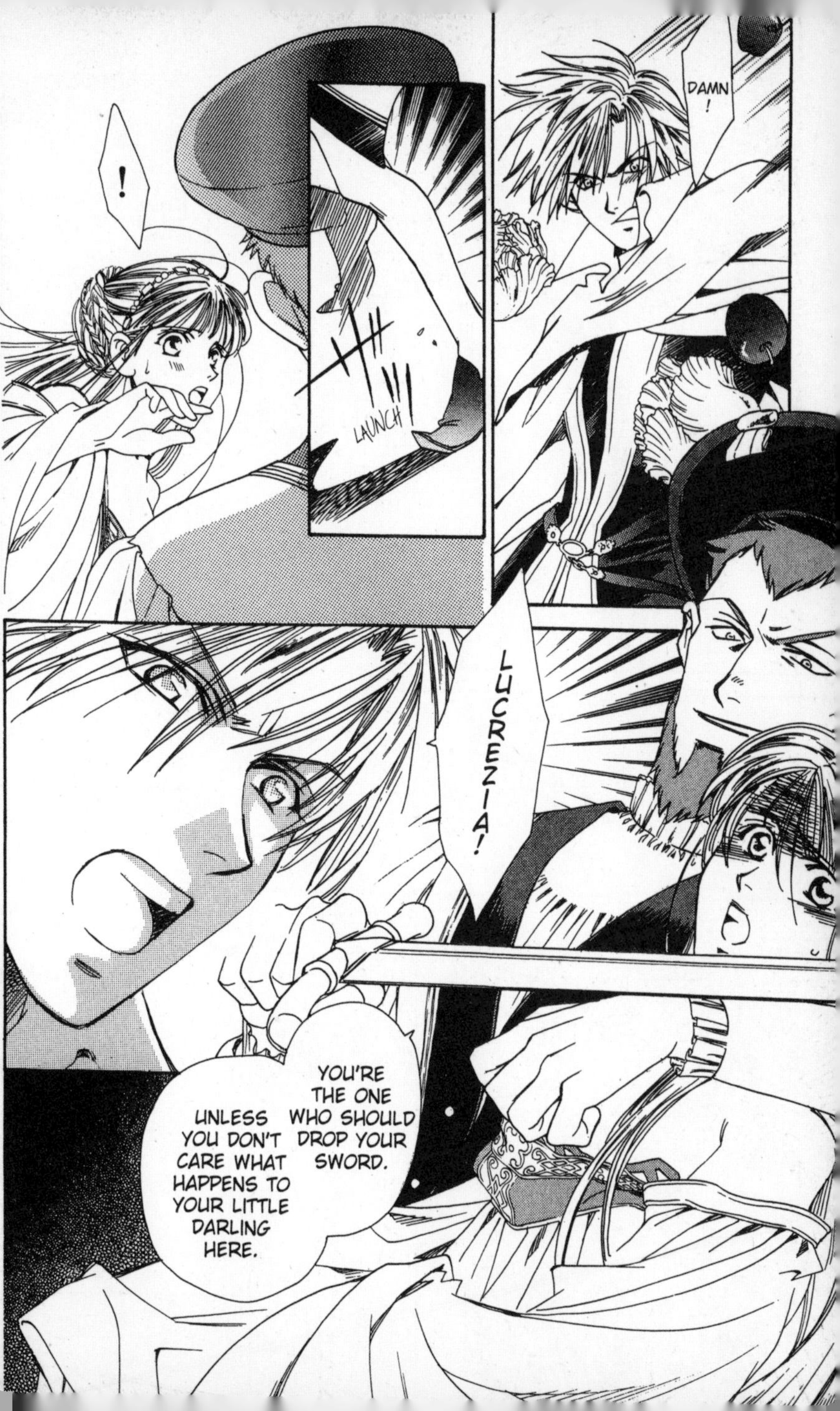
DAMN!
LAUNCH
!
LUCREZIA!
YOU'RE THE ONE WHO SHOULD DROP YOUR SWORD.
UNLESS YOU DON'T CARE WHAT HAPPENS TO YOUR LITTLE DARLING HERE.

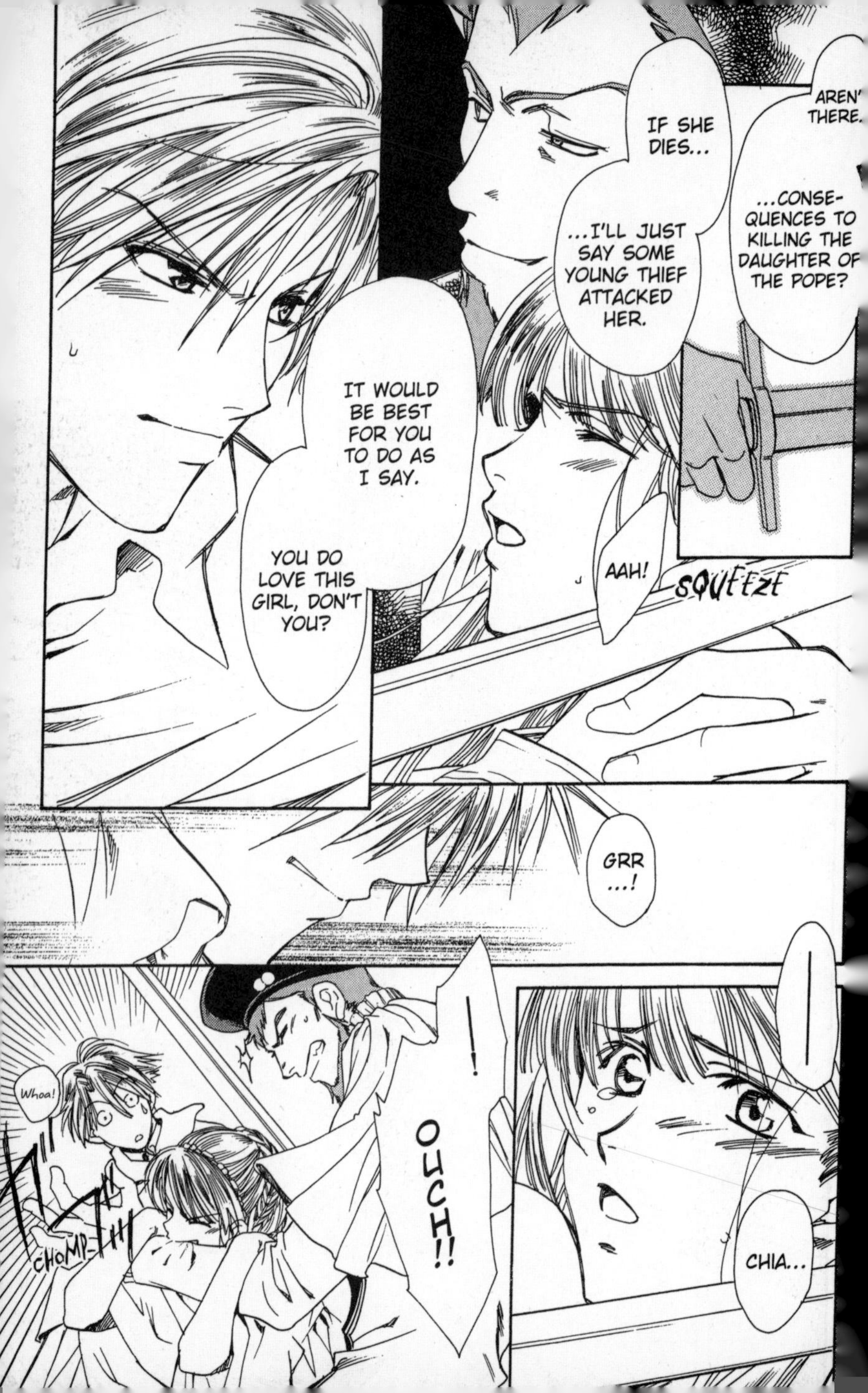
AREN' THERE.
...CONSE-QUENCES TO KILLING THE DAUGHTER OF THE POPE?
IF SHE DIES...
...I'LL JUST SAY SOME YOUNG THIEF ATTACKED HER.
IT WOULD BE BEST FOR YOU TO DO AS I SAY.
YOU DO LOVE THIS GIRL, DON'T YOU?
AAH!
SQUEEZE
GRR ...!
!
CHIA...
!
OUCH!!
Whoa!
CHOMP

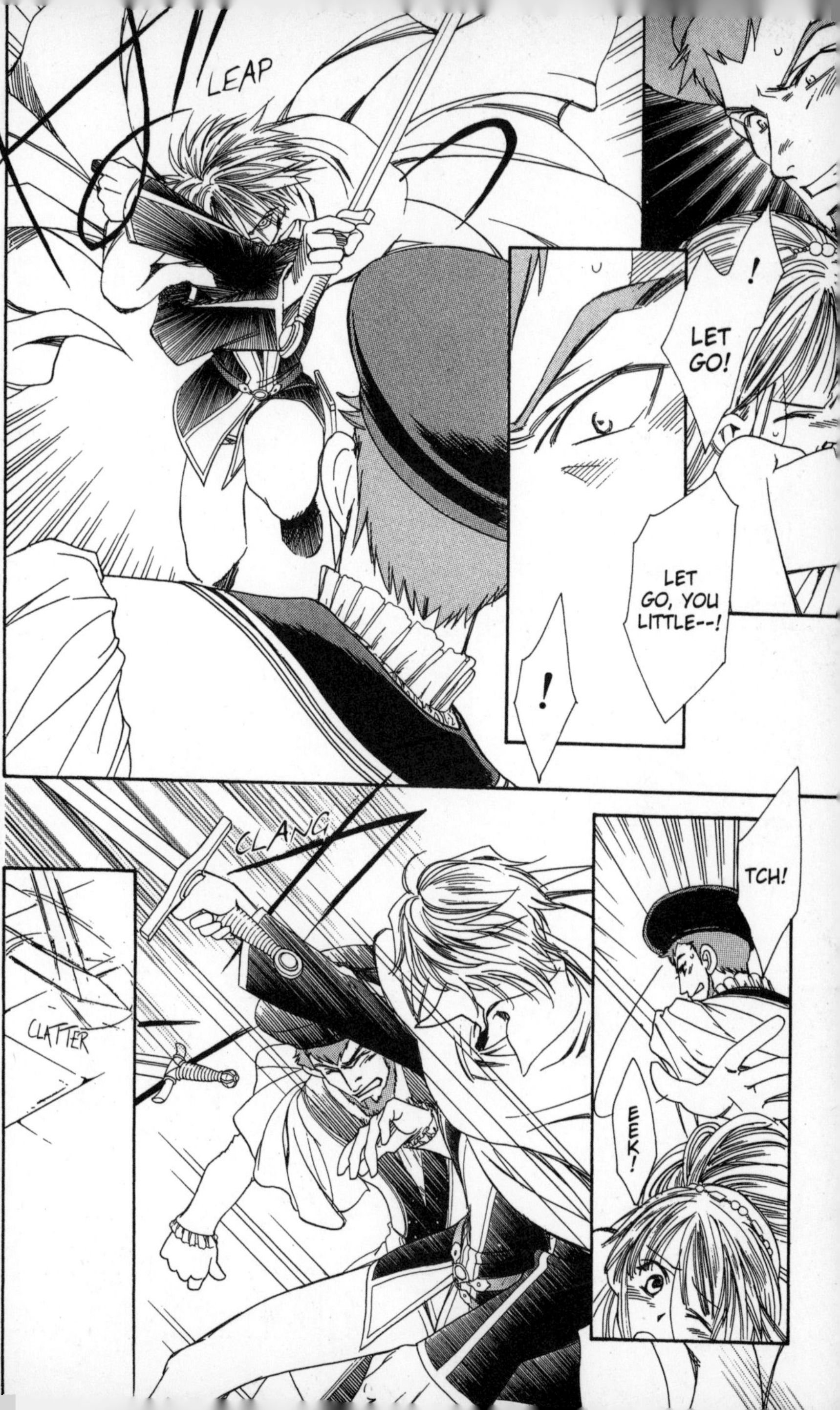
!
LET GO!
LET GO, YOU LITTLE--!
!
LEAP
TCH!
EEK!
CLANG
CLATTER

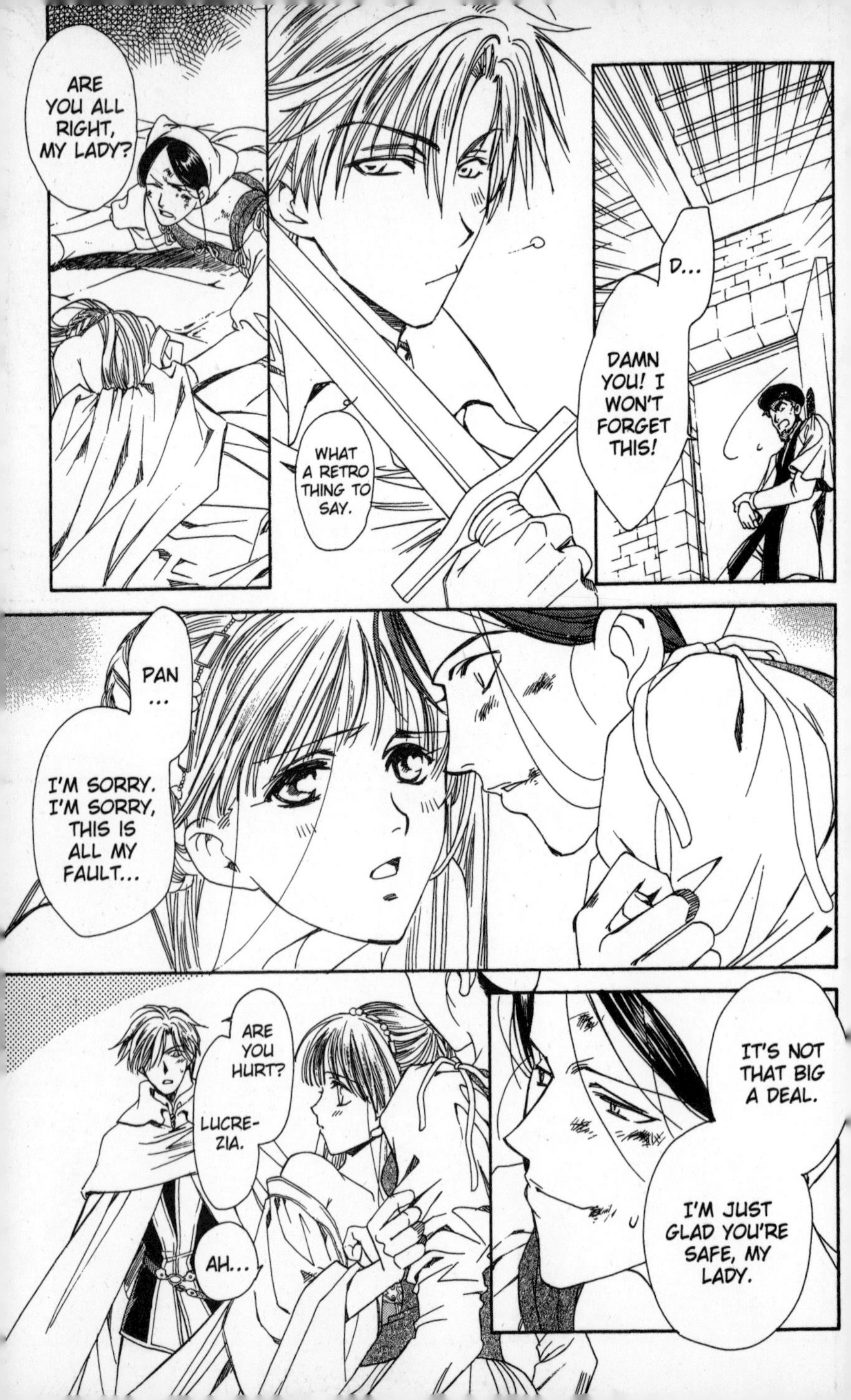
D...
DAMN YOU! I WON'T FORGET THIS!
WHAT A RETRO THING TO SAY.
ARE YOU ALL RIGHT, MY LADY?
PAN...
I'M SORRY. I'M SORRY, THIS IS ALL MY FAULT...
IT'S NOT THAT BIG A DEAL.
I'M JUST GLAD YOU'RE SAFE, MY LADY.
ARE YOU HURT?
LUCREZIA.
AH...

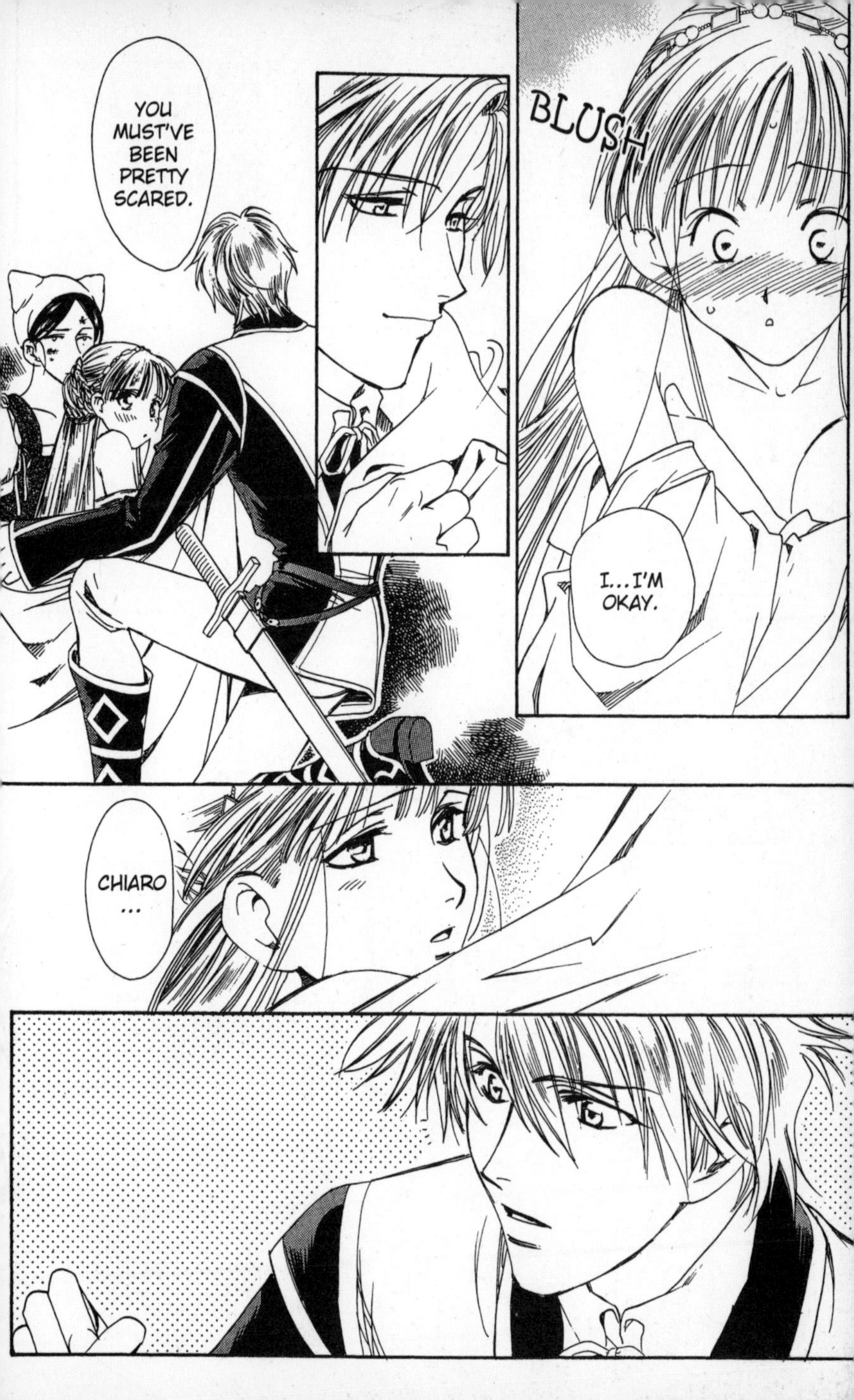
BLUSH
I...I'M OKAY.
YOU MUST'VE BEEN PRETTY SCARED.
CHIARO ...

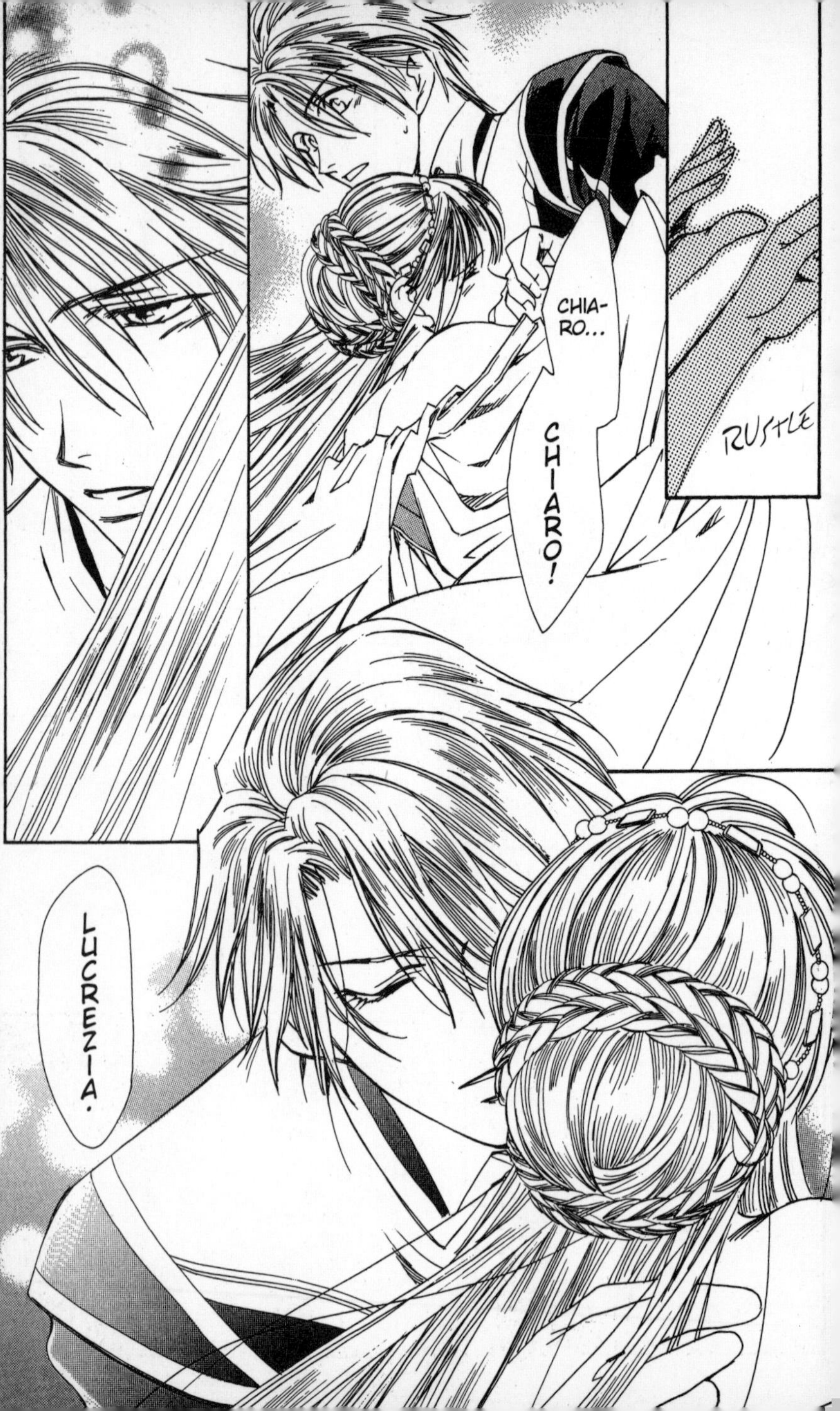
RUSTLE
CHIARO...
CHIARO!
LUCREZIA.

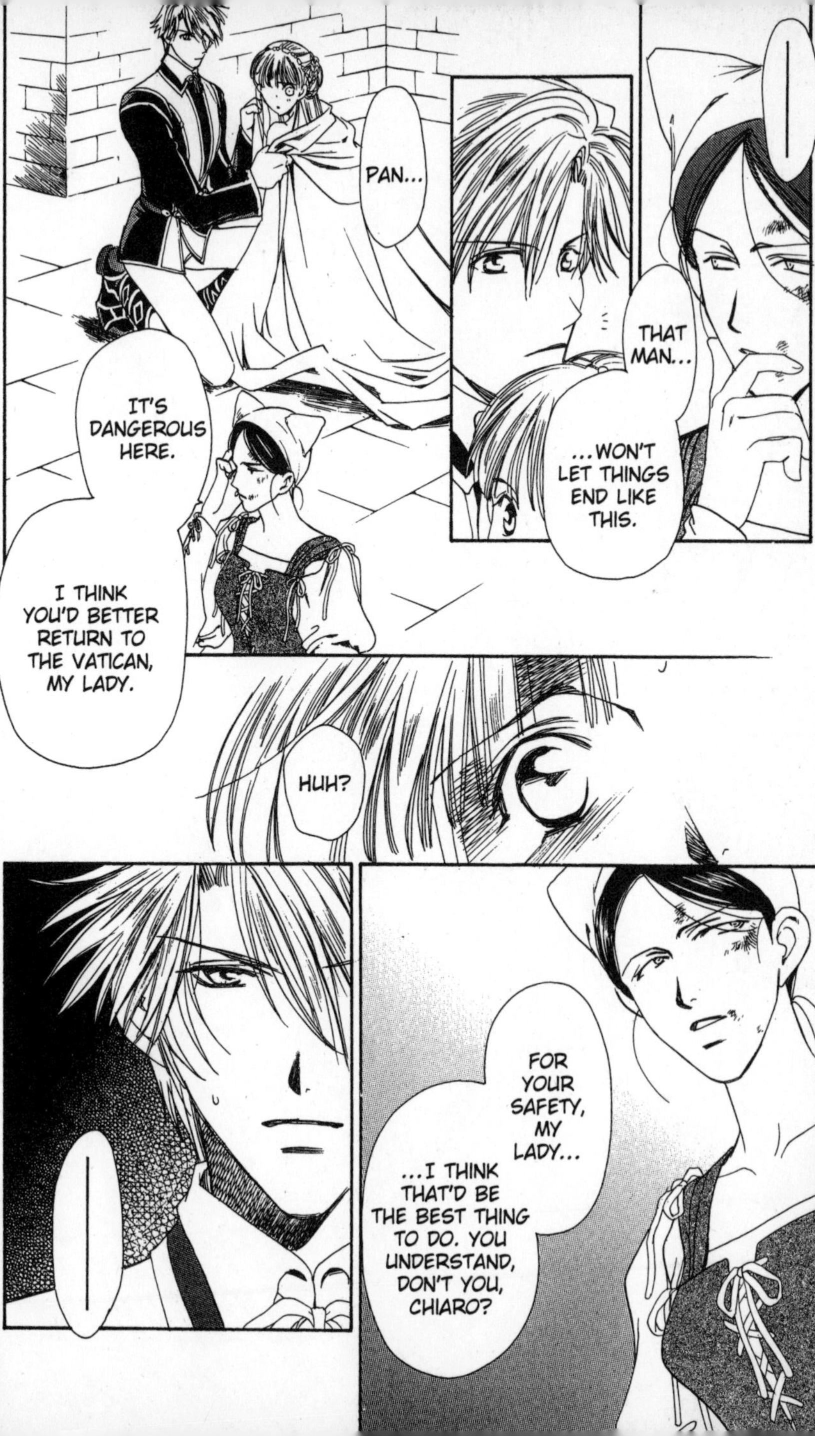
THAT MAN...
...WON'T LET THINGS END LIKE THIS.
PAN...
IT'S DANGEROUS HERE.
I THINK YOU'D BETTER RETURN TO THE VATICAN, MY LADY.
HUH?
FOR YOUR SAFETY, MY LADY...
...I THINK THAT'D BE THE BEST THING TO DO. YOU UNDERSTAND, DON'T YOU, CHIARO?

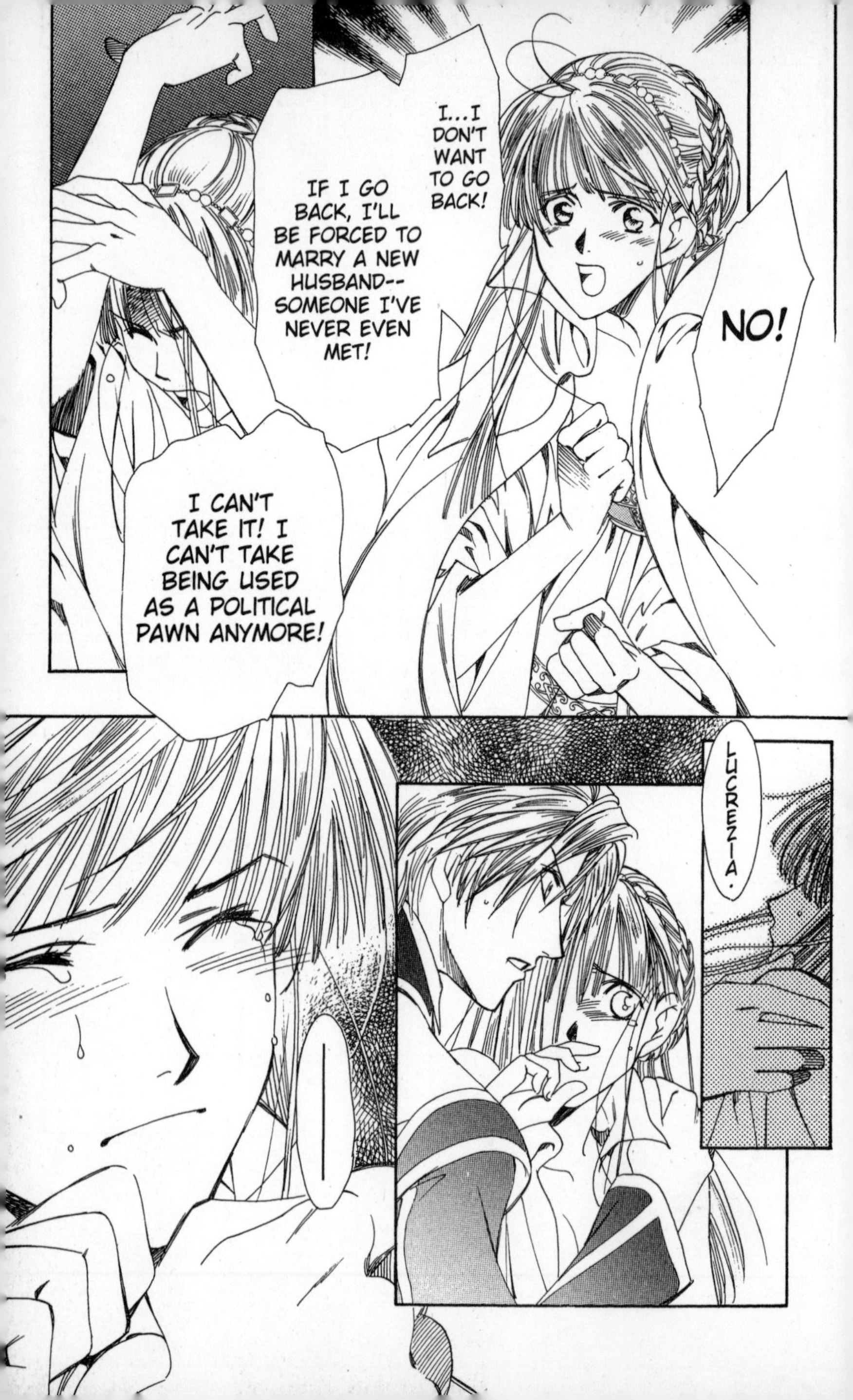
NO!
I...I DON'T WANT TO GO BACK!
IF I GO BACK, I'LL BE FORCED TO MARRY A NEW HUSBAND--SOMEONE I'VE NEVER EVEN MET!
I CAN'T TAKE IT! I CAN'T TAKE BEING USED AS A POLITICAL PAWN ANYMORE!
LUCREZIA.

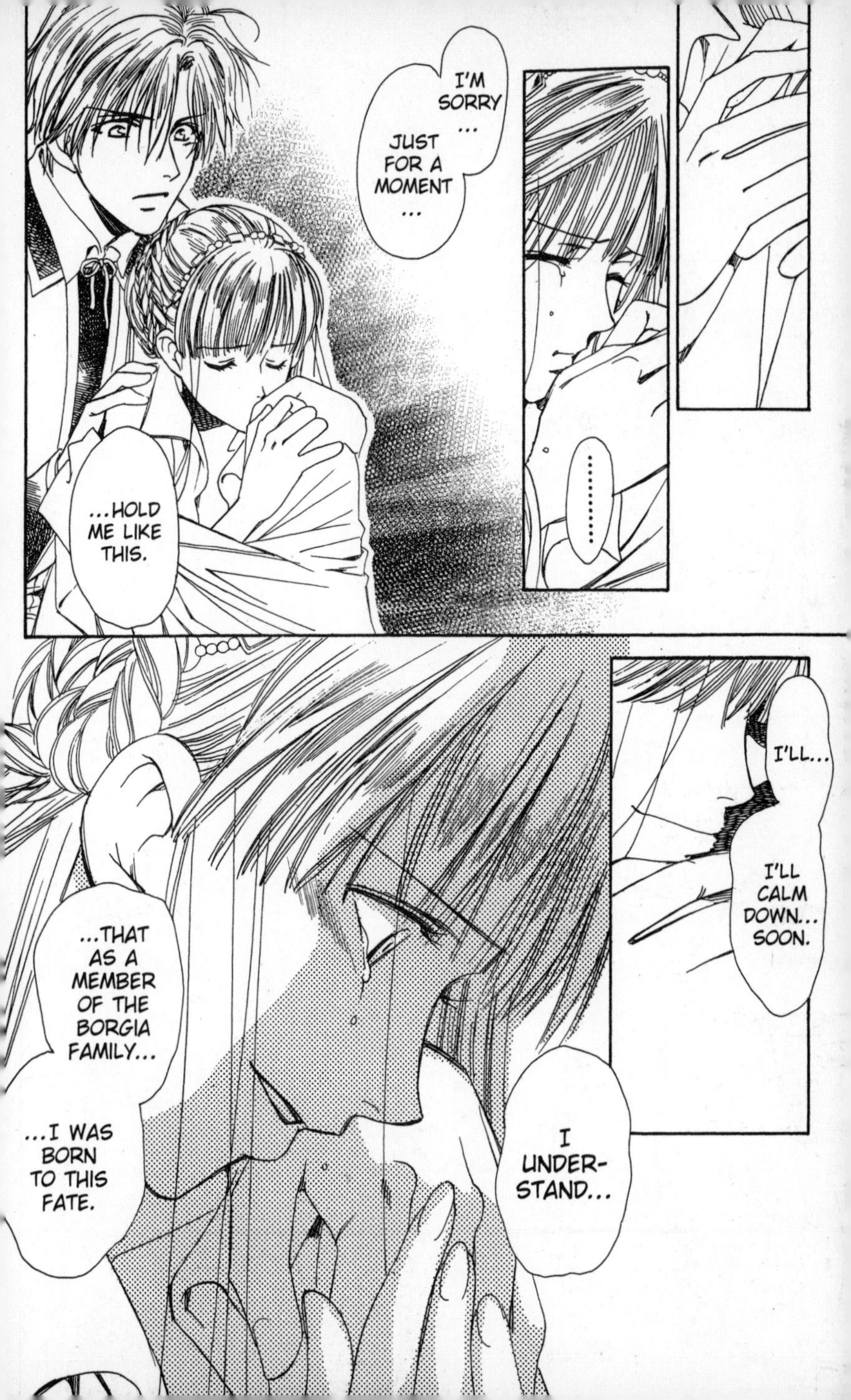
......
I'M SORRY ... JUST FOR A MOMENT ...
...HOLD ME LIKE THIS.
I'LL...
I'LL CALM DOWN... SOON.
I UNDER-STAND...
...THAT AS A MEMBER OF THE BORGIA FAMILY...
...I WAS BORN TO THIS FATE.

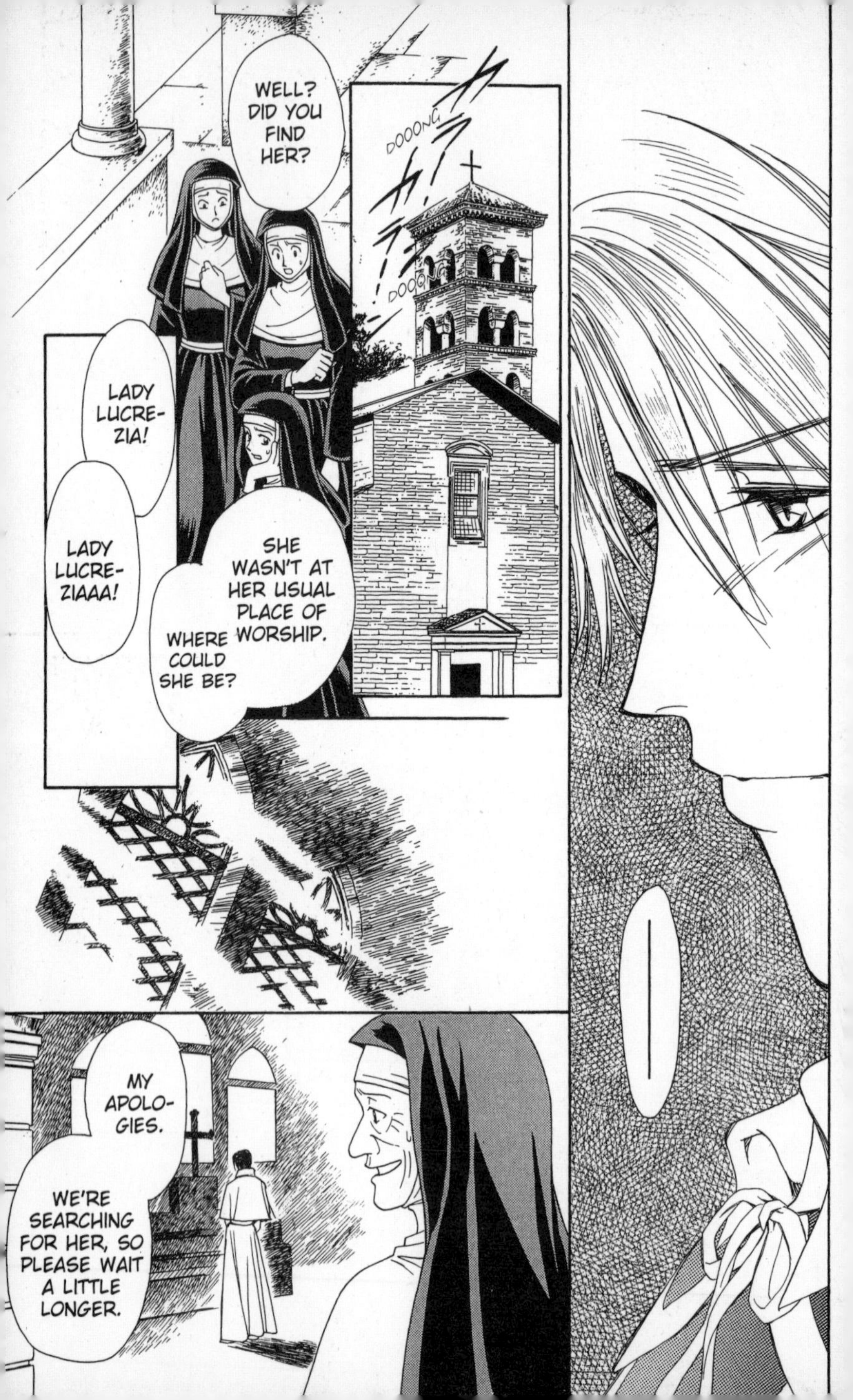
DOOONG
DOOONG
WELL? DID YOU FIND HER?
SHE WASN'T AT HER USUAL PLACE OF WORSHIP.
WHERE COULD SHE BE?
LADY LUCREZIA!
LADY LUCREZIAAA!
MY APOLOGIES.
WE'RE SEARCHING FOR HER, SO PLEASE WAIT A LITTLE LONGER.

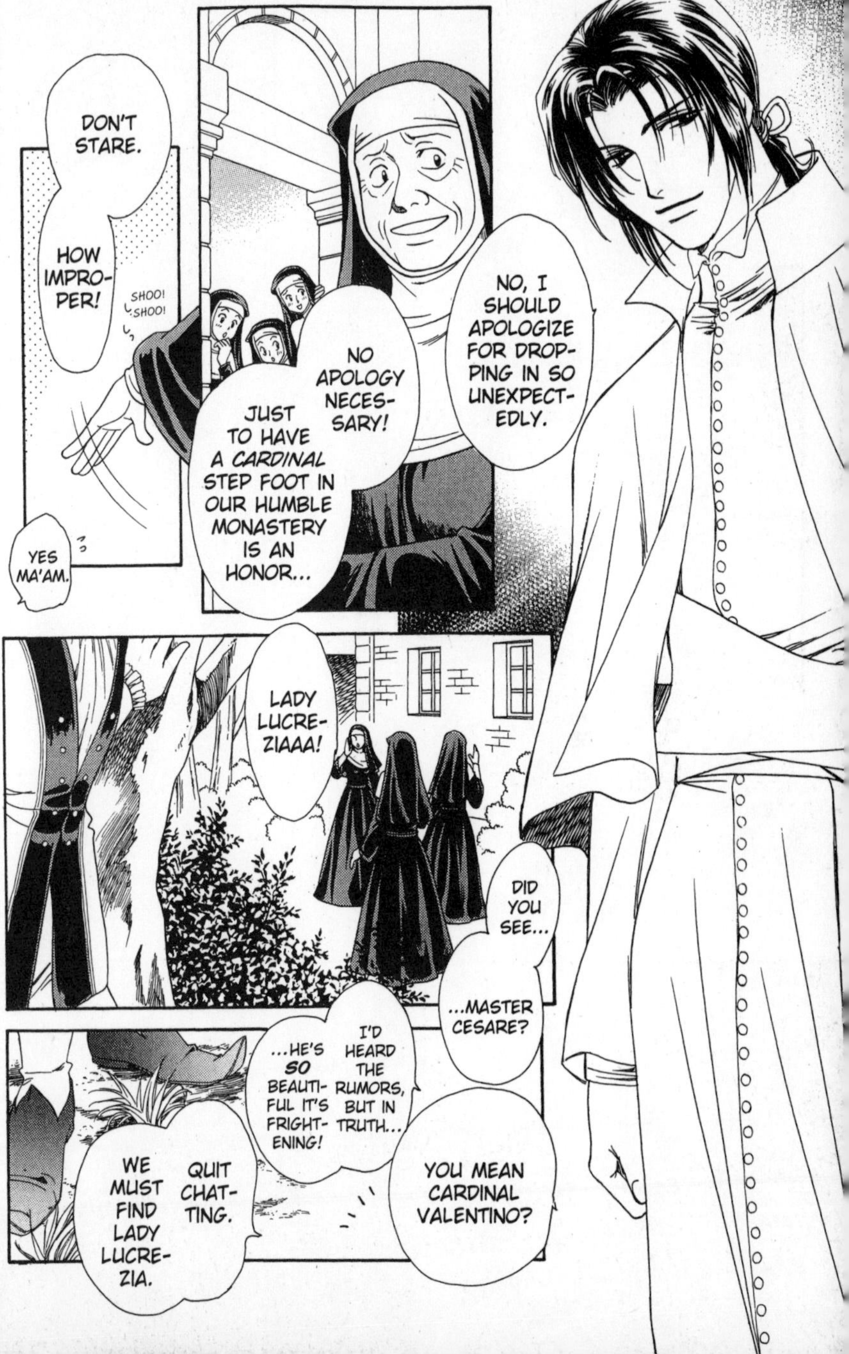
NO, I SHOULD APOLOGIZE FOR DROPPING IN SO UNEXPECTEDLY.
NO APOLOGY NECESSARY!
JUST TO HAVE A *CARDINAL* STEP FOOT IN OUR HUMBLE MONASTERY IS AN HONOR...
DON'T STARE.
HOW IMPROPER!
SHOO! SHOO!
YES MA'AM.
LADY LUCREZIAAA!
DID YOU SEE...
...MASTER CESARE?
YOU MEAN CARDINAL VALENTINO?
I'D HEARD THE RUMORS, BUT IN TRUTH...
...HE'S *SO* BEAUTIFUL IT'S FRIGHTENING!
QUIT CHATTING.
WE MUST FIND LADY LUCREZIA.

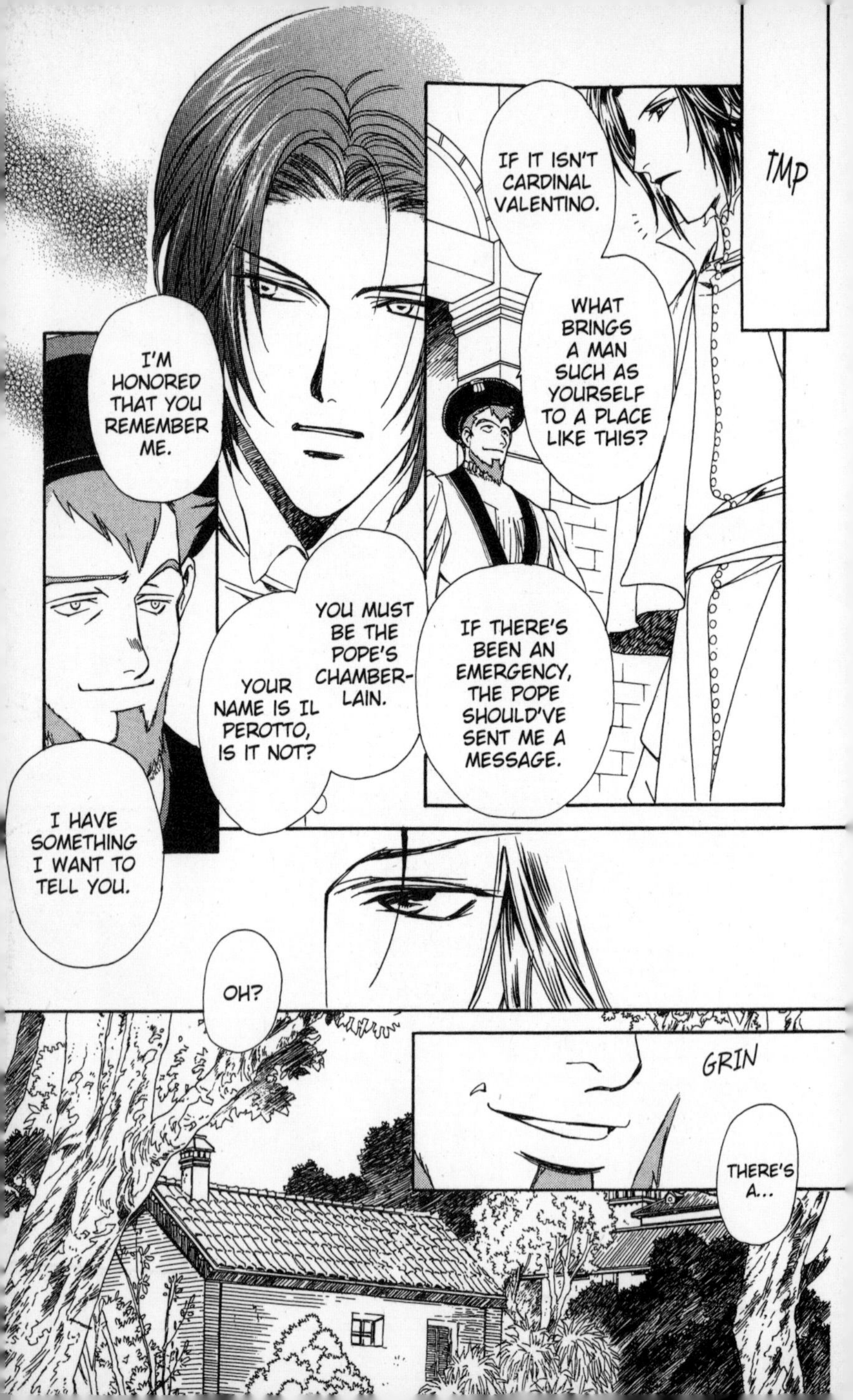
TMP
IF IT ISN'T CARDINAL VALENTINO.
WHAT BRINGS A MAN SUCH AS YOURSELF TO A PLACE LIKE THIS?
IF THERE'S BEEN AN EMERGENCY, THE POPE SHOULD'VE SENT ME A MESSAGE.
YOU MUST BE THE POPE'S CHAMBER-LAIN.
YOUR NAME IS IL PEROTTO, IS IT NOT?
I'M HONORED THAT YOU REMEMBER ME.
I HAVE SOMETHING I WANT TO TELL YOU.
OH?
GRIN
THERE'S A...

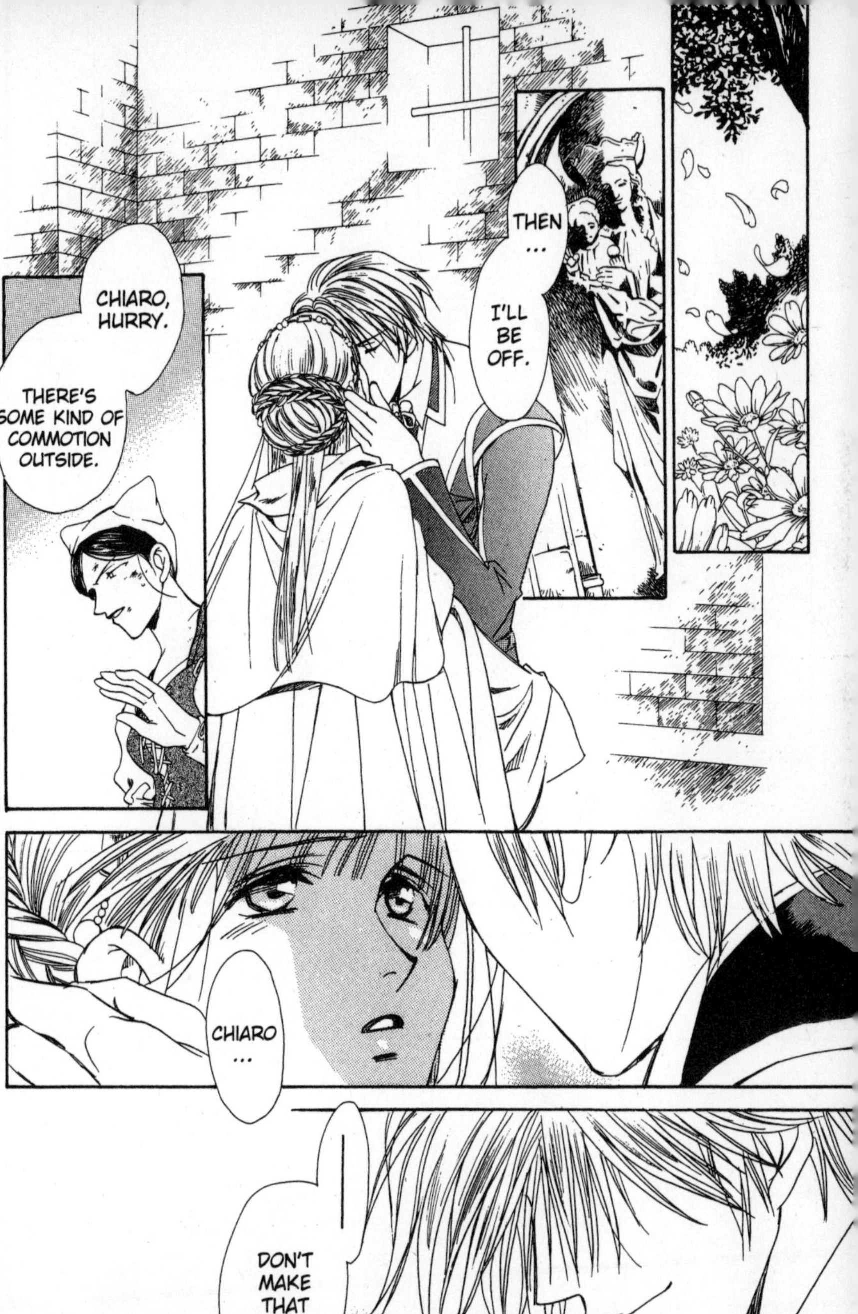
THEN... I'LL BE OFF.
CHIARO, HURRY.
THERE'S SOME KIND OF COMMOTION OUTSIDE.
CHIARO...
DON'T MAKE THAT FACE...

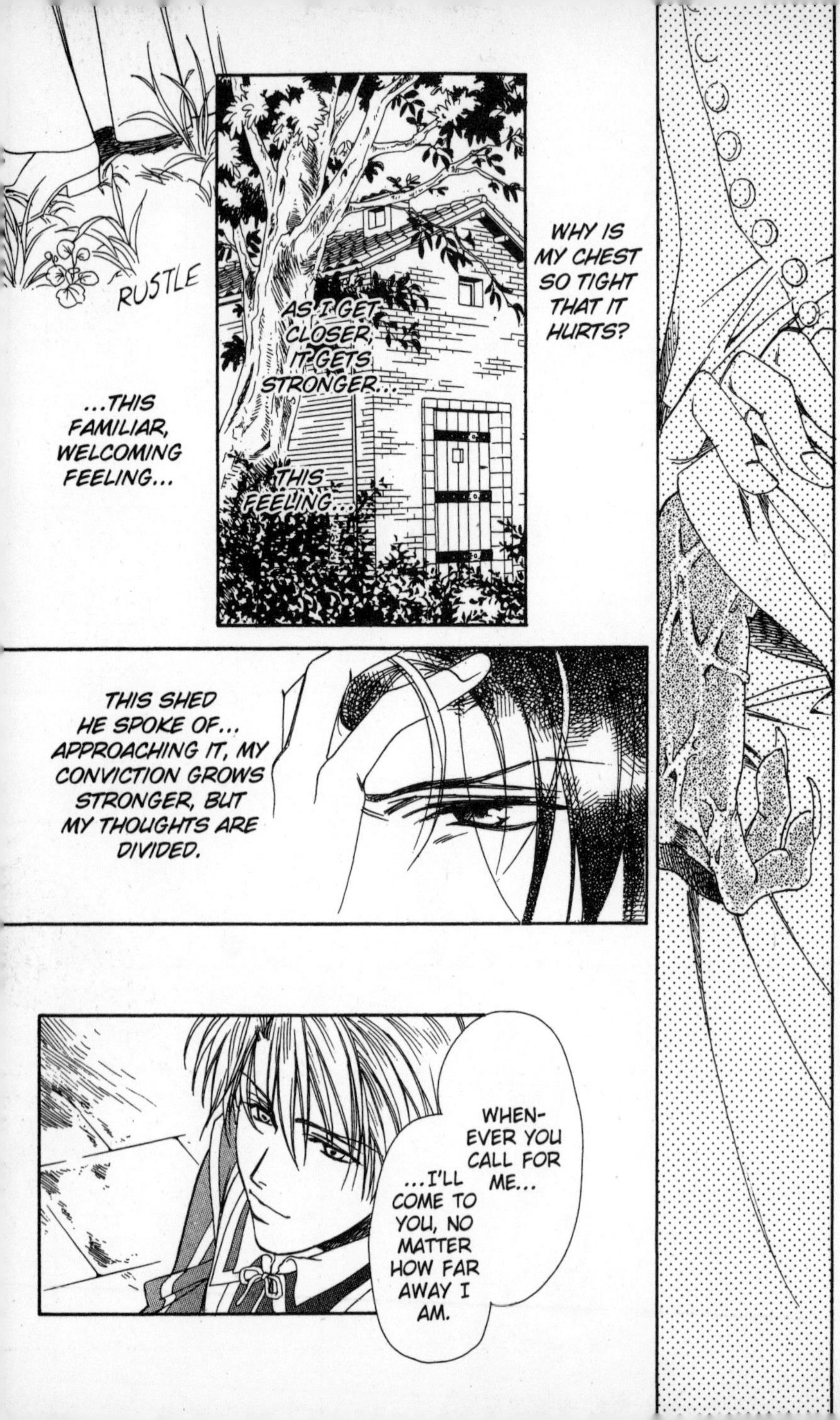
WHY IS MY CHEST SO TIGHT THAT IT HURTS?
AS I GET CLOSER, IT GETS STRONGER...
THIS FEELING...
RUSTLE
...THIS FAMILIAR, WELCOMING FEELING...
THIS SHED HE SPOKE OF... APPROACHING IT, MY CONVICTION GROWS STRONGER, BUT MY THOUGHTS ARE DIVIDED.
WHEN-EVER YOU CALL FOR ME...
...I'LL COME TO YOU, NO MATTER HOW FAR AWAY I AM.

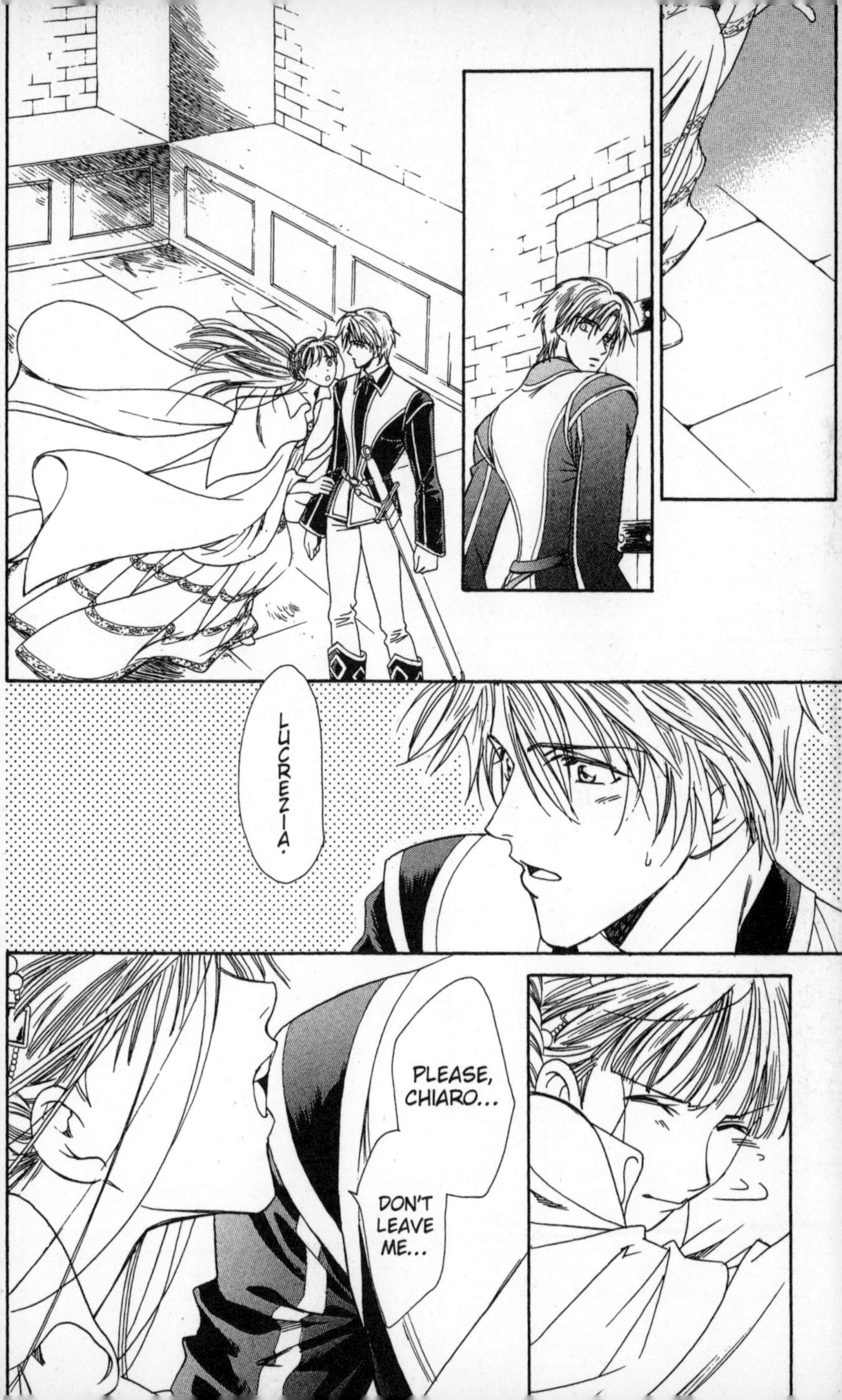
LUCREZIA.
PLEASE, CHIARO...
DON'T LEAVE ME...

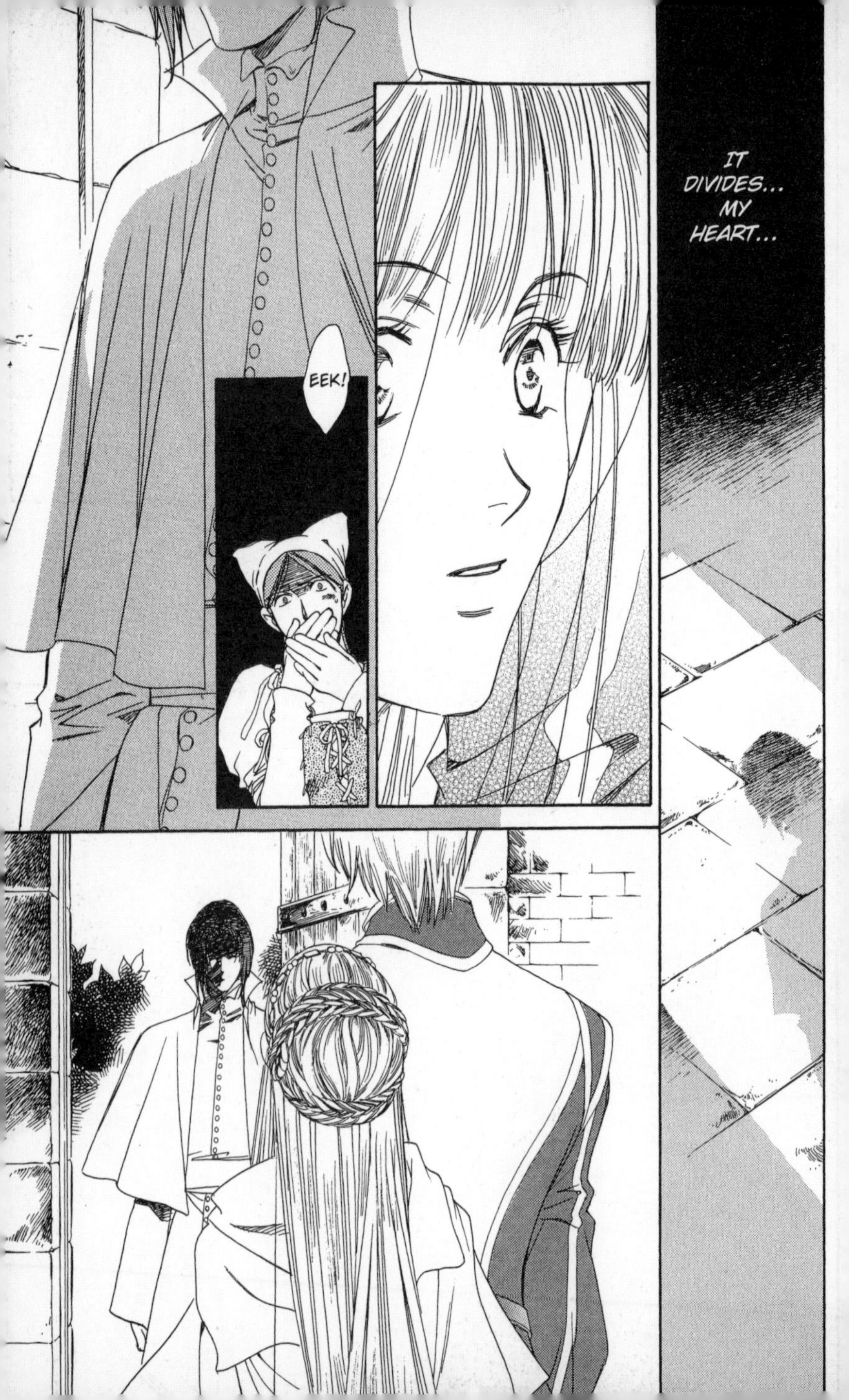
IT DIVIDES... MY HEART...
EEK!

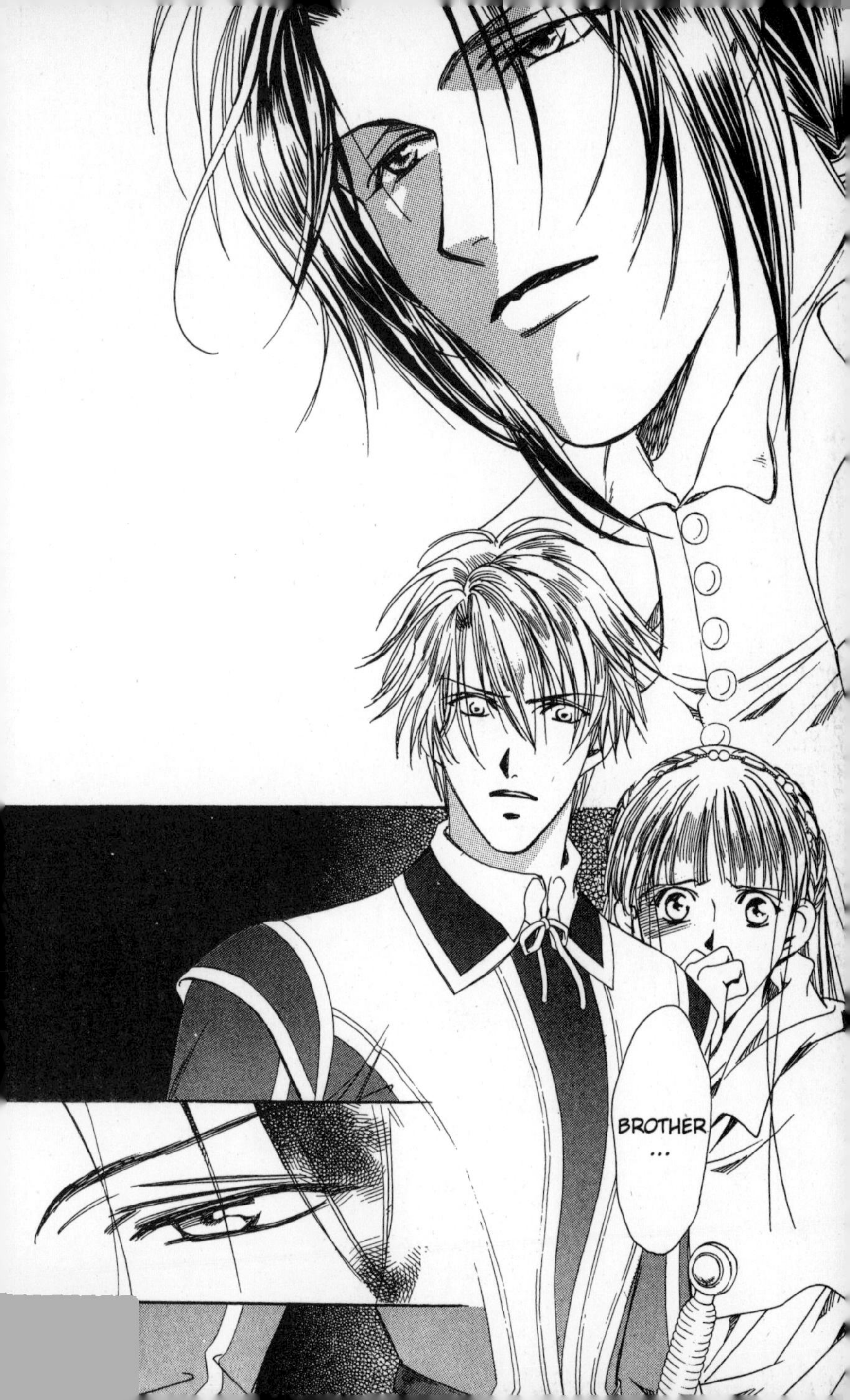
BROTHER ...

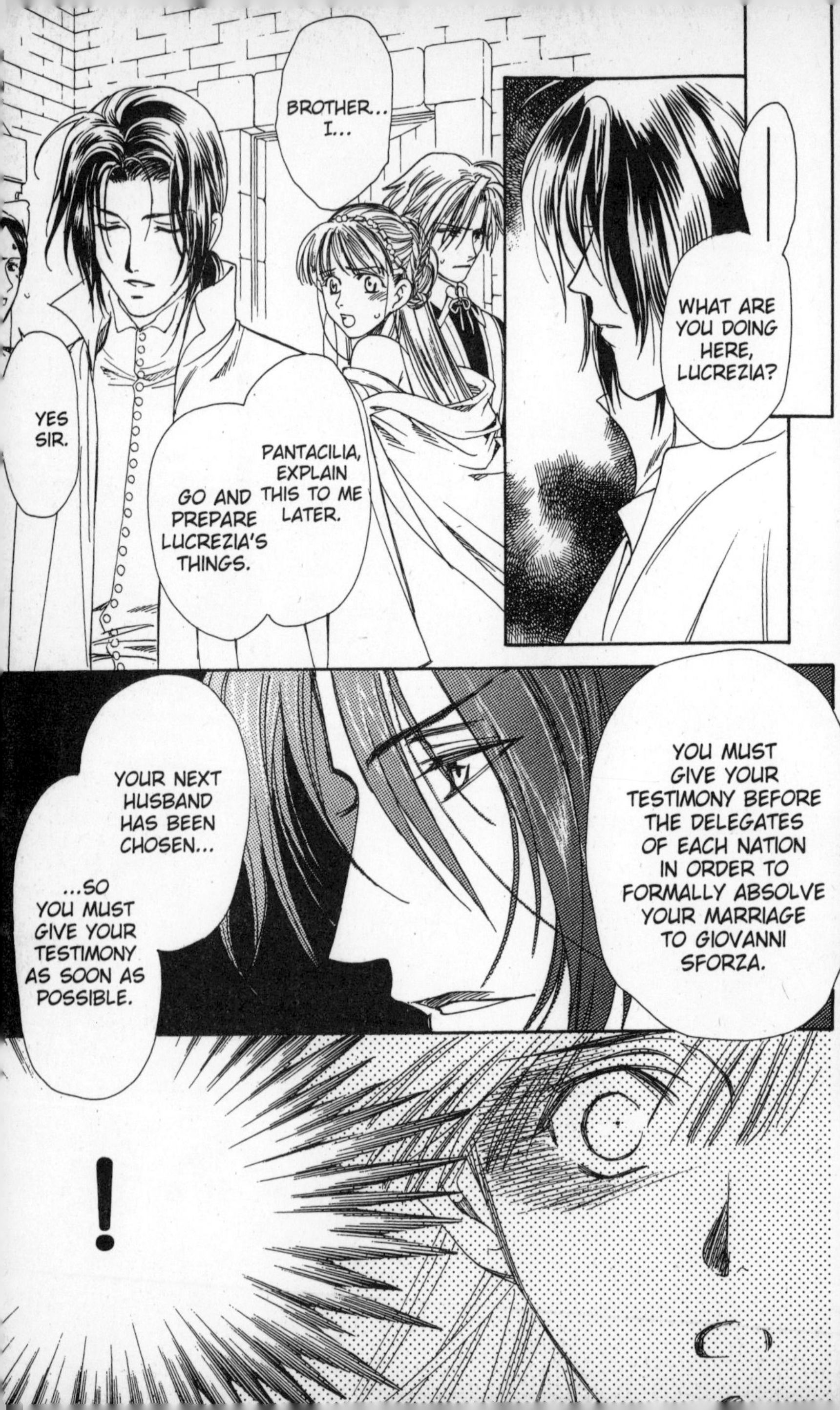
WHAT ARE YOU DOING HERE, LUCREZIA?
BROTHER... I...
PANTACILIA, EXPLAIN THIS TO ME LATER.
GO AND PREPARE LUCREZIA'S THINGS.
YES SIR.
YOU MUST GIVE YOUR TESTIMONY BEFORE THE DELEGATES OF EACH NATION IN ORDER TO FORMALLY ABSOLVE YOUR MARRIAGE TO GIOVANNI SFORZA.
YOUR NEXT HUSBAND HAS BEEN CHOSEN...
...SO YOU MUST GIVE YOUR TESTIMONY AS SOON AS POSSIBLE.
!

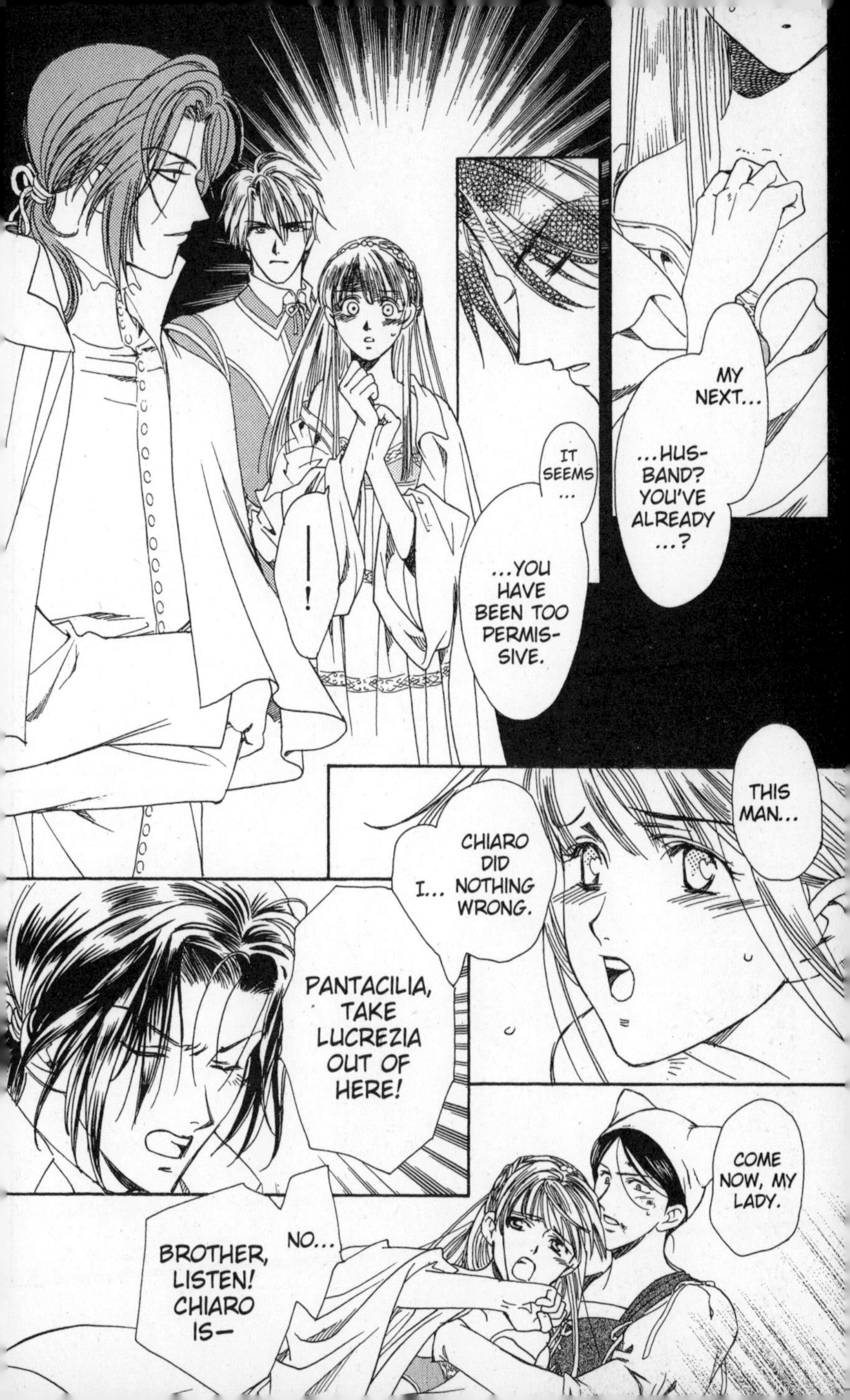
MY NEXT...
...HUS-BAND? YOU'VE ALREADY ...?
IT SEEMS ...
...YOU HAVE BEEN TOO PERMIS-SIVE.
!
THIS MAN...
I... CHIARO DID NOTHING WRONG.
PANTACILIA, TAKE LUCREZIA OUT OF HERE!
COME NOW, MY LADY.
NO...
BROTHER, LISTEN! CHIARO IS—

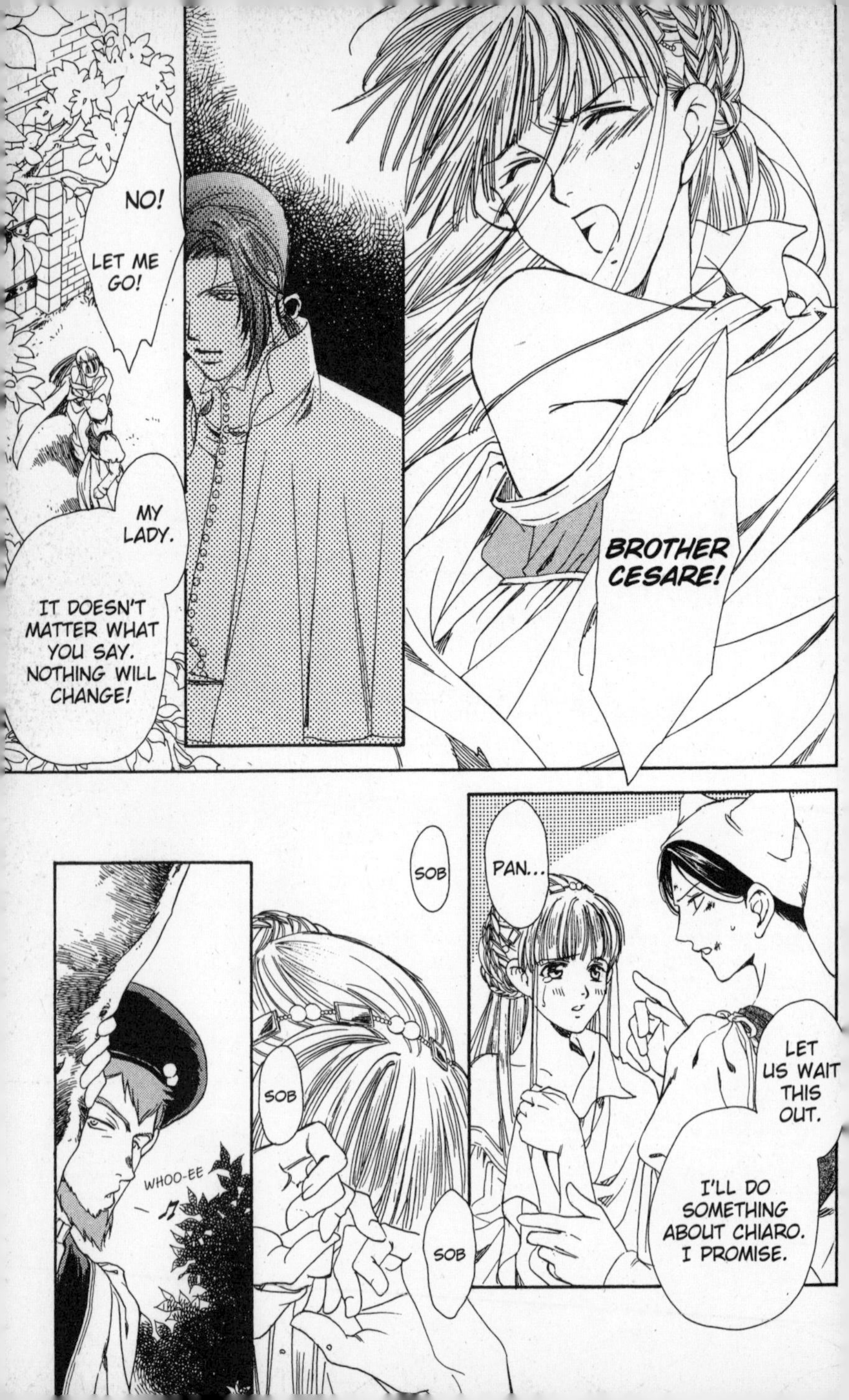
BROTHER CESARE!
NO!
LET ME GO!
MY LADY.
IT DOESN'T MATTER WHAT YOU SAY. NOTHING WILL CHANGE!
PAN...
LET US WAIT THIS OUT.
I'LL DO SOMETHING ABOUT CHIARO. I PROMISE.
SOB
SOB
SOB
WHOO-EE

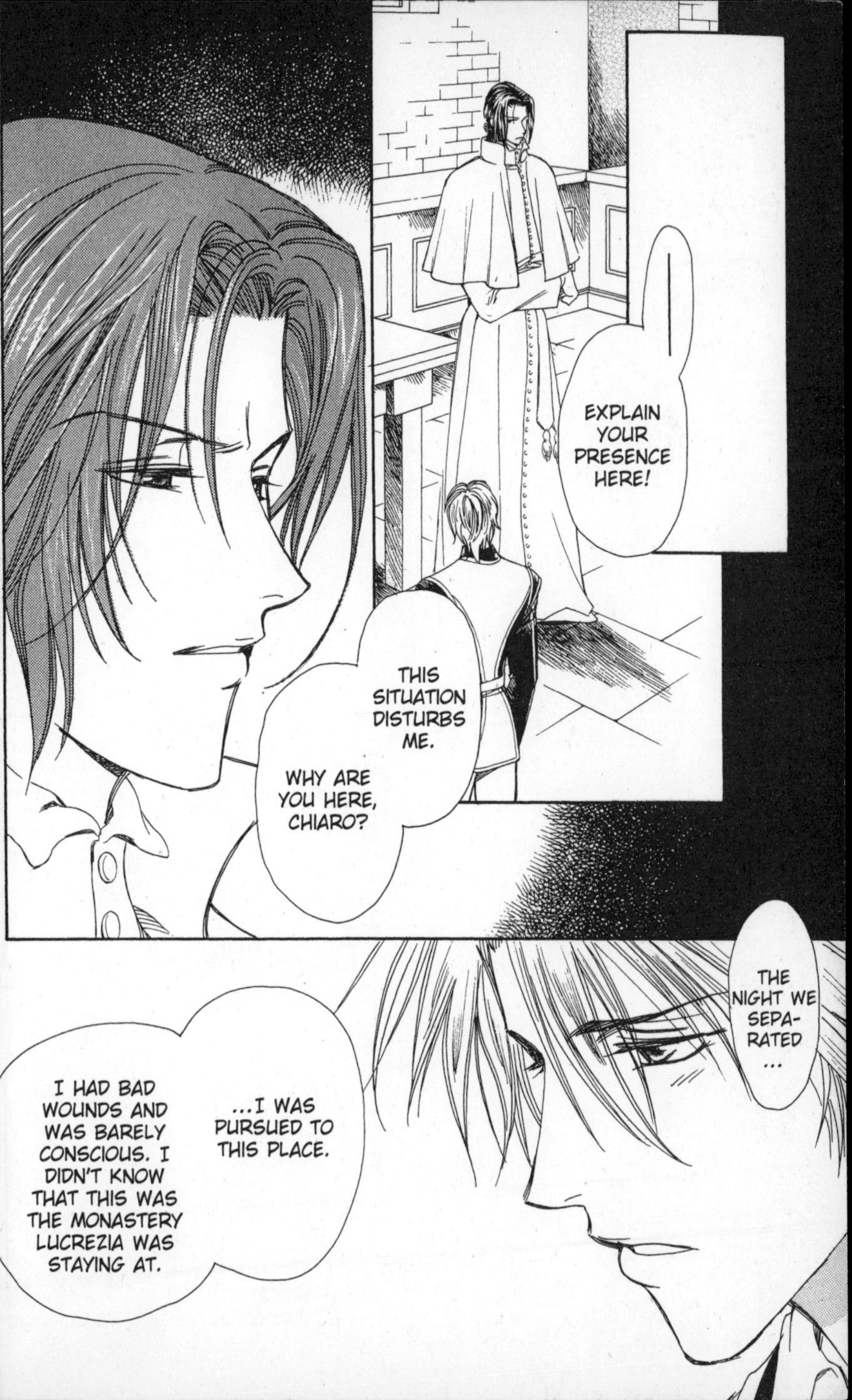
EXPLAIN YOUR PRESENCE HERE!
THIS SITUATION DISTURBS ME.
WHY ARE YOU HERE, CHIARO?
THE NIGHT WE SEPA-RATED ...
...I WAS PURSUED TO THIS PLACE.
I HAD BAD WOUNDS AND WAS BARELY CONSCIOUS. I DIDN'T KNOW THAT THIS WAS THE MONASTERY LUCREZIA WAS STAYING AT.

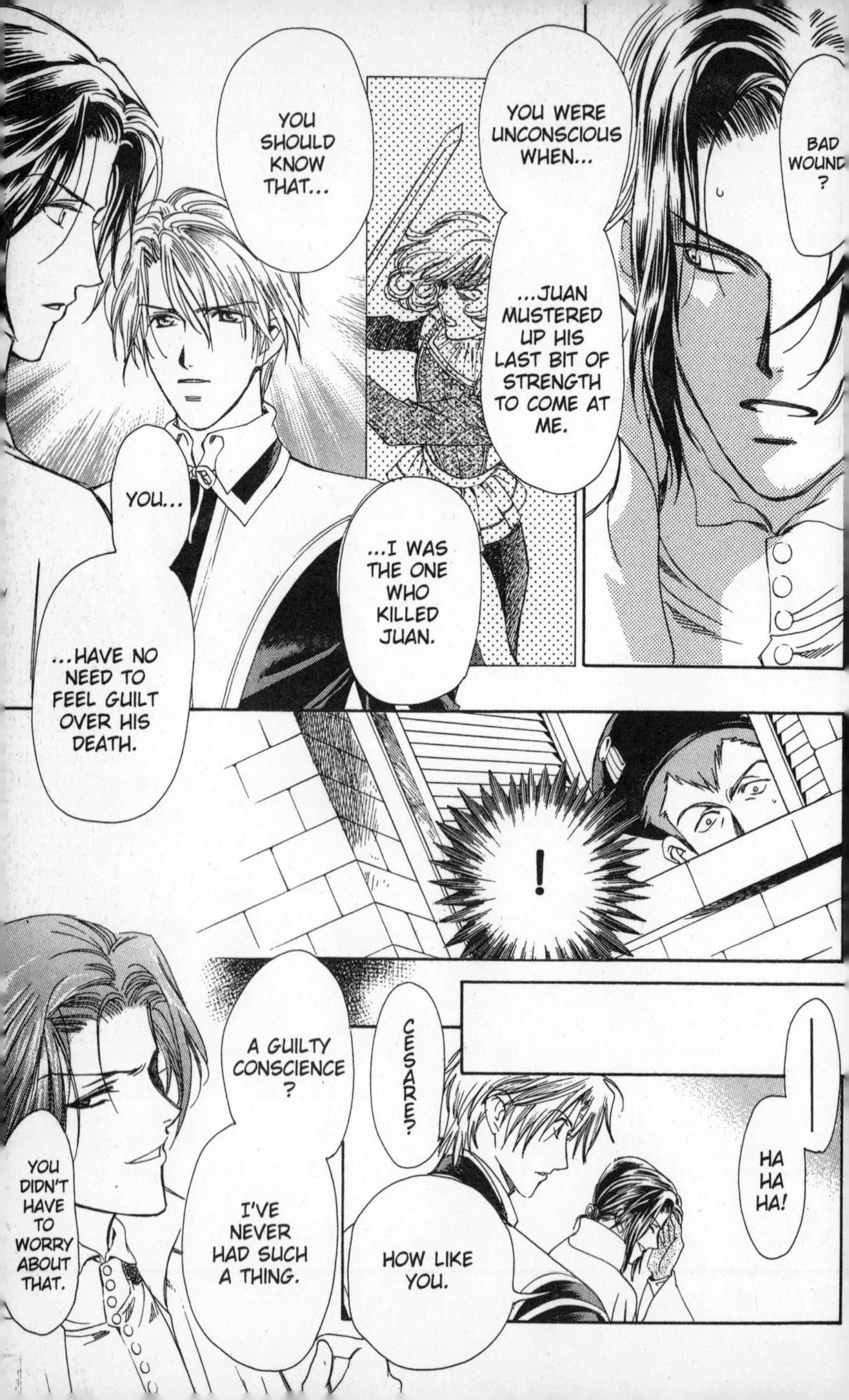
BAD WOUND?
YOU WERE UNCONSCIOUS WHEN...
...JUAN MUSTERED UP HIS LAST BIT OF STRENGTH TO COME AT ME.
YOU SHOULD KNOW THAT...
...I WAS THE ONE WHO KILLED JUAN.
YOU...
...HAVE NO NEED TO FEEL GUILT OVER HIS DEATH.
!
HA HA HA!
CESARE?
HOW LIKE YOU.
A GUILTY CONSCIENCE?
I'VE NEVER HAD SUCH A THING.
YOU DIDN'T HAVE TO WORRY ABOUT THAT.

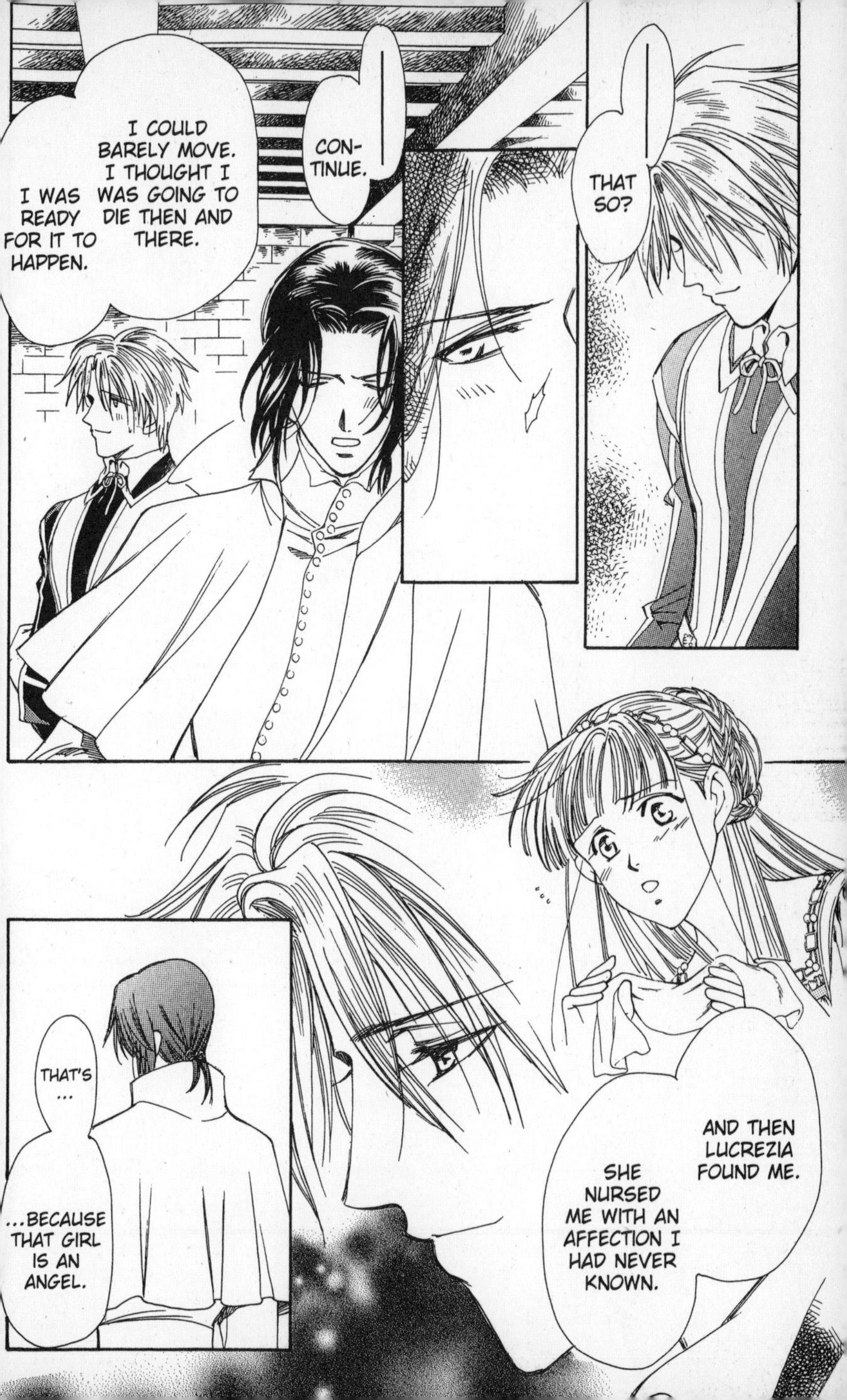
THAT SO?
CON-TINUE.
I COULD BARELY MOVE. I THOUGHT I WAS GOING TO DIE THEN AND THERE.
I WAS READY FOR IT TO HAPPEN.
AND THEN LUCREZIA FOUND ME.
SHE NURSED ME WITH AN AFFECTION I HAD NEVER KNOWN.
...
THAT'S ...
...BECAUSE THAT GIRL IS AN ANGEL.

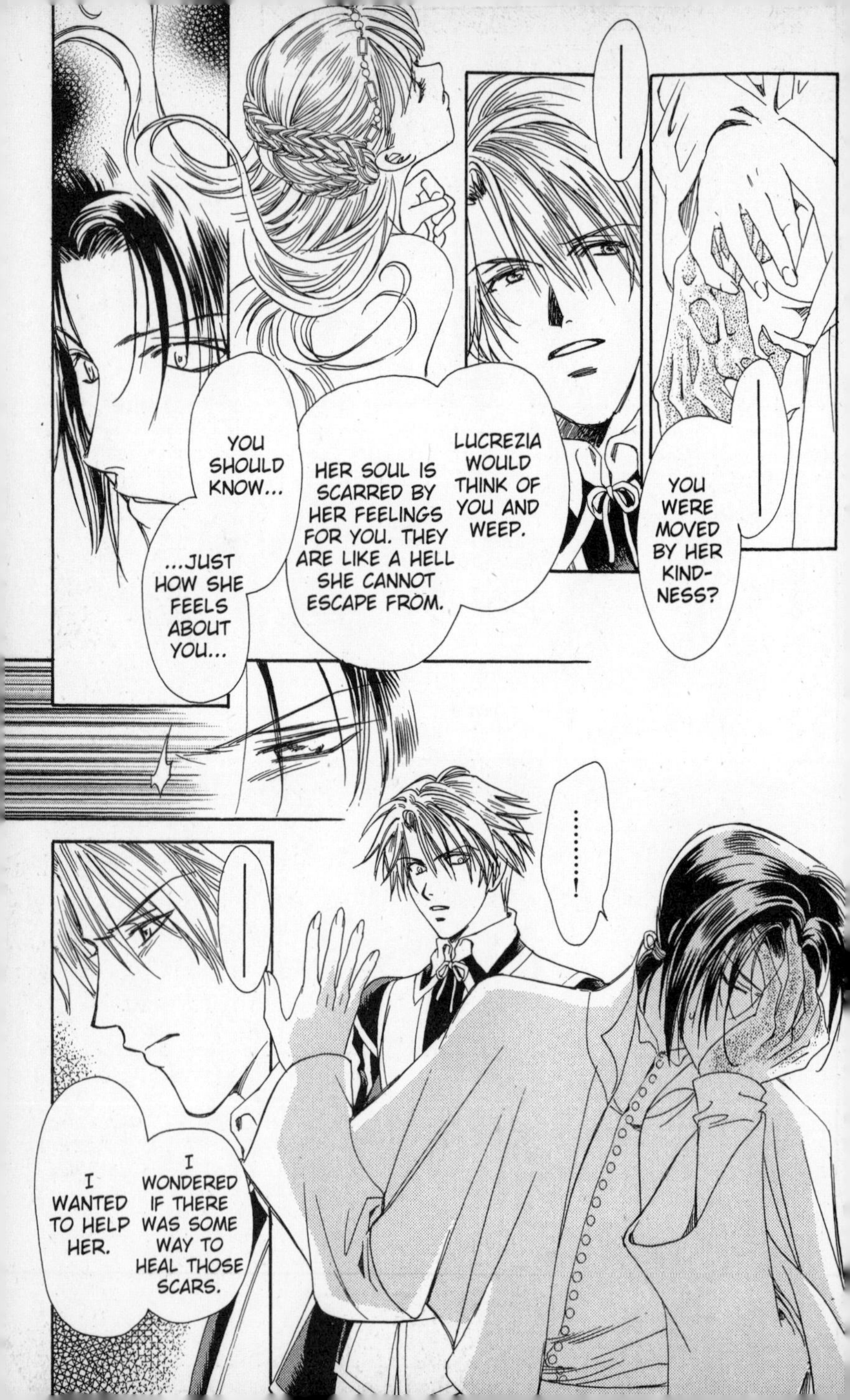
YOU WERE MOVED BY HER KINDNESS?
LUCREZIA WOULD THINK OF YOU AND WEEP.
HER SOUL IS SCARRED BY HER FEELINGS FOR YOU. THEY ARE LIKE A HELL SHE CANNOT ESCAPE FROM.
YOU SHOULD KNOW...
...JUST HOW SHE FEELS ABOUT YOU...
......!
I WONDERED IF THERE WAS SOME WAY TO HEAL THOSE SCARS.
I WANTED TO HELP HER.

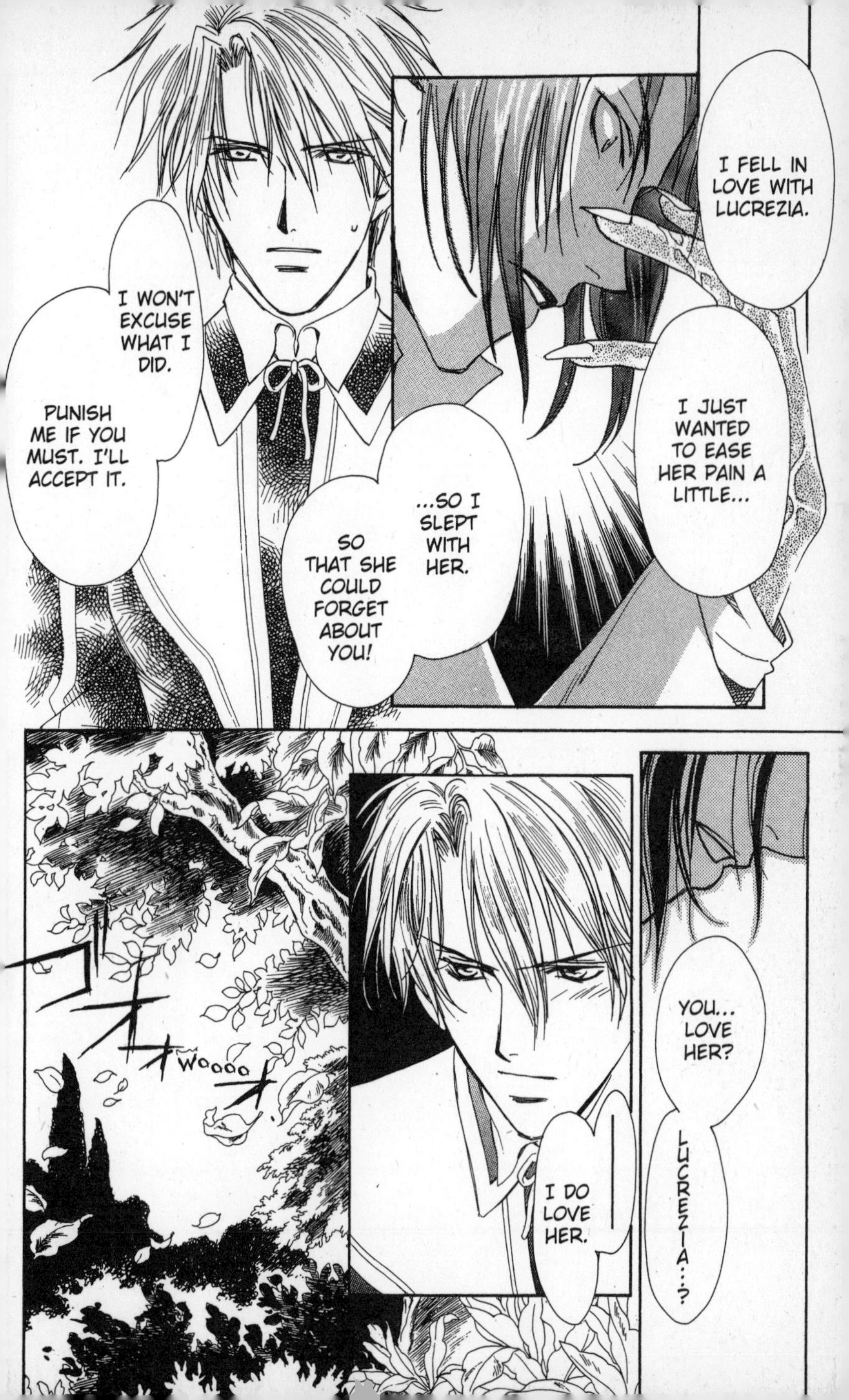
I FELL IN LOVE WITH LUCREZIA.
I JUST WANTED TO EASE HER PAIN A LITTLE...
...SO I SLEPT WITH HER.
SO THAT SHE COULD FORGET ABOUT YOU!
I WON'T EXCUSE WHAT I DID.
PUNISH ME IF YOU MUST. I'LL ACCEPT IT.
YOU... LOVE HER?
LUCREZIA...?
I DO LOVE HER.
Woooo

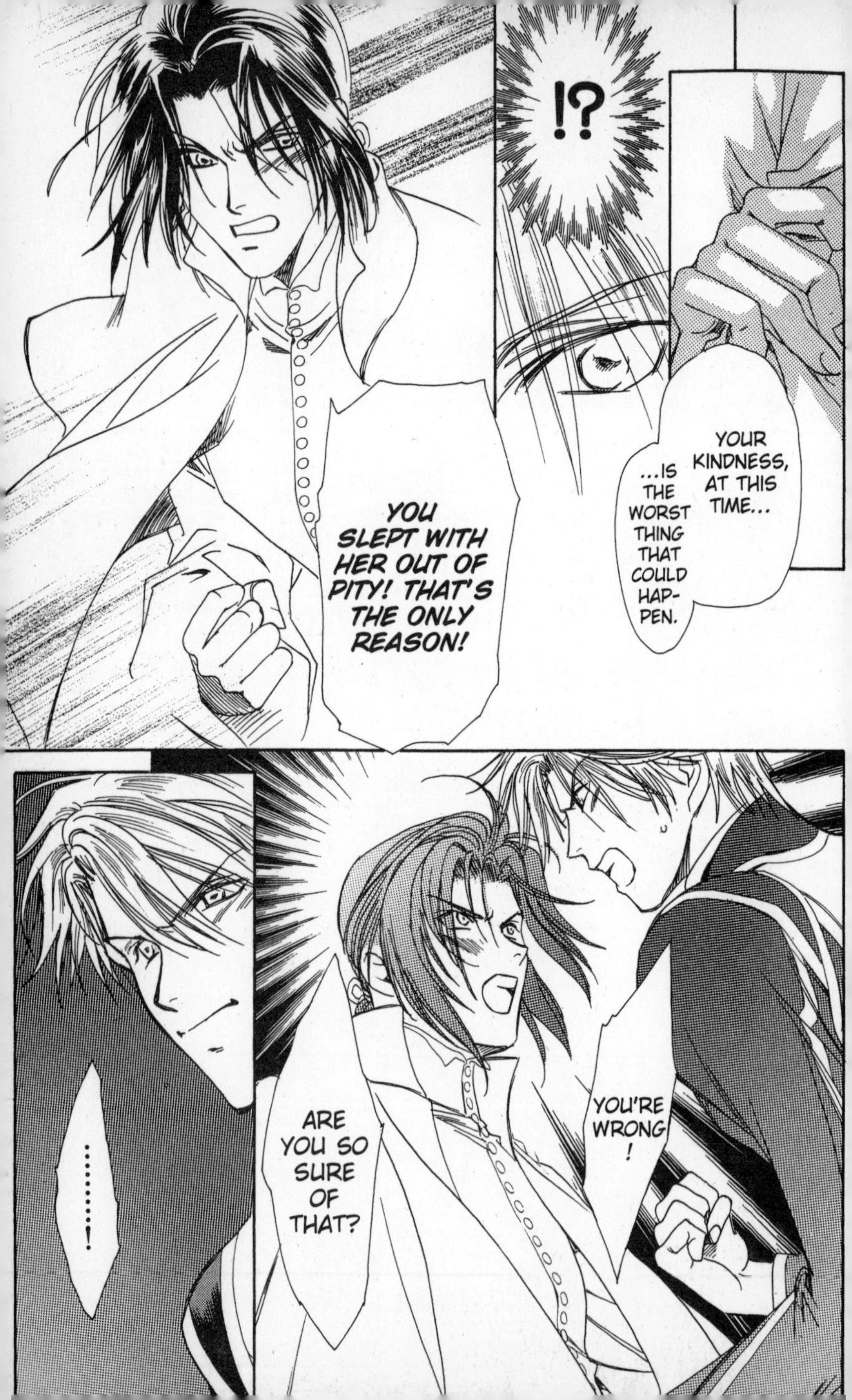
YOUR KINDNESS, AT THIS TIME...
...IS THE WORST THING THAT COULD HAP-PEN.
!?
YOU SLEPT WITH HER OUT OF PITY! THAT'S THE ONLY REASON!
YOU'RE WRONG!
ARE YOU SO SURE OF THAT?
......!

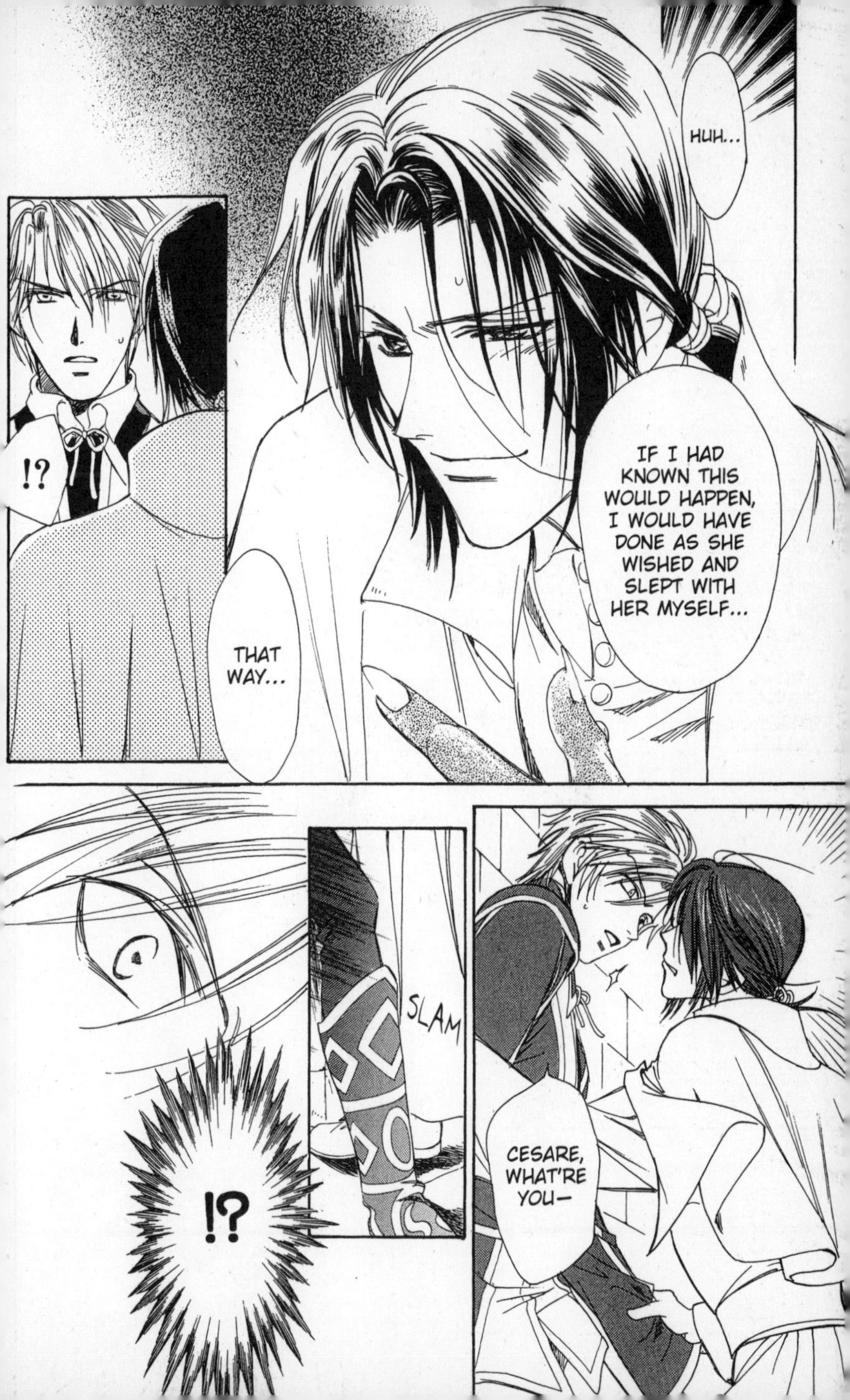
HUH...
IF I HAD KNOWN THIS WOULD HAPPEN, I WOULD HAVE DONE AS SHE WISHED AND SLEPT WITH HER MYSELF...
THAT WAY...
!?
CESARE, WHAT'RE YOU—
SLAM
!?

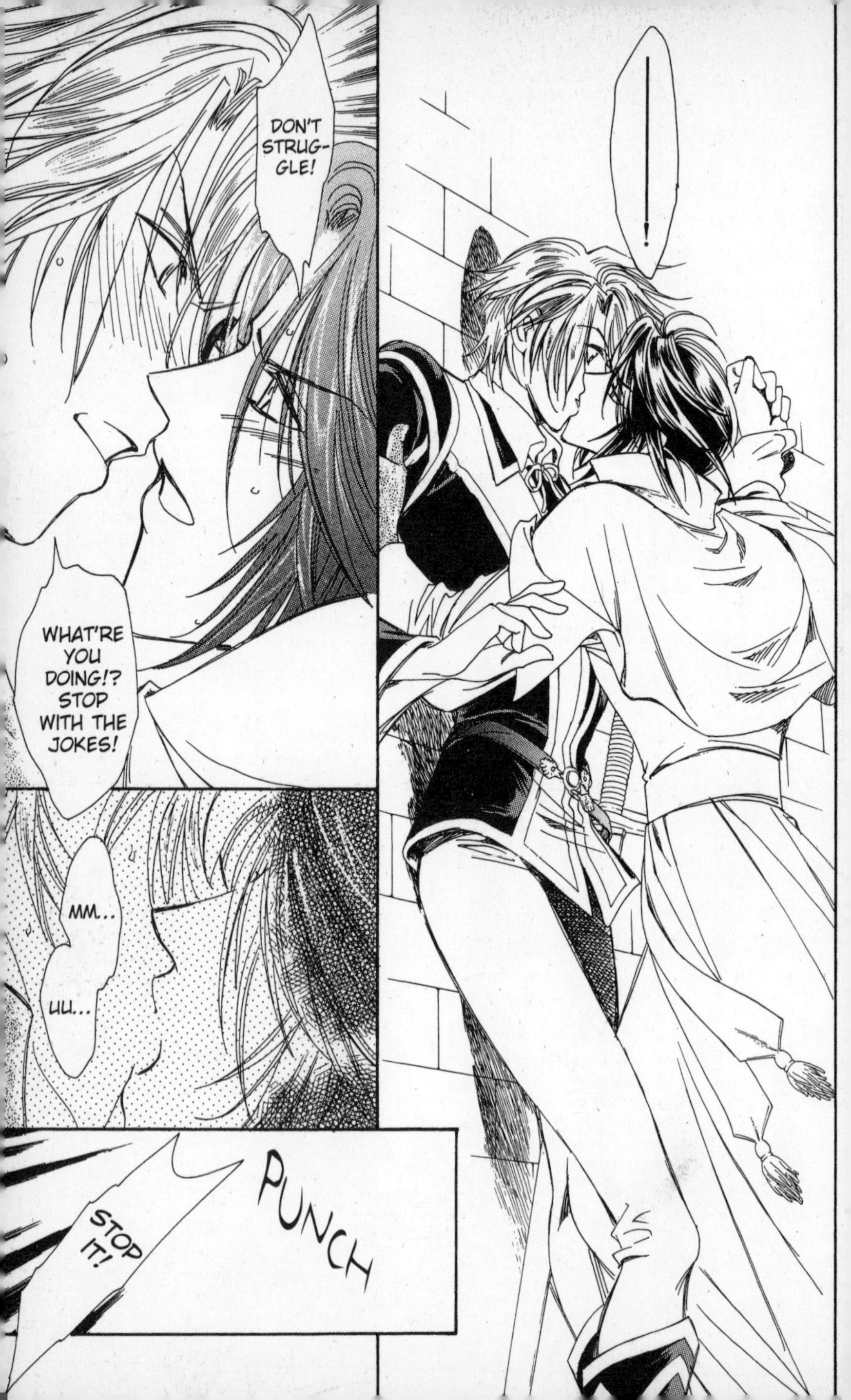
!
DON'T STRUG-GLE!
WHAT'RE YOU DOING!? STOP WITH THE JOKES!
MM...
UU...
PUNCH
STOP IT!

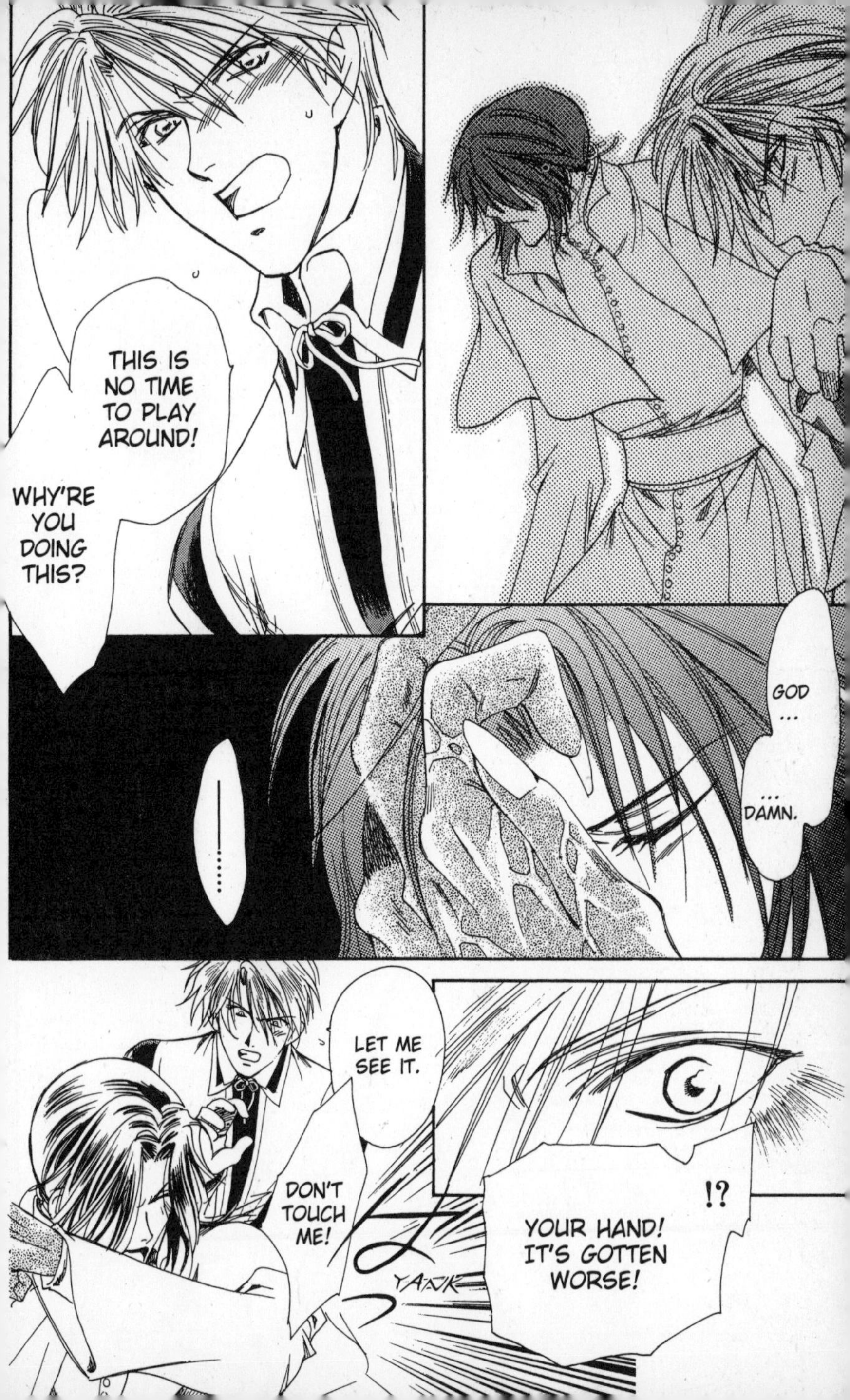
THIS IS NO TIME TO PLAY AROUND!
WHY'RE YOU DOING THIS?
GOD ...
... DAMN.
!......
LET ME SEE IT.
DON'T TOUCH ME!
YANK
!?
YOUR HAND! IT'S GOTTEN WORSE!

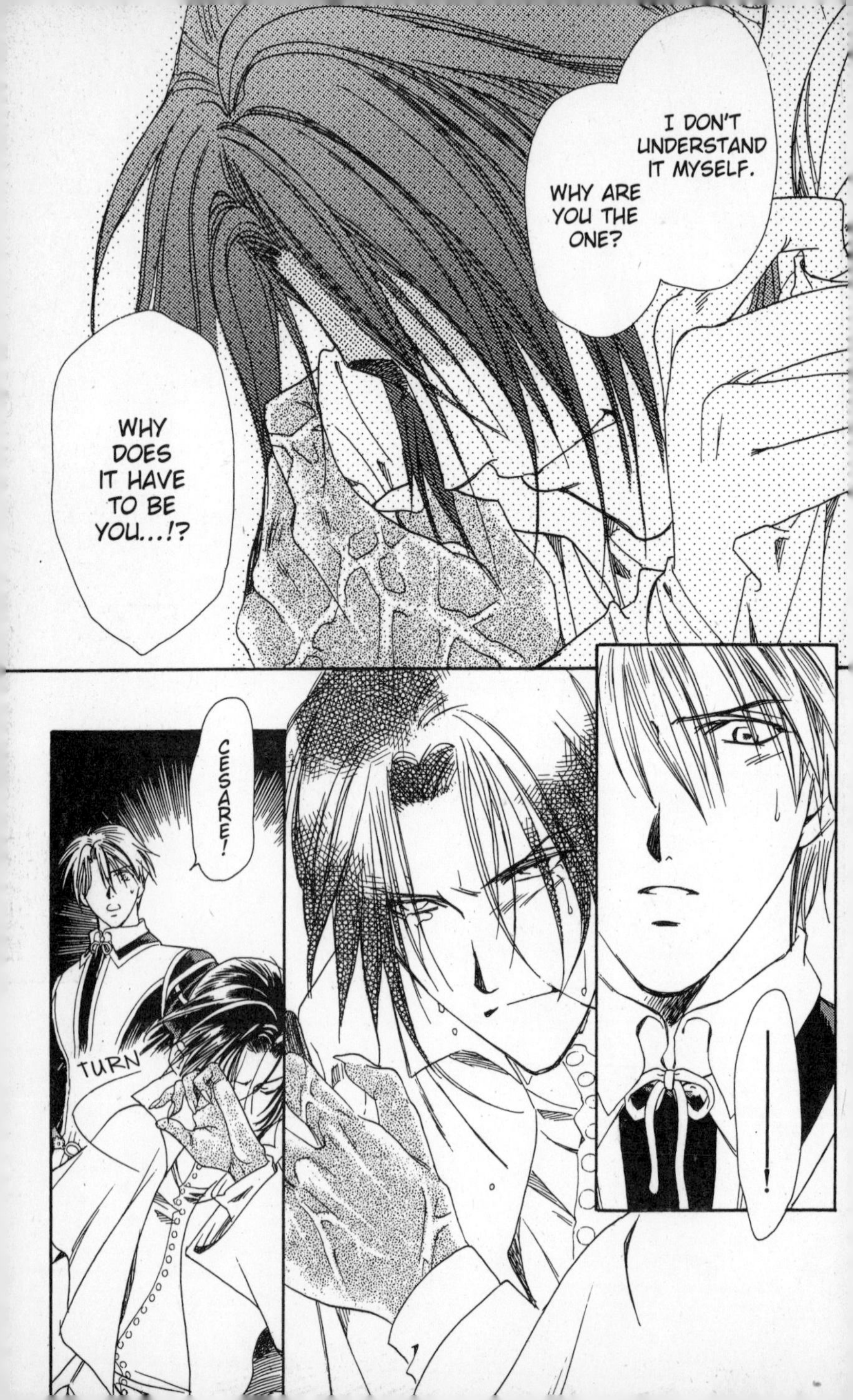
I DON'T UNDERSTAND IT MYSELF.
WHY ARE YOU THE ONE?
WHY DOES IT HAVE TO BE YOU...!?
!
CESARE!
TURN

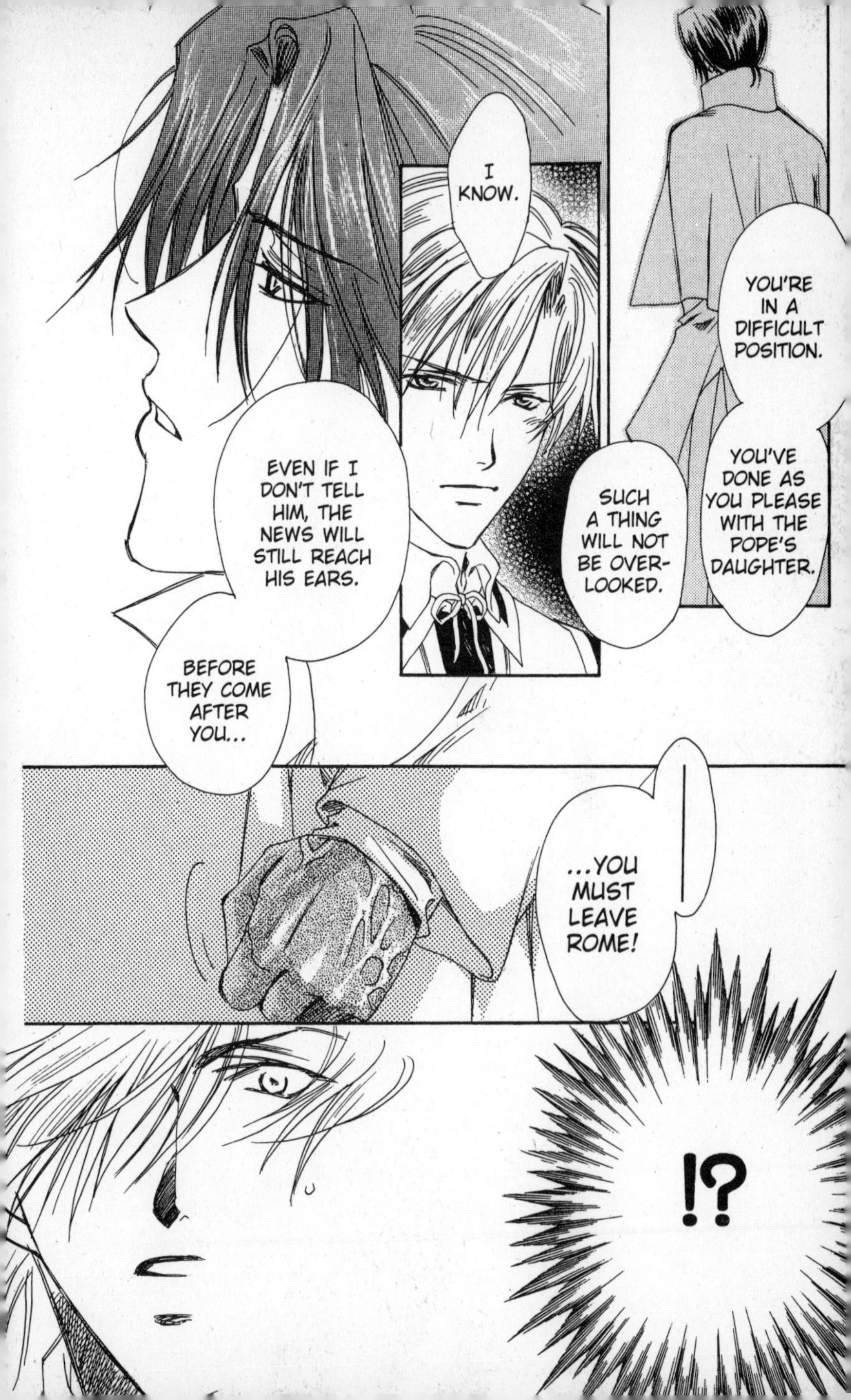
YOU'RE IN A DIFFICULT POSITION.
YOU'VE DONE AS YOU PLEASE WITH THE POPE'S DAUGHTER.
SUCH A THING WILL NOT BE OVER-LOOKED.
I KNOW.
EVEN IF I DON'T TELL HIM, THE NEWS WILL STILL REACH HIS EARS.
BEFORE THEY COME AFTER YOU...
...YOU MUST LEAVE ROME!
!?

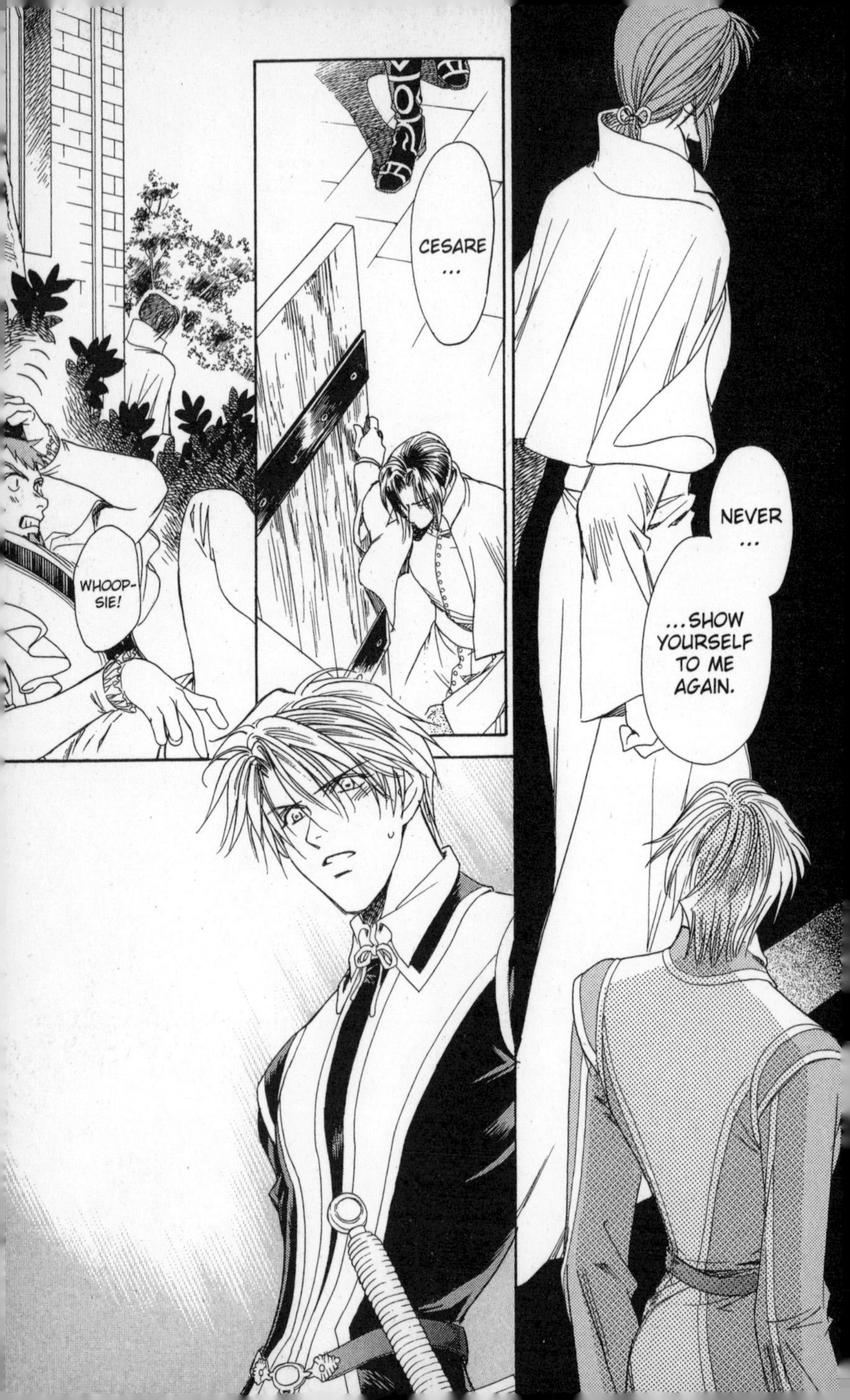
NEVER ...
...SHOW YOURSELF TO ME AGAIN.
CESARE ...
WHOOP-SIE!

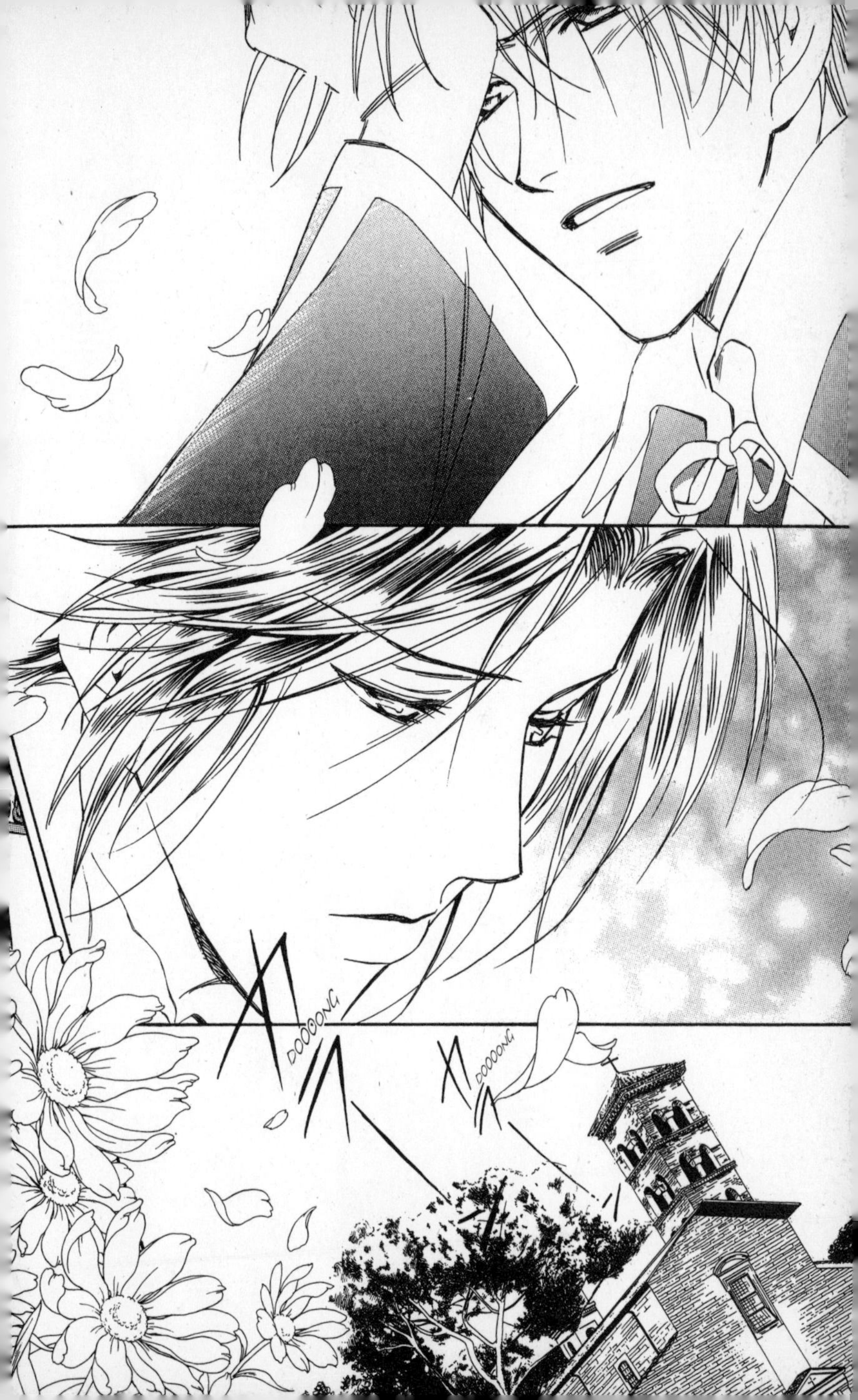
DOOOONG
DOOOONG

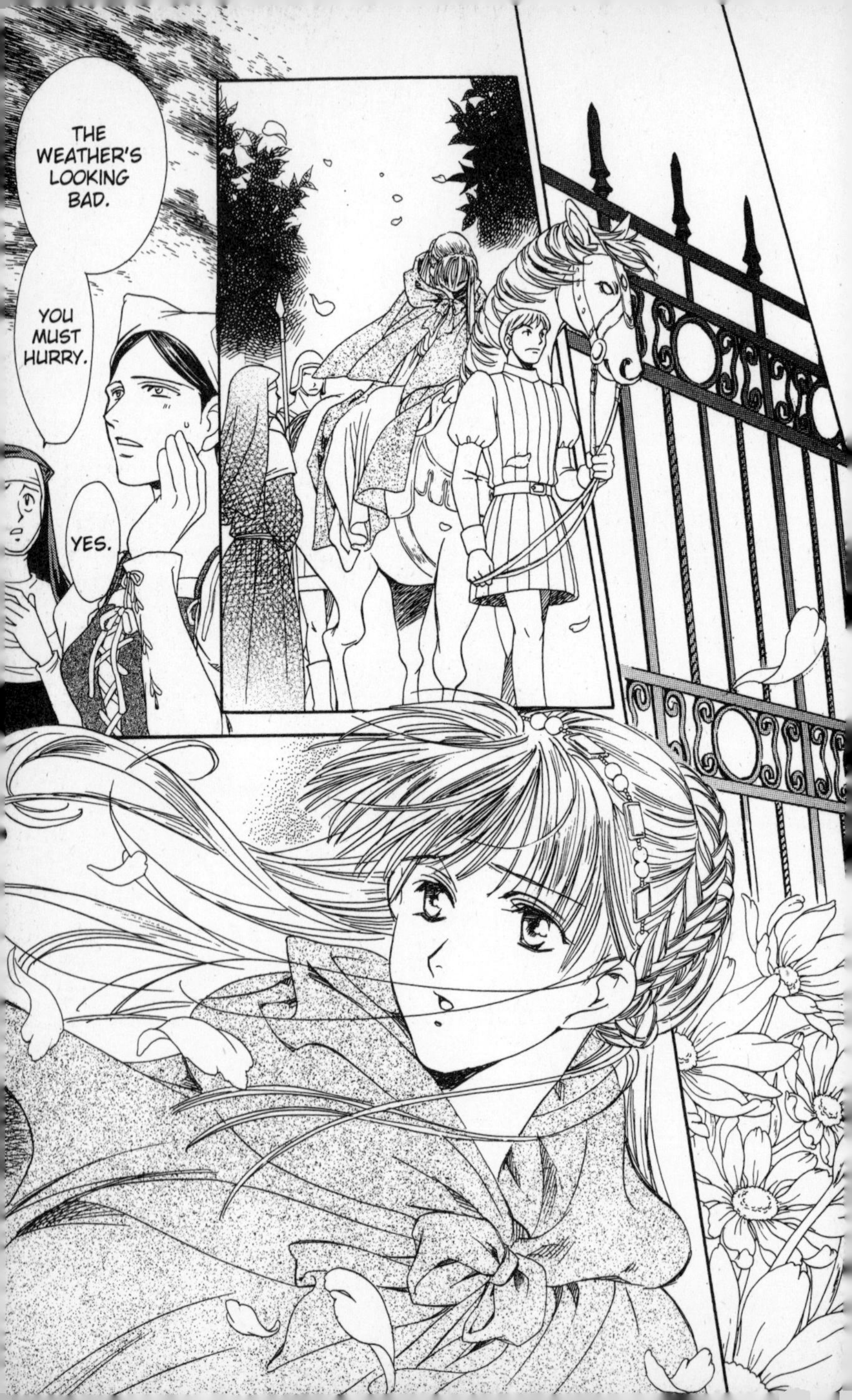
THE WEATHER'S LOOKING BAD.
YOU MUST HURRY.
YES.

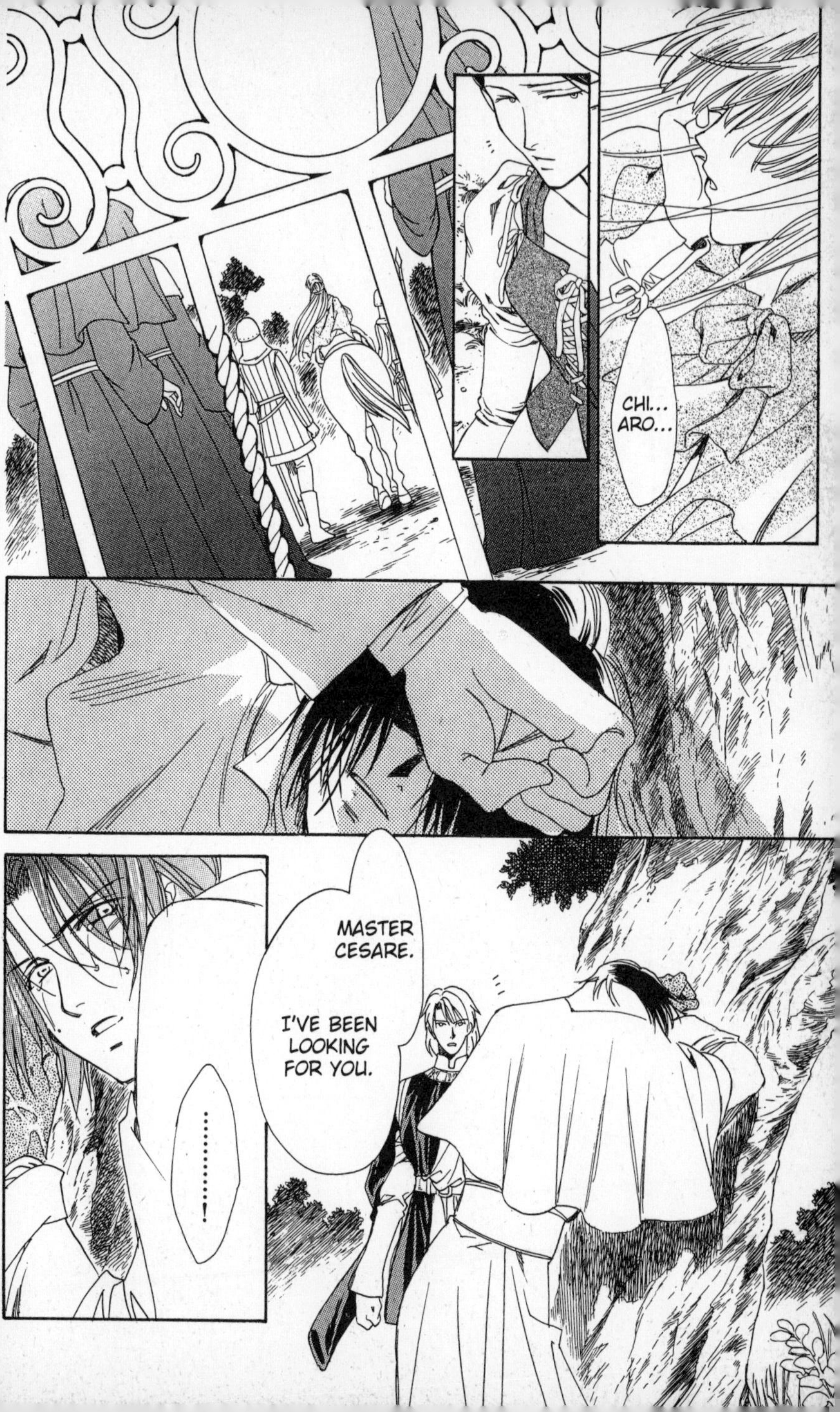
CHI... ARO...
MASTER CESARE.
I'VE BEEN LOOKING FOR YOU.
......!

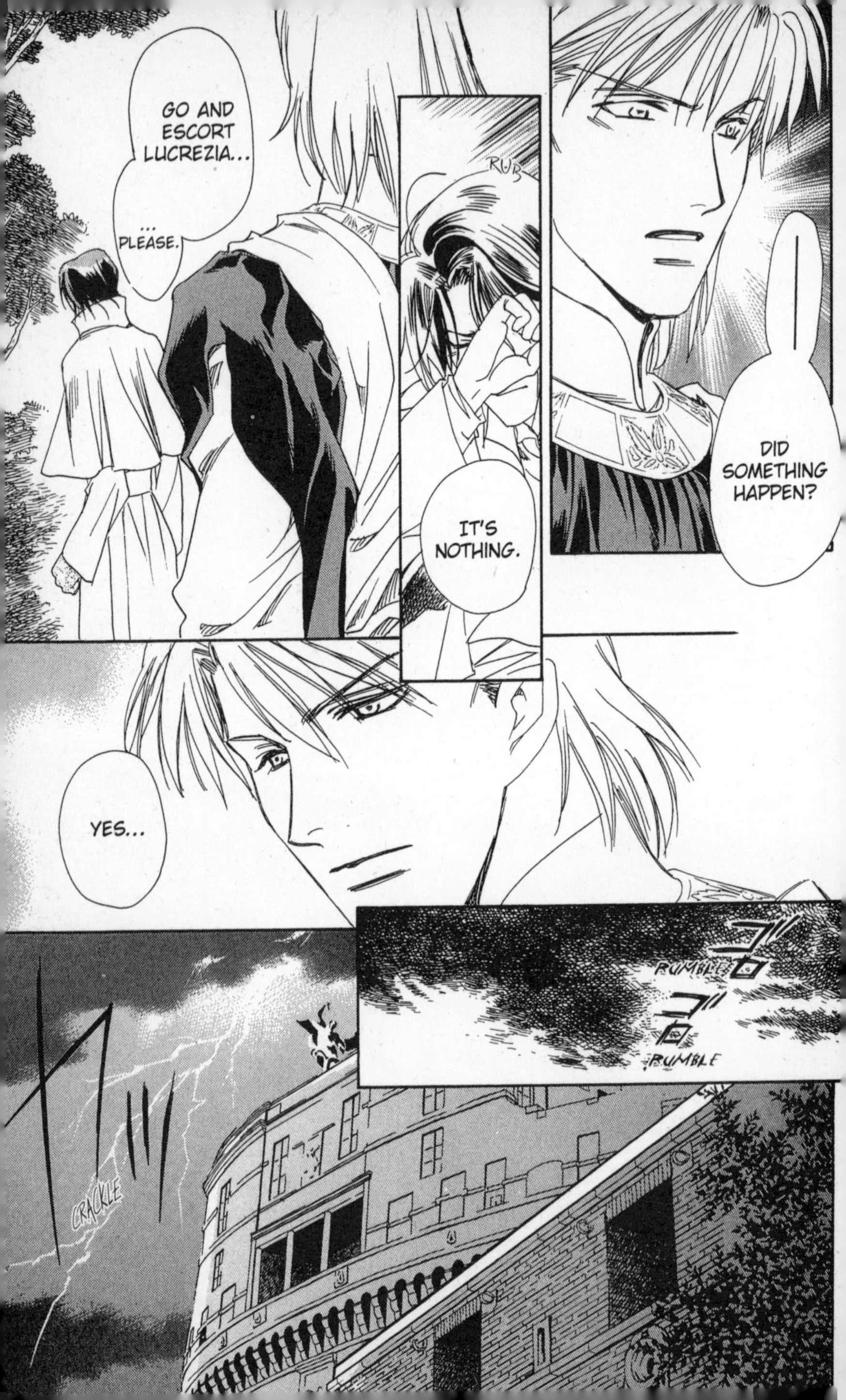
DID SOMETHING HAPPEN?
RUB
IT'S NOTHING.
GO AND ESCORT LUCREZIA...
... PLEASE.
YES...
RUMBLE
RUMBLE
CRACKLE

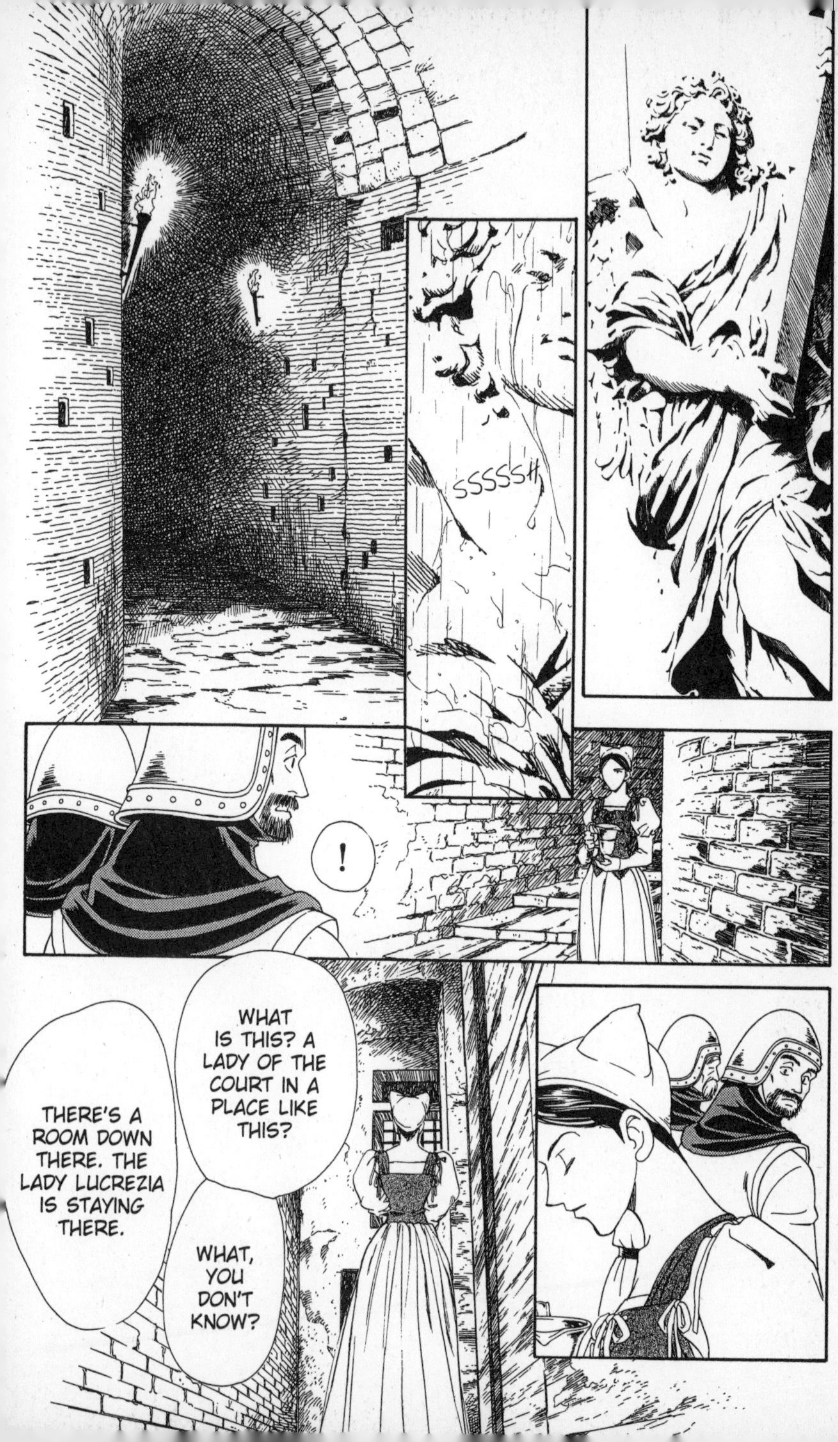
SSSSSH
!
WHAT IS THIS? A LADY OF THE COURT IN A PLACE LIKE THIS?
WHAT, YOU DON'T KNOW?
THERE'S A ROOM DOWN THERE. THE LADY LUCREZIA IS STAYING THERE.

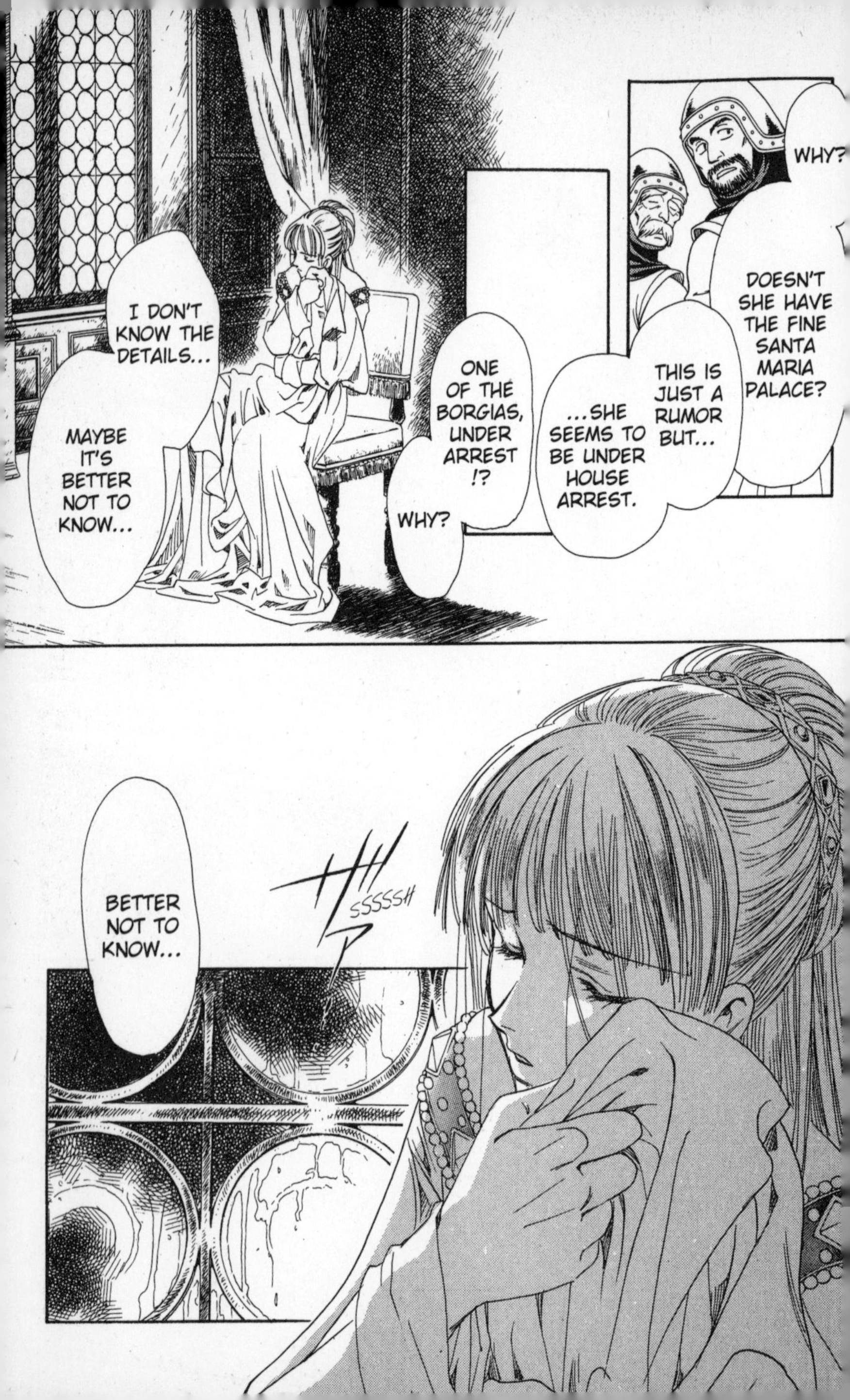
WHY?
DOESN'T SHE HAVE THE FINE SANTA MARIA PALACE?
THIS IS JUST A RUMOR BUT...
...SHE SEEMS TO BE UNDER HOUSE ARREST.
ONE OF THE BORGIAS, UNDER ARREST!?
WHY?
I DON'T KNOW THE DETAILS...
MAYBE IT'S BETTER NOT TO KNOW...
SSSSSH
BETTER NOT TO KNOW...

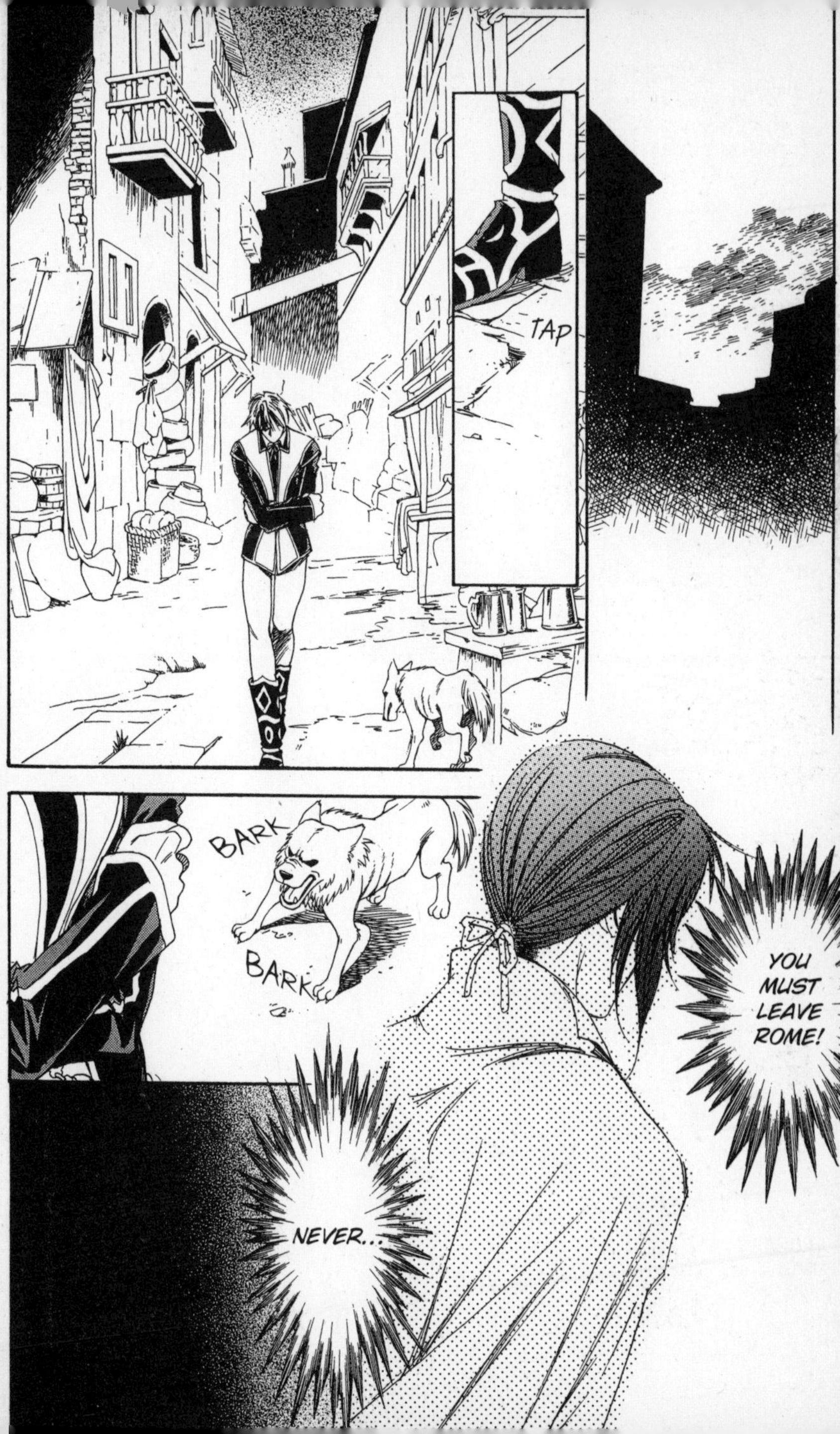
TAP
YOU MUST LEAVE ROME!
NEVER...
BARK
BARK

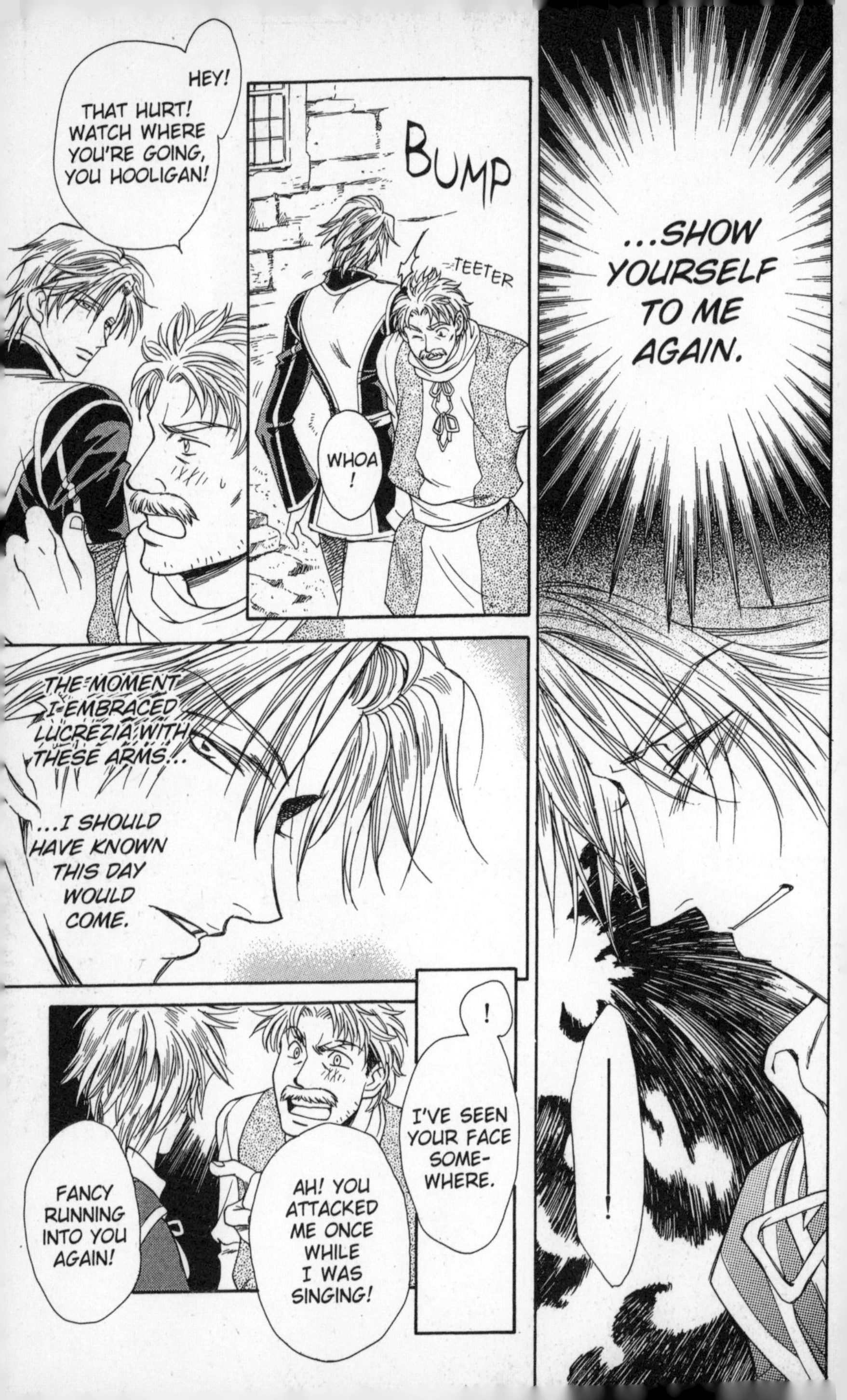
...SHOW YOURSELF TO ME AGAIN.
!
BUMP
TEETER
WHOA!
HEY! THAT HURT! WATCH WHERE YOU'RE GOING, YOU HOOLIGAN!
THE MOMENT I EMBRACED LUCREZIA WITH THESE ARMS...
...I SHOULD HAVE KNOWN THIS DAY WOULD COME.
!
I'VE SEEN YOUR FACE SOME-WHERE.
AH! YOU ATTACKED ME ONCE WHILE I WAS SINGING!
FANCY RUNNING INTO YOU AGAIN!

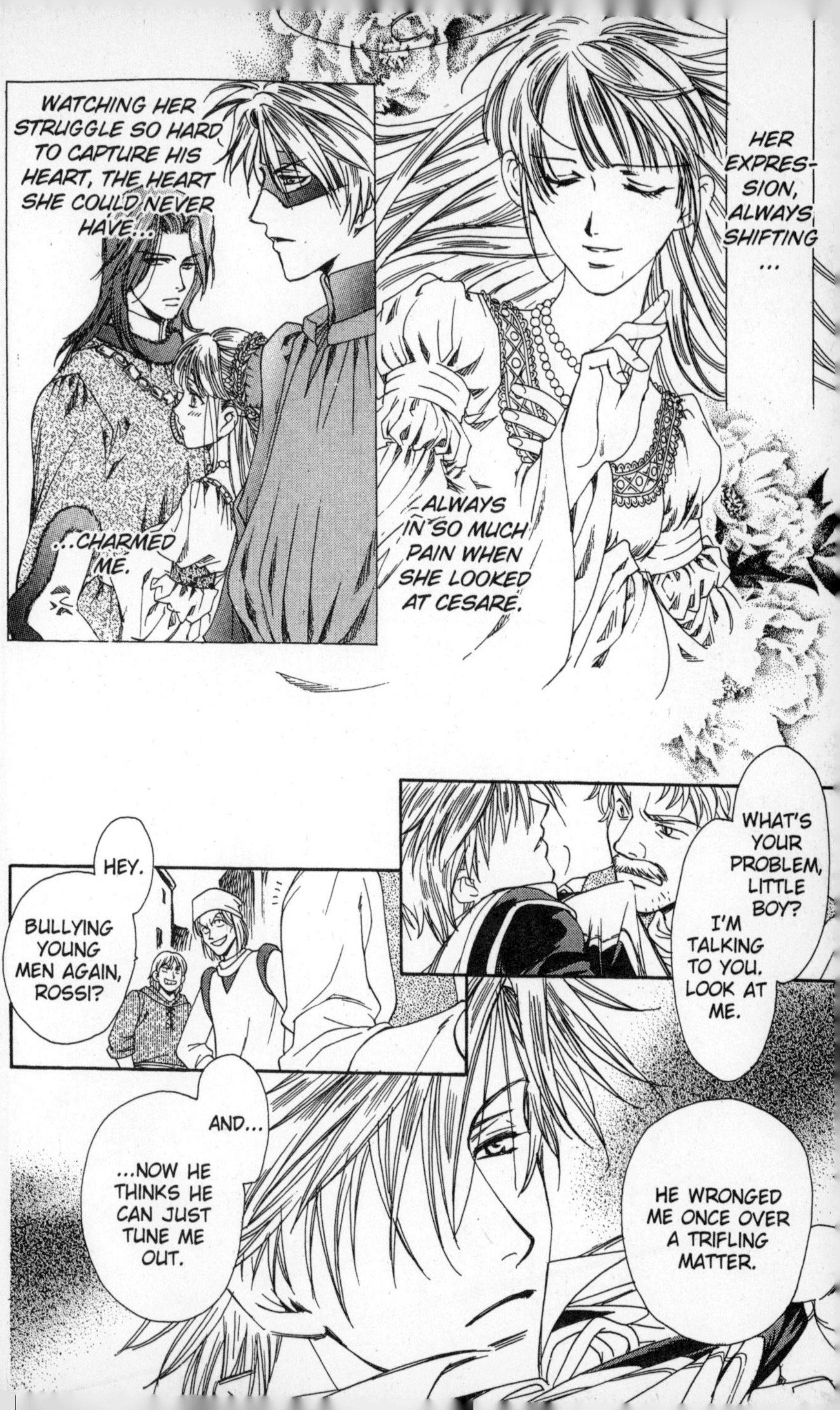
HER EXPRES-SION, ALWAYS SHIFTING...
ALWAYS IN SO MUCH PAIN WHEN SHE LOOKED AT CESARE.
WATCHING HER STRUGGLE SO HARD TO CAPTURE HIS HEART, THE HEART SHE COULD NEVER HAVE...
...CHARMED ME.
WHAT'S YOUR PROBLEM, LITTLE BOY?
I'M TALKING TO YOU. LOOK AT ME.
HEY.
BULLYING YOUNG MEN AGAIN, ROSSI?
HE WRONGED ME ONCE OVER A TRIFLING MATTER.
AND...
...NOW HE THINKS HE CAN JUST TUNE ME OUT.

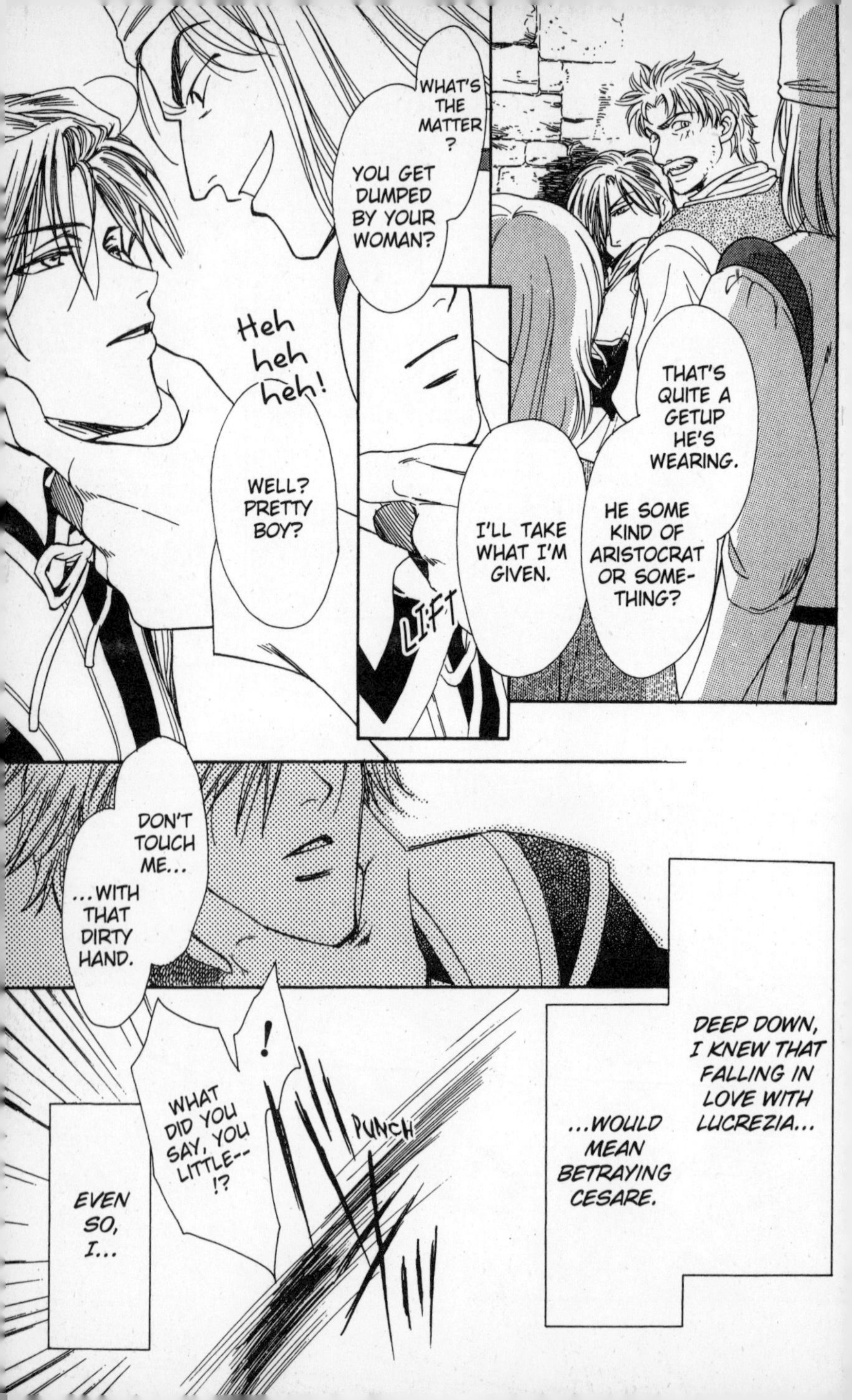
THAT'S QUITE A GETUP HE'S WEARING.
HE SOME KIND OF ARISTOCRAT OR SOME-THING?
WHAT'S THE MATTER?
YOU GET DUMPED BY YOUR WOMAN?
I'LL TAKE WHAT I'M GIVEN.
LIFT
Heh heh heh!
WELL? PRETTY BOY?
DEEP DOWN, I KNEW THAT FALLING IN LOVE WITH LUCREZIA...
...WOULD MEAN BETRAYING CESARE.
DON'T TOUCH ME...
...WITH THAT DIRTY HAND.
!
PUNCH
WHAT DID YOU SAY, YOU LITTLE--!?
EVEN SO, I...

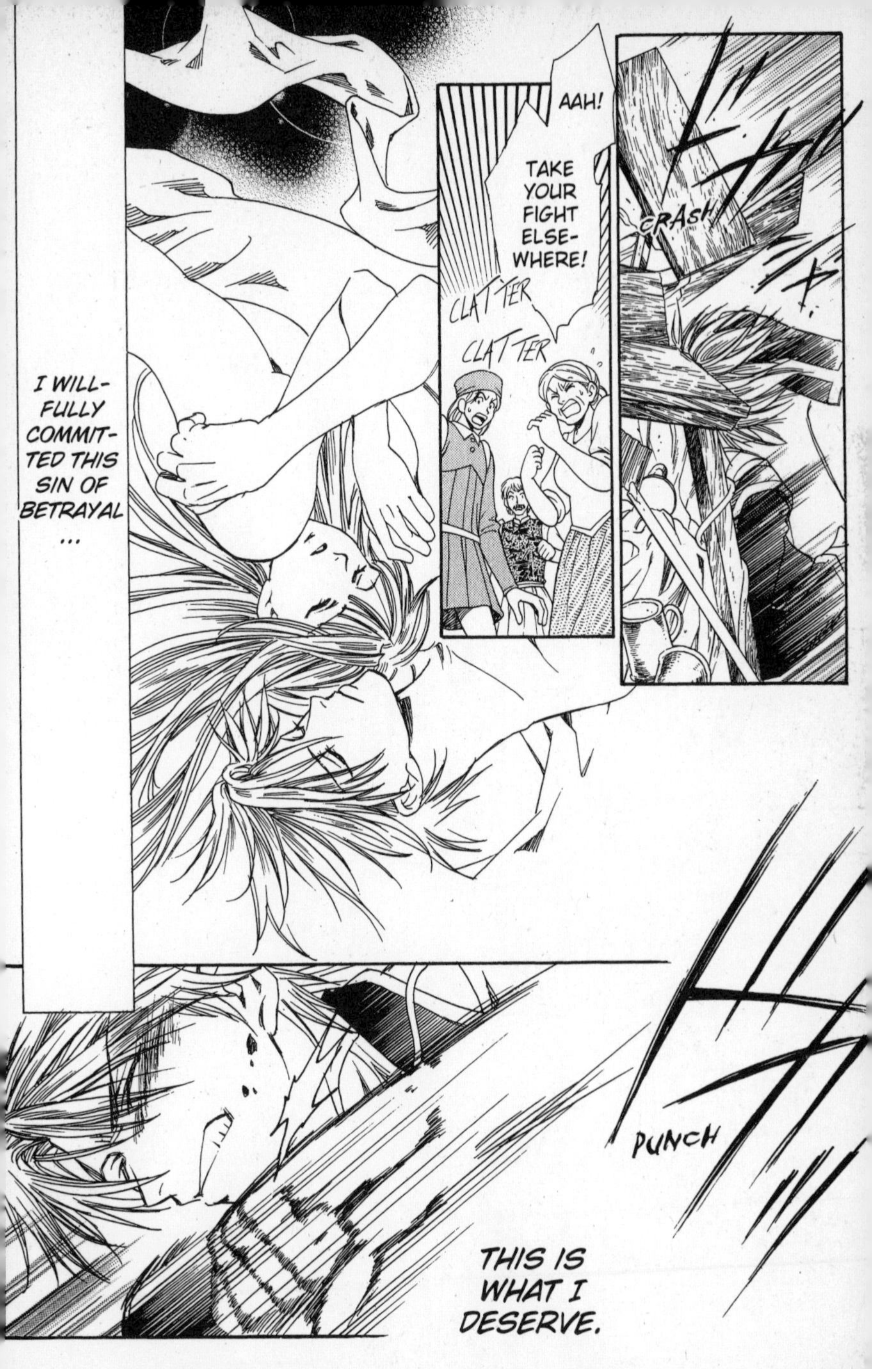
CRASH
AAH!
TAKE YOUR FIGHT ELSE-WHERE!
CLATTER
CLATTER
I WILL-FULLY COMMIT-TED THIS SIN OF BETRAYAL ...
PUNCH
THIS IS WHAT I DESERVE.

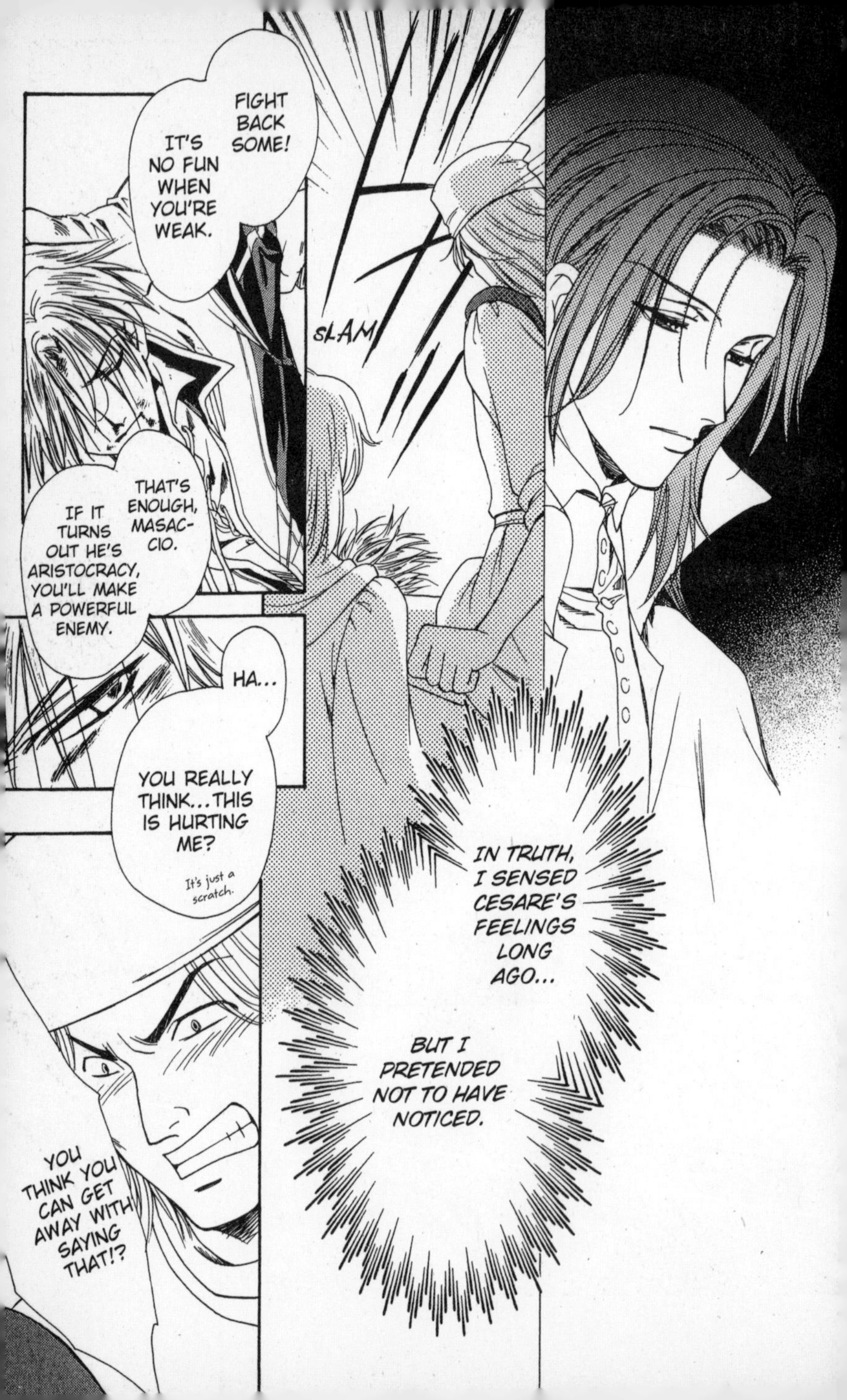
IN TRUTH, I SENSED CESARE'S FEELINGS LONG AGO...
BUT I PRETENDED NOT TO HAVE NOTICED.
SLAM
FIGHT BACK SOME!
IT'S NO FUN WHEN YOU'RE WEAK.
THAT'S ENOUGH, MASACCIO.
IF IT TURNS OUT HE'S ARISTOCRACY, YOU'LL MAKE A POWERFUL ENEMY.
HA...
YOU REALLY THINK...THIS IS HURTING ME?
It's just a scratch.
YOU THINK YOU CAN GET AWAY WITH SAYING THAT!?

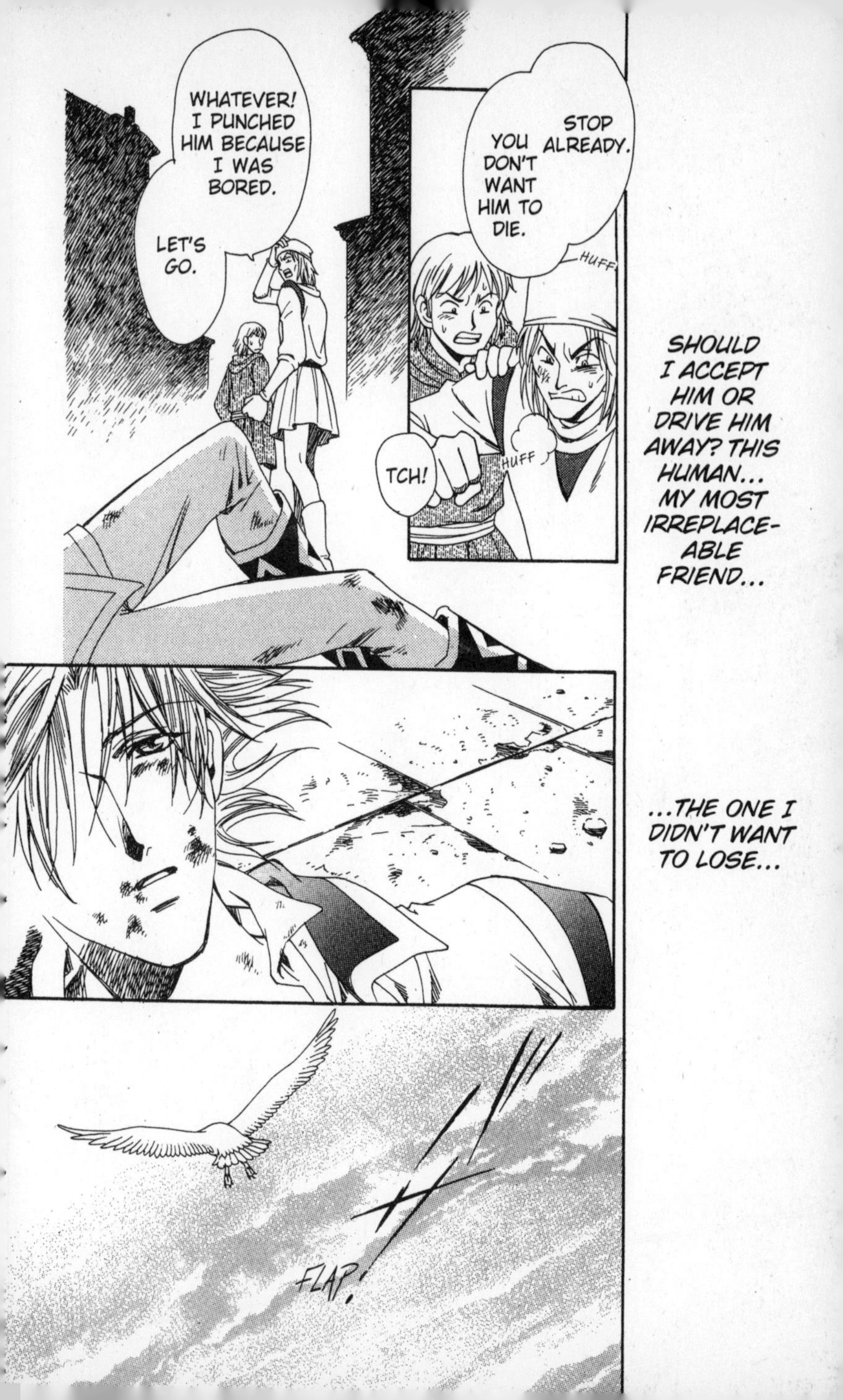

STOP ALREADY.
YOU DON'T WANT HIM TO DIE.
HUFF
HUFF
TCH!
WHATEVER! I PUNCHED HIM BECAUSE I WAS BORED.
LET'S GO.
SHOULD I ACCEPT HIM OR DRIVE HIM AWAY? THIS HUMAN... MY MOST IRREPLACE-ABLE FRIEND...
...THE ONE I DIDN'T WANT TO LOSE...
FLAP!

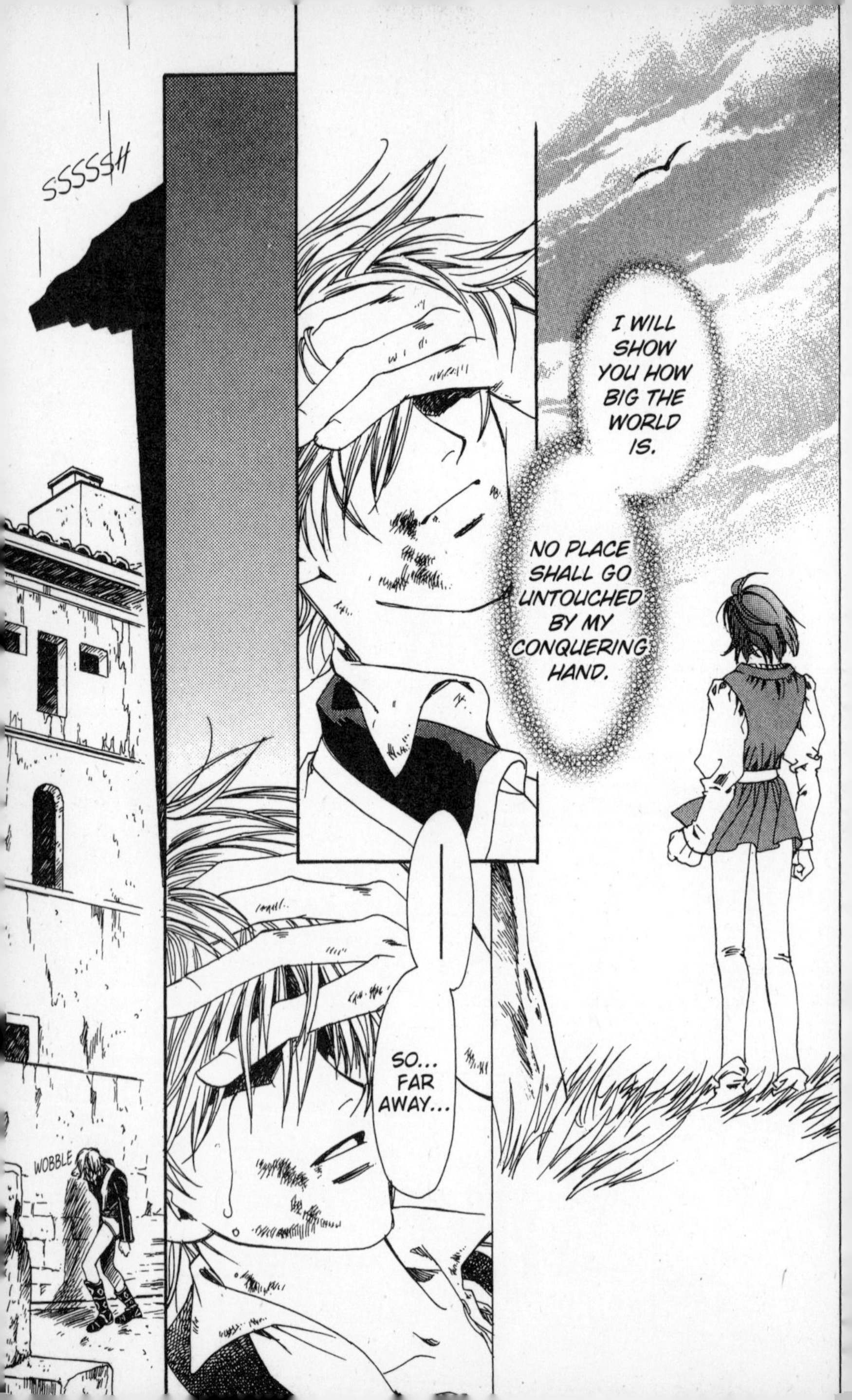
I WILL SHOW YOU HOW BIG THE WORLD IS.
NO PLACE SHALL GO UNTOUCHED BY MY CONQUERING HAND.
SO... FAR AWAY...
SSSSSH
WOBBLE

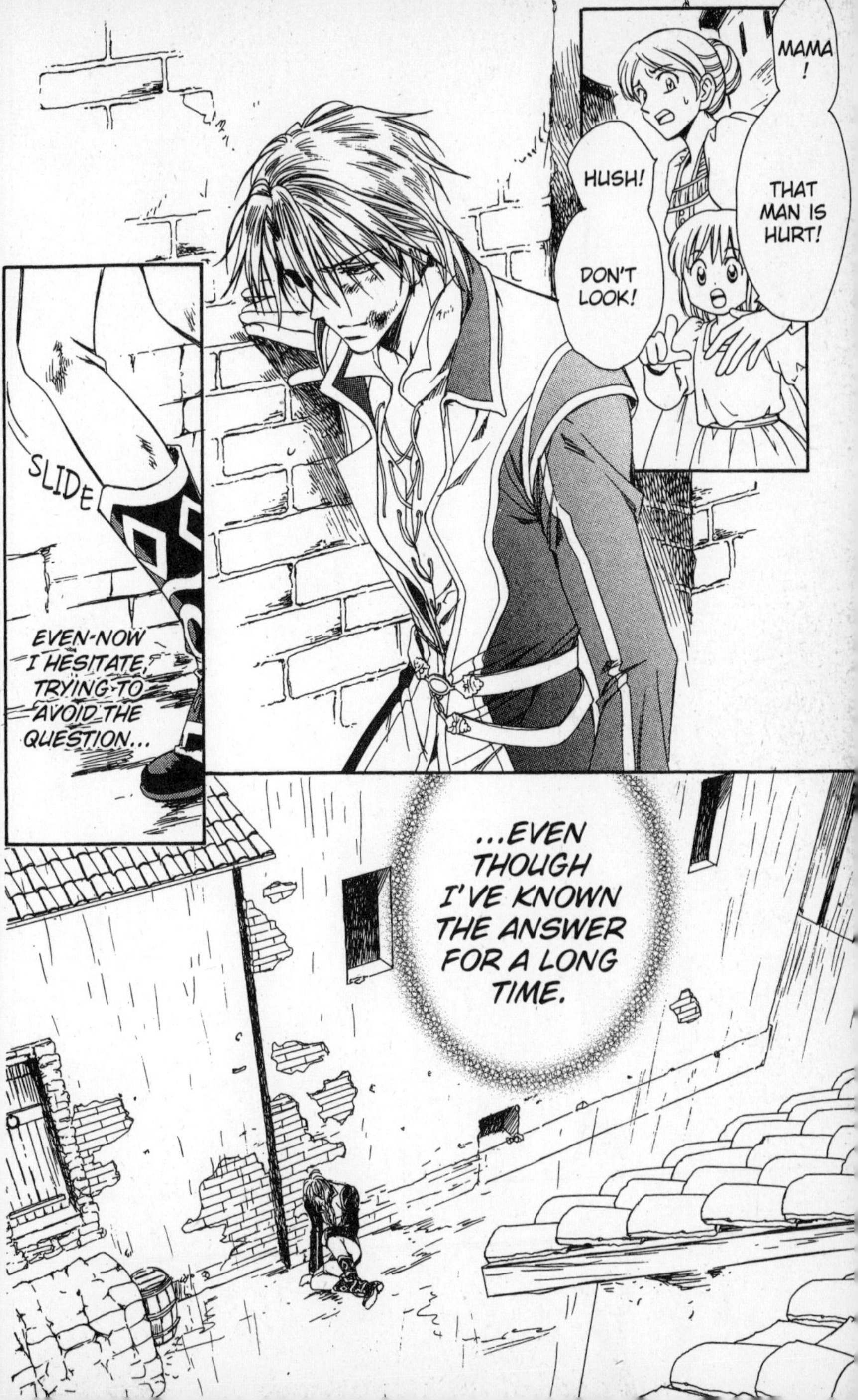
MAMA!
THAT MAN IS HURT!
HUSH!
DON'T LOOK!
SLIDE
EVEN NOW I HESITATE, TRYING TO AVOID THE QUESTION...
...EVEN THOUGH I'VE KNOWN THE ANSWER FOR A LONG TIME.

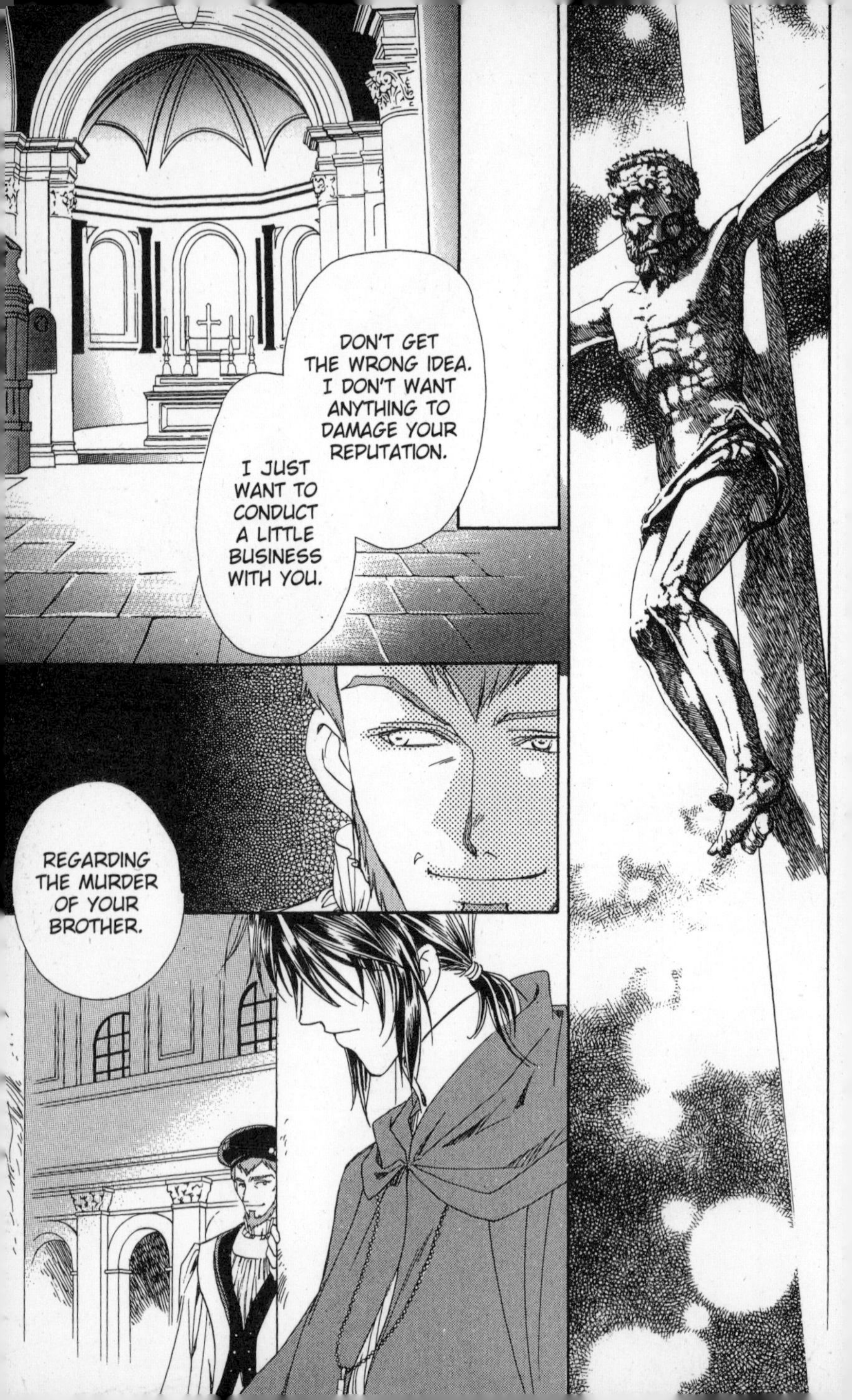
DON'T GET THE WRONG IDEA. I DON'T WANT ANYTHING TO DAMAGE YOUR REPUTATION.
I JUST WANT TO CONDUCT A LITTLE BUSINESS WITH YOU.
REGARDING THE MURDER OF YOUR BROTHER.

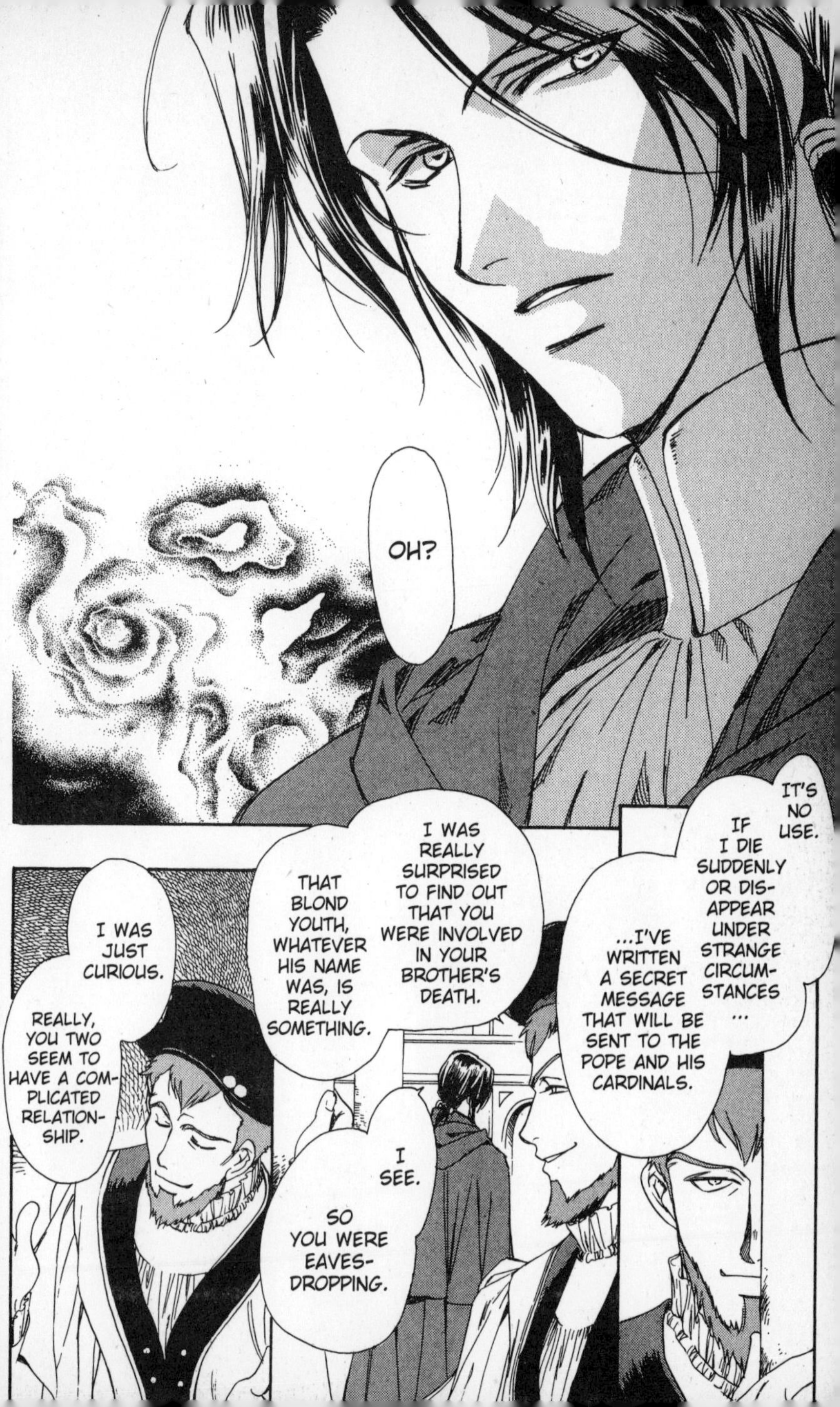
OH?
IT'S NO USE.
IF I DIE SUDDENLY OR DIS-APPEAR UNDER STRANGE CIRCUM-STANCES...
...I'VE WRITTEN A SECRET MESSAGE THAT WILL BE SENT TO THE POPE AND HIS CARDINALS.
I WAS REALLY SURPRISED TO FIND OUT THAT YOU WERE INVOLVED IN YOUR BROTHER'S DEATH.
THAT BLOND YOUTH, WHATEVER HIS NAME WAS, IS REALLY SOMETHING.
I SEE.
SO YOU WERE EAVES-DROPPING.
I WAS JUST CURIOUS.
REALLY, YOU TWO SEEM TO HAVE A COM-PLICATED RELATION-SHIP.

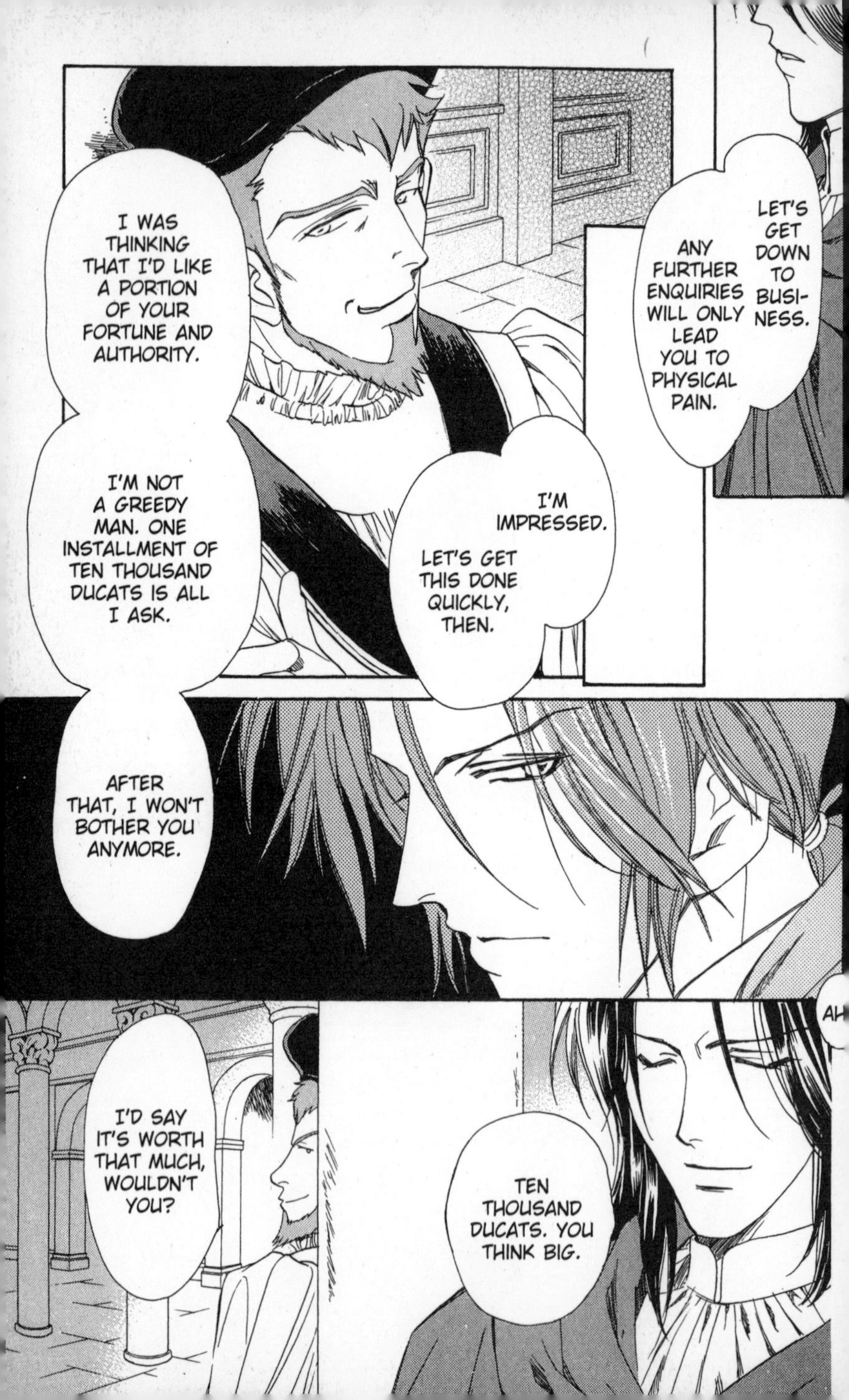
LET'S GET DOWN TO BUSINESS.
ANY FURTHER ENQUIRIES WILL ONLY LEAD YOU TO PHYSICAL PAIN.
I'M IMPRESSED.
LET'S GET THIS DONE QUICKLY, THEN.
I WAS THINKING THAT I'D LIKE A PORTION OF YOUR FORTUNE AND AUTHORITY.
I'M NOT A GREEDY MAN. ONE INSTALLMENT OF TEN THOUSAND DUCATS IS ALL I ASK.
AFTER THAT, I WON'T BOTHER YOU ANYMORE.
AH
TEN THOUSAND DUCATS. YOU THINK BIG.
I'D SAY IT'S WORTH THAT MUCH, WOULDN'T YOU?

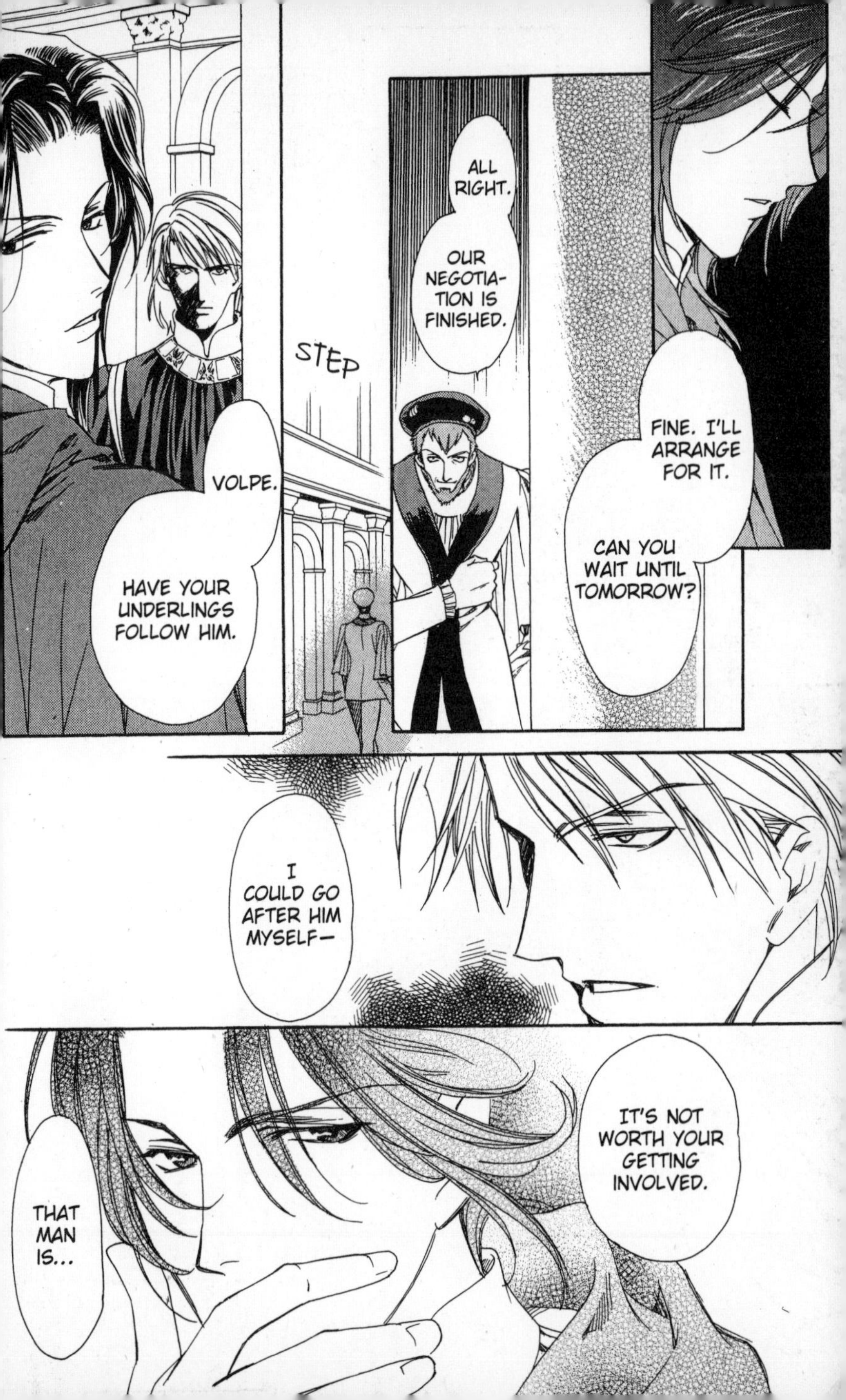
FINE. I'LL ARRANGE FOR IT.
CAN YOU WAIT UNTIL TOMORROW?
ALL RIGHT.
OUR NEGOTIA-TION IS FINISHED.
STEP
VOLPE.
HAVE YOUR UNDERLINGS FOLLOW HIM.
I COULD GO AFTER HIM MYSELF—
IT'S NOT WORTH YOUR GETTING INVOLVED.
THAT MAN IS...

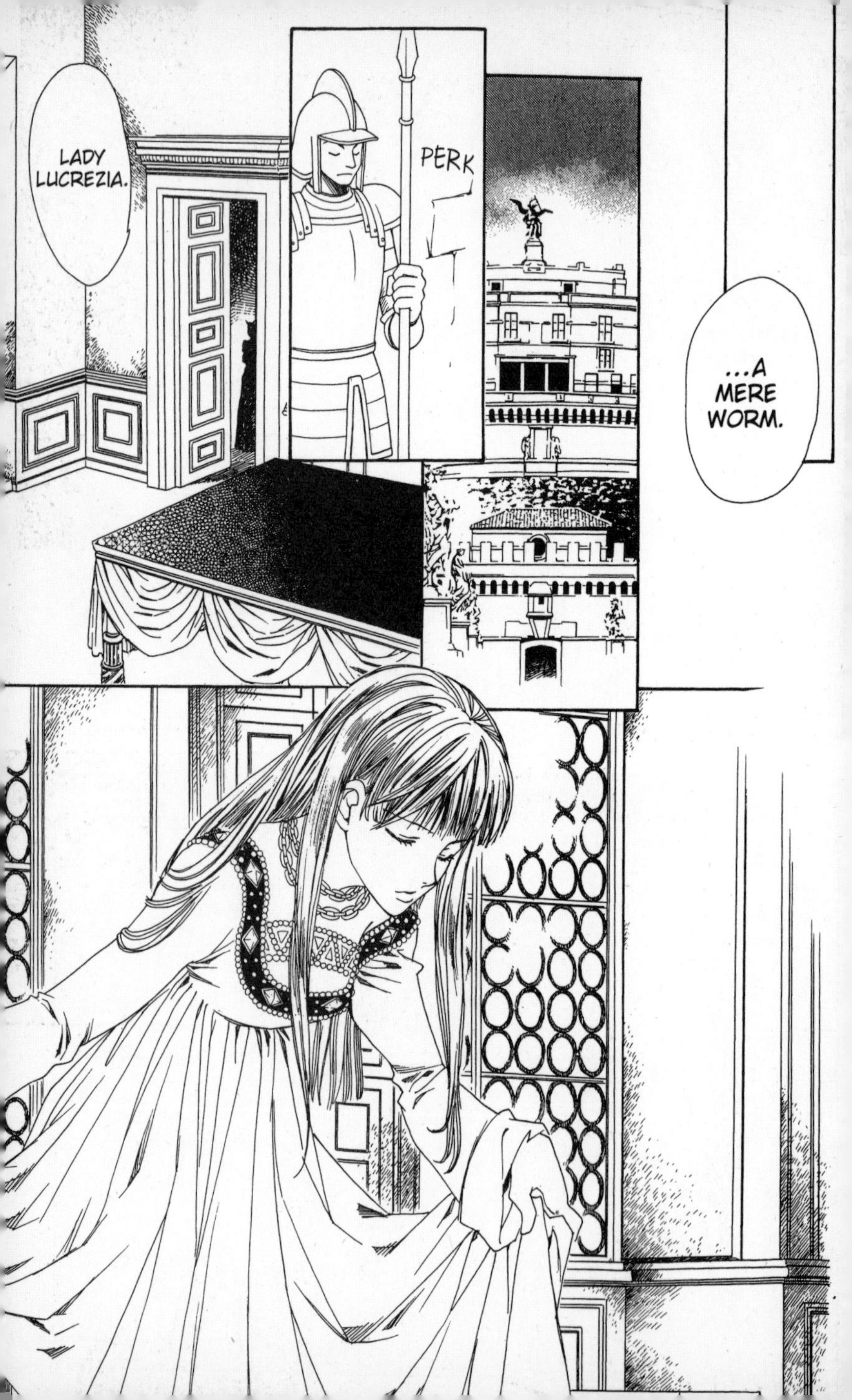
...A MERE WORM.
PERK
LADY LUCREZIA.

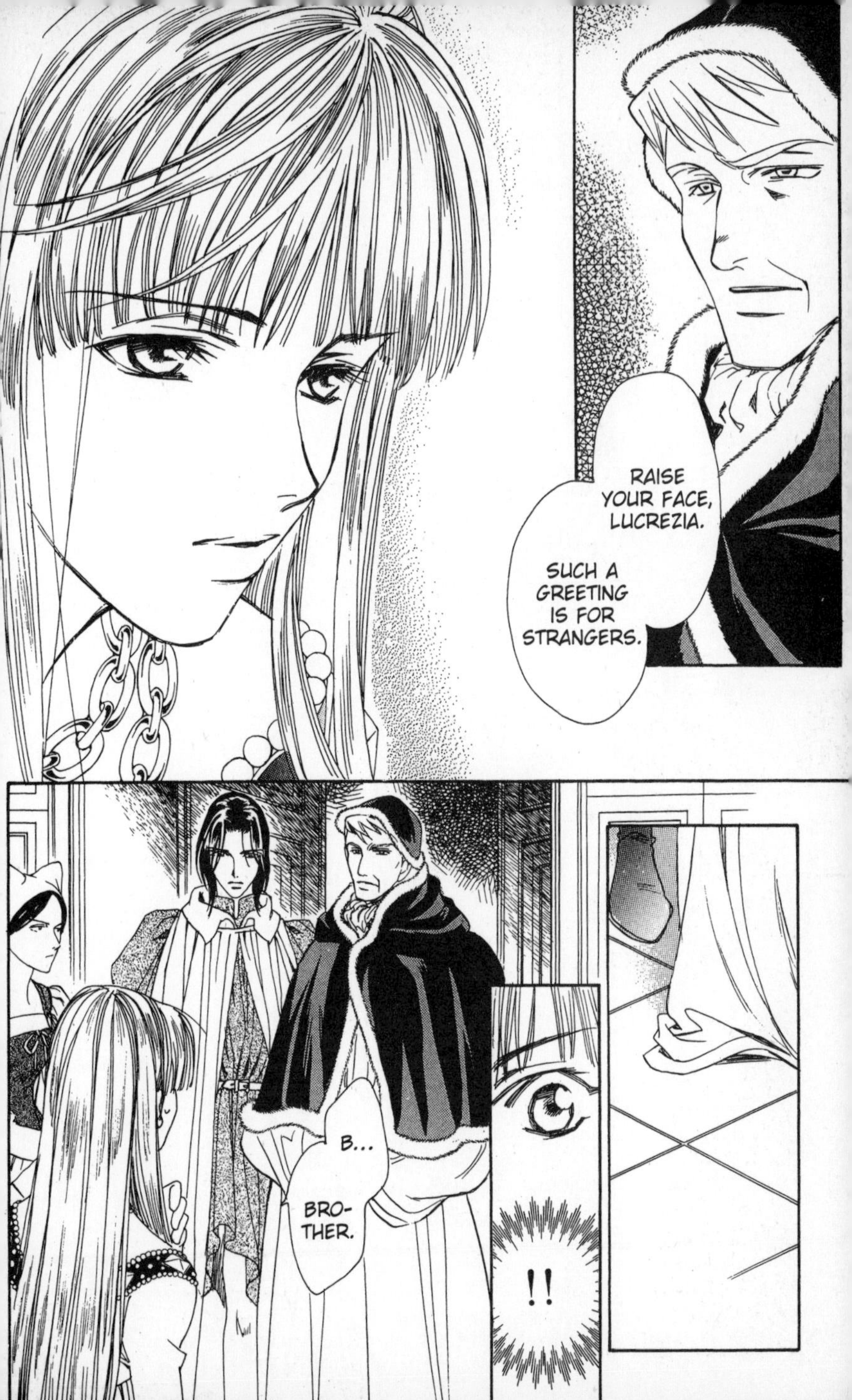
RAISE YOUR FACE, LUCREZIA.
SUCH A GREETING IS FOR STRANGERS.
!!
B...
BRO-THER.

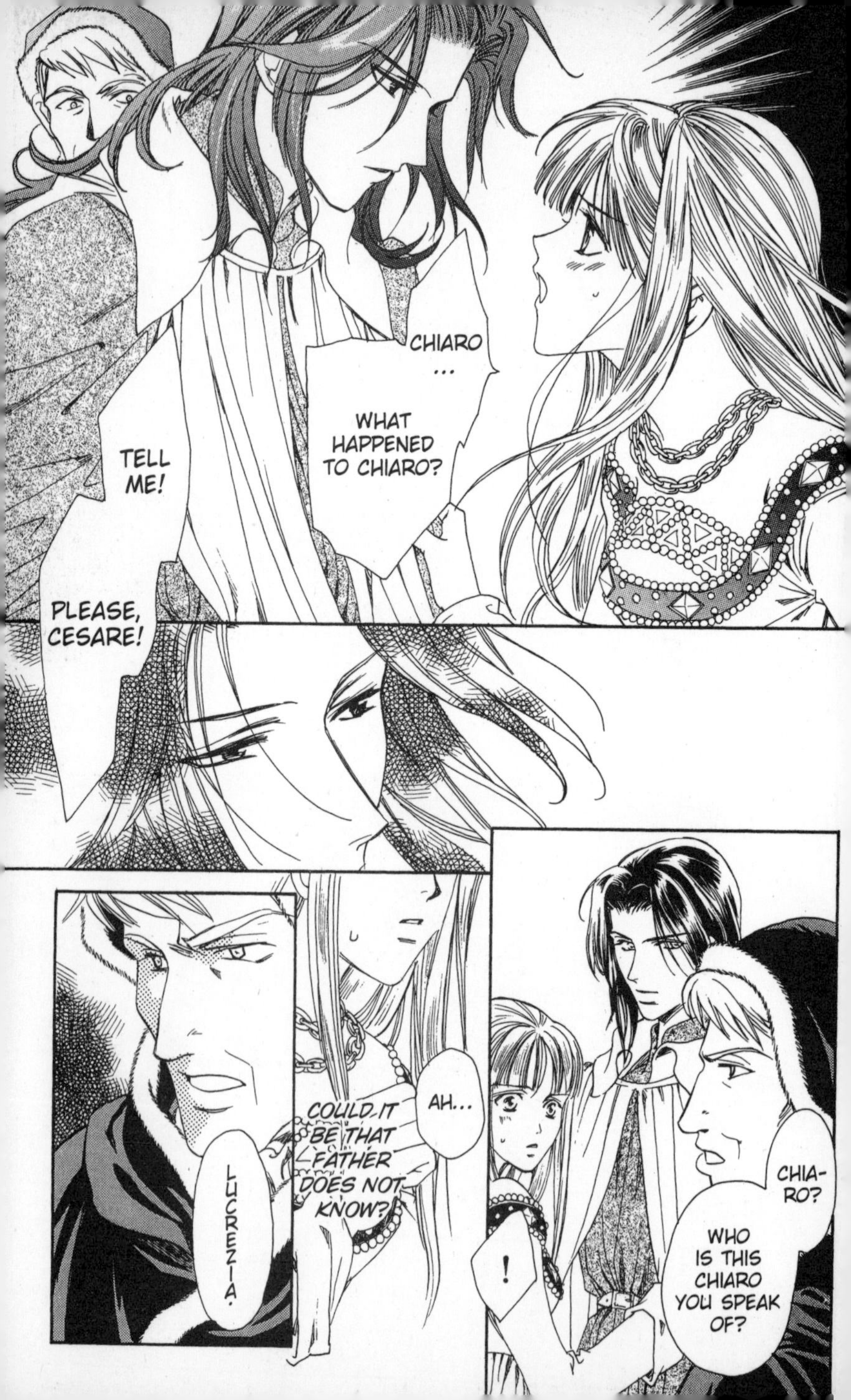
CHIARO ...
WHAT HAPPENED TO CHIARO?
TELL ME!
PLEASE, CESARE!
CHIARO?
WHO IS THIS CHIARO YOU SPEAK OF?
!
AH...
COULD IT BE THAT FATHER DOES NOT KNOW?
LUCREZIA.

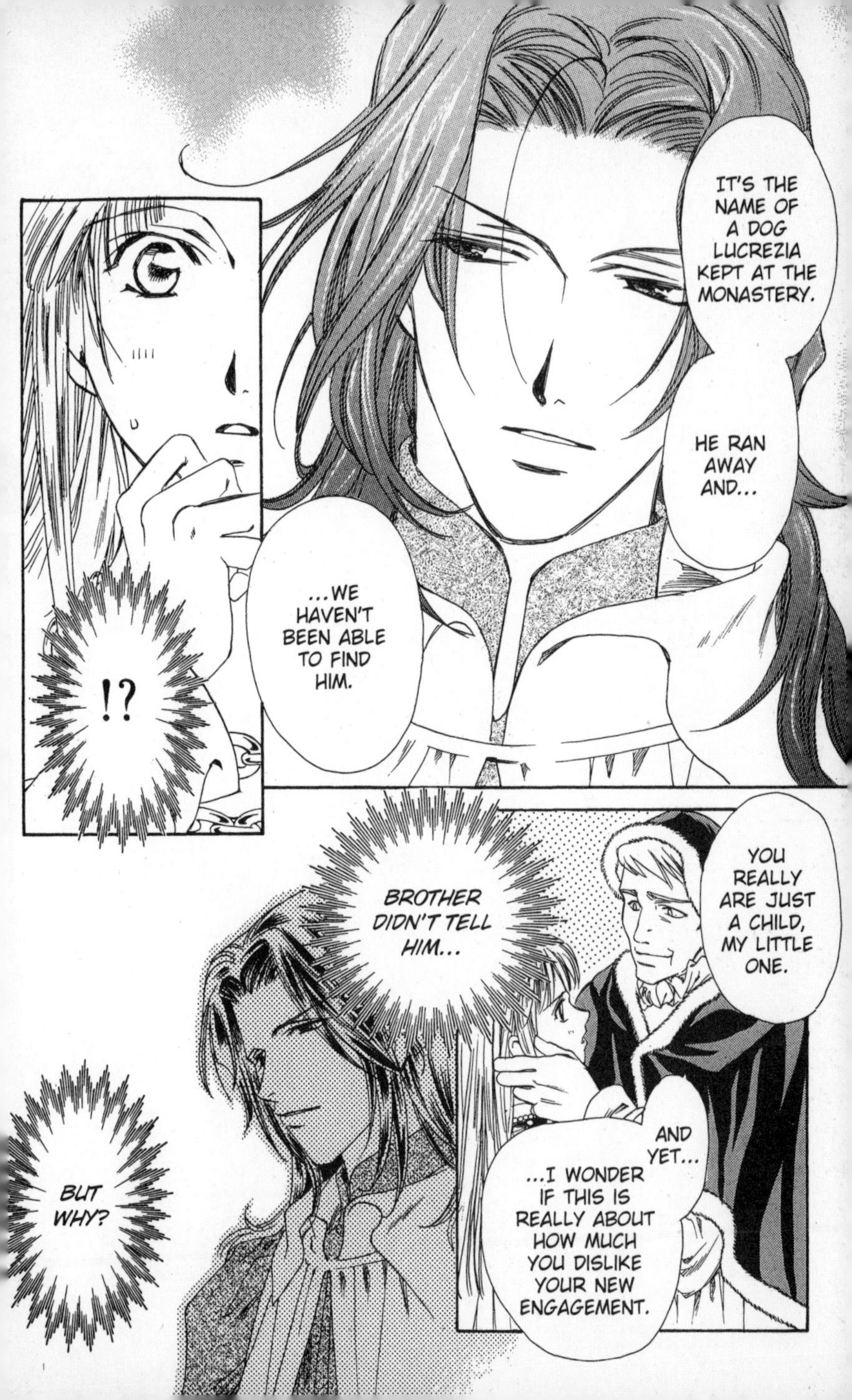
IT'S THE NAME OF A DOG LUCREZIA KEPT AT THE MONASTERY.
HE RAN AWAY AND...
...WE HAVEN'T BEEN ABLE TO FIND HIM.
!?
YOU REALLY ARE JUST A CHILD, MY LITTLE ONE.
AND YET...
...I WONDER IF THIS IS REALLY ABOUT HOW MUCH YOU DISLIKE YOUR NEW ENGAGEMENT.
BROTHER DIDN'T TELL HIM...
BUT WHY?

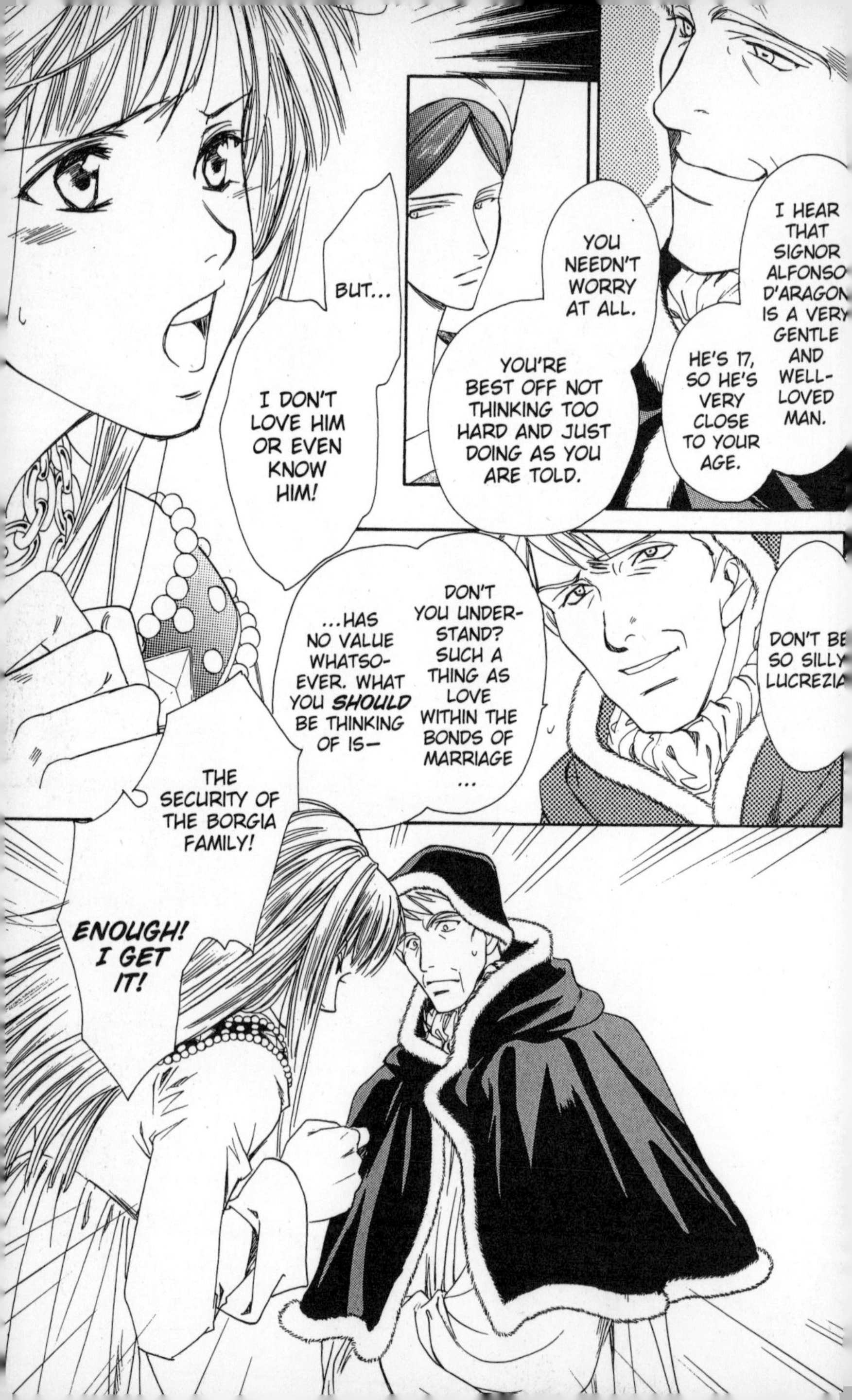
I HEAR THAT SIGNOR ALFONSO D'ARAGON IS A VERY GENTLE AND WELL-LOVED MAN.
HE'S 17, SO HE'S VERY CLOSE TO YOUR AGE.
YOU NEEDN'T WORRY AT ALL.
YOU'RE BEST OFF NOT THINKING TOO HARD AND JUST DOING AS YOU ARE TOLD.
BUT...
I DON'T LOVE HIM OR EVEN KNOW HIM!
DON'T BE SO SILLY LUCREZIA
DON'T YOU UNDERSTAND? SUCH A THING AS LOVE WITHIN THE BONDS OF MARRIAGE...
...HAS NO VALUE WHATSOEVER. WHAT YOU *SHOULD* BE THINKING OF IS—
THE SECURITY OF THE BORGIA FAMILY!
ENOUGH! I GET IT!

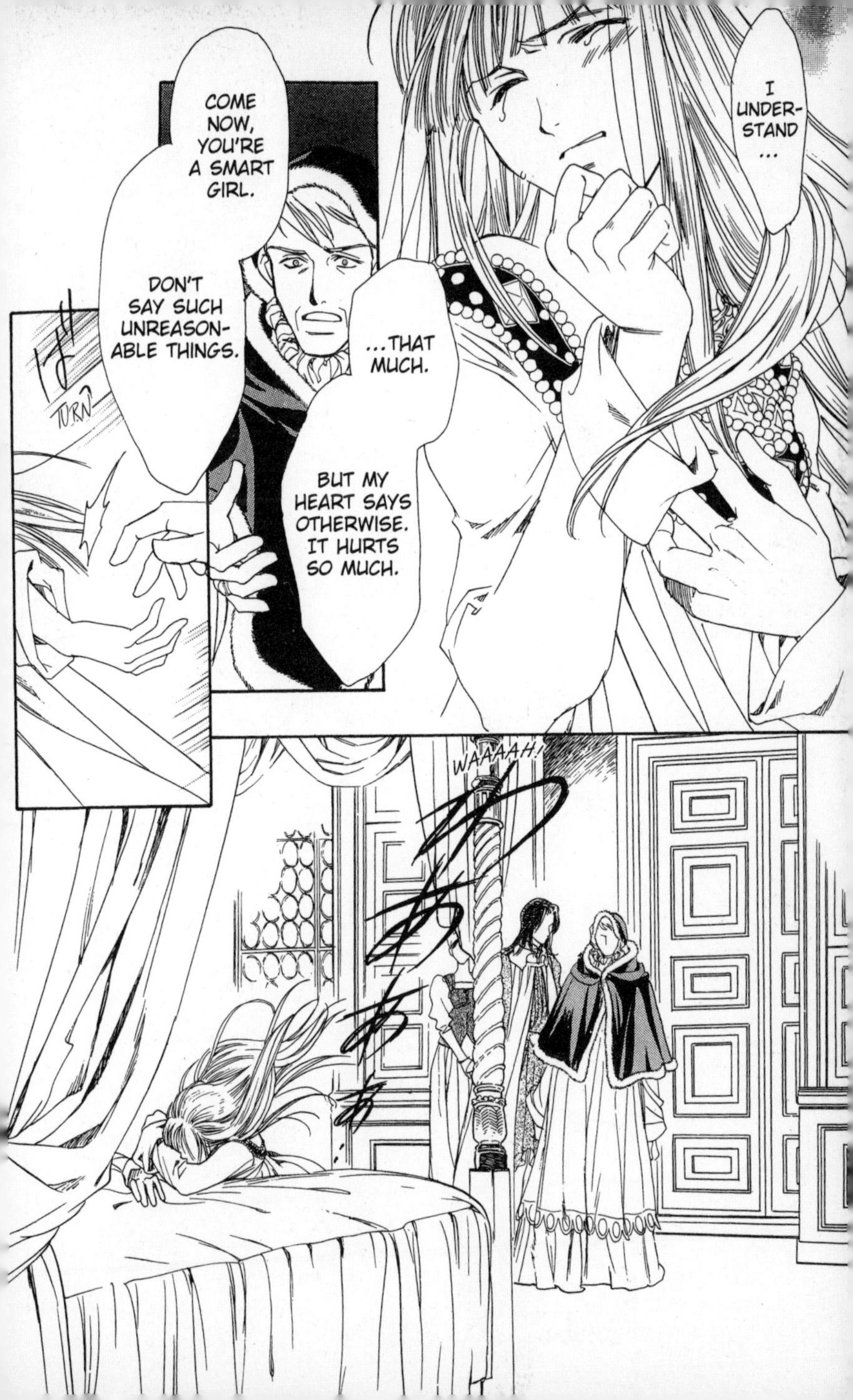
I UNDERSTAND...
...THAT MUCH.
BUT MY HEART SAYS OTHERWISE. IT HURTS SO MUCH.
COME NOW, YOU'RE A SMART GIRL.
DON'T SAY SUCH UNREASONABLE THINGS.
TURN
WAAAAH!

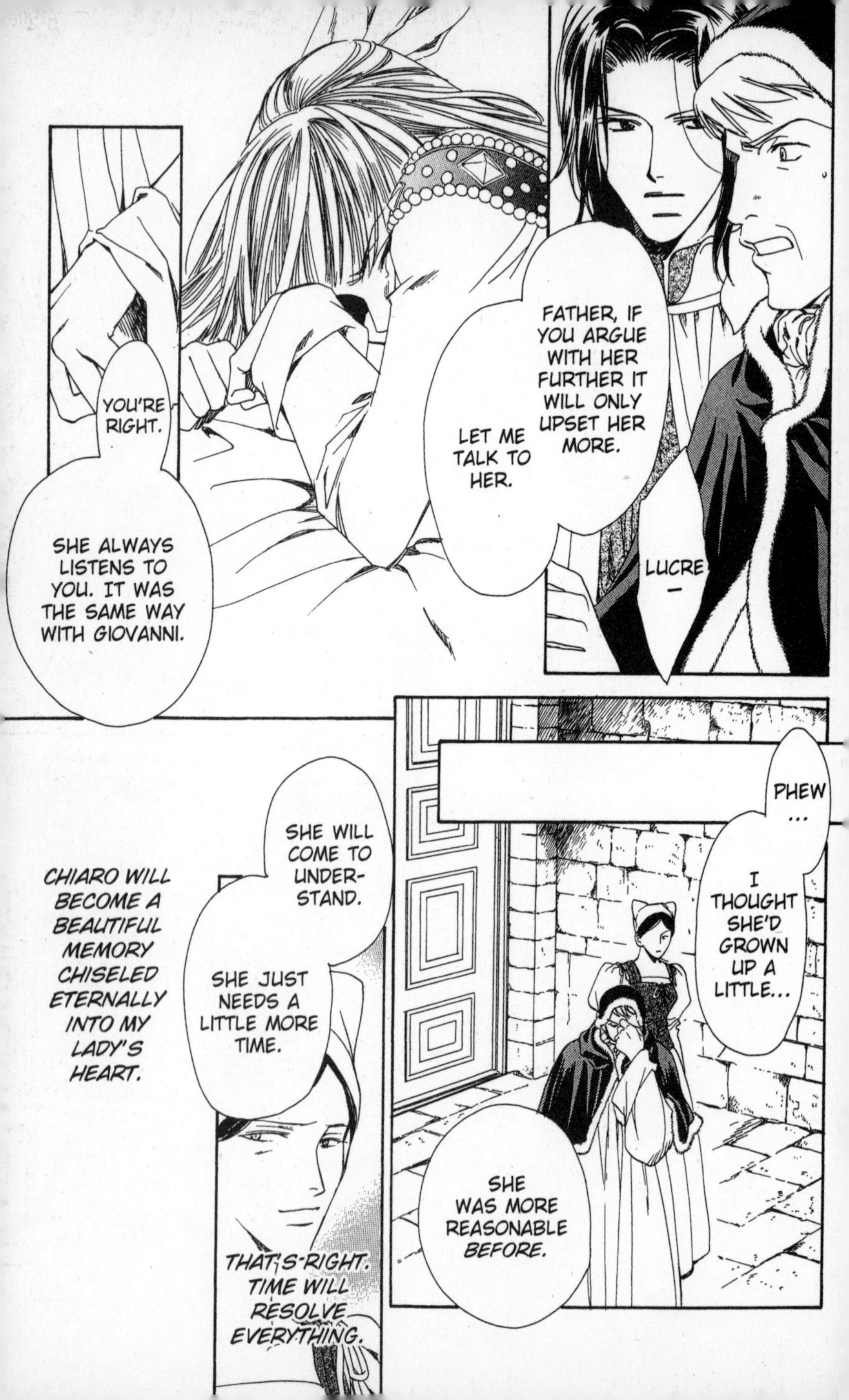

FATHER, IF YOU ARGUE WITH HER FURTHER IT WILL ONLY UPSET HER MORE.
LET ME TALK TO HER.
LUCRE—
YOU'RE RIGHT.
SHE ALWAYS LISTENS TO YOU. IT WAS THE SAME WAY WITH GIOVANNI.
PHEW...
I THOUGHT SHE'D GROWN UP A LITTLE...
SHE WAS MORE REASONABLE BEFORE.
SHE WILL COME TO UNDER-STAND.
SHE JUST NEEDS A LITTLE MORE TIME.
CHIARO WILL BECOME A BEAUTIFUL MEMORY CHISELED ETERNALLY INTO MY LADY'S HEART.
THAT'S RIGHT. TIME WILL RESOLVE EVERYTHING.

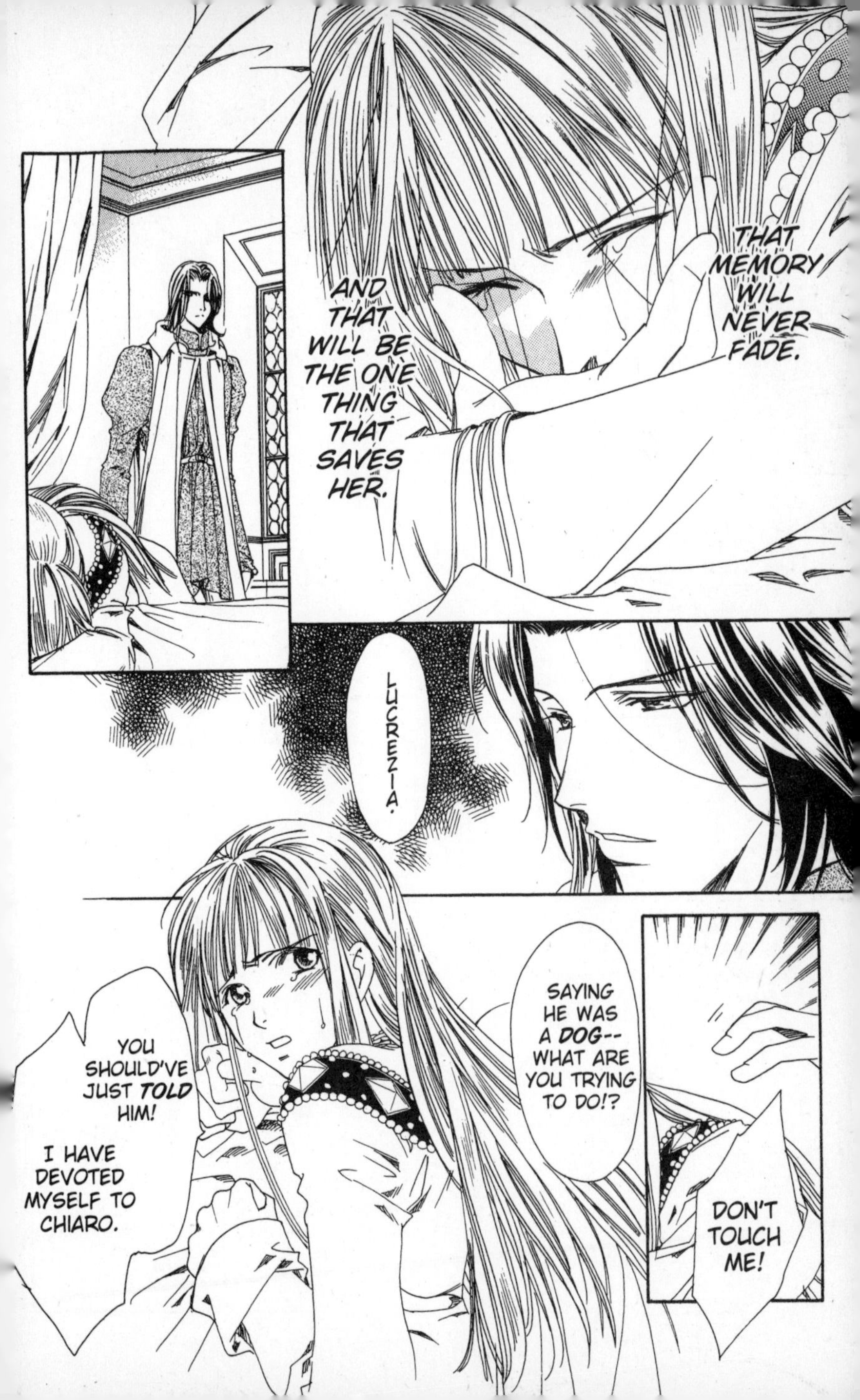
THAT MEMORY WILL NEVER FADE.
AND THAT WILL BE THE ONE THING THAT SAVES HER.
LUCREZIA.
DON'T TOUCH ME!
SAYING HE WAS A *DOG*--WHAT ARE YOU TRYING TO DO!?
YOU SHOULD'VE JUST *TOLD* HIM!
I HAVE DEVOTED MYSELF TO CHIARO.

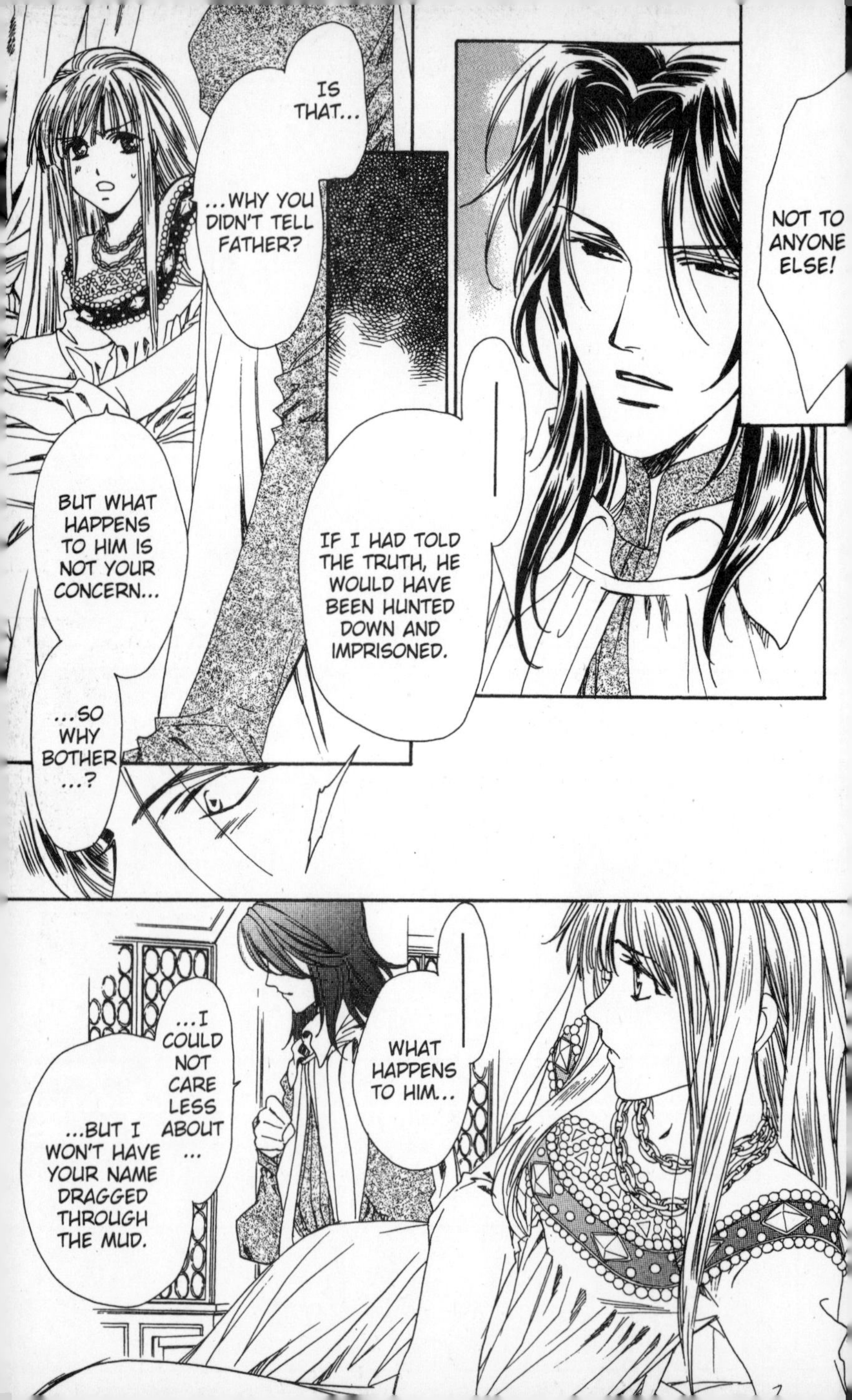
NOT TO ANYONE ELSE!
IS THAT...
...WHY YOU DIDN'T TELL FATHER?
IF I HAD TOLD THE TRUTH, HE WOULD HAVE BEEN HUNTED DOWN AND IMPRISONED.
BUT WHAT HAPPENS TO HIM IS NOT YOUR CONCERN...
...SO WHY BOTHER ...?
WHAT HAPPENS TO HIM...
...I COULD NOT CARE LESS ABOUT ...
...BUT I WON'T HAVE YOUR NAME DRAGGED THROUGH THE MUD.

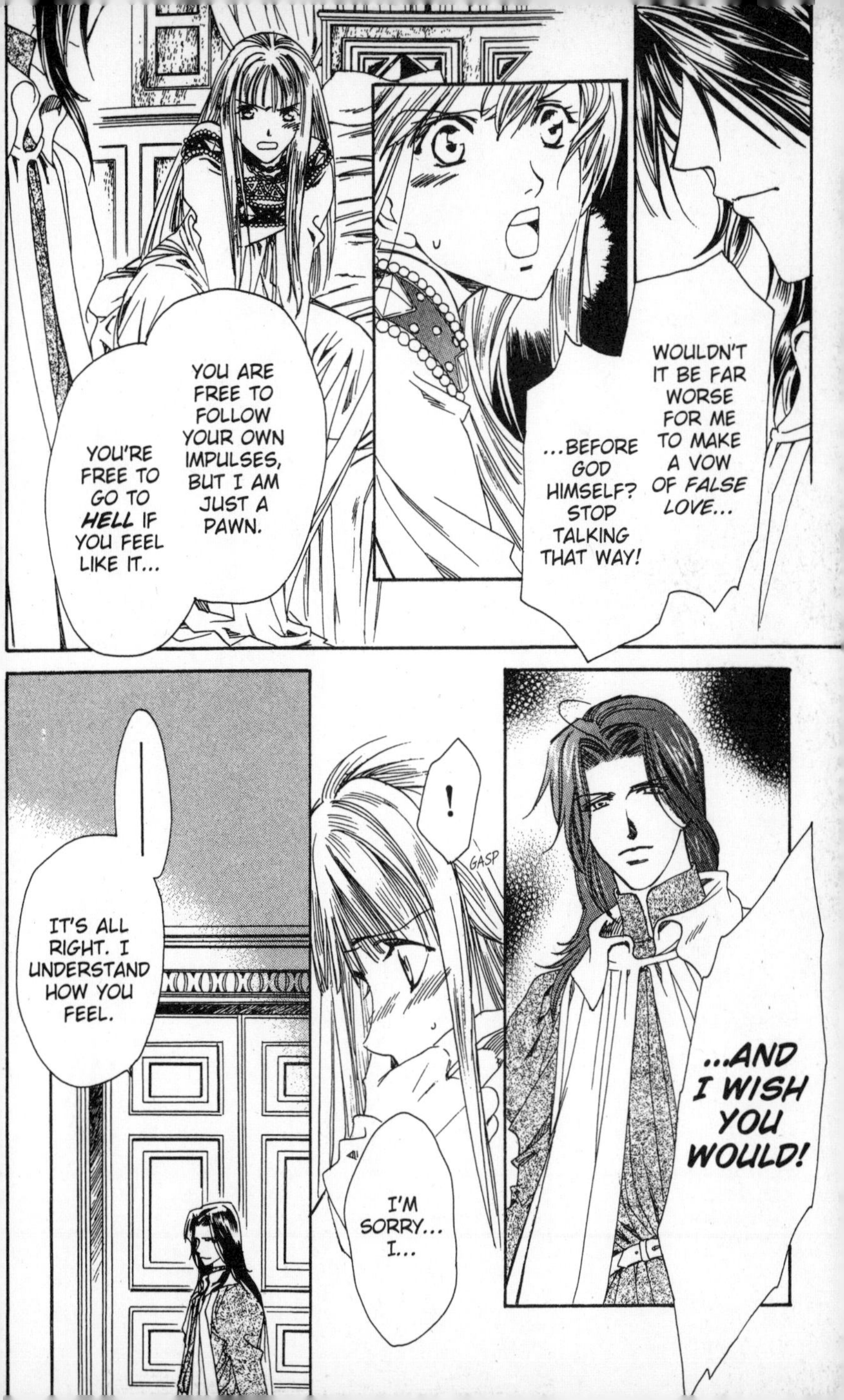
WOULDN'T IT BE FAR WORSE FOR ME TO MAKE A VOW OF *FALSE* LOVE...
...BEFORE GOD HIMSELF? STOP TALKING THAT WAY!
YOU ARE FREE TO FOLLOW YOUR OWN IMPULSES, BUT I AM JUST A PAWN.
YOU'RE FREE TO GO TO ***HELL*** IF YOU FEEL LIKE IT...
...AND I WISH YOU WOULD!
!
GASP
I'M SORRY... I...
IT'S ALL RIGHT. I UNDERSTAND HOW YOU FEEL.

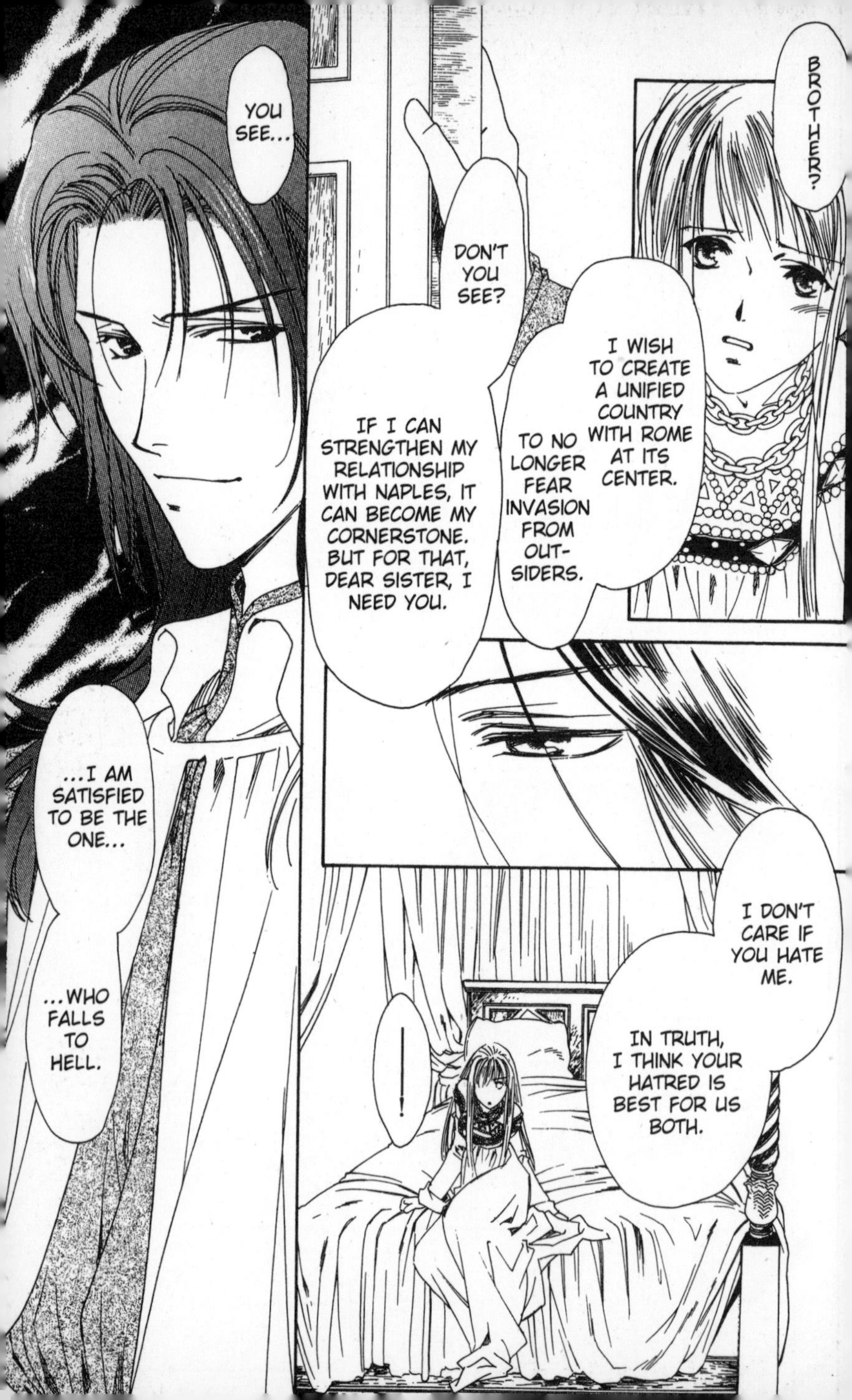
BROTHER?
I WISH TO CREATE A UNIFIED COUNTRY WITH ROME AT ITS CENTER.
TO NO LONGER FEAR INVASION FROM OUT-SIDERS.
DON'T YOU SEE?
IF I CAN STRENGTHEN MY RELATIONSHIP WITH NAPLES, IT CAN BECOME MY CORNERSTONE. BUT FOR THAT, DEAR SISTER, I NEED YOU.
I DON'T CARE IF YOU HATE ME.
IN TRUTH, I THINK YOUR HATRED IS BEST FOR US BOTH.
!
YOU SEE...
...I AM SATISFIED TO BE THE ONE...
...WHO FALLS TO HELL.

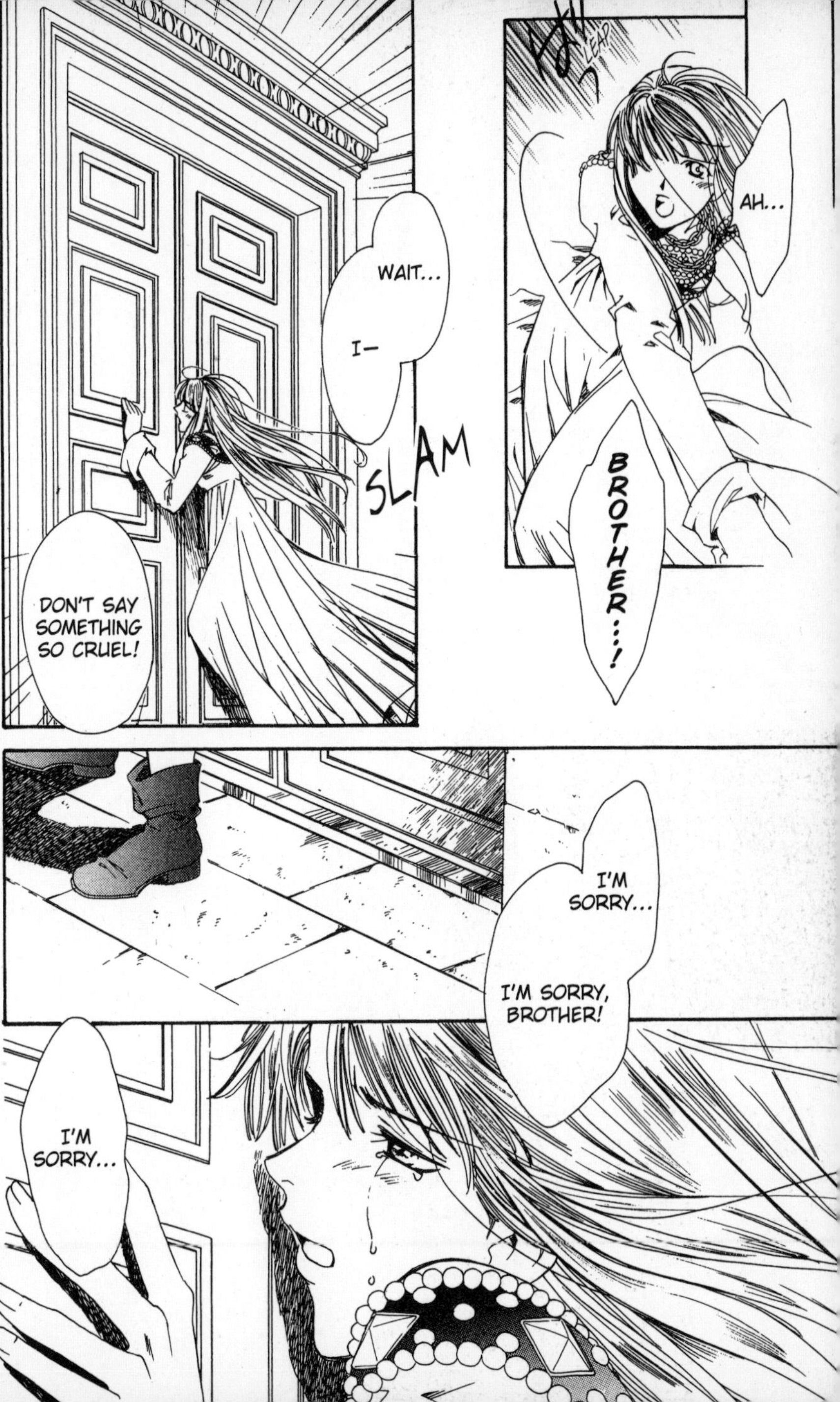
LEAP
AH...
BROTHER...!
WAIT...
I—
SLAM
DON'T SAY SOMETHING SO CRUEL!
I'M SORRY...
I'M SORRY, BROTHER!
I'M SORRY...

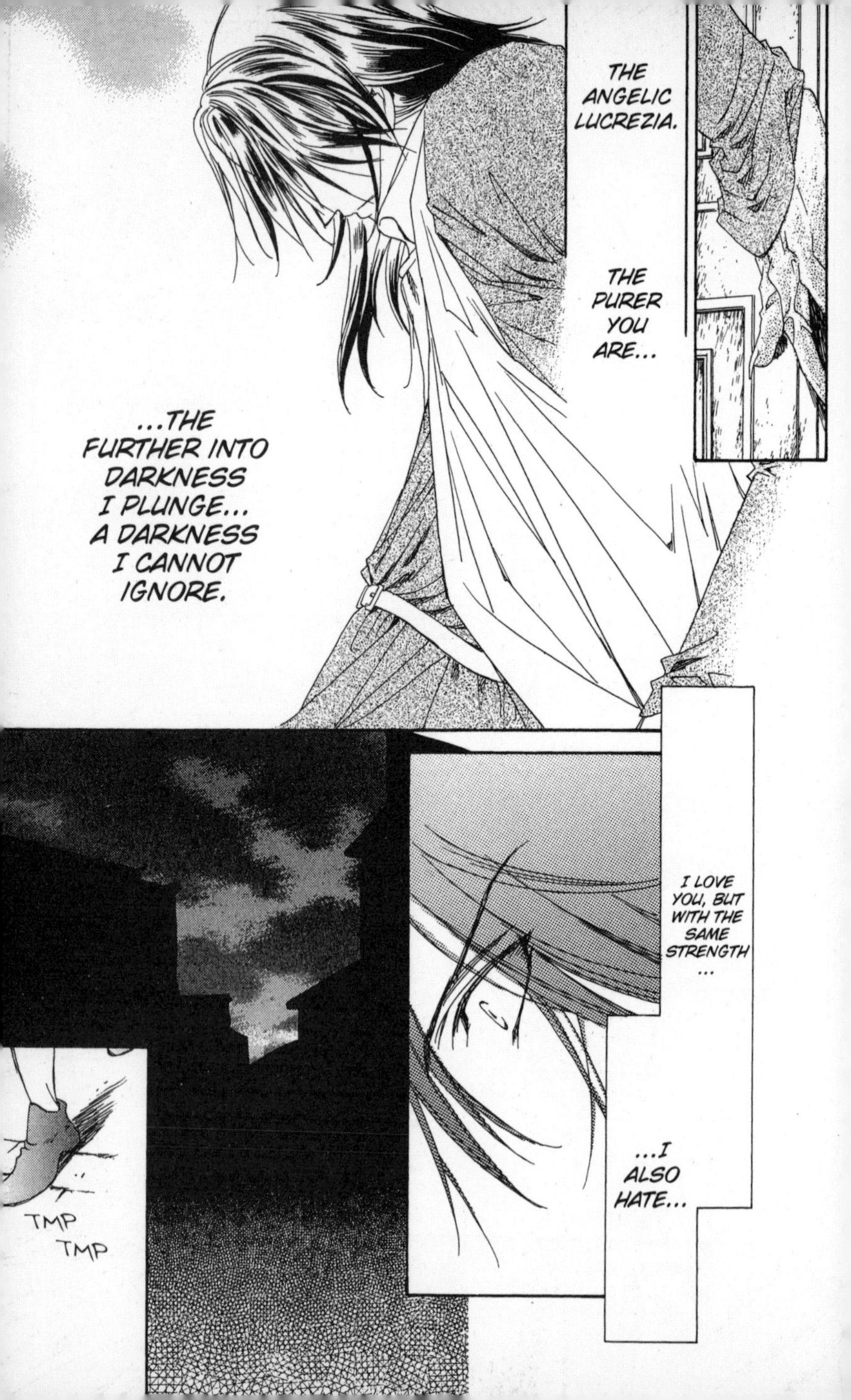
THE ANGELIC LUCREZIA.
THE PURER YOU ARE...
...THE FURTHER INTO DARKNESS I PLUNGE... A DARKNESS I CANNOT IGNORE.
I LOVE YOU, BUT WITH THE SAME STRENGTH ...
...I ALSO HATE...
TMP TMP

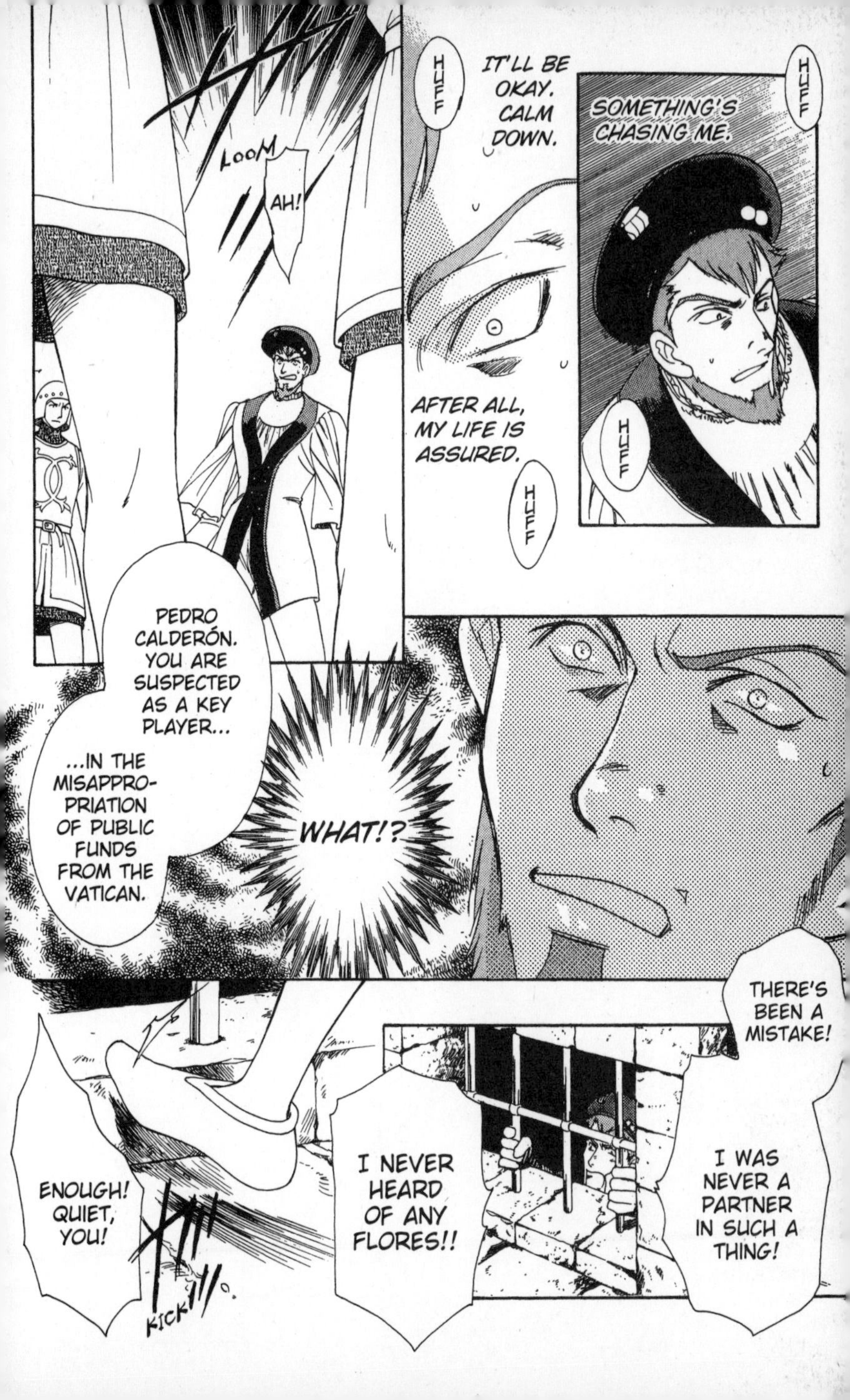
HUFF
SOMETHING'S CHASING ME.
HUFF
HUFF
IT'LL BE OKAY. CALM DOWN.
AFTER ALL, MY LIFE IS ASSURED.
HUFF
LOOM
AH!
PEDRO CALDERÓN. YOU ARE SUSPECTED AS A KEY PLAYER...
...IN THE MISAPPRO-PRIATION OF PUBLIC FUNDS FROM THE VATICAN.
WHAT!?
THERE'S BEEN A MISTAKE!
I WAS NEVER A PARTNER IN SUCH A THING!
I NEVER HEARD OF ANY FLORES!!
ENOUGH! QUIET, YOU!
KICK

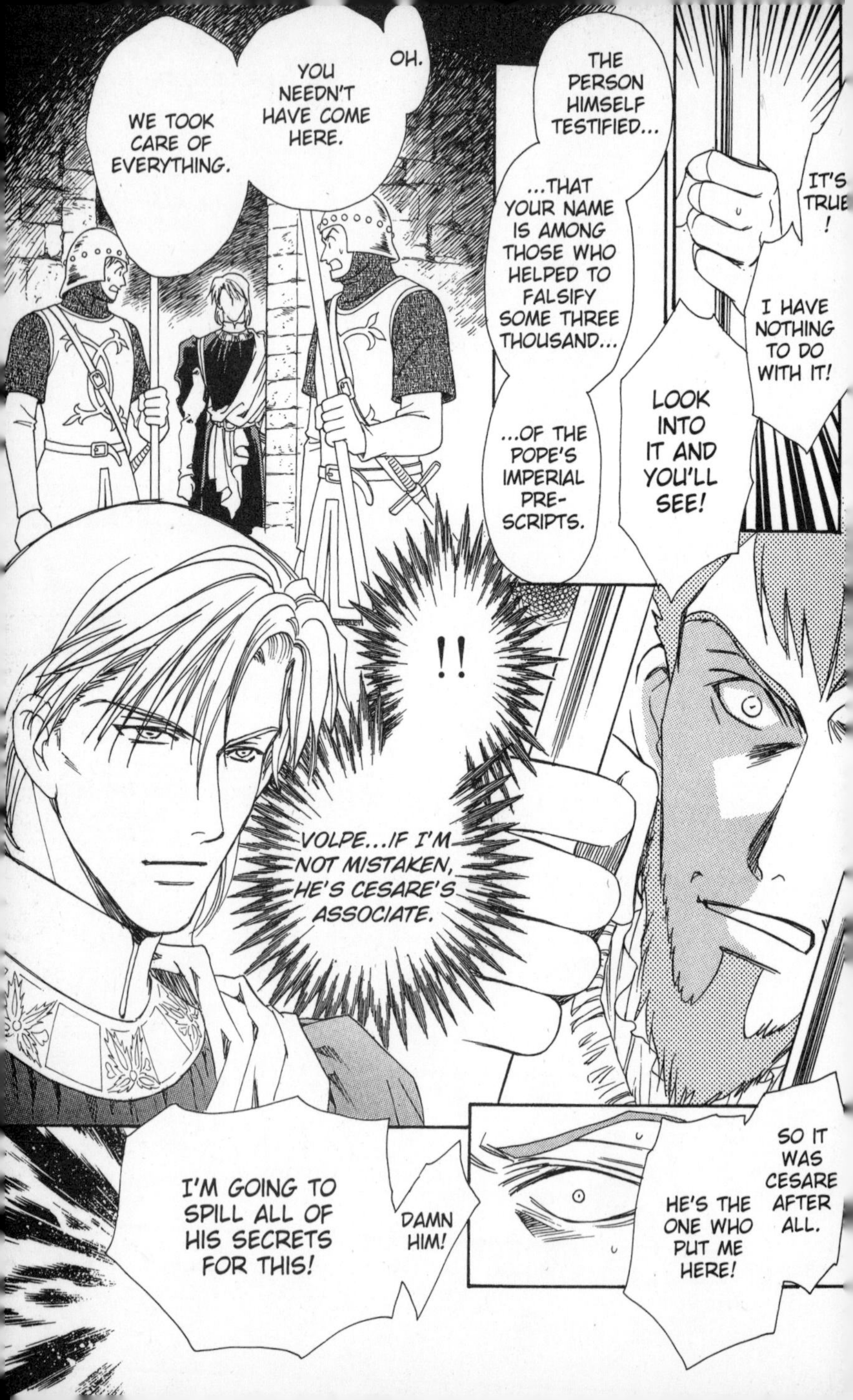
IT'S TRUE!
I HAVE NOTHING TO DO WITH IT!
LOOK INTO IT AND YOU'LL SEE!
THE PERSON HIMSELF TESTIFIED...
...THAT YOUR NAME IS AMONG THOSE WHO HELPED TO FALSIFY SOME THREE THOUSAND...
...OF THE POPE'S IMPERIAL PRE-SCRIPTS.
OH.
YOU NEEDN'T HAVE COME HERE.
WE TOOK CARE OF EVERYTHING.
!!
VOLPE...IF I'M NOT MISTAKEN, HE'S CESARE'S ASSOCIATE.
SO IT WAS CESARE AFTER ALL.
HE'S THE ONE WHO PUT ME HERE!
DAMN HIM!
I'M GOING TO SPILL ALL OF HIS SECRETS FOR THIS!

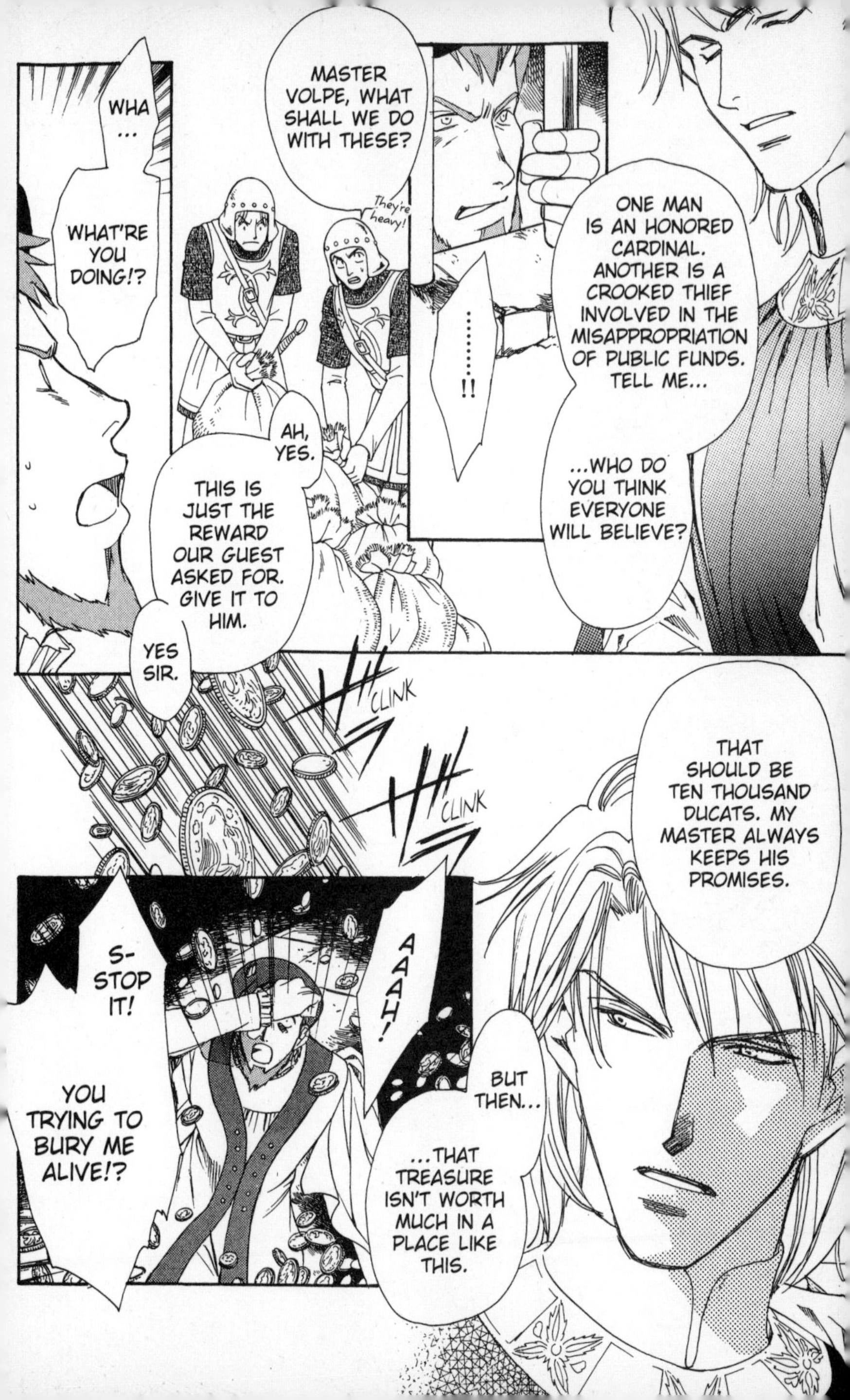

ONE MAN IS AN HONORED CARDINAL. ANOTHER IS A CROOKED THIEF INVOLVED IN THE MISAPPROPRIATION OF PUBLIC FUNDS. TELL ME...
...WHO DO YOU THINK EVERYONE WILL BELIEVE?
......!!
MASTER VOLPE, WHAT SHALL WE DO WITH THESE?
They're heavy!
AH, YES.
THIS IS JUST THE REWARD OUR GUEST ASKED FOR. GIVE IT TO HIM.
YES SIR.
WHA...
WHAT'RE YOU DOING!?
CLINK
CLINK
THAT SHOULD BE TEN THOUSAND DUCATS. MY MASTER ALWAYS KEEPS HIS PROMISES.
BUT THEN...
...THAT TREASURE ISN'T WORTH MUCH IN A PLACE LIKE THIS.
AAAAH!
S-STOP IT!
YOU TRYING TO BURY ME ALIVE!?

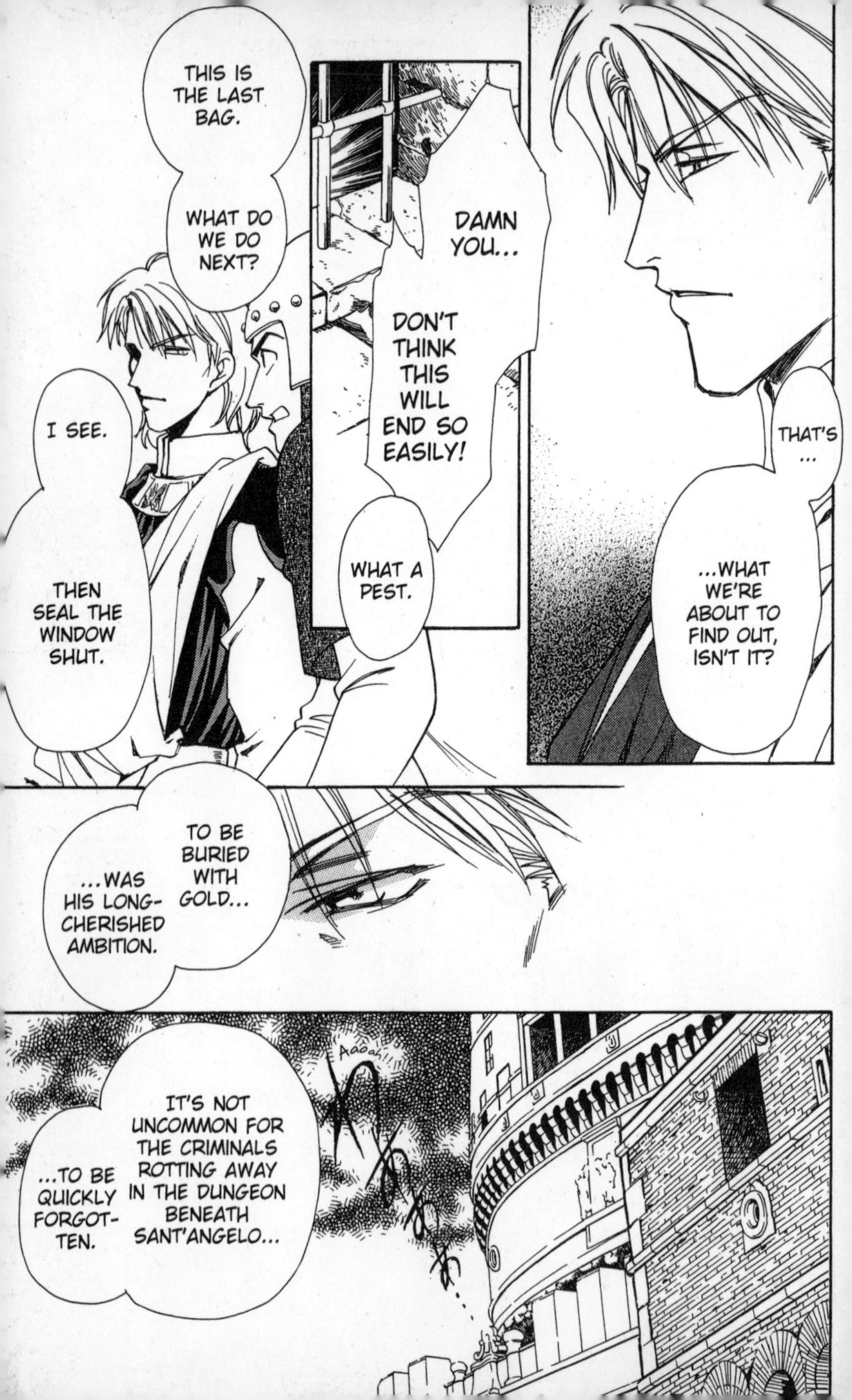
THAT'S...
...WHAT WE'RE ABOUT TO FIND OUT, ISN'T IT?
DAMN YOU...
DON'T THINK THIS WILL END SO EASILY!
WHAT A PEST.
THIS IS THE LAST BAG.
WHAT DO WE DO NEXT?
I SEE.
THEN SEAL THE WINDOW SHUT.
TO BE BURIED WITH GOLD...
...WAS HIS LONG-CHERISHED AMBITION.
Aaaah!!
IT'S NOT UNCOMMON FOR THE CRIMINALS ROTTING AWAY IN THE DUNGEON BENEATH SANT'ANGELO...
...TO BE QUICKLY FORGOT-TEN.

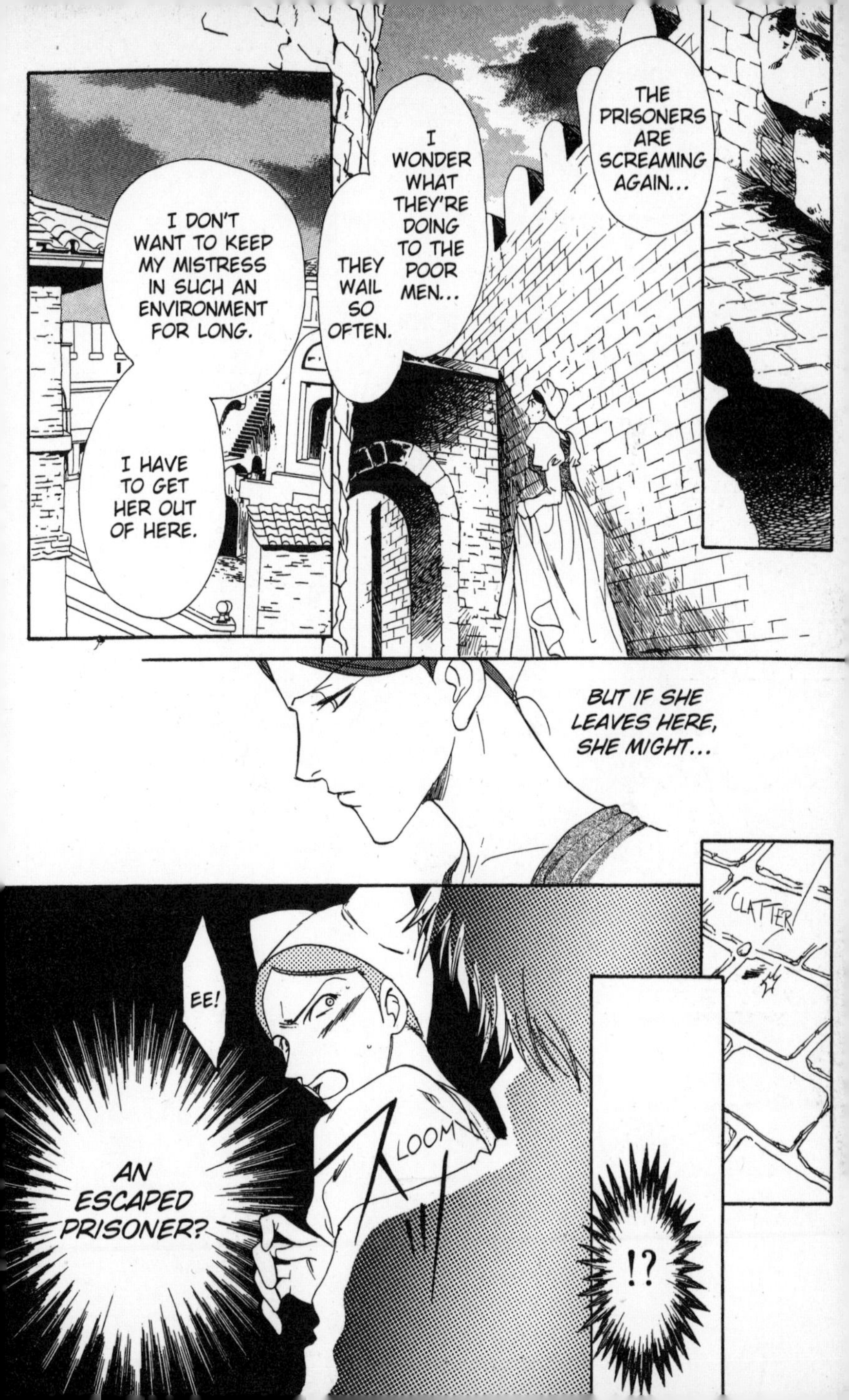
THE PRISONERS ARE SCREAMING AGAIN...
I WONDER WHAT THEY'RE DOING TO THE POOR MEN...
THEY WAIL SO OFTEN.
I DON'T WANT TO KEEP MY MISTRESS IN SUCH AN ENVIRONMENT FOR LONG.
I HAVE TO GET HER OUT OF HERE.
BUT IF SHE LEAVES HERE, SHE MIGHT...
CLATTER
!?
EE!
LOOM
AN ESCAPED PRISONER?

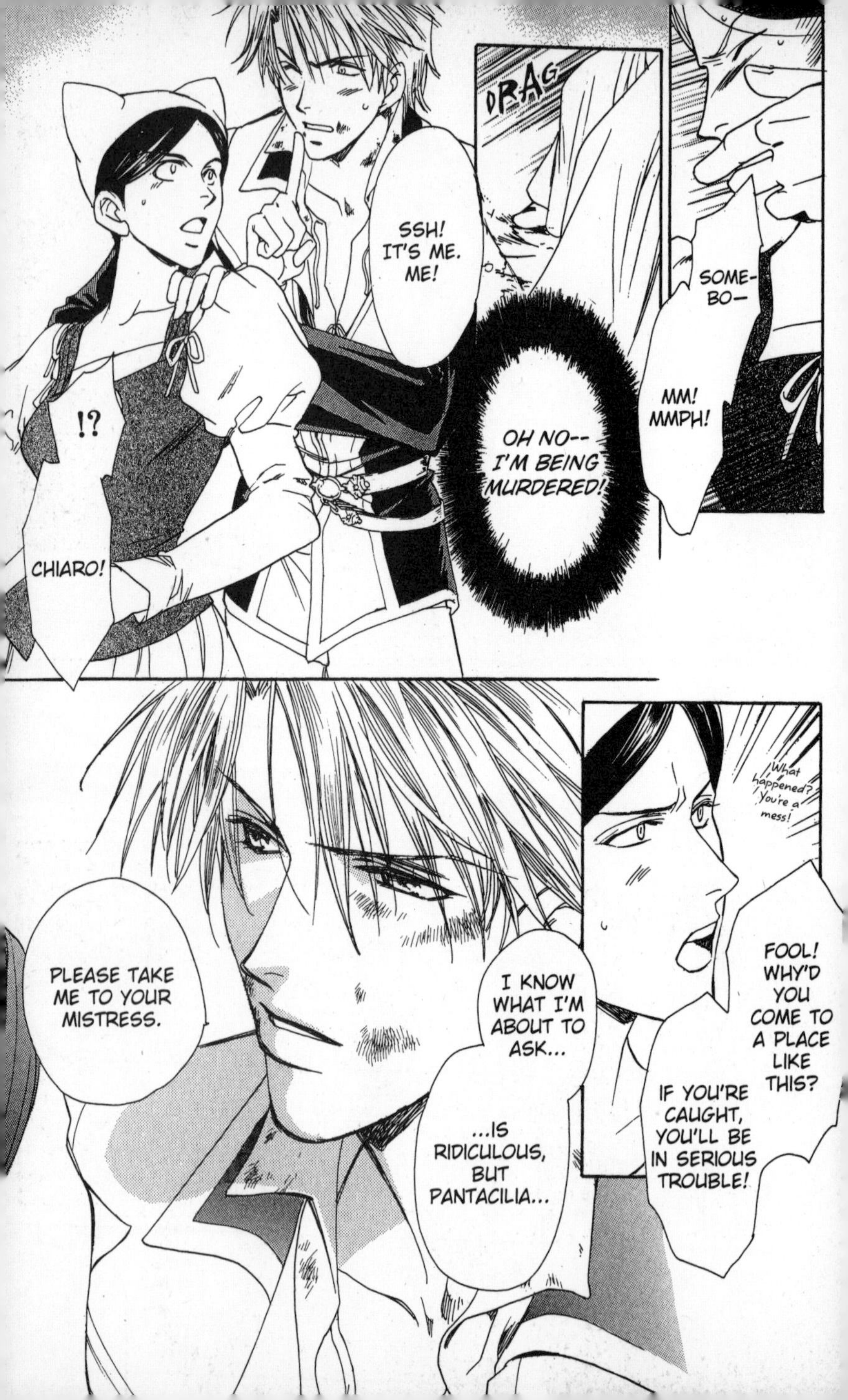
SOME-BO—
MM! MMPH!
DRAG
OH NO-- I'M BEING MURDERED!
SSH! IT'S ME. ME!
!?
CHIARO!
What happened? You're a mess!
FOOL! WHY'D YOU COME TO A PLACE LIKE THIS?
IF YOU'RE CAUGHT, YOU'LL BE IN SERIOUS TROUBLE!
I KNOW WHAT I'M ABOUT TO ASK...
...IS RIDICULOUS, BUT PANTACILIA...
PLEASE TAKE ME TO YOUR MISTRESS.

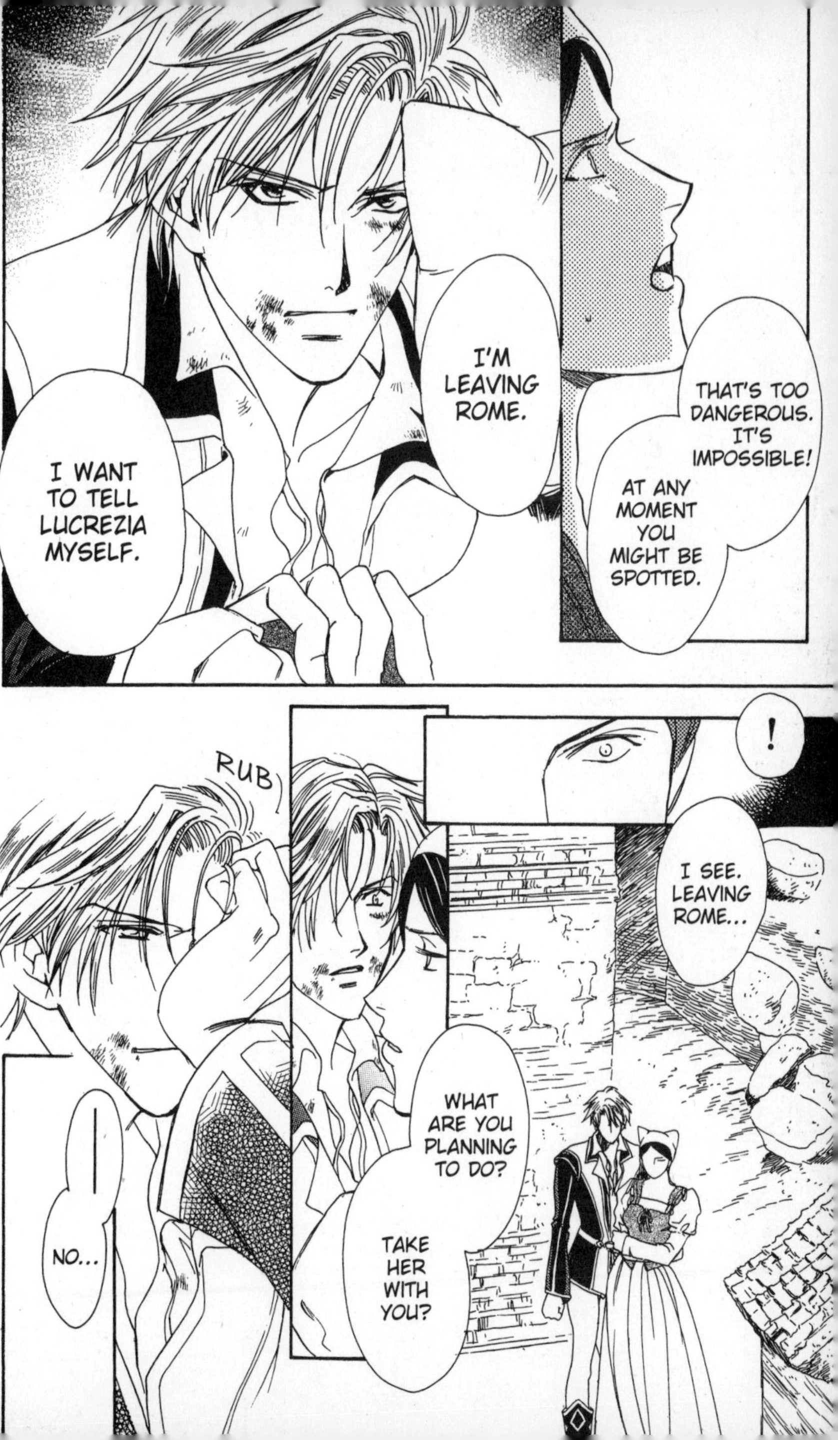
THAT'S TOO DANGEROUS. IT'S IMPOSSIBLE!
AT ANY MOMENT YOU MIGHT BE SPOTTED.
I'M LEAVING ROME.
I WANT TO TELL LUCREZIA MYSELF.
!
I SEE. LEAVING ROME...
WHAT ARE YOU PLANNING TO DO?
TAKE HER WITH YOU?
RUB
NO...

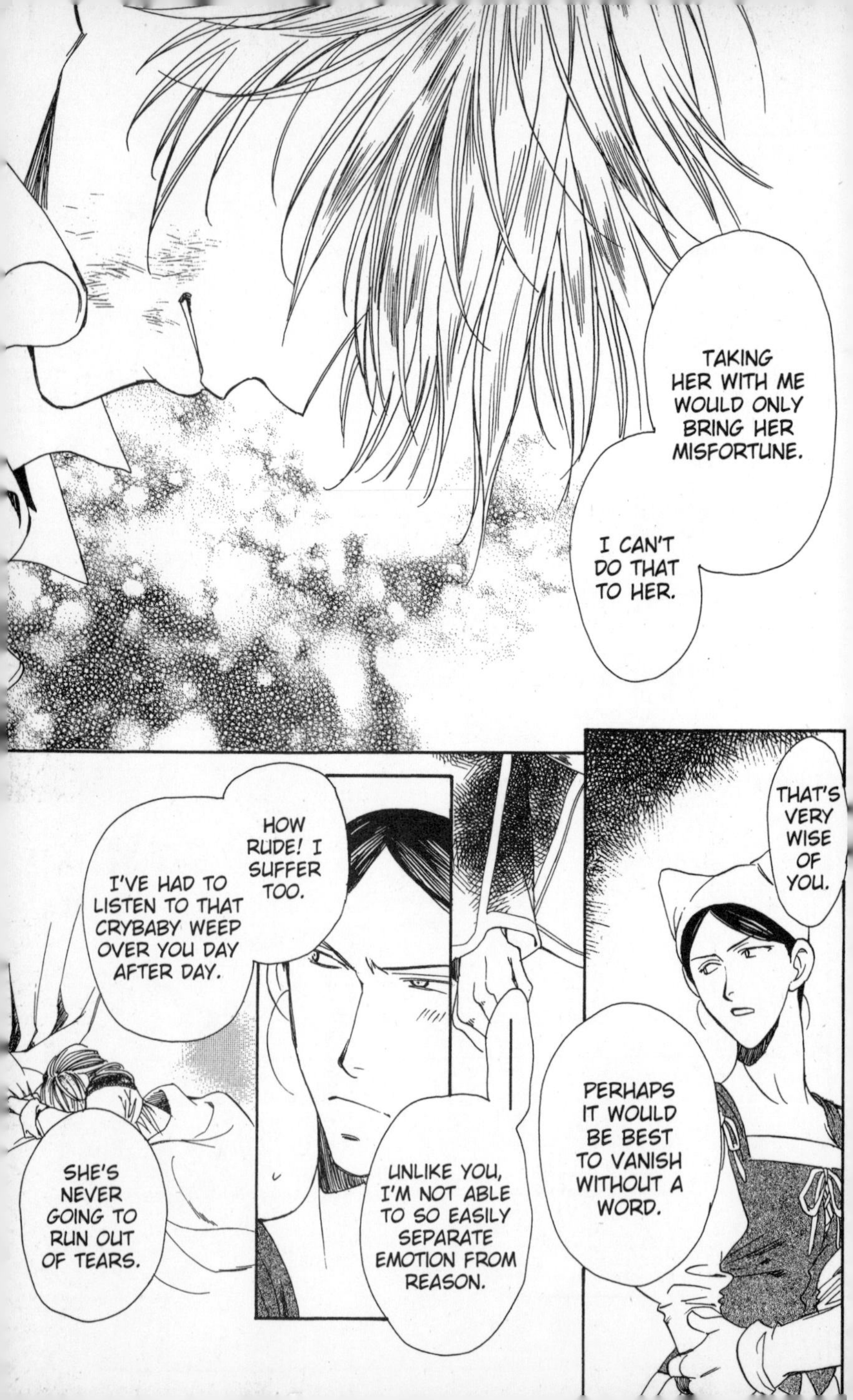
TAKING HER WITH ME WOULD ONLY BRING HER MISFORTUNE.
I CAN'T DO THAT TO HER.
THAT'S VERY WISE OF YOU.
PERHAPS IT WOULD BE BEST TO VANISH WITHOUT A WORD.
UNLIKE YOU, I'M NOT ABLE TO SO EASILY SEPARATE EMOTION FROM REASON.
HOW RUDE! I SUFFER TOO.
I'VE HAD TO LISTEN TO THAT CRYBABY WEEP OVER YOU DAY AFTER DAY.
SHE'S NEVER GOING TO RUN OUT OF TEARS.

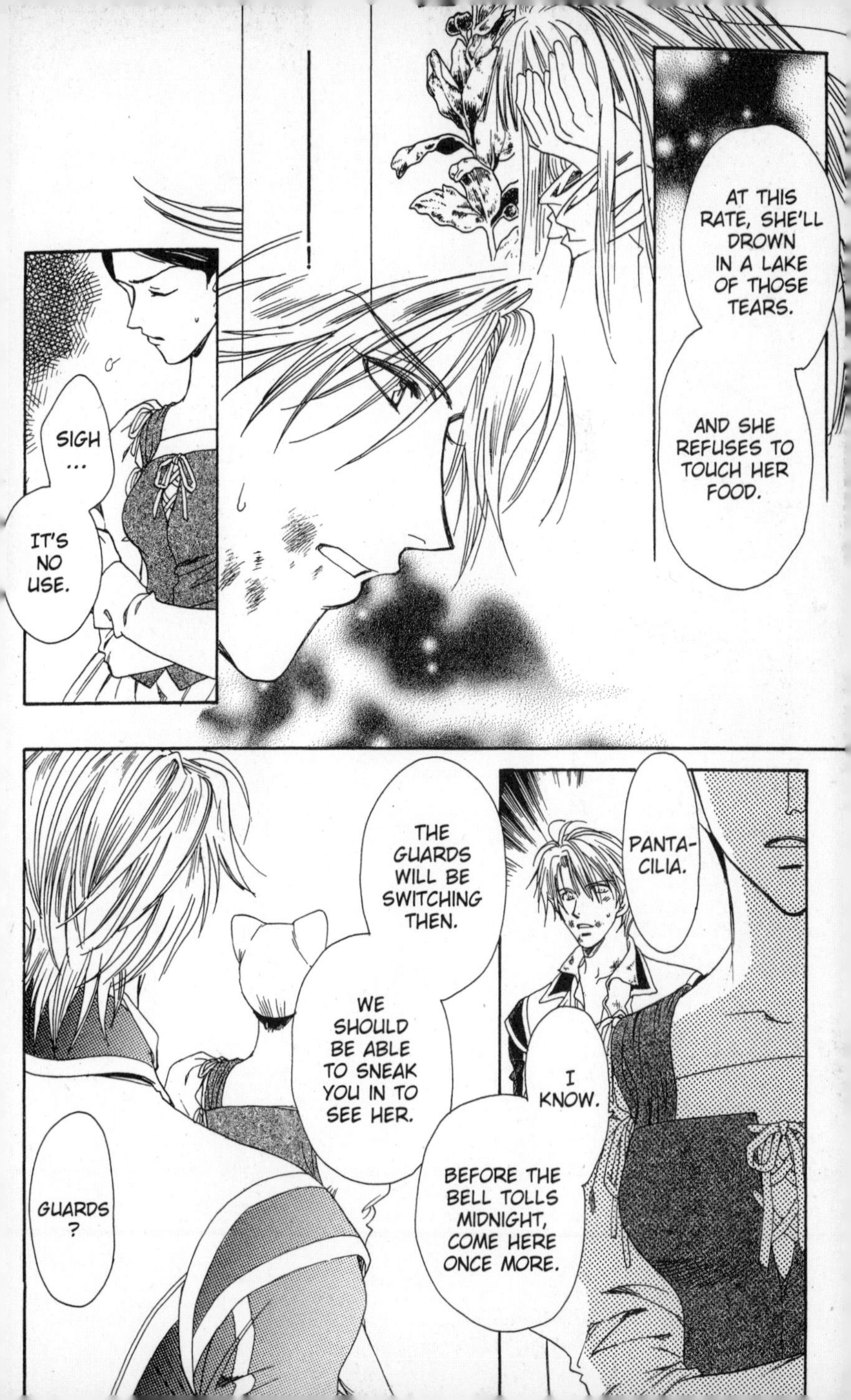
AT THIS RATE, SHE'LL DROWN IN A LAKE OF THOSE TEARS.
AND SHE REFUSES TO TOUCH HER FOOD.
SIGH ...
IT'S NO USE.
PANTA-CILIA.
I KNOW.
BEFORE THE BELL TOLLS MIDNIGHT, COME HERE ONCE MORE.
THE GUARDS WILL BE SWITCHING THEN.
WE SHOULD BE ABLE TO SNEAK YOU IN TO SEE HER.
GUARDS?

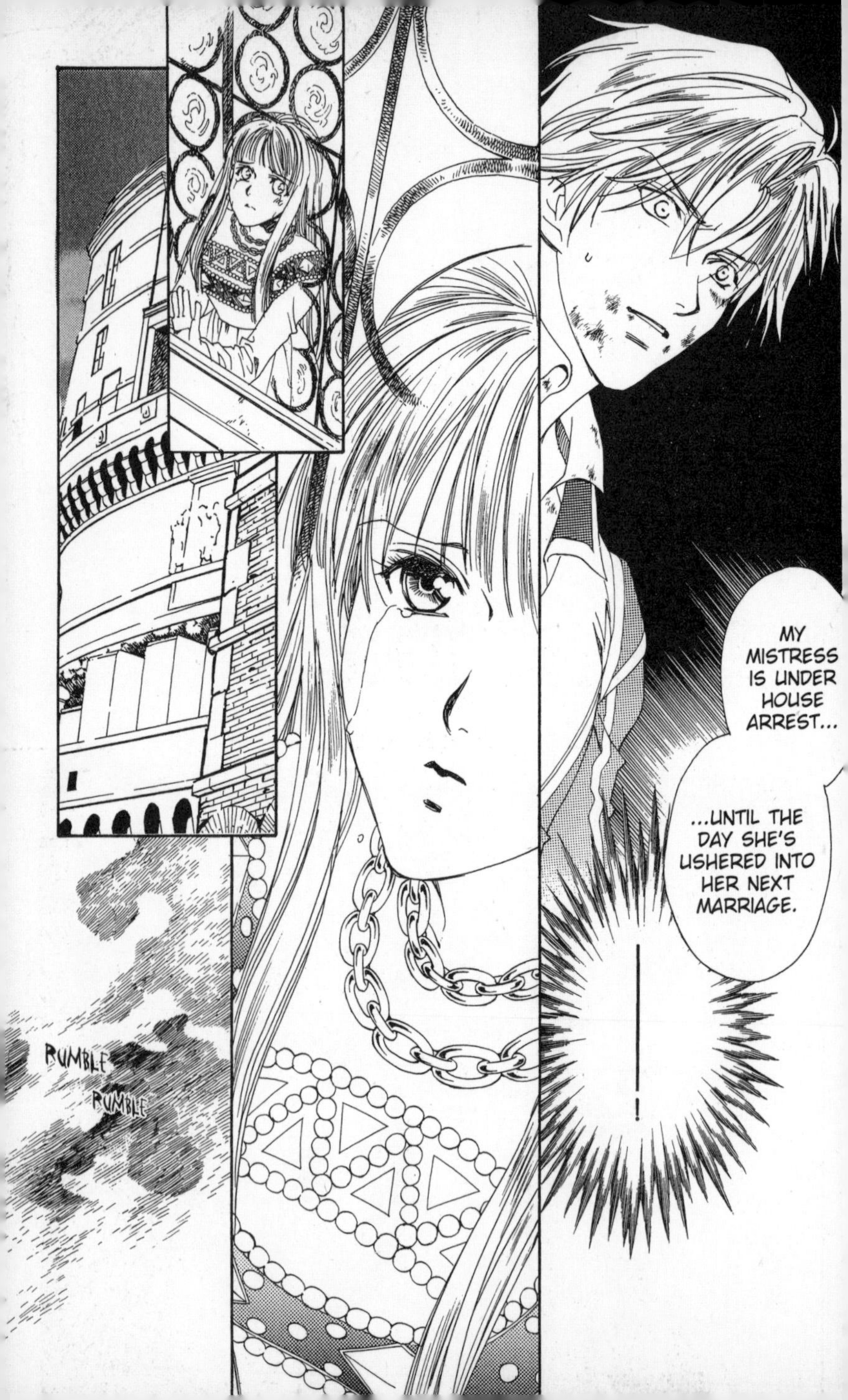
MY MISTRESS IS UNDER HOUSE ARREST...
...UNTIL THE DAY SHE'S USHERED INTO HER NEXT MARRIAGE.
!
RUMBLE
RUMBLE

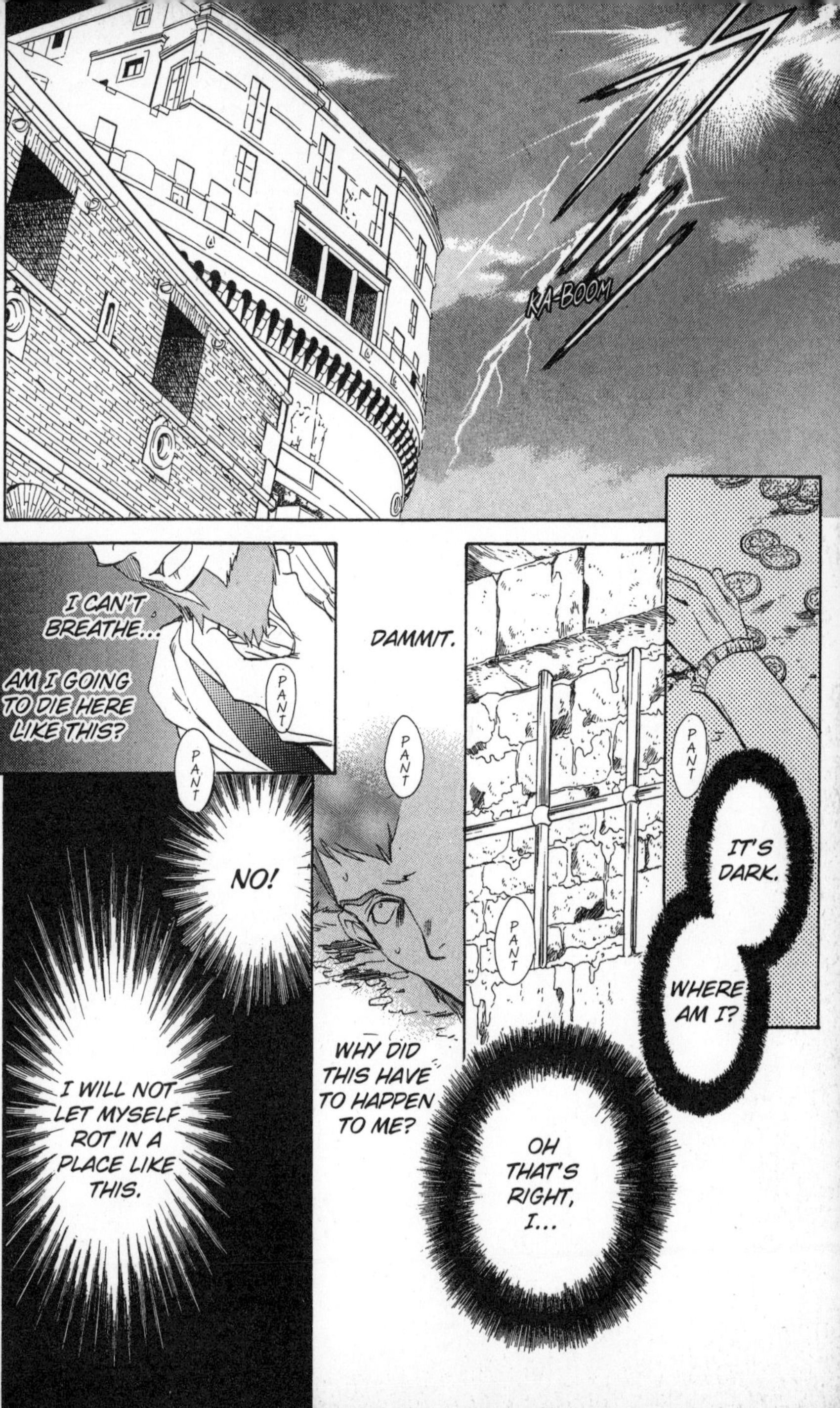
KA-BOOM
PANT
IT'S DARK.
WHERE AM I?
PANT
OH THAT'S RIGHT, I...
DAMMIT.
PANT
WHY DID THIS HAVE TO HAPPEN TO ME?
I CAN'T BREATHE...
AM I GOING TO DIE HERE LIKE THIS?
PANT
PANT
NO!
I WILL NOT LET MYSELF ROT IN A PLACE LIKE THIS.

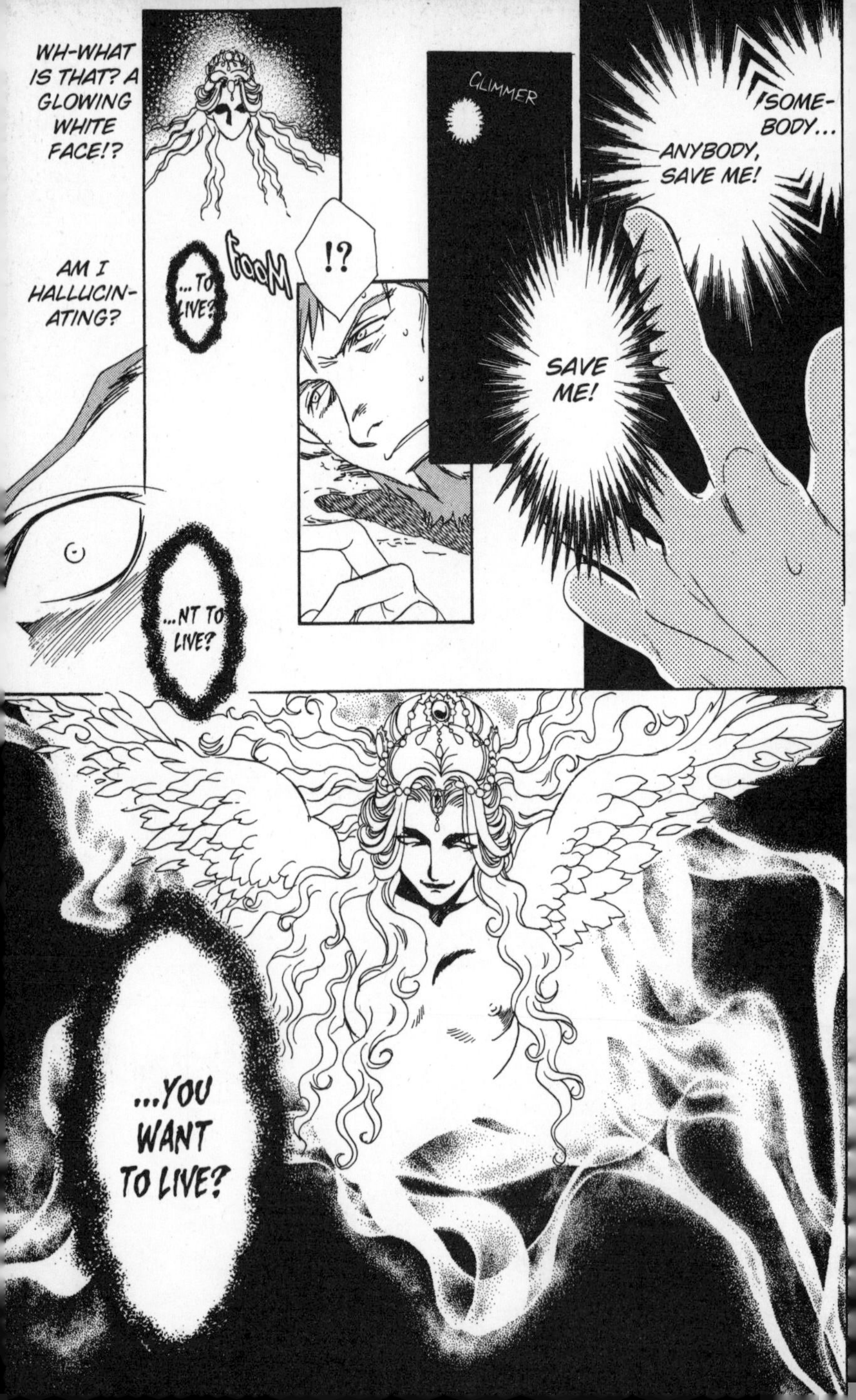
SOMEBODY... ANYBODY, SAVE ME!
SAVE ME!
GLIMMER
!?
WH-WHAT IS THAT? A GLOWING WHITE FACE!?
FOOM
...TO LIVE?
AM I HALLUCINATING?
...NT TO LIVE?
...YOU WANT TO LIVE?

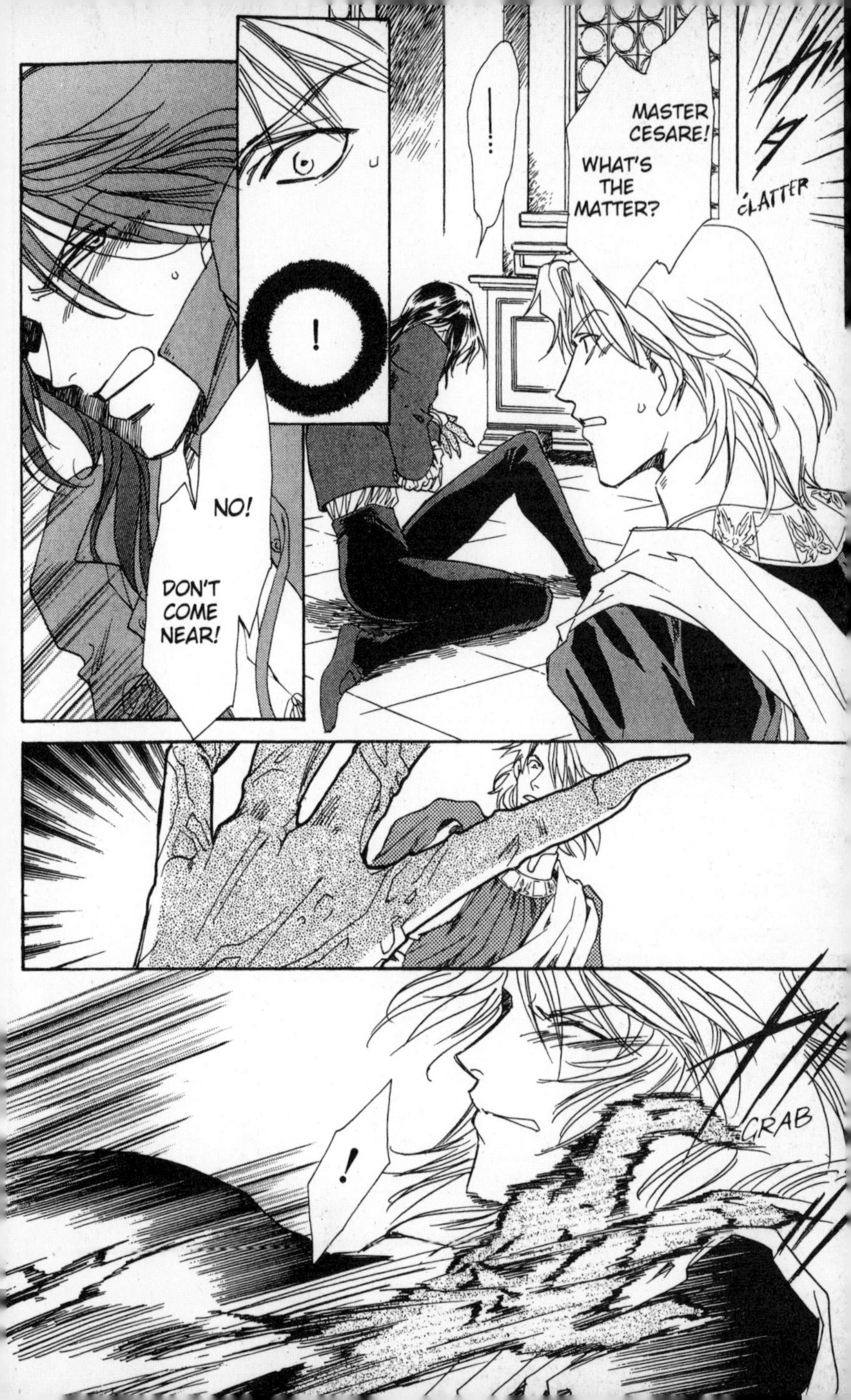
CLATTER
MASTER CESARE!
WHAT'S THE MATTER?
!...
!
NO!
DON'T COME NEAR!
GRAB
!

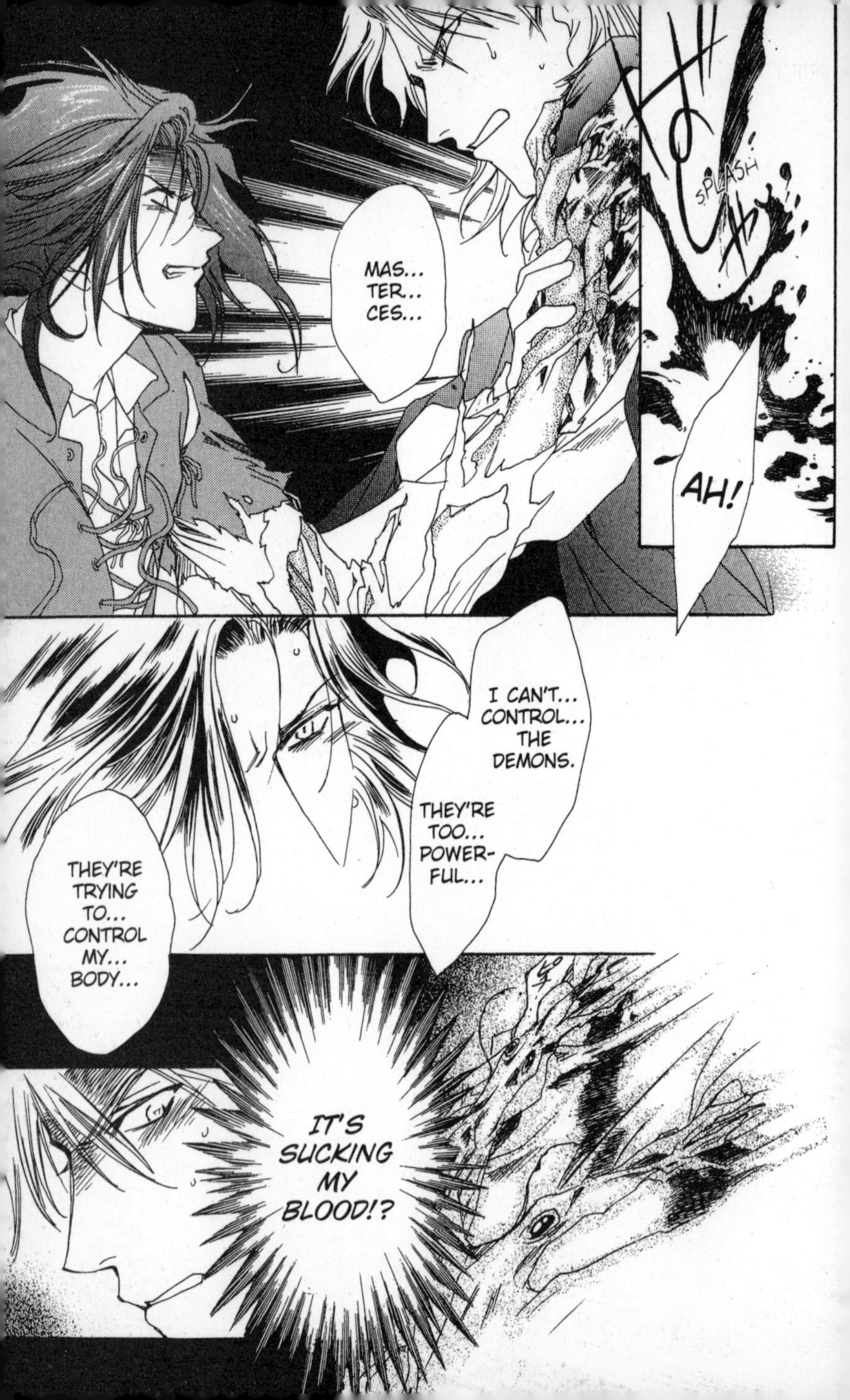
SPLASH
AH!
MAS... TER... CES...
I CAN'T... CONTROL... THE DEMONS.
THEY'RE TOO... POWERFUL...
THEY'RE TRYING TO... CONTROL MY... BODY...
IT'S SUCKING MY BLOOD!?

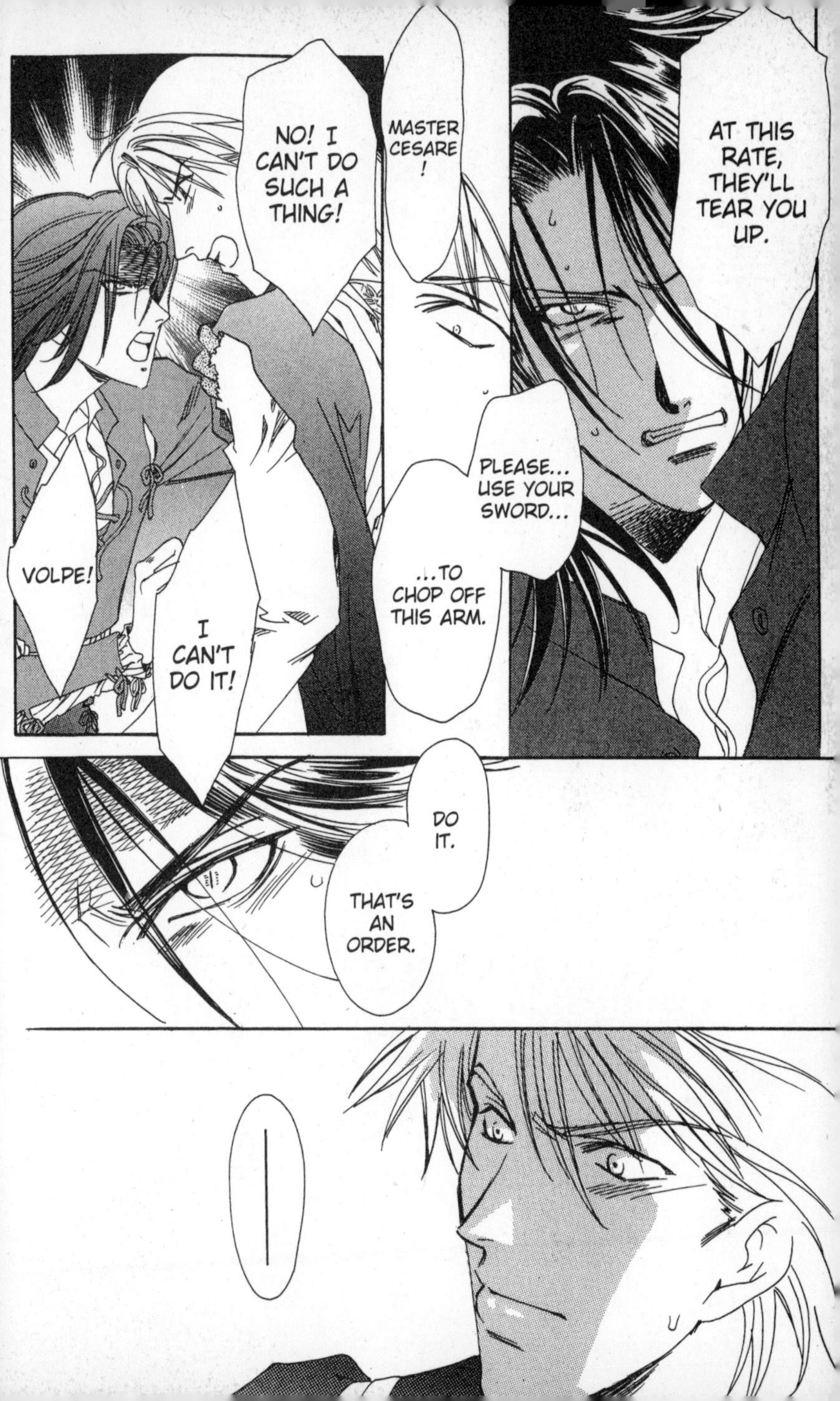

AT THIS RATE, THEY'LL TEAR YOU UP.
MASTER CESARE!
PLEASE... USE YOUR SWORD...
...TO CHOP OFF THIS ARM.
NO! I CAN'T DO SUCH A THING!
VOLPE!
I CAN'T DO IT!
DO IT.
THAT'S AN ORDER.
—

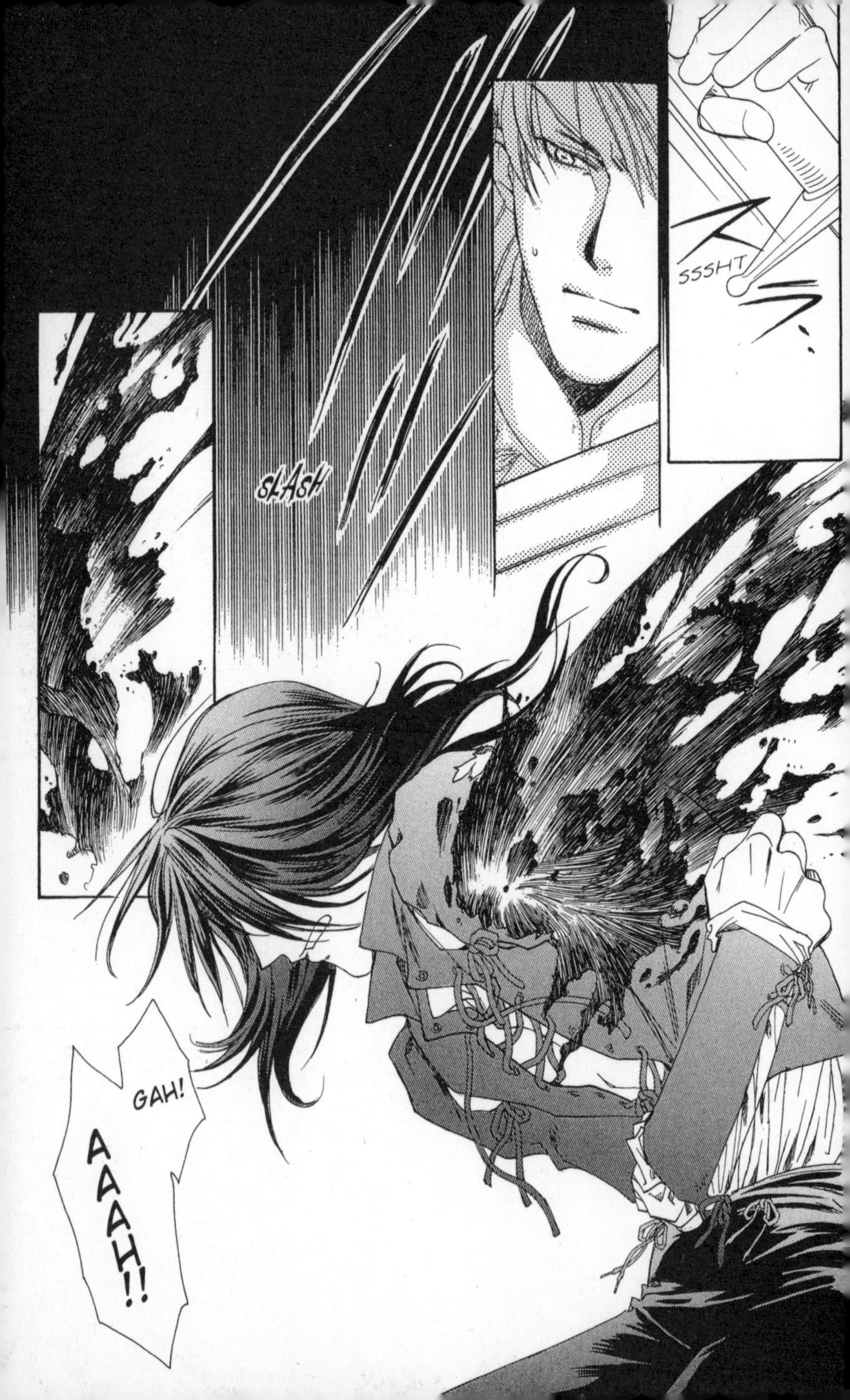
SSSHT
SLASH
GAH!
AAAAH!!

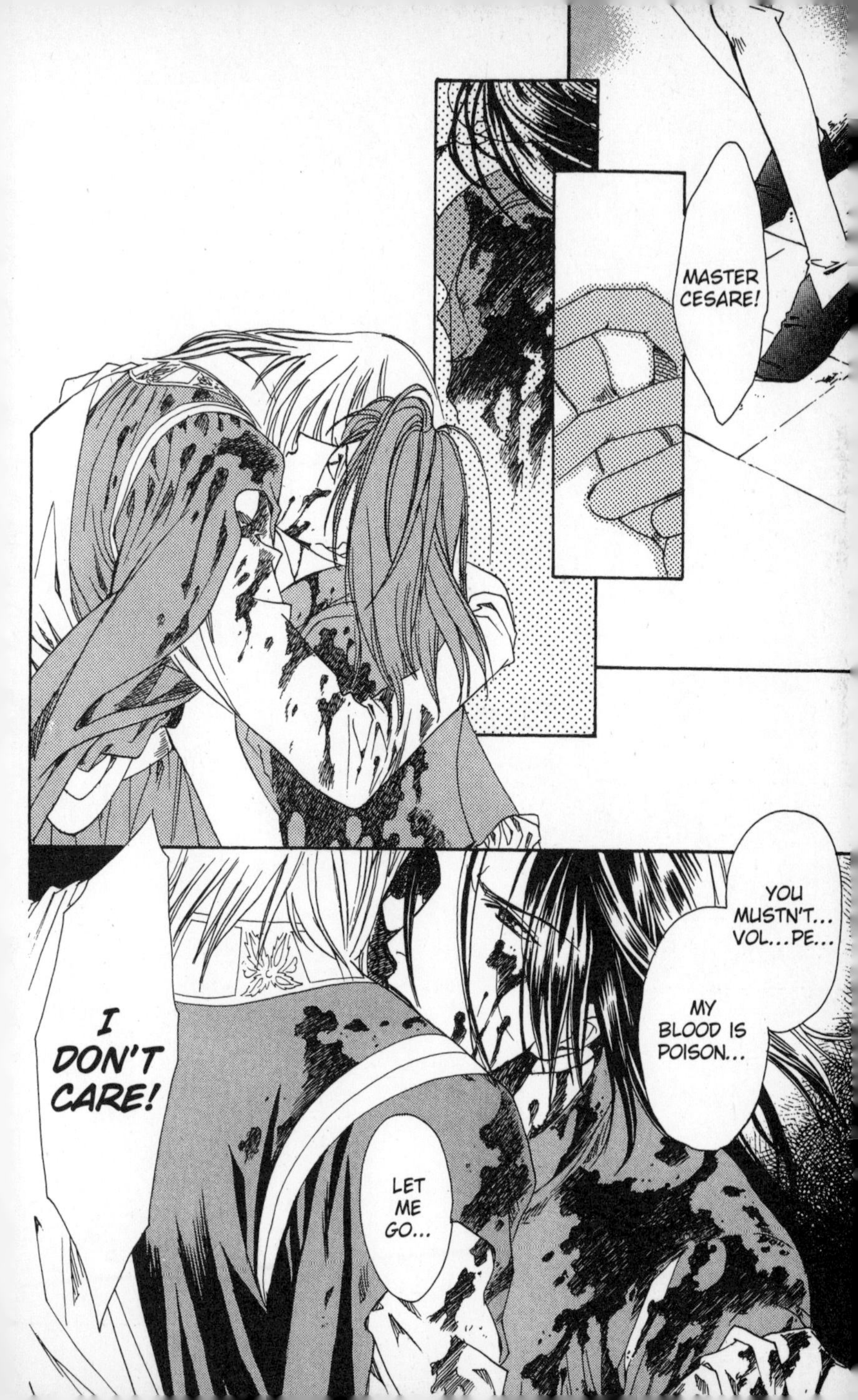
MASTER CESARE!
YOU MUSTN'T... VOL...PE...
MY BLOOD IS POISON...
I DON'T CARE!
LET ME GO...

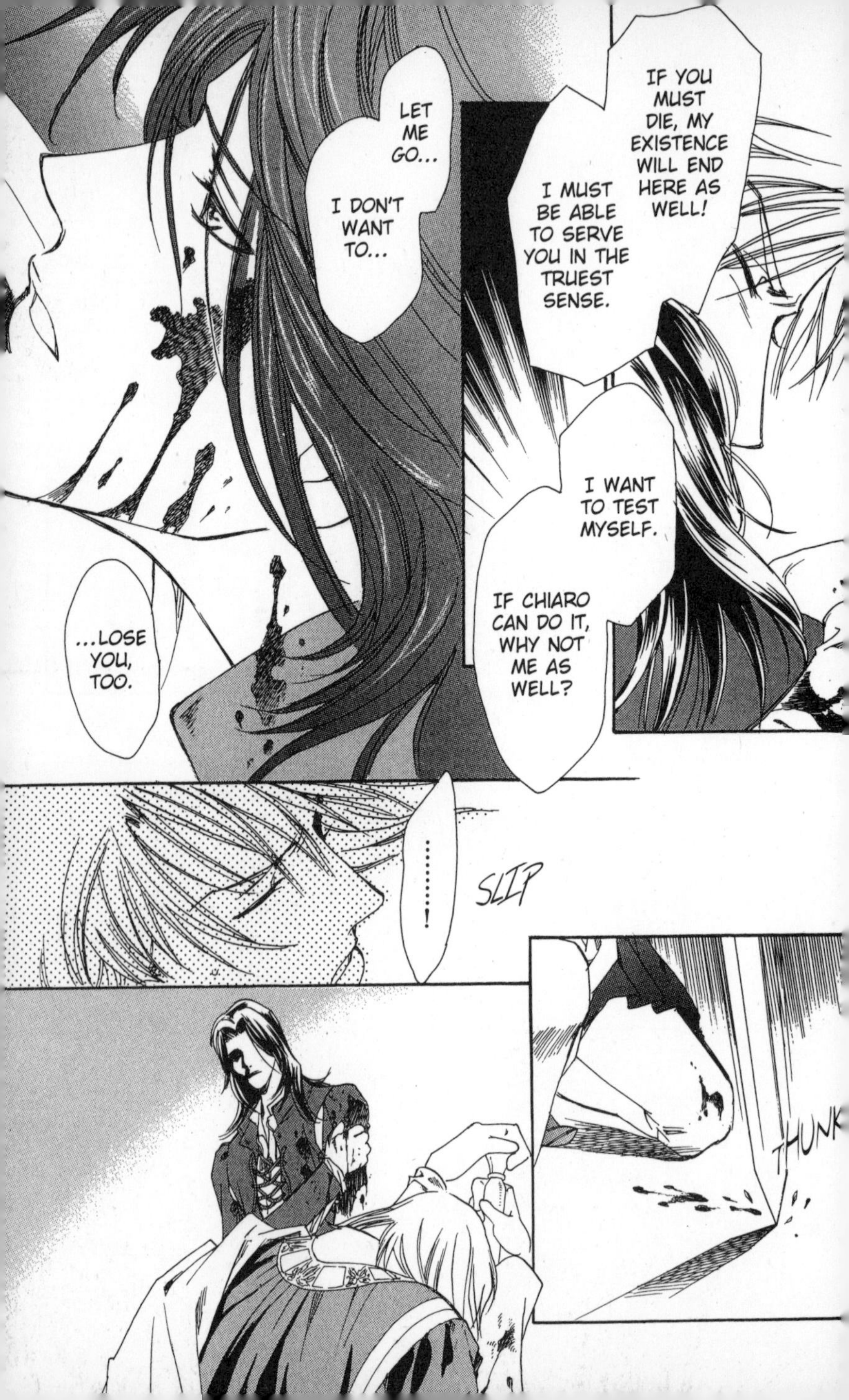
IF YOU MUST DIE, MY EXISTENCE WILL END HERE AS WELL!
I MUST BE ABLE TO SERVE YOU IN THE TRUEST SENSE.
I WANT TO TEST MYSELF.
IF CHIARO CAN DO IT, WHY NOT ME AS WELL?
LET ME GO...
I DON'T WANT TO...
...LOSE YOU, TOO.
......!
SLIP
THUNK

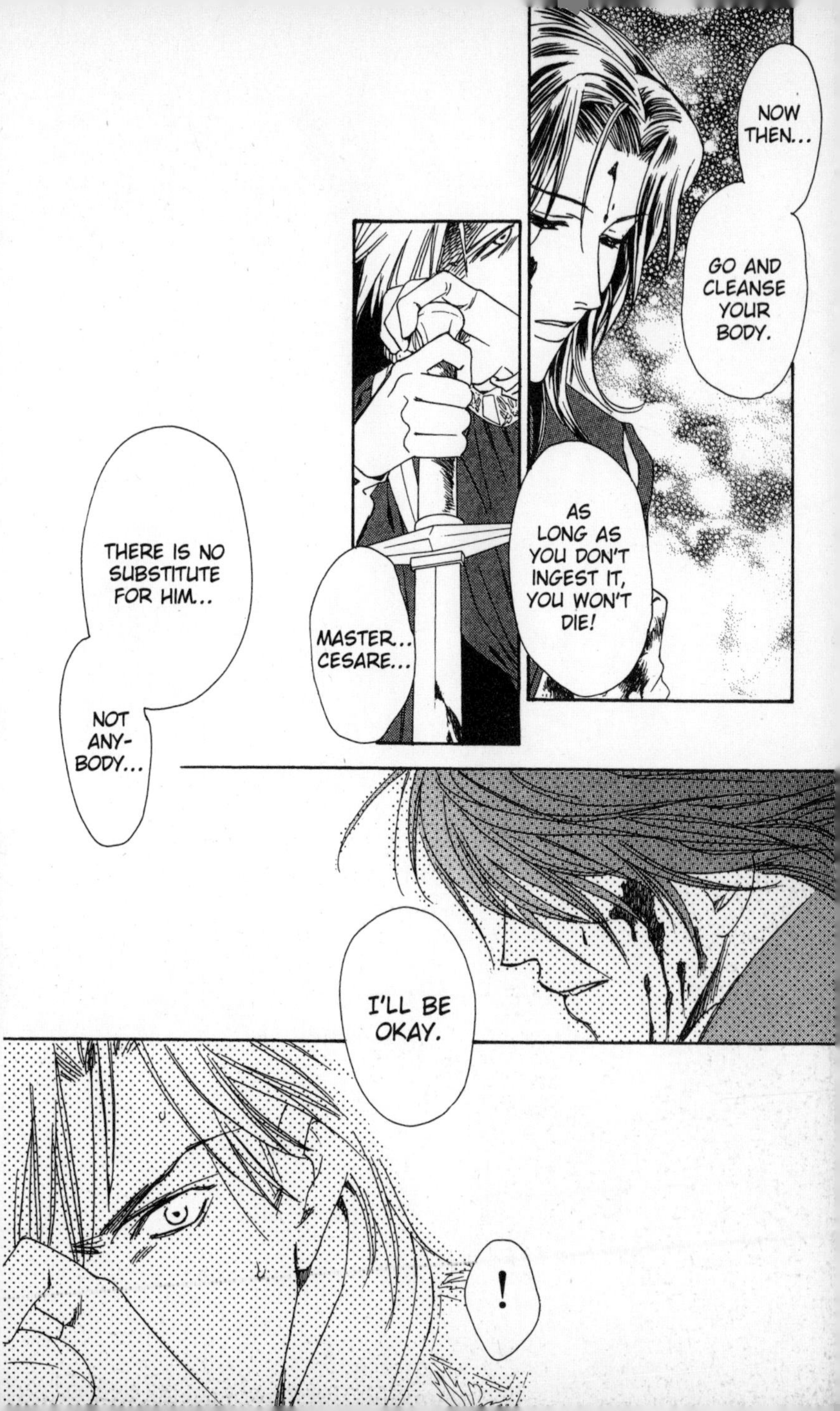
NOW THEN...
GO AND CLEANSE YOUR BODY.
AS LONG AS YOU DON'T INGEST IT, YOU WON'T DIE!
MASTER... CESARE...
THERE IS NO SUBSTITUTE FOR HIM...
NOT ANY-BODY...
I'LL BE OKAY.
!

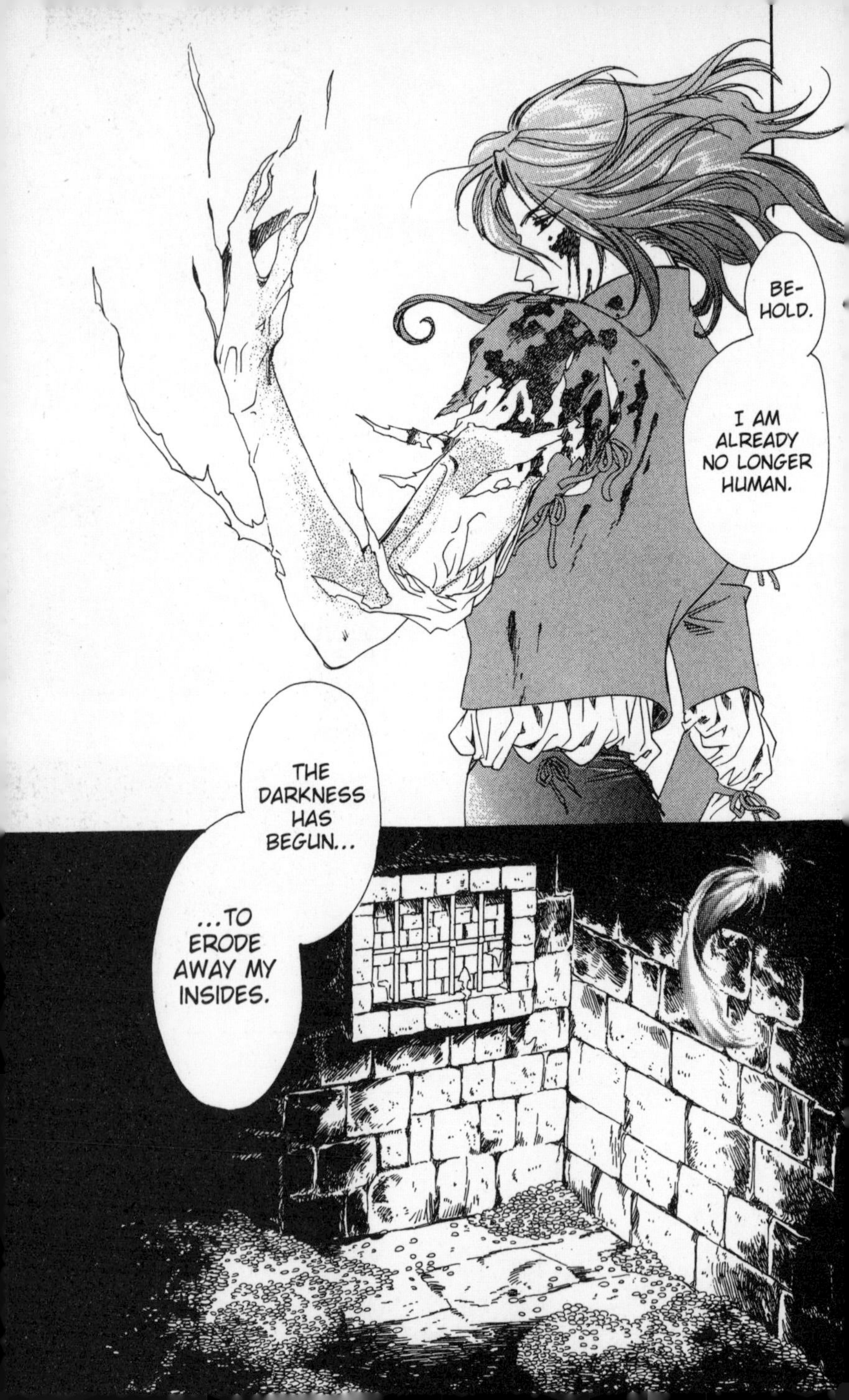
BE-HOLD.
I AM ALREADY NO LONGER HUMAN.
THE DARKNESS HAS BEGUN...
...TO ERODE AWAY MY INSIDES.

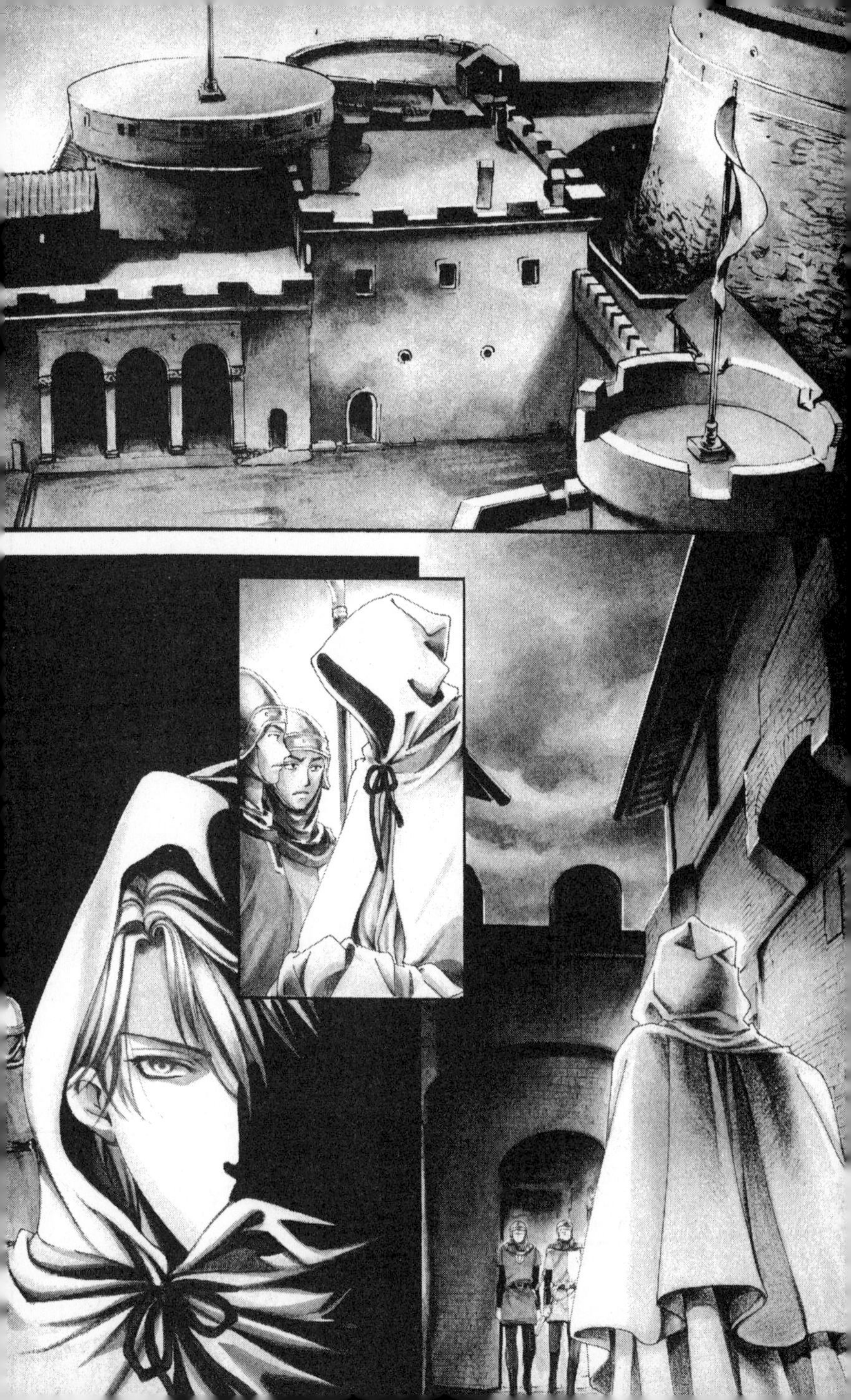

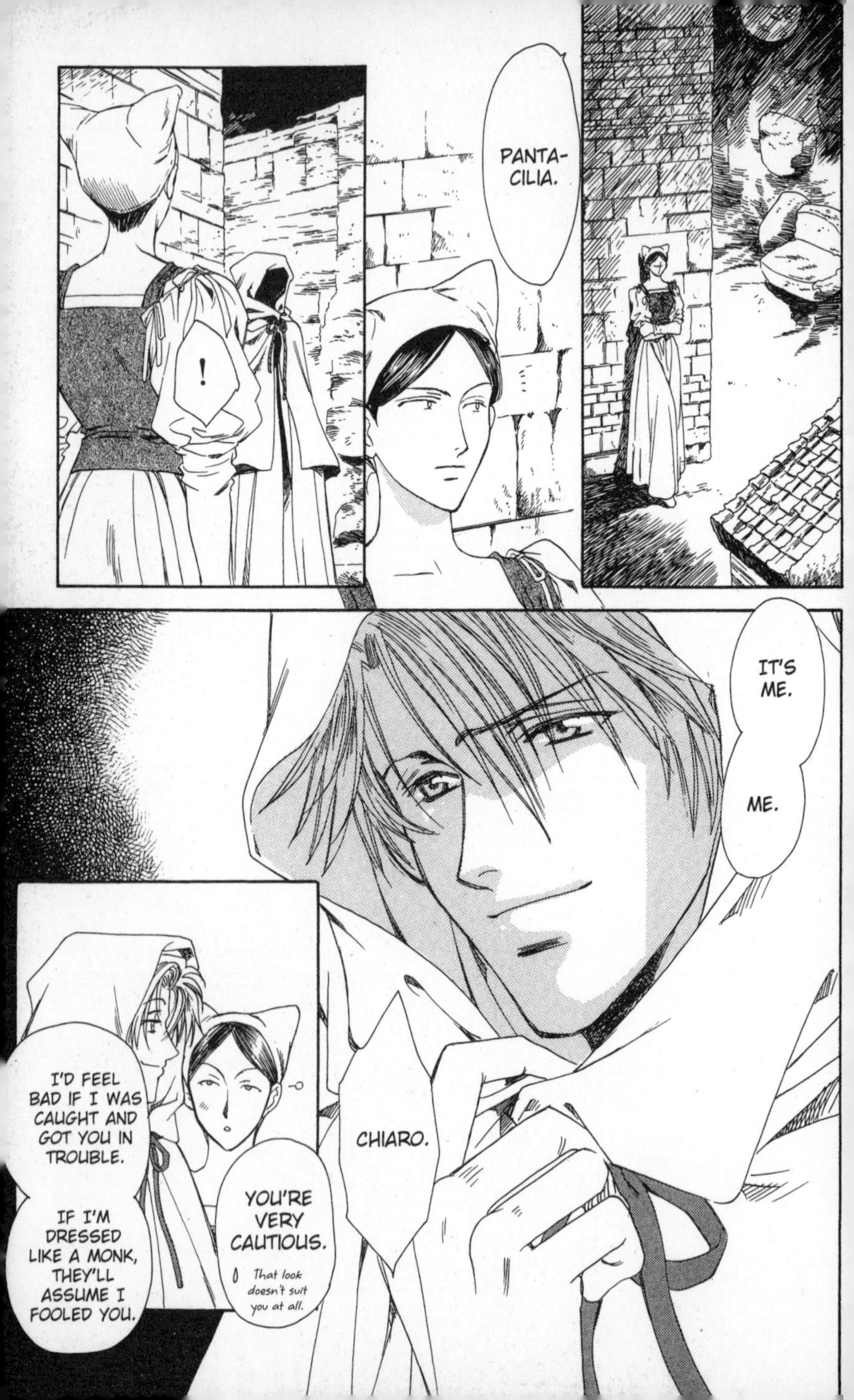
PANTA-CILIA.
!
IT'S ME.
ME.
CHIARO.
YOU'RE VERY CAUTIOUS.
That look doesn't suit you at all.
I'D FEEL BAD IF I WAS CAUGHT AND GOT YOU IN TROUBLE.
IF I'M DRESSED LIKE A MONK, THEY'LL ASSUME I FOOLED YOU.

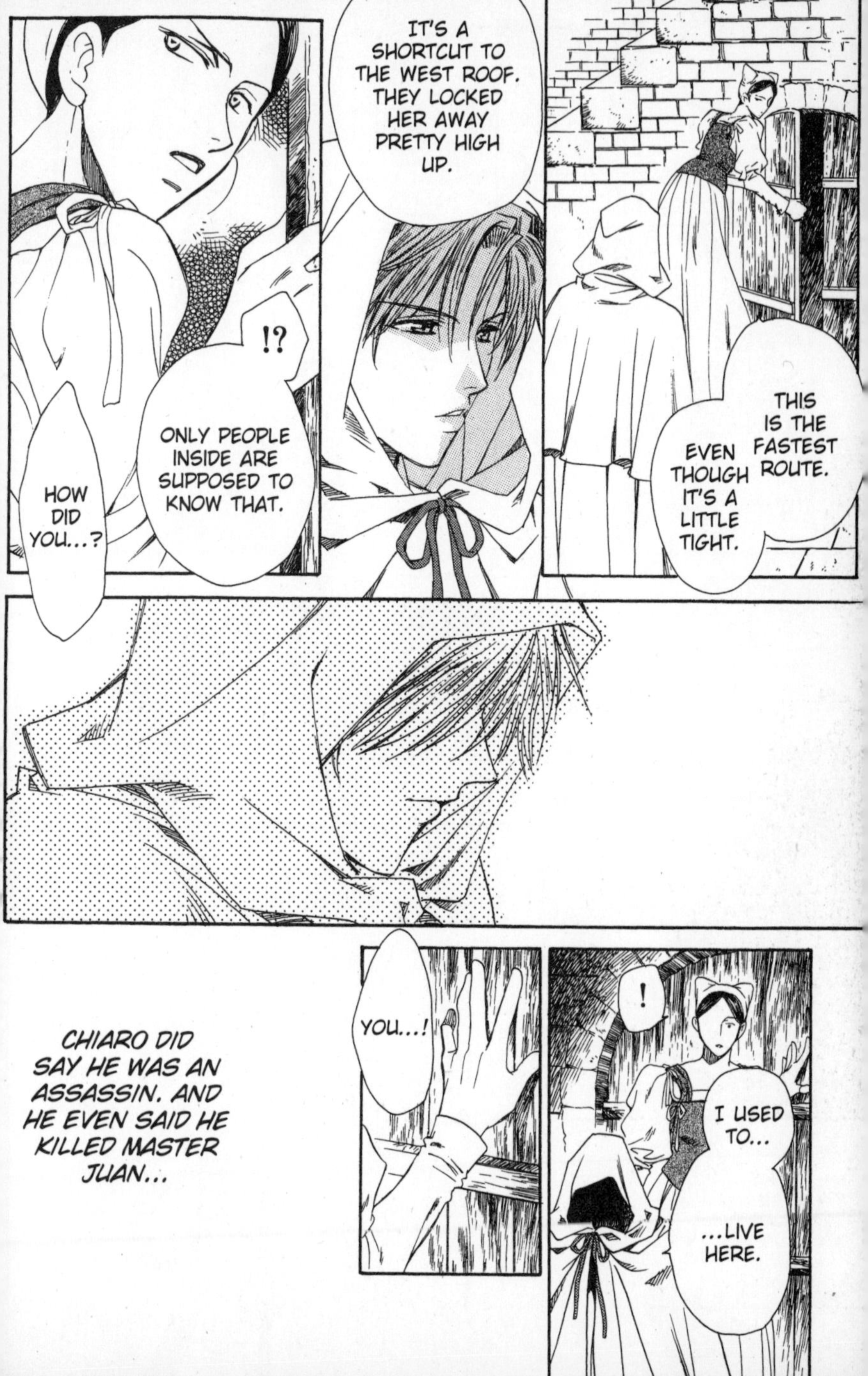
THIS IS THE FASTEST ROUTE.
EVEN THOUGH IT'S A LITTLE TIGHT.
IT'S A SHORTCUT TO THE WEST ROOF. THEY LOCKED HER AWAY PRETTY HIGH UP.
!?
ONLY PEOPLE INSIDE ARE SUPPOSED TO KNOW THAT.
HOW DID YOU...?
!
I USED TO...
...LIVE HERE.
YOU...!
CHIARO DID SAY HE WAS AN ASSASSIN. AND HE EVEN SAID HE KILLED MASTER JUAN...

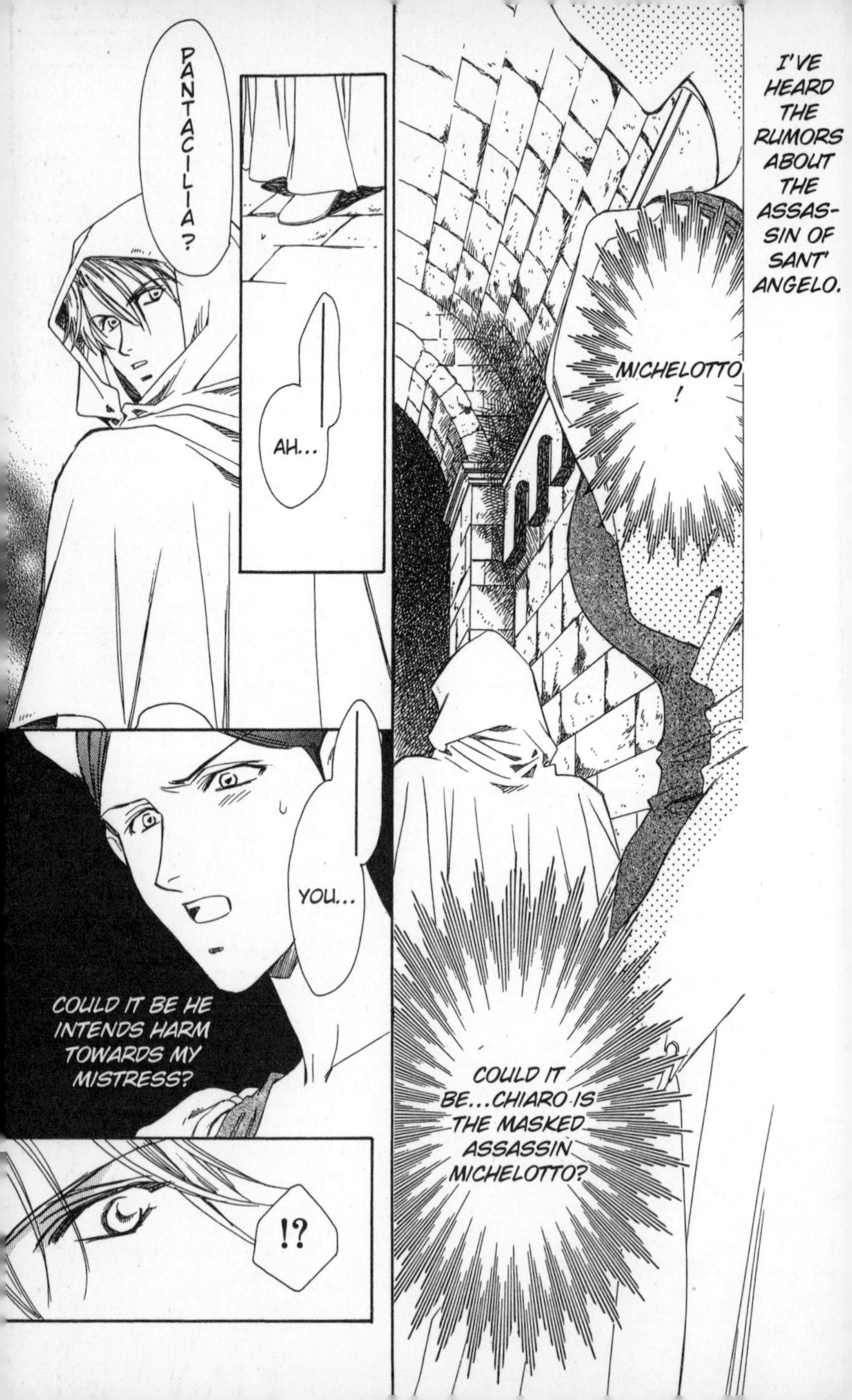

I'VE HEARD THE RUMORS ABOUT THE ASSAS-SIN OF SANT' ANGELO.
MICHELOTTO!
COULD IT BE...CHIARO IS THE MASKED ASSASSIN MICHELOTTO?
AH...
PANTACILIA?
YOU...
COULD IT BE HE INTENDS HARM TOWARDS MY MISTRESS?
!?

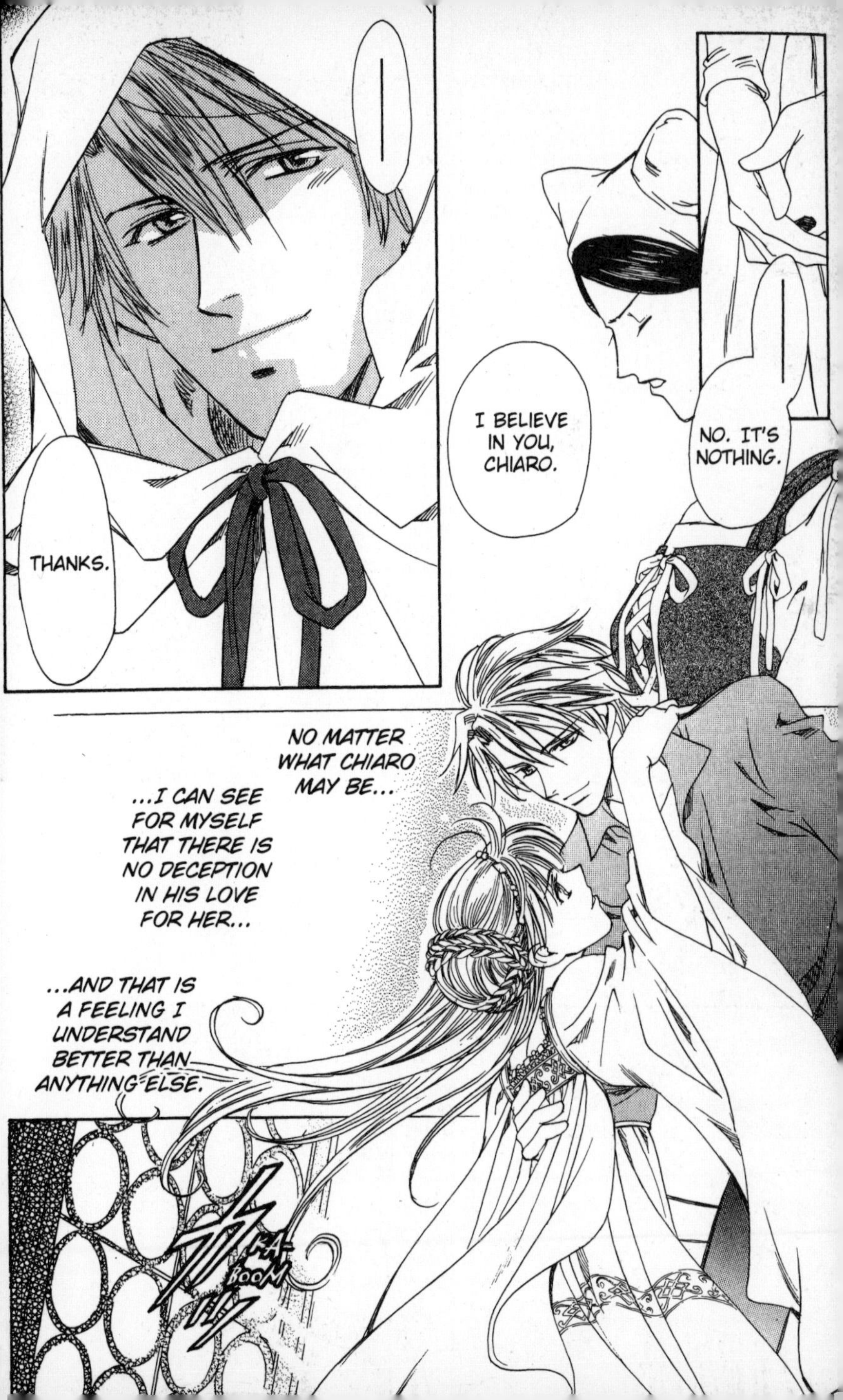
NO. IT'S NOTHING.
I BELIEVE IN YOU, CHIARO.
...
THANKS.
NO MATTER WHAT CHIARO MAY BE...
...I CAN SEE FOR MYSELF THAT THERE IS NO DECEPTION IN HIS LOVE FOR HER...
...AND THAT IS A FEELING I UNDERSTAND BETTER THAN ANYTHING ELSE.
KA-BOOM

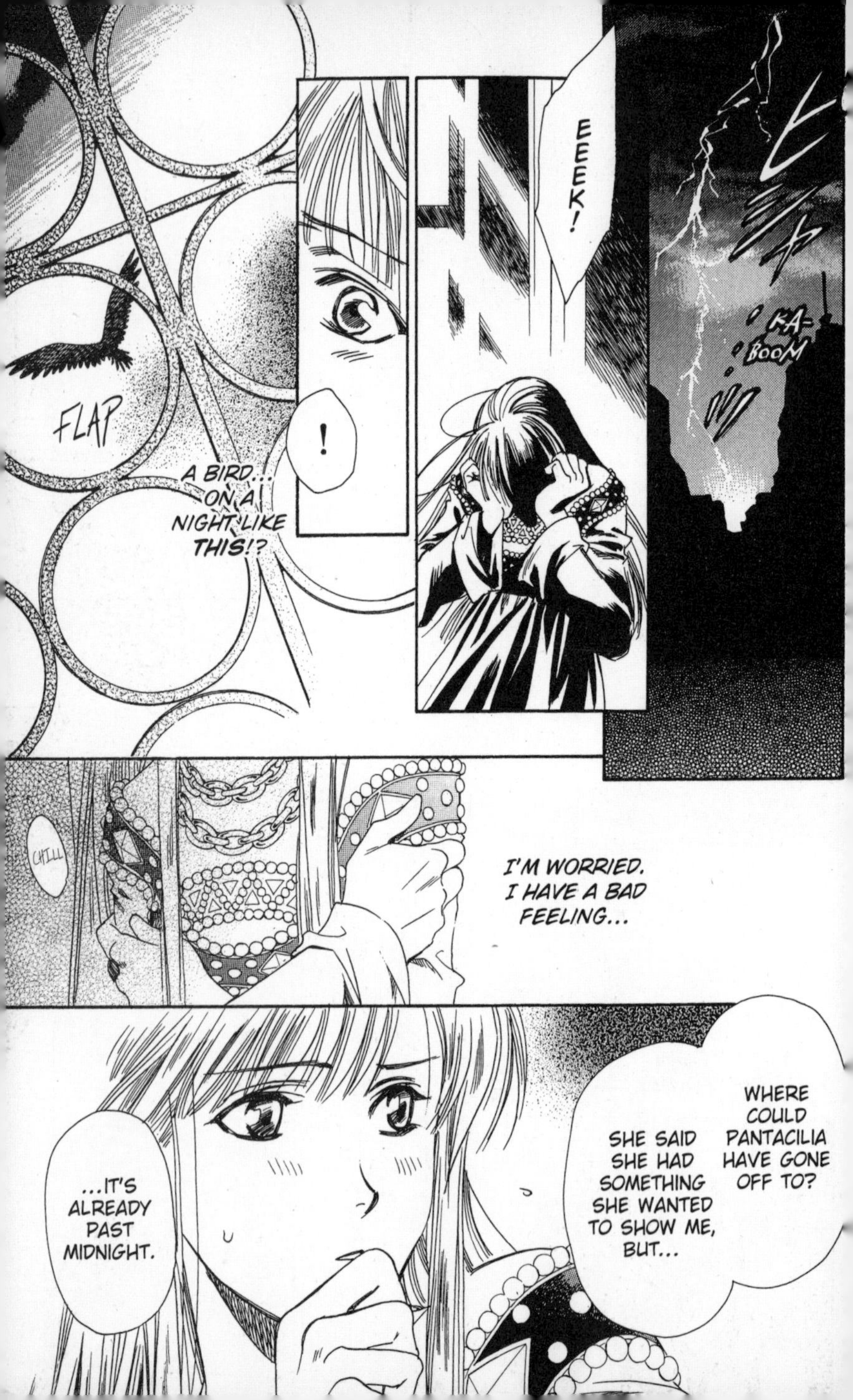
KA-BOOM
EEEK!
!
FLAP
A BIRD... ON A NIGHT LIKE THIS!?
I'M WORRIED. I HAVE A BAD FEELING...
CHILL
WHERE COULD PANTACILIA HAVE GONE OFF TO?
SHE SAID SHE HAD SOMETHING SHE WANTED TO SHOW ME, BUT...
...IT'S ALREADY PAST MIDNIGHT.

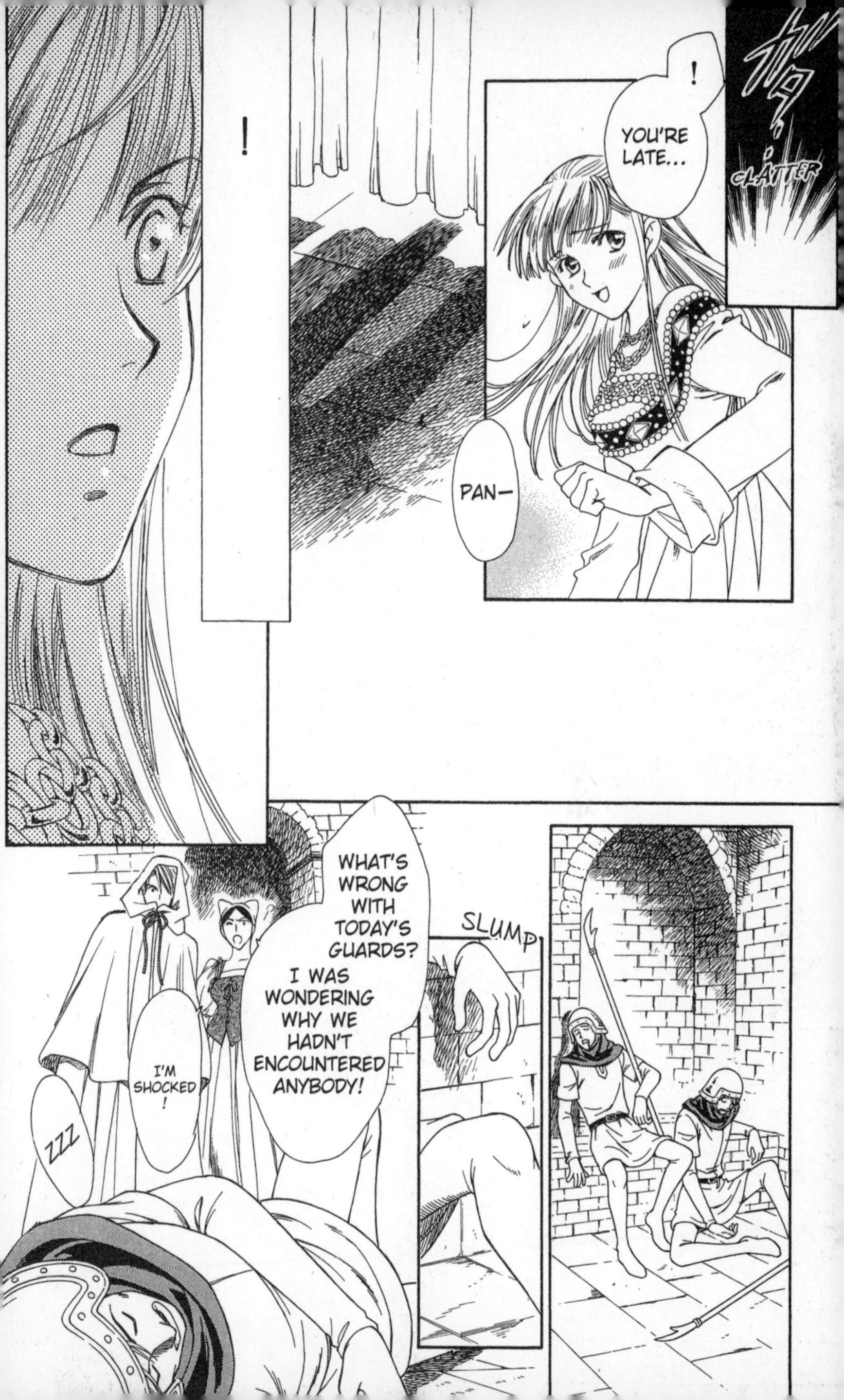
CLATTER
!
YOU'RE LATE...
PAN—
!
SLUMP
WHAT'S WRONG WITH TODAY'S GUARDS? I WAS WONDERING WHY WE HADN'T ENCOUNTERED ANYBODY!
I'M SHOCKED!
ZZZ

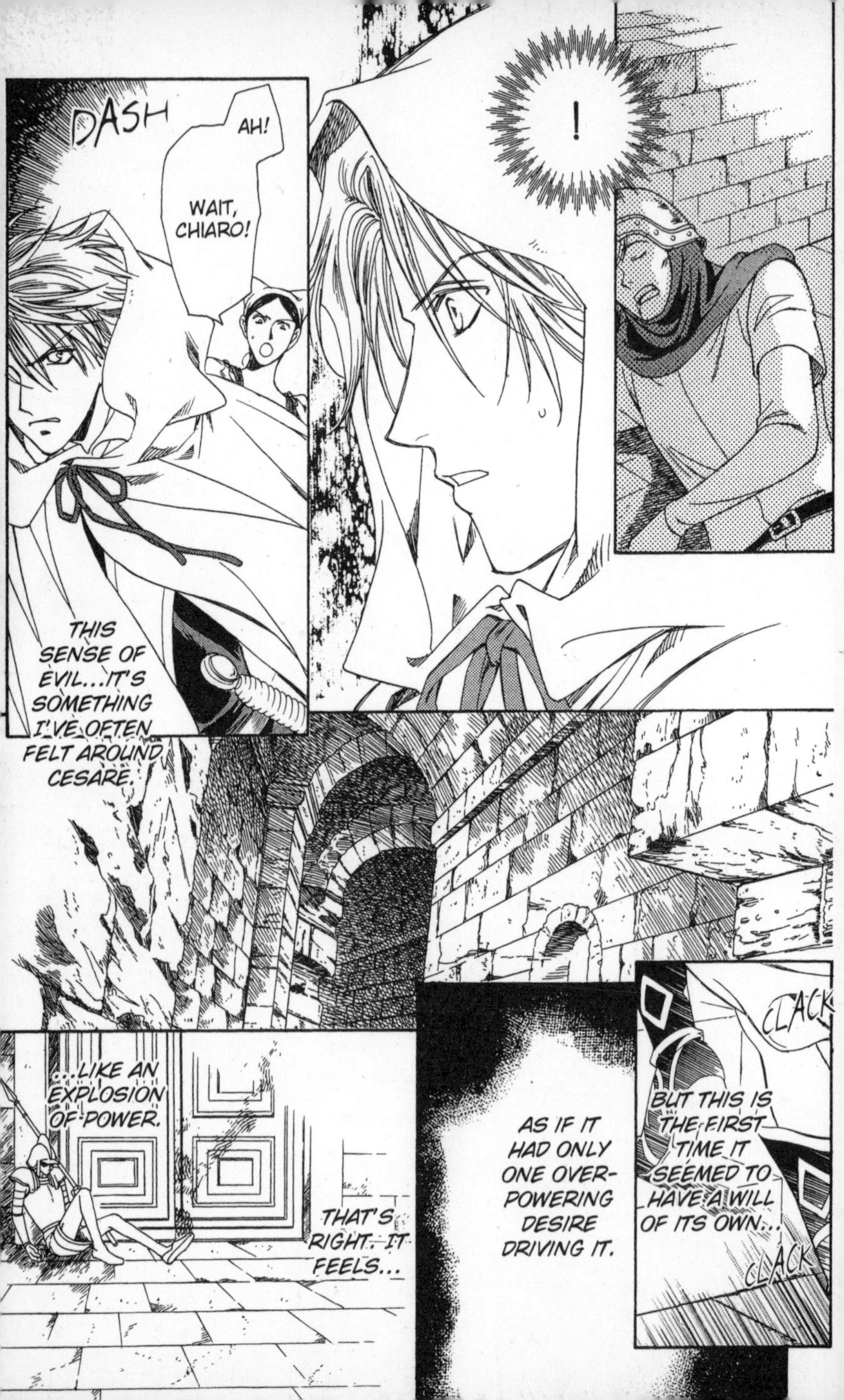
!
DASH
AH!
WAIT, CHIARO!
THIS SENSE OF EVIL...IT'S SOMETHING I'VE OFTEN FELT AROUND CESARE.
CLACK
BUT THIS IS THE FIRST TIME IT SEEMED TO HAVE A WILL OF ITS OWN...
CLACK
AS IF IT HAD ONLY ONE OVER-POWERING DESIRE DRIVING IT.
THAT'S RIGHT. IT FEELS...
...LIKE AN EXPLOSION OF POWER.

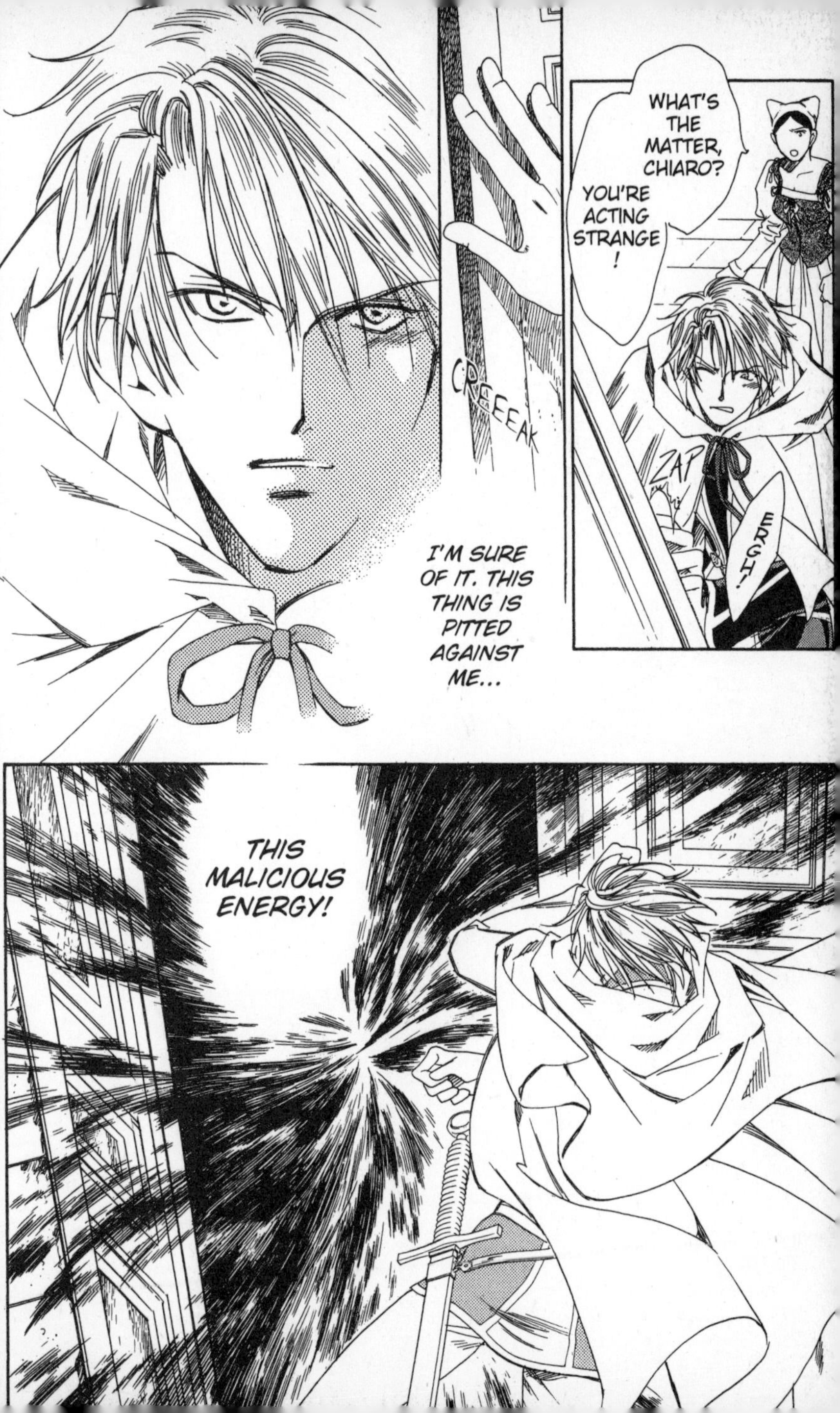
WHAT'S THE MATTER, CHIARO? YOU'RE ACTING STRANGE!
ZAP
ERGH!
CREEEAK
I'M SURE OF IT. THIS THING IS PITTED AGAINST ME...
THIS MALICIOUS ENERGY!

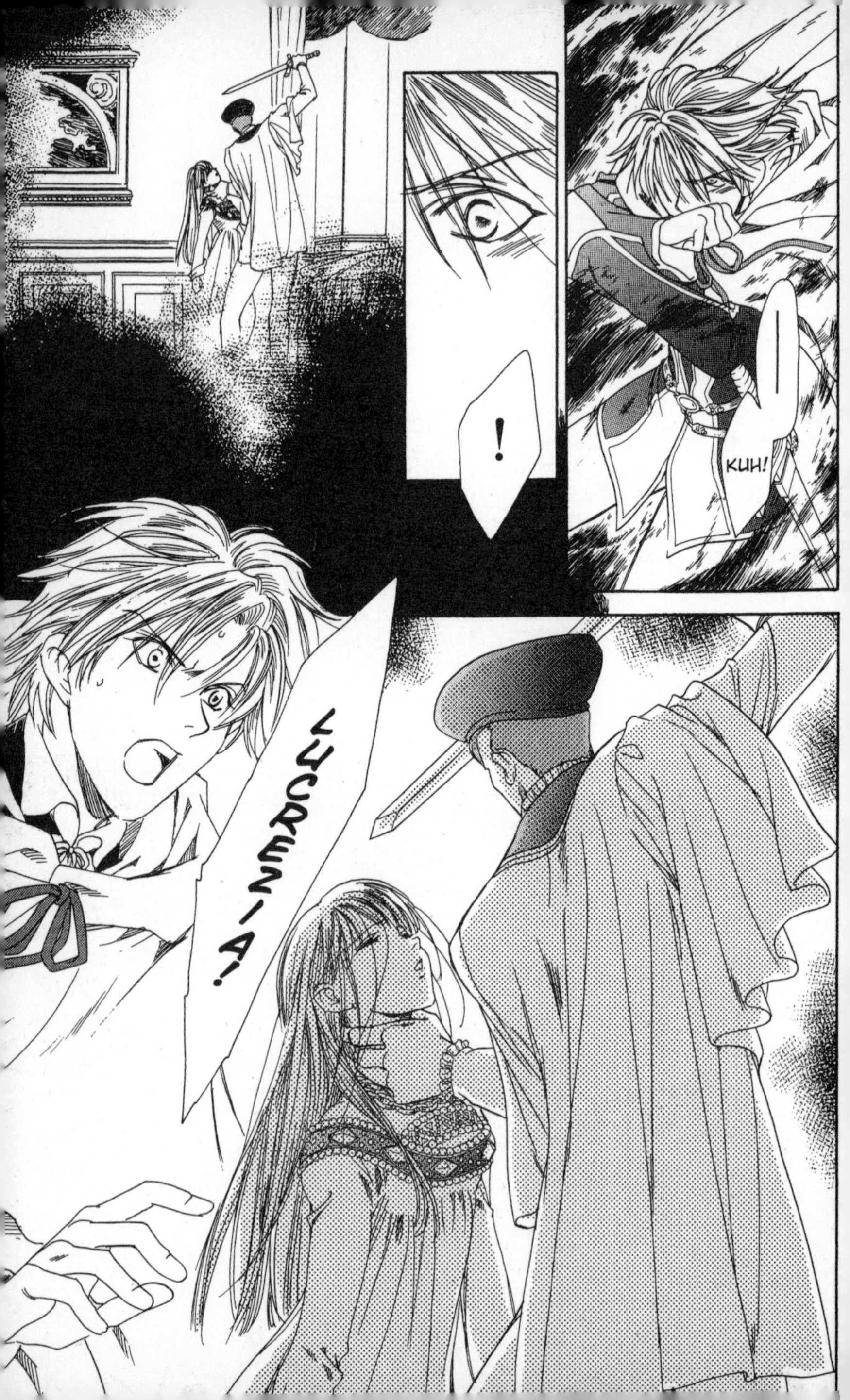
KUH!
!
LUCREZIA!

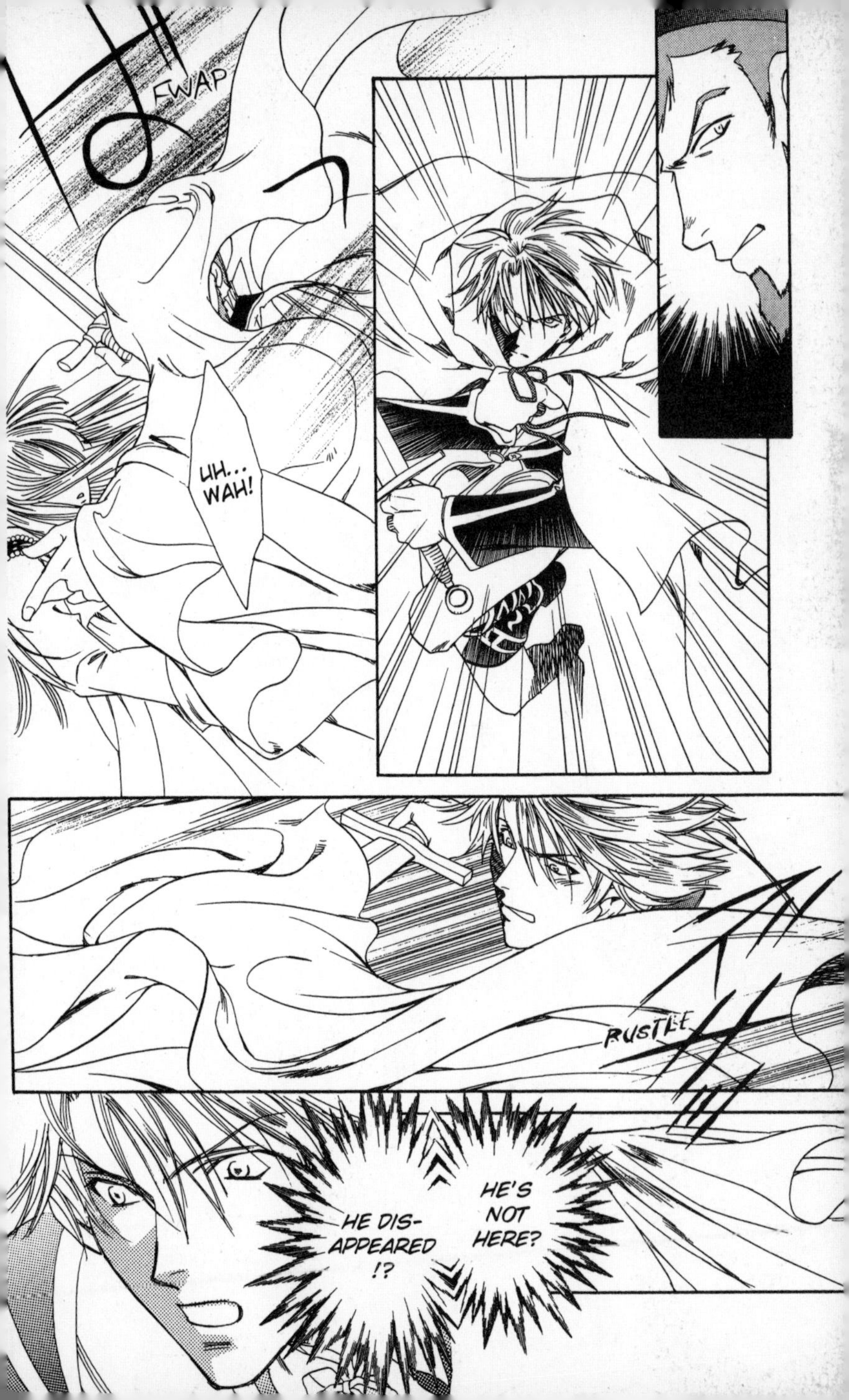
FWAP
UH... WAH!
RUSTLE
HE'S NOT HERE?
HE DIS-APPEARED !?

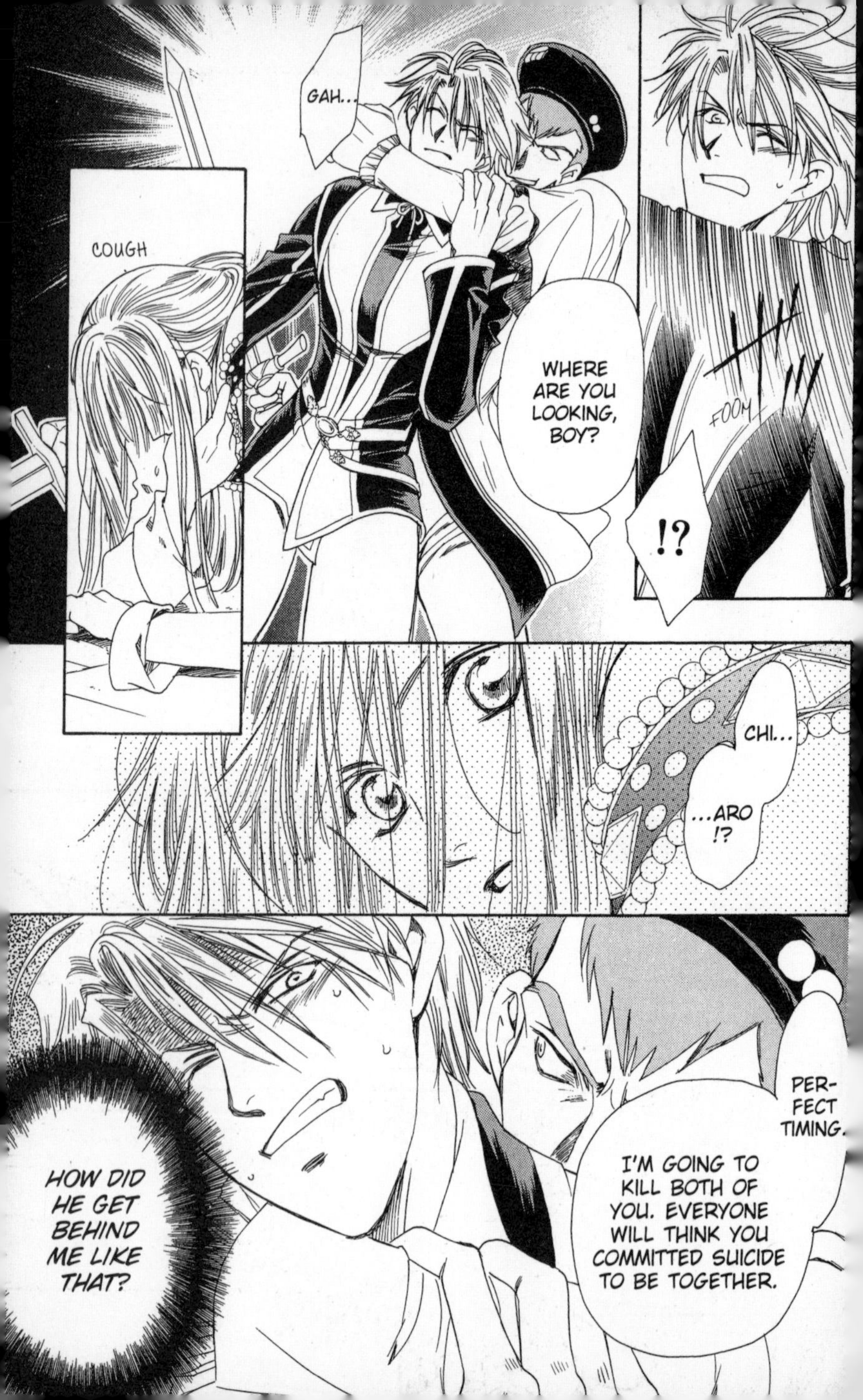
FOOM
!?
GAH...
WHERE ARE YOU LOOKING, BOY?
COUGH
CHI...
...ARO !?
PER-FECT TIMING.
I'M GOING TO KILL BOTH OF YOU. EVERYONE WILL THINK YOU COMMITTED SUICIDE TO BE TOGETHER.
HOW DID HE GET BEHIND ME LIKE THAT?

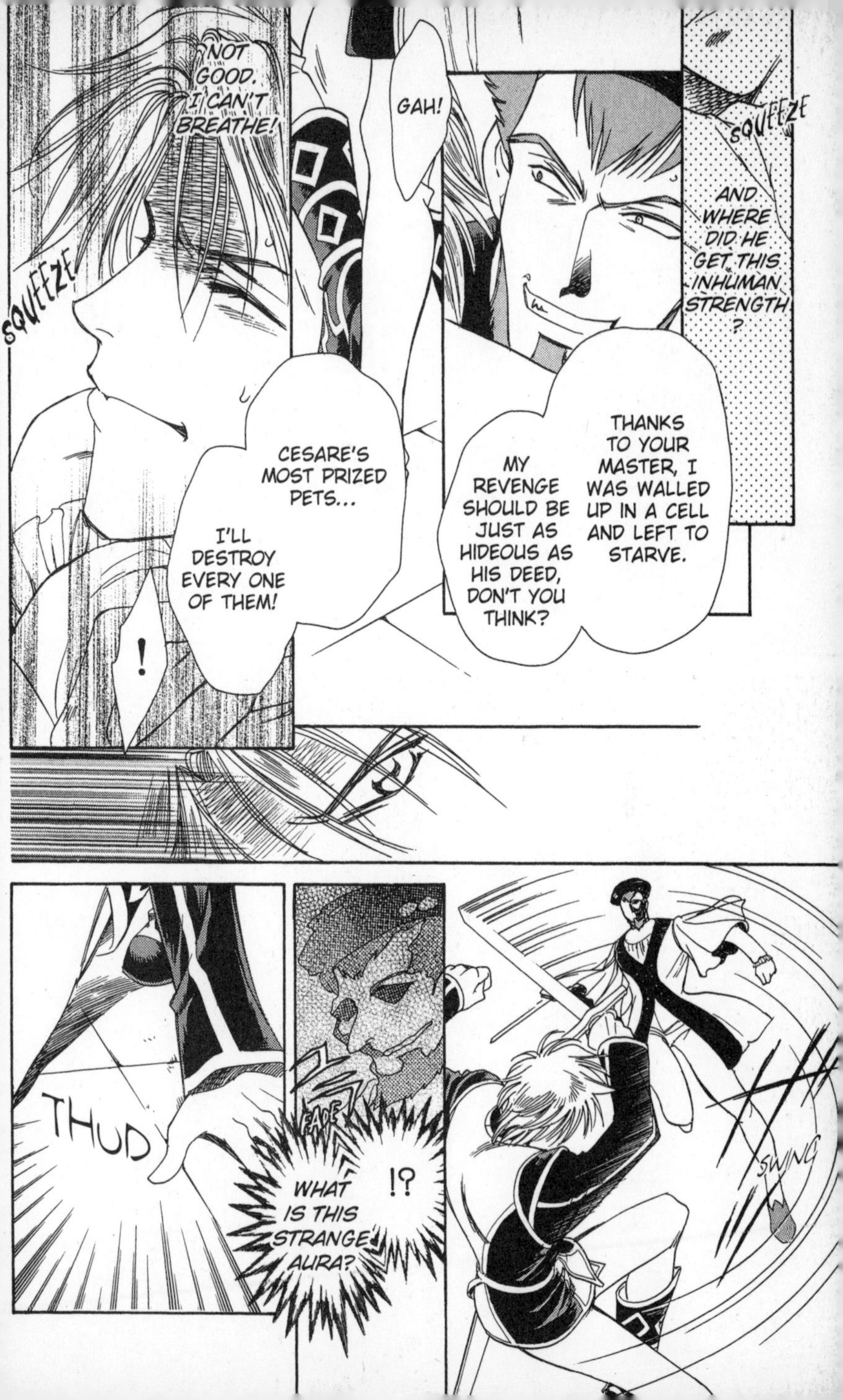
SQUEEZE
AND WHERE DID HE GET THIS INHUMAN STRENGTH?
GAH!
THANKS TO YOUR MASTER, I WAS WALLED UP IN A CELL AND LEFT TO STARVE.
MY REVENGE SHOULD BE JUST AS HIDEOUS AS HIS DEED, DON'T YOU THINK?
NOT GOOD. I CAN'T BREATHE!
SQUEEZE
CESARE'S MOST PRIZED PETS...
I'LL DESTROY EVERY ONE OF THEM!
!
SWING
!?
WHAT IS THIS STRANGE AURA?
FADE
THUD

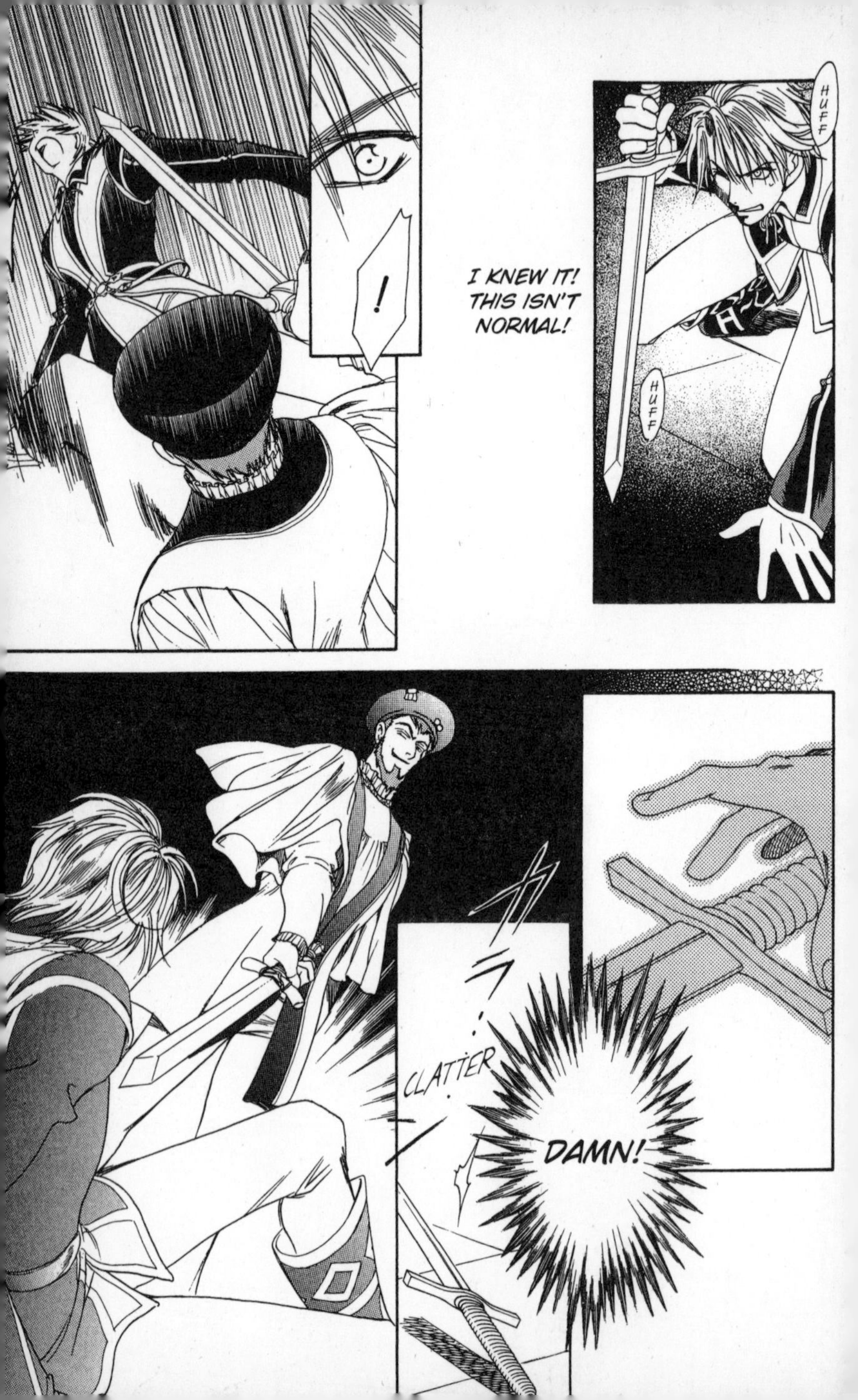
HUFF
HUFF
I KNEW IT! THIS ISN'T NORMAL!
!
DAMN!
CLATTER

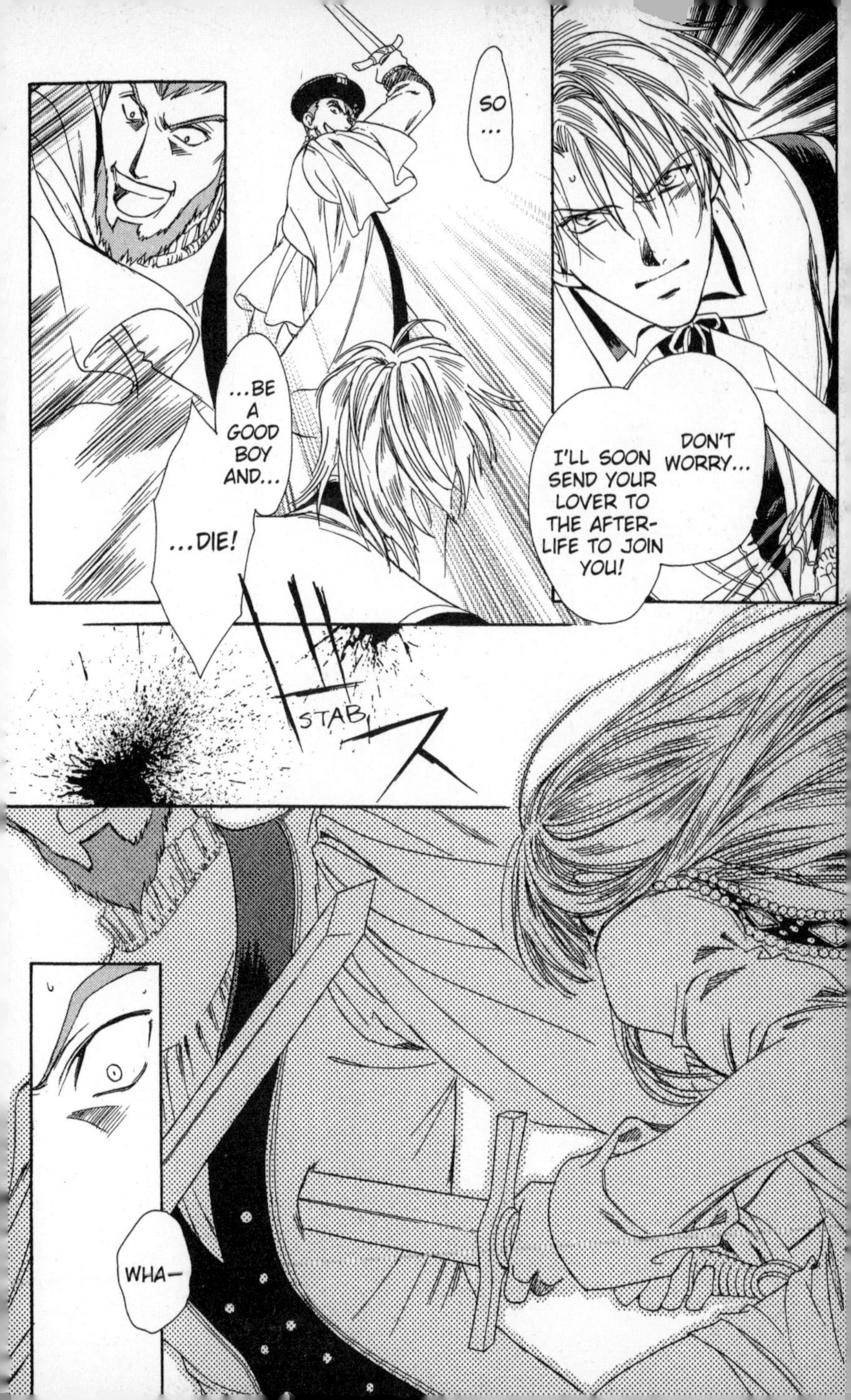
DON'T WORRY...
I'LL SOON SEND YOUR LOVER TO THE AFTER-LIFE TO JOIN YOU!
SO...
...BE A GOOD BOY AND...
...DIE!
STAB
WHA-

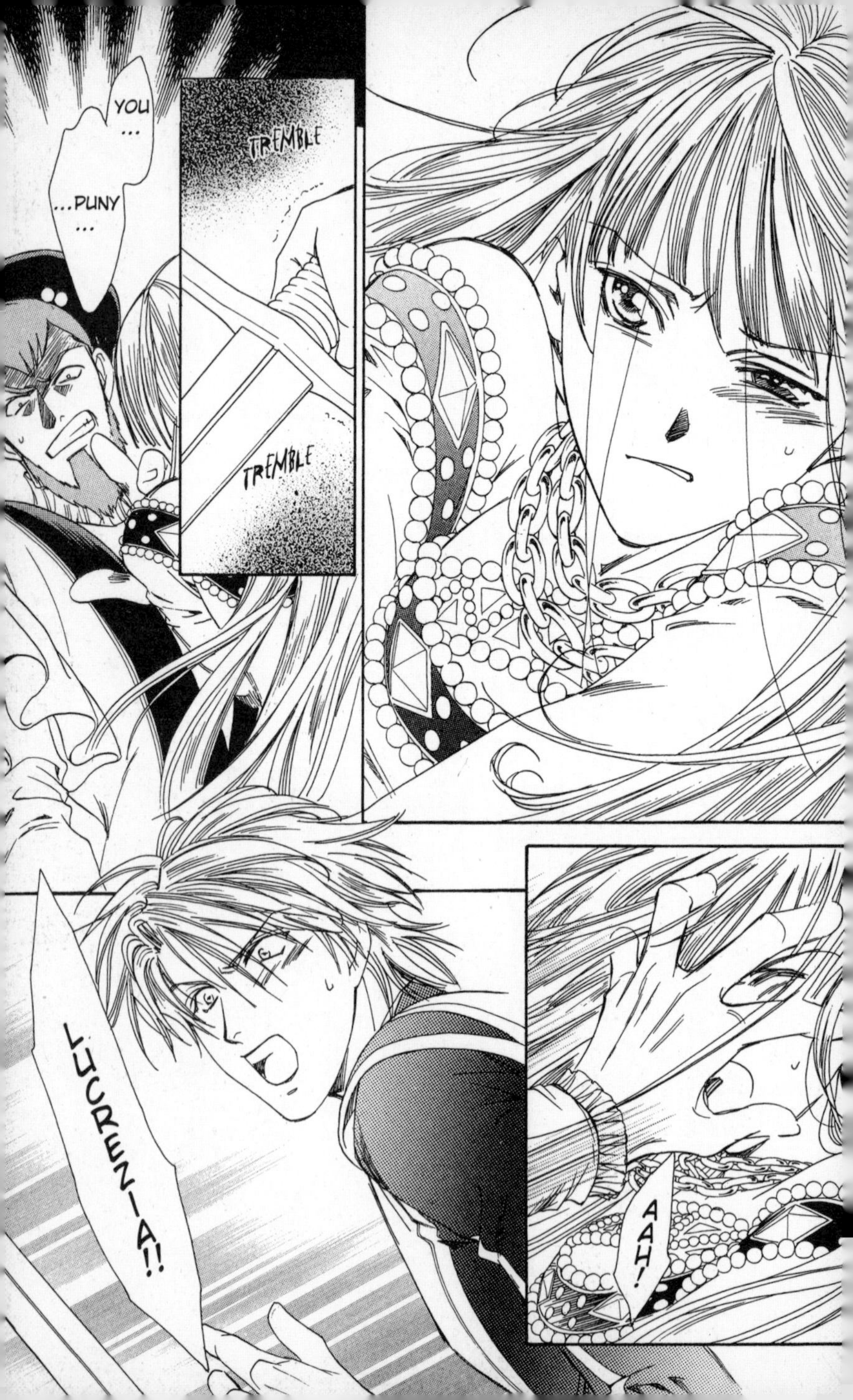
TREMBLE
TREMBLE
YOU ... ...PUNY ...
AAH!
LUCREZIA!!

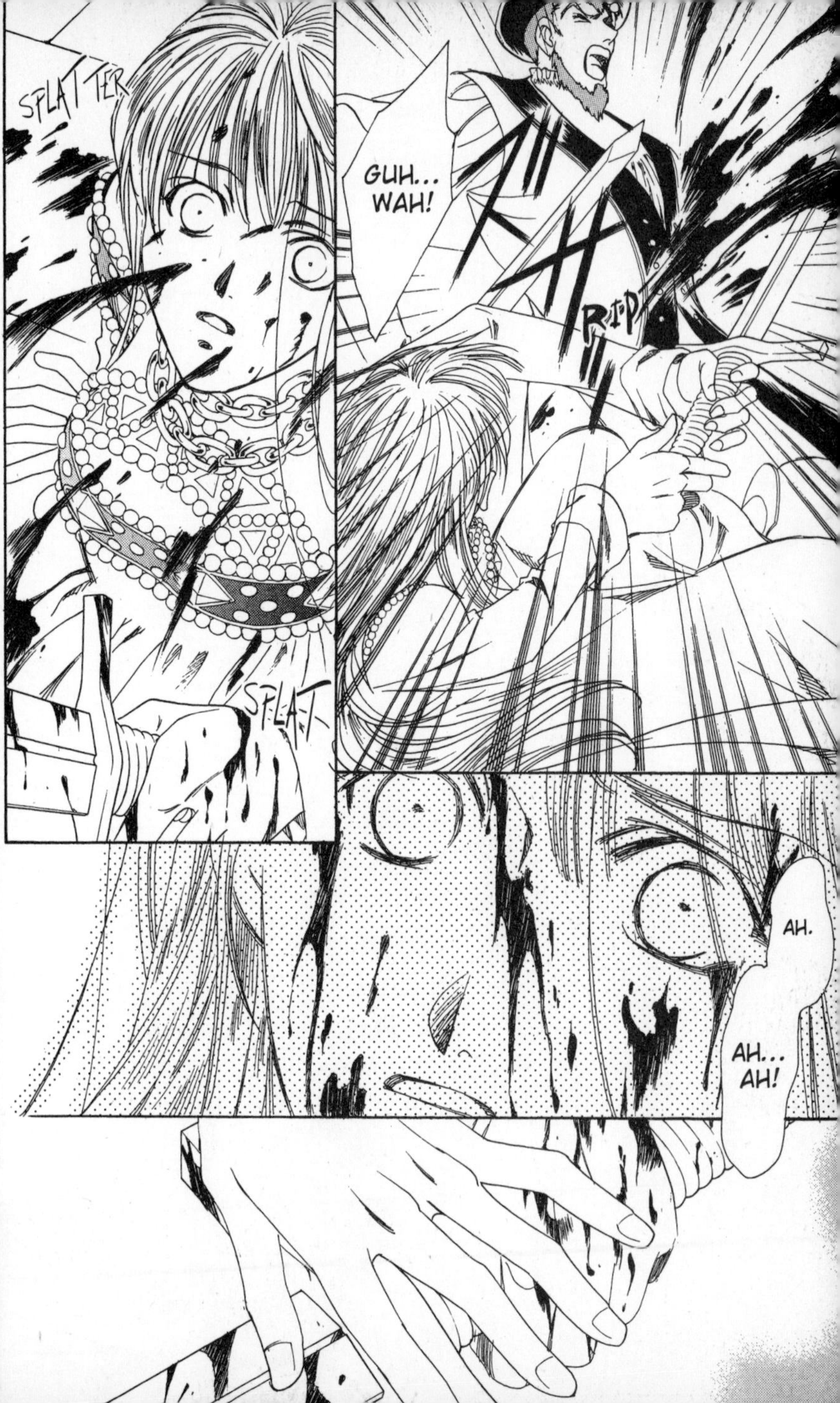
GUH...
WAH!
RIP
SPLATTER
SPLAT
AH.
AH...
AH!

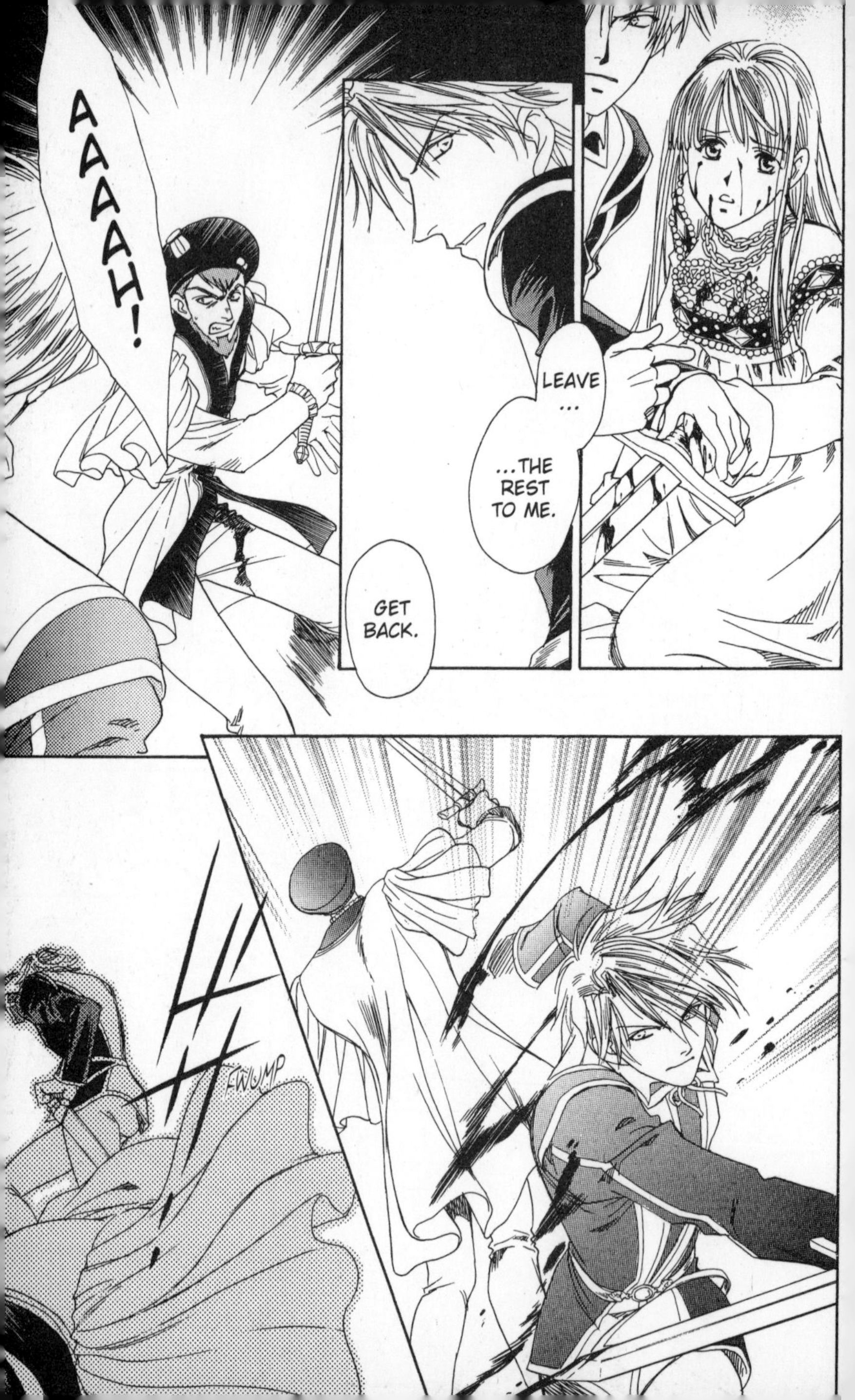
LEAVE...
...THE REST TO ME.
GET BACK.
AAAAAH!
FWUMP

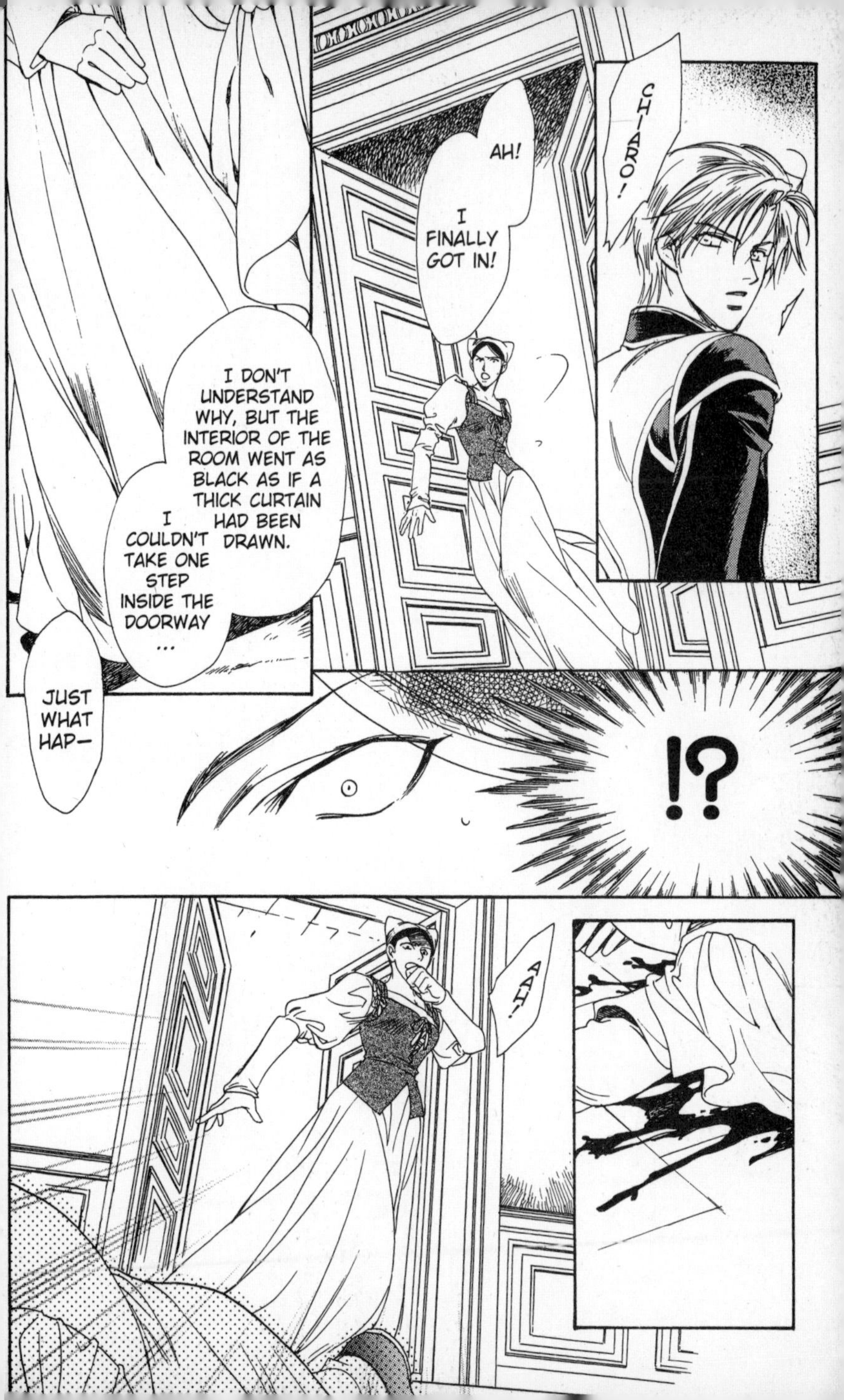
CHIARO!
AH!
I FINALLY GOT IN!
I DON'T UNDERSTAND WHY, BUT THE INTERIOR OF THE ROOM WENT AS BLACK AS IF A THICK CURTAIN HAD BEEN DRAWN.
I COULDN'T TAKE ONE STEP INSIDE THE DOORWAY...
JUST WHAT HAP—
!?
AAH!

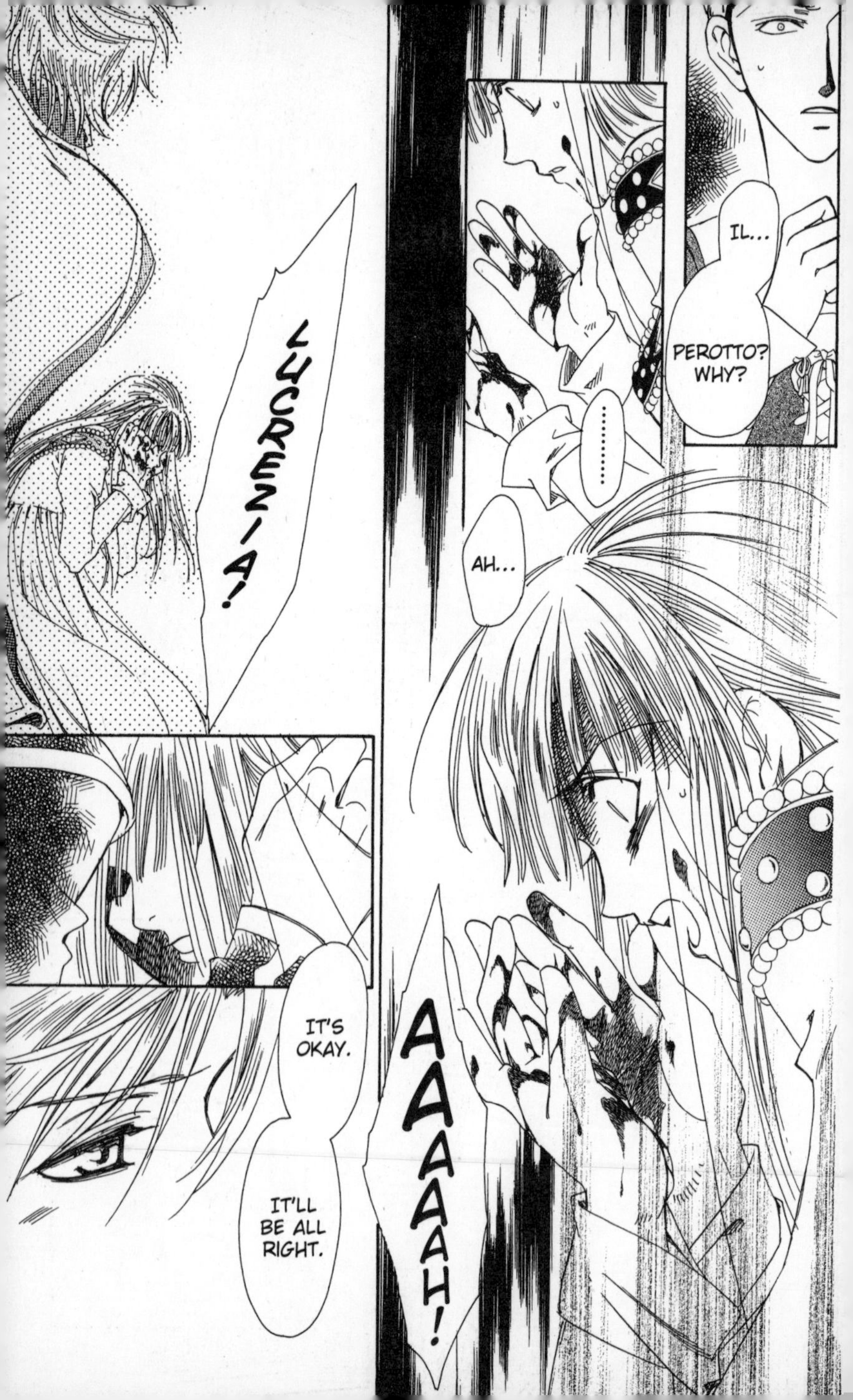
IL...
PEROTTO? WHY?
......
AH...
AAAAAH!
LUCREZIA!
IT'S OKAY.
IT'LL BE ALL RIGHT.

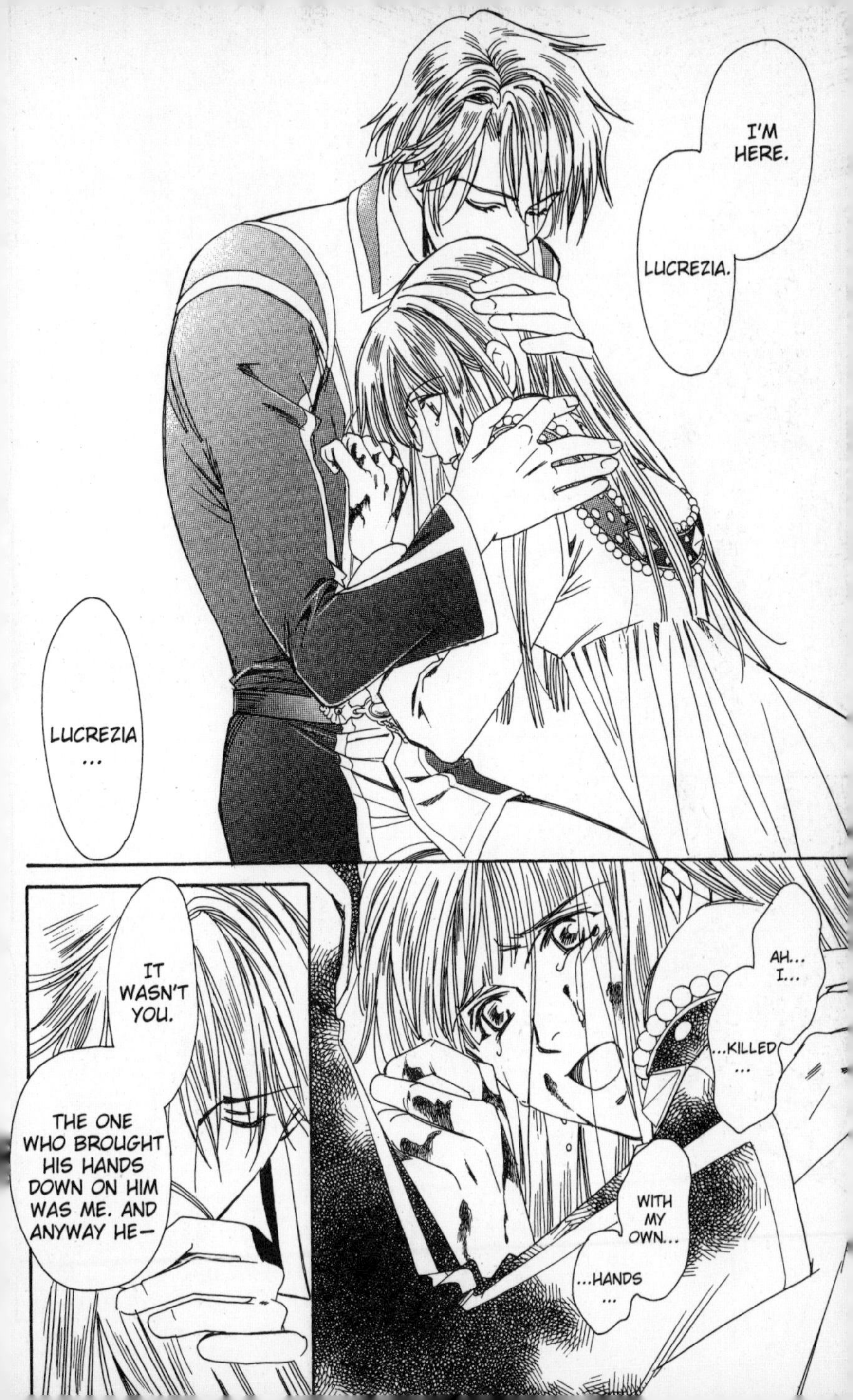
I'M HERE.
LUCREZIA.
LUCREZIA ...
AH... I...
...KILLED ...
WITH MY OWN...
...HANDS ...
IT WASN'T YOU.
THE ONE WHO BROUGHT HIS HANDS DOWN ON HIM WAS ME. AND ANYWAY HE—

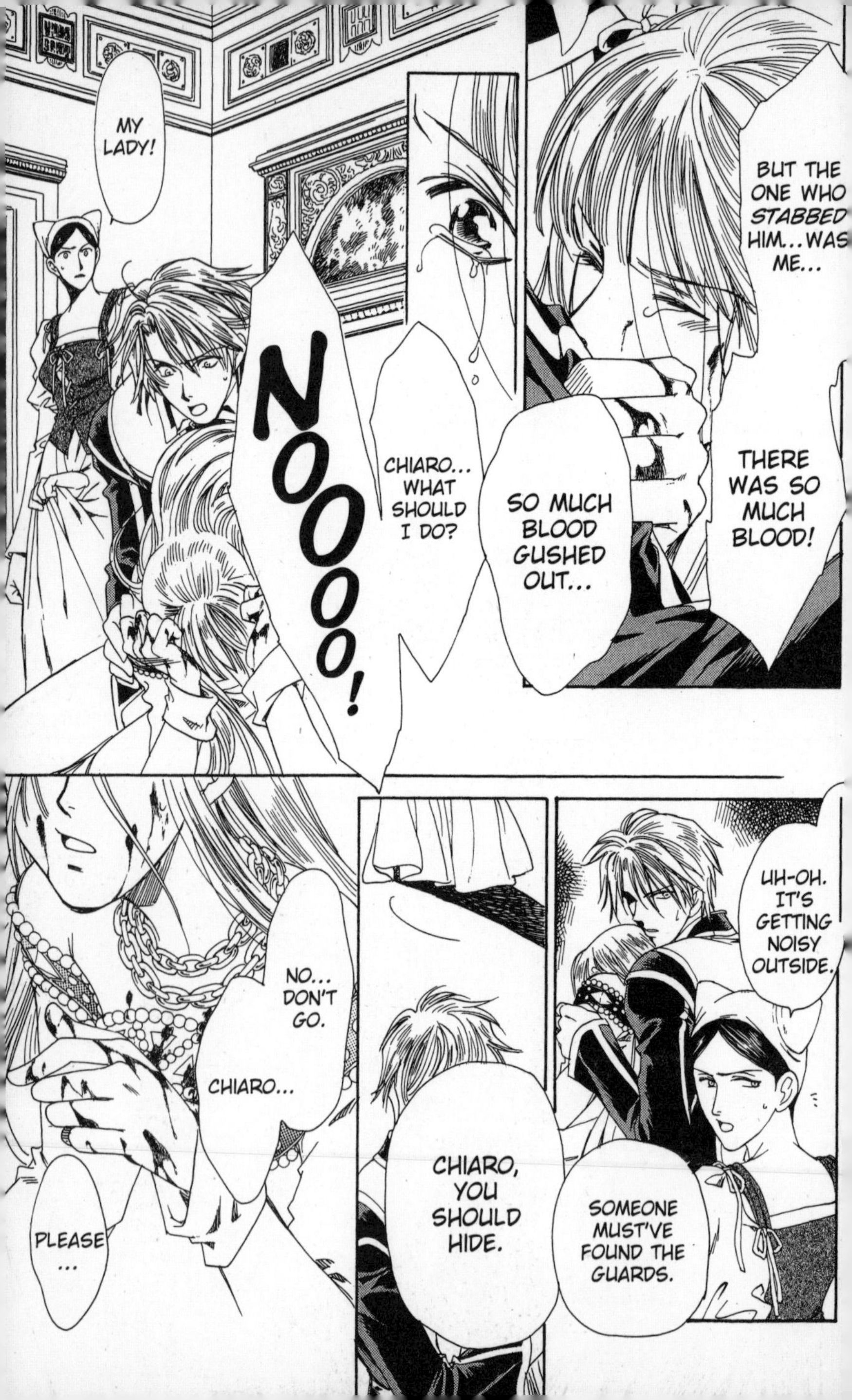
BUT THE ONE WHO STABBED HIM...WAS ME...
THERE WAS SO MUCH BLOOD!
SO MUCH BLOOD GUSHED OUT...
CHIARO... WHAT SHOULD I DO?
NOOOO!
MY LADY!
UH-OH. IT'S GETTING NOISY OUTSIDE.
SOMEONE MUST'VE FOUND THE GUARDS.
CHIARO, YOU SHOULD HIDE.
NO... DON'T GO.
CHIARO...
PLEASE...

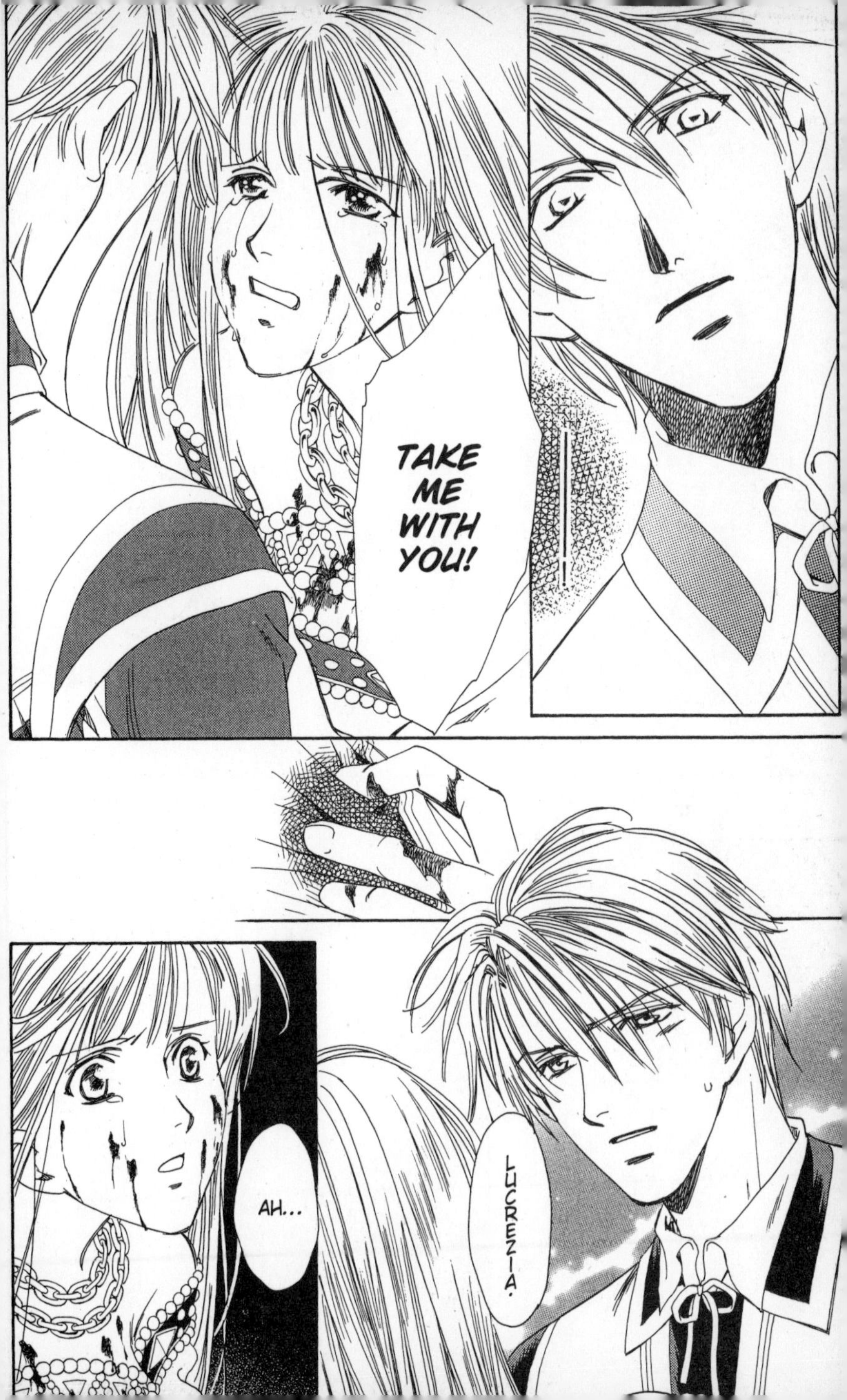
TAKE ME WITH YOU!
LUCREZIA.
AH...

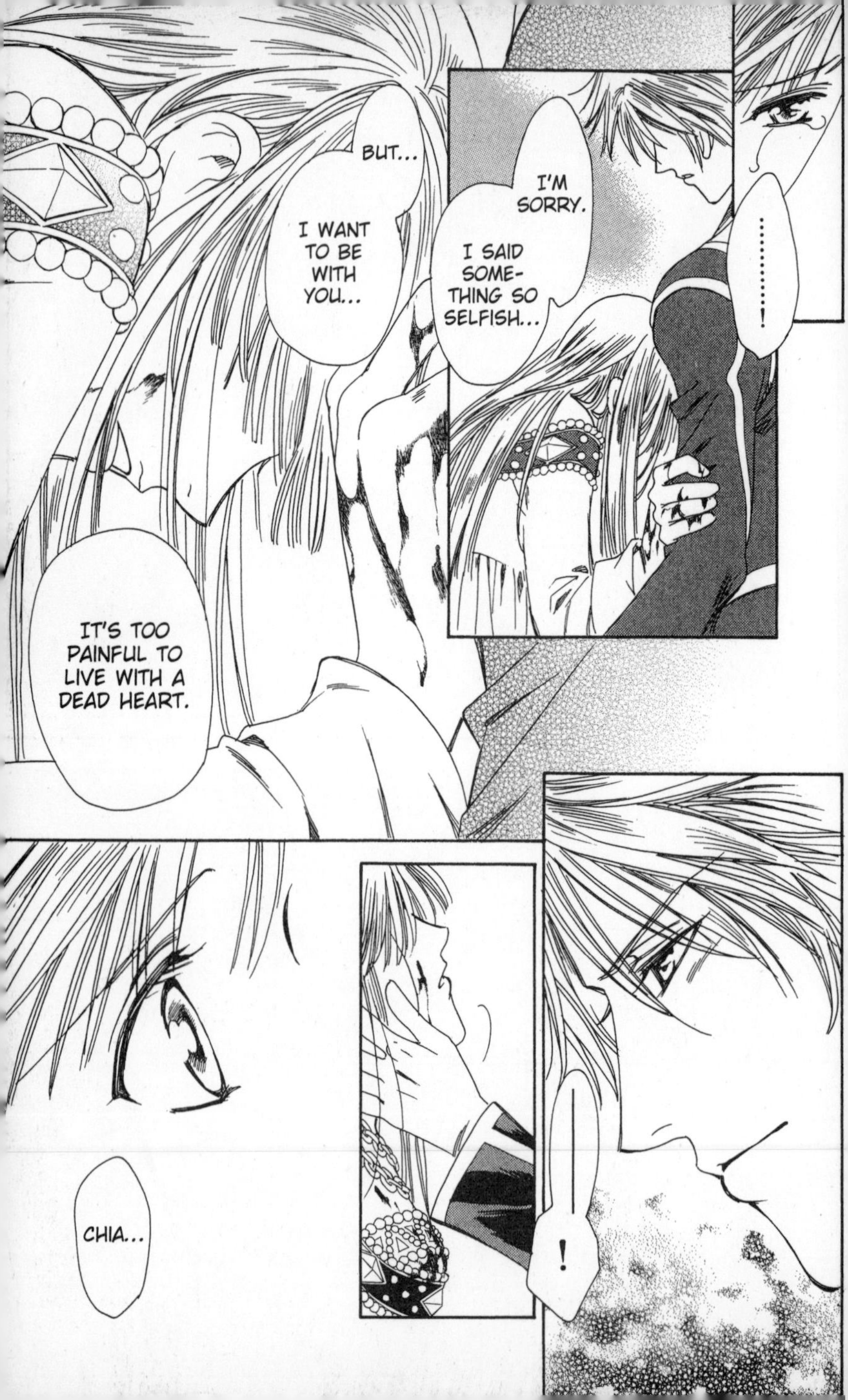
......!
I'M SORRY.
I SAID SOME-THING SO SELFISH...
BUT...
I WANT TO BE WITH YOU...
IT'S TOO PAINFUL TO LIVE WITH A DEAD HEART.
!
CHIA...

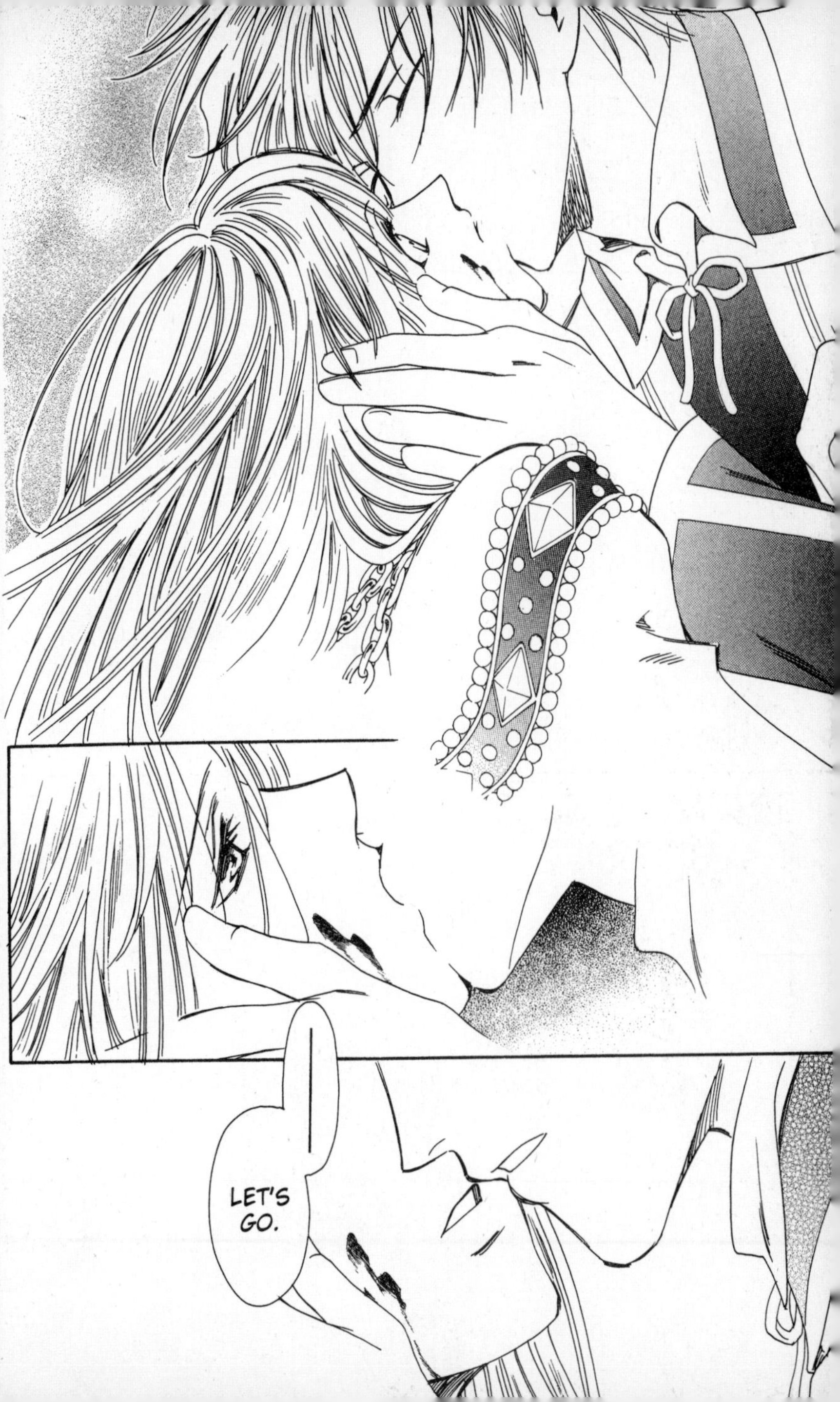
LET'S GO.

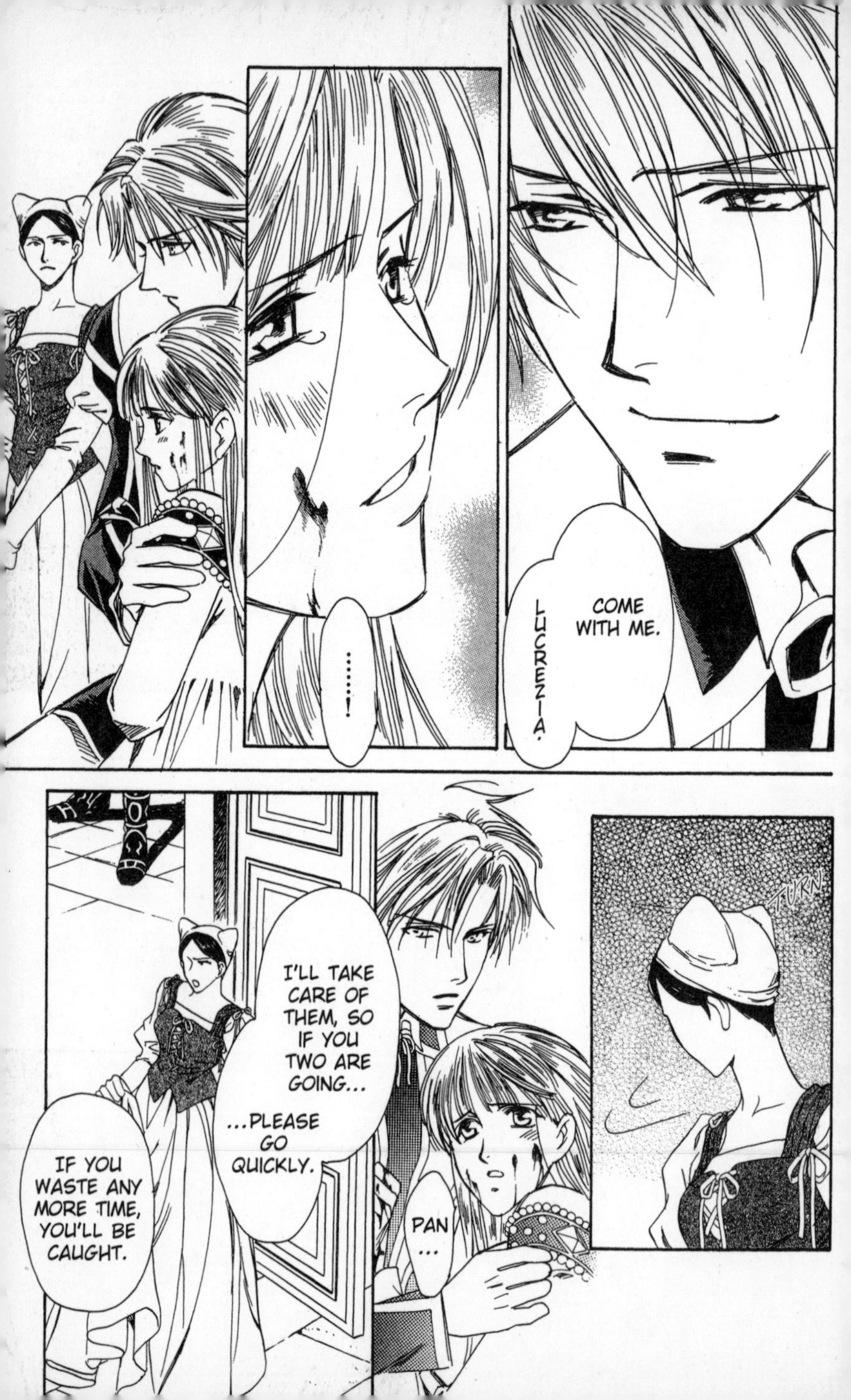
COME WITH ME.
LUCREZIA.
......!
TURN
I'LL TAKE CARE OF THEM, SO IF YOU TWO ARE GOING...
...PLEASE GO QUICKLY.
IF YOU WASTE ANY MORE TIME, YOU'LL BE CAUGHT.
PAN...

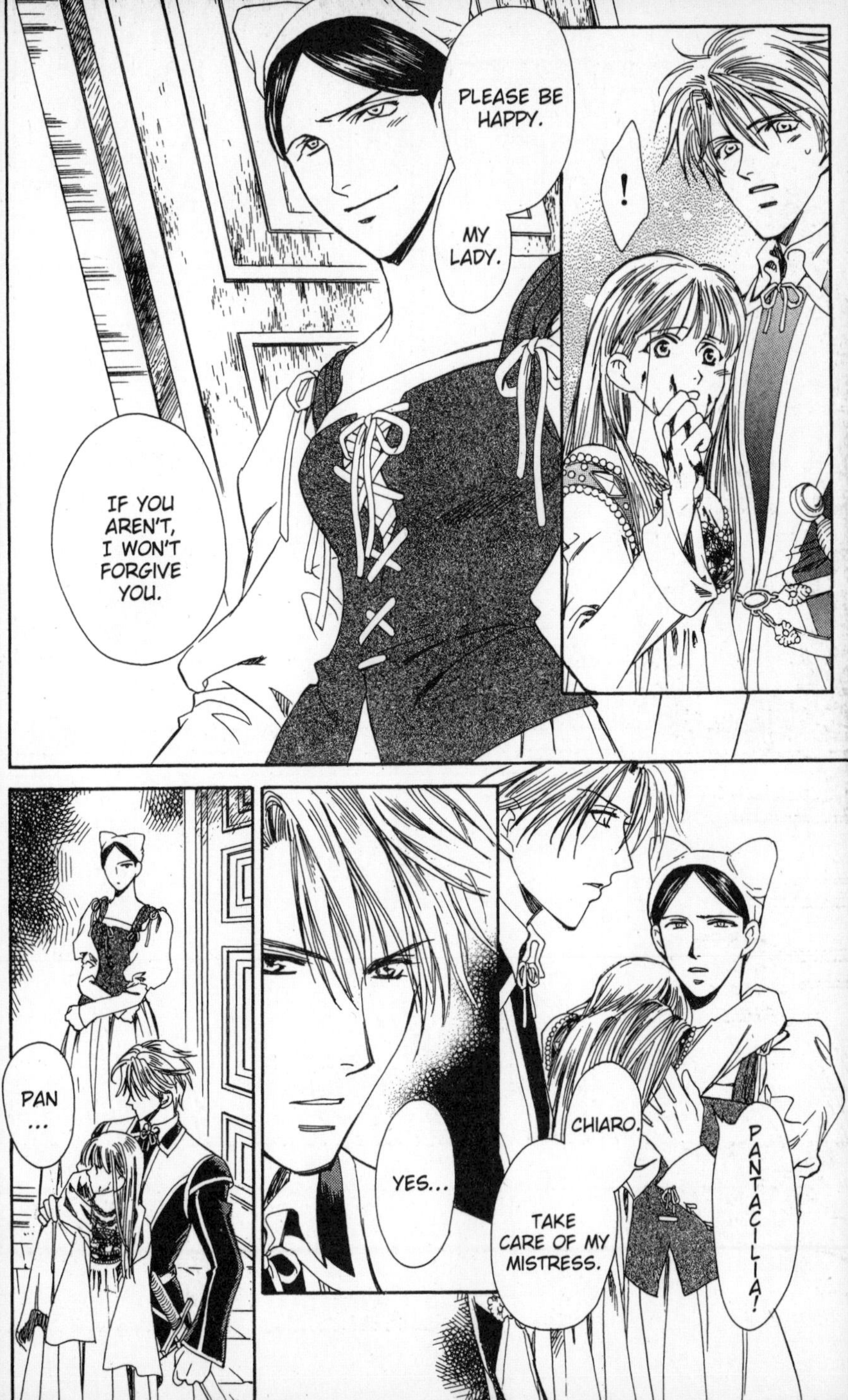
PLEASE BE HAPPY.
MY LADY.
!
IF YOU AREN'T, I WON'T FORGIVE YOU.
PANTACILIA!
CHIARO.
TAKE CARE OF MY MISTRESS.
YES...
PAN...

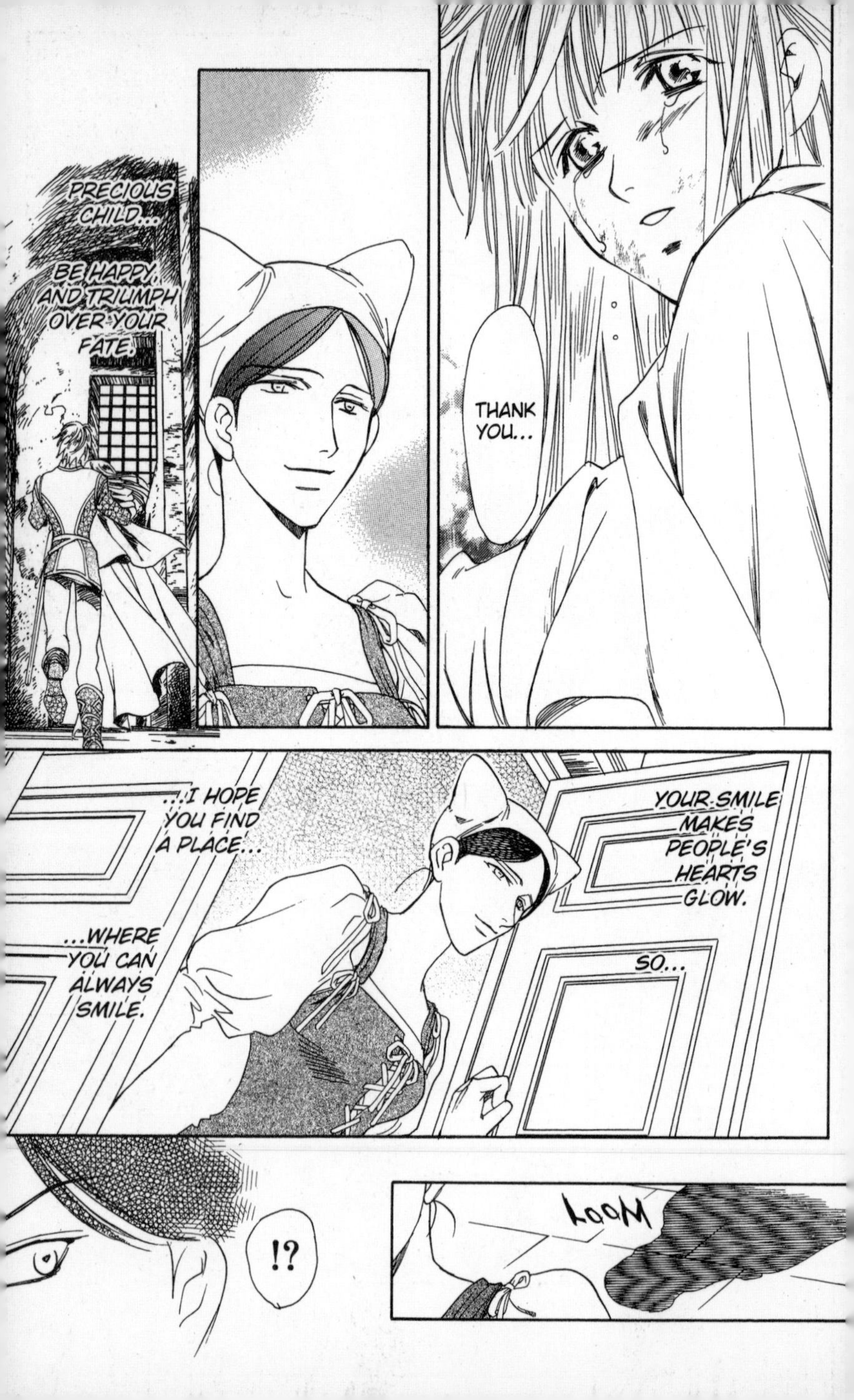
THANK YOU...
PRECIOUS CHILD...
BE HAPPY AND TRIUMPH OVER YOUR FATE.
YOUR SMILE MAKES PEOPLE'S HEARTS GLOW.
SO...
...I HOPE YOU FIND A PLACE...
...WHERE YOU CAN ALWAYS SMILE.
!?

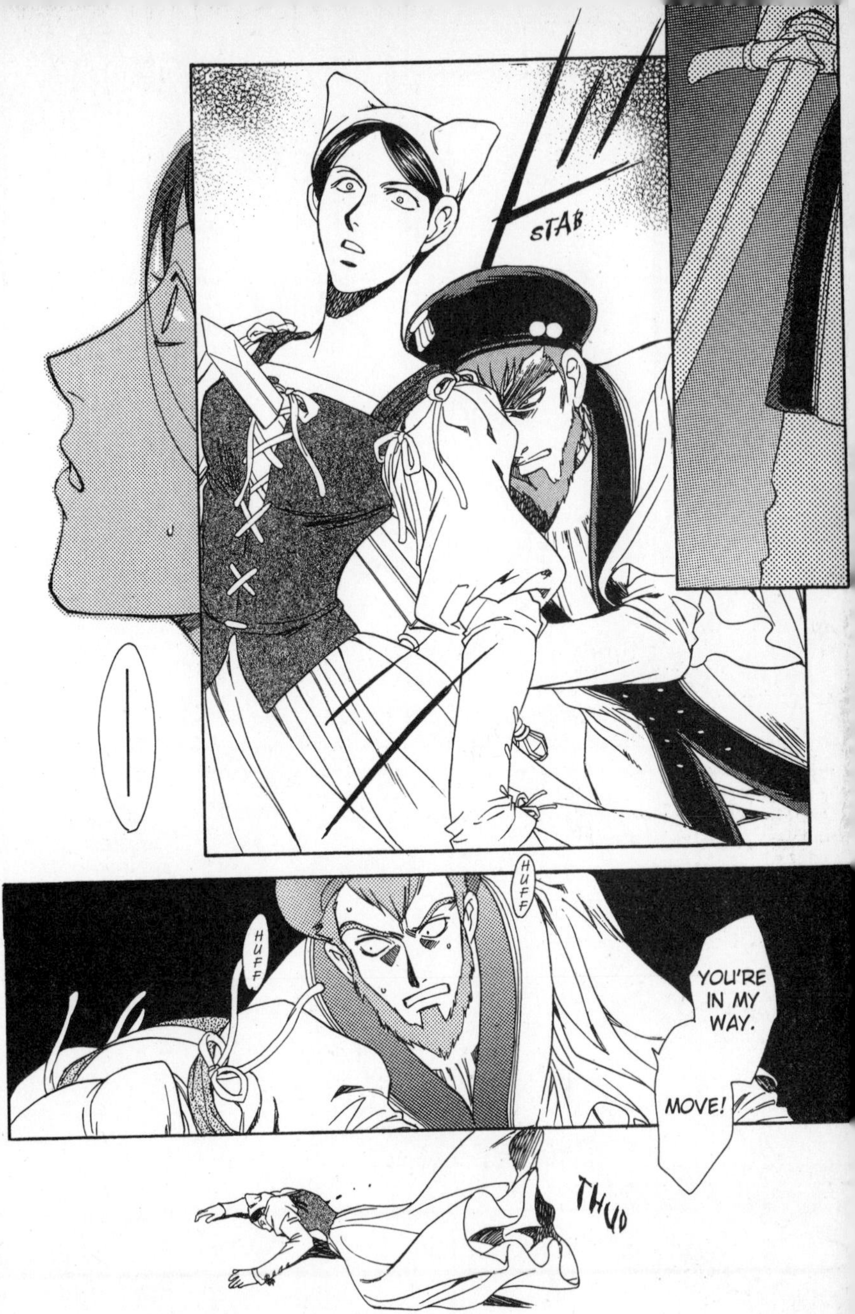
STAB
—
HUFF
HUFF
YOU'RE IN MY WAY.
MOVE!
THUD

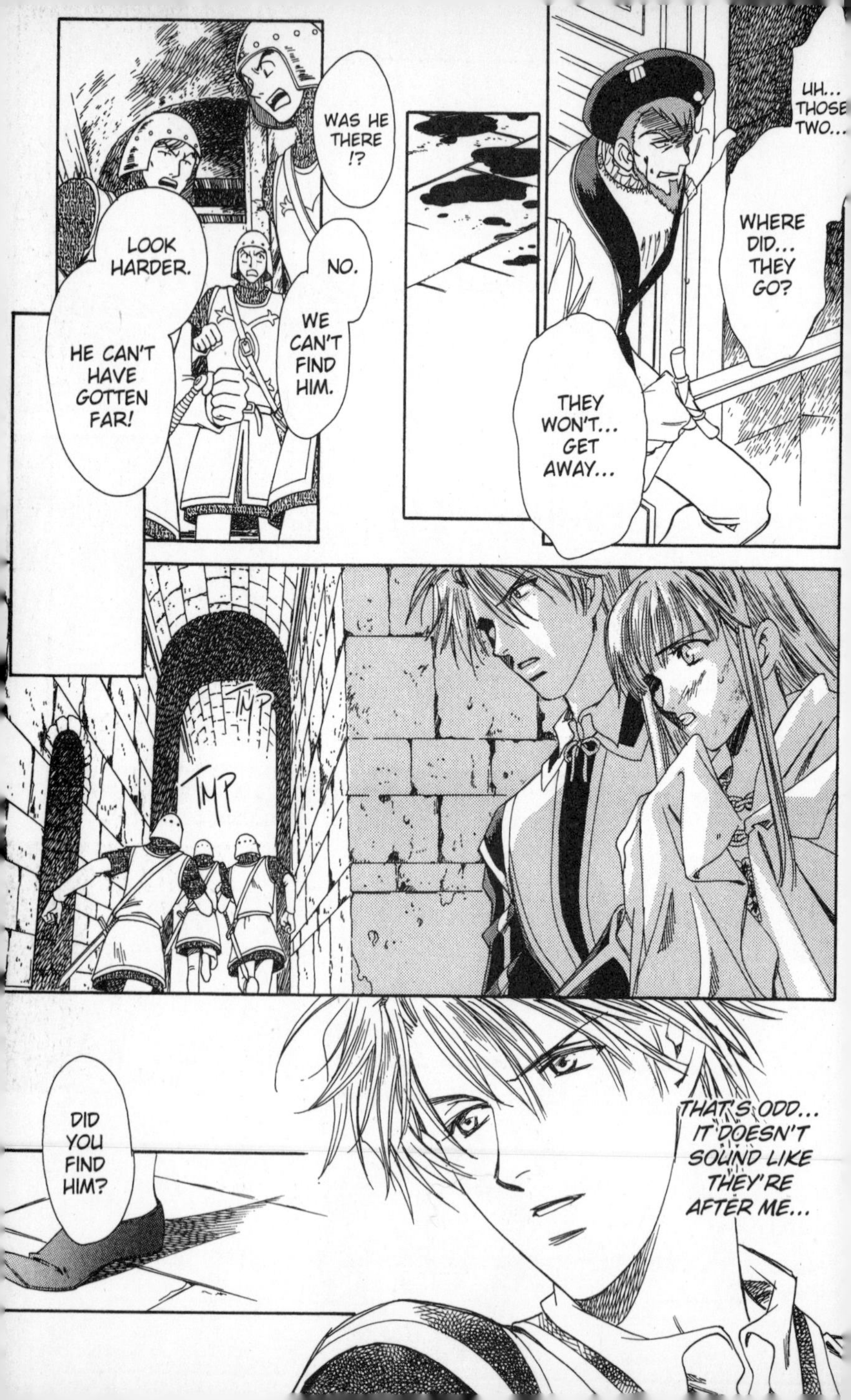

UH... THOSE TWO...
WHERE DID... THEY GO?
THEY WON'T... GET AWAY...
WAS HE THERE !?
NO.
WE CAN'T FIND HIM.
LOOK HARDER.
HE CAN'T HAVE GOTTEN FAR!
TMP
TMP
THAT'S ODD... IT DOESN'T SOUND LIKE THEY'RE AFTER ME...
DID YOU FIND HIM?

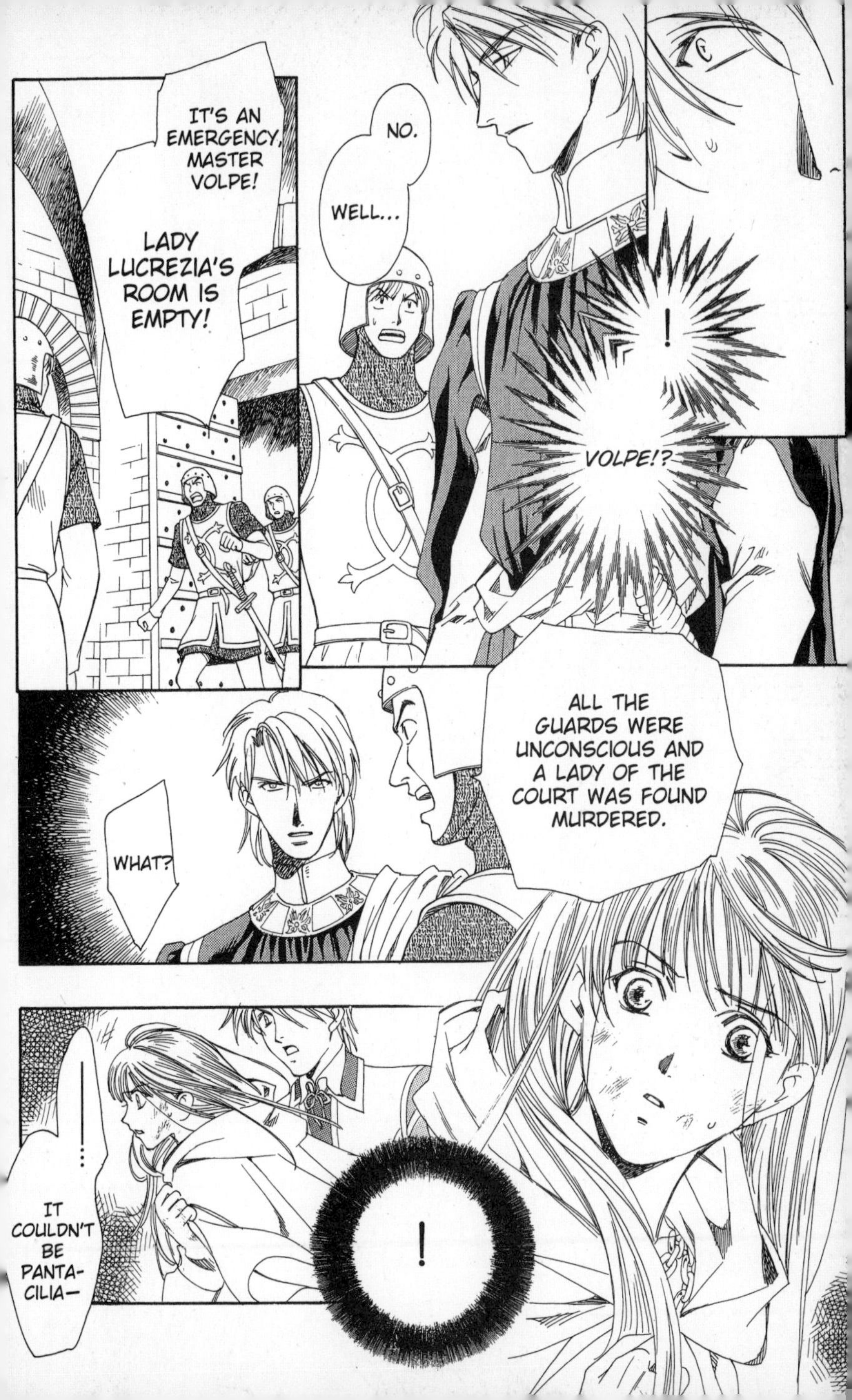
!
VOLPE!?
NO.
WELL...
IT'S AN EMERGENCY, MASTER VOLPE!
LADY LUCREZIA'S ROOM IS EMPTY!
ALL THE GUARDS WERE UNCONSCIOUS AND A LADY OF THE COURT WAS FOUND MURDERED.
WHAT?
!
......
IT COULDN'T BE PANTACILIA—

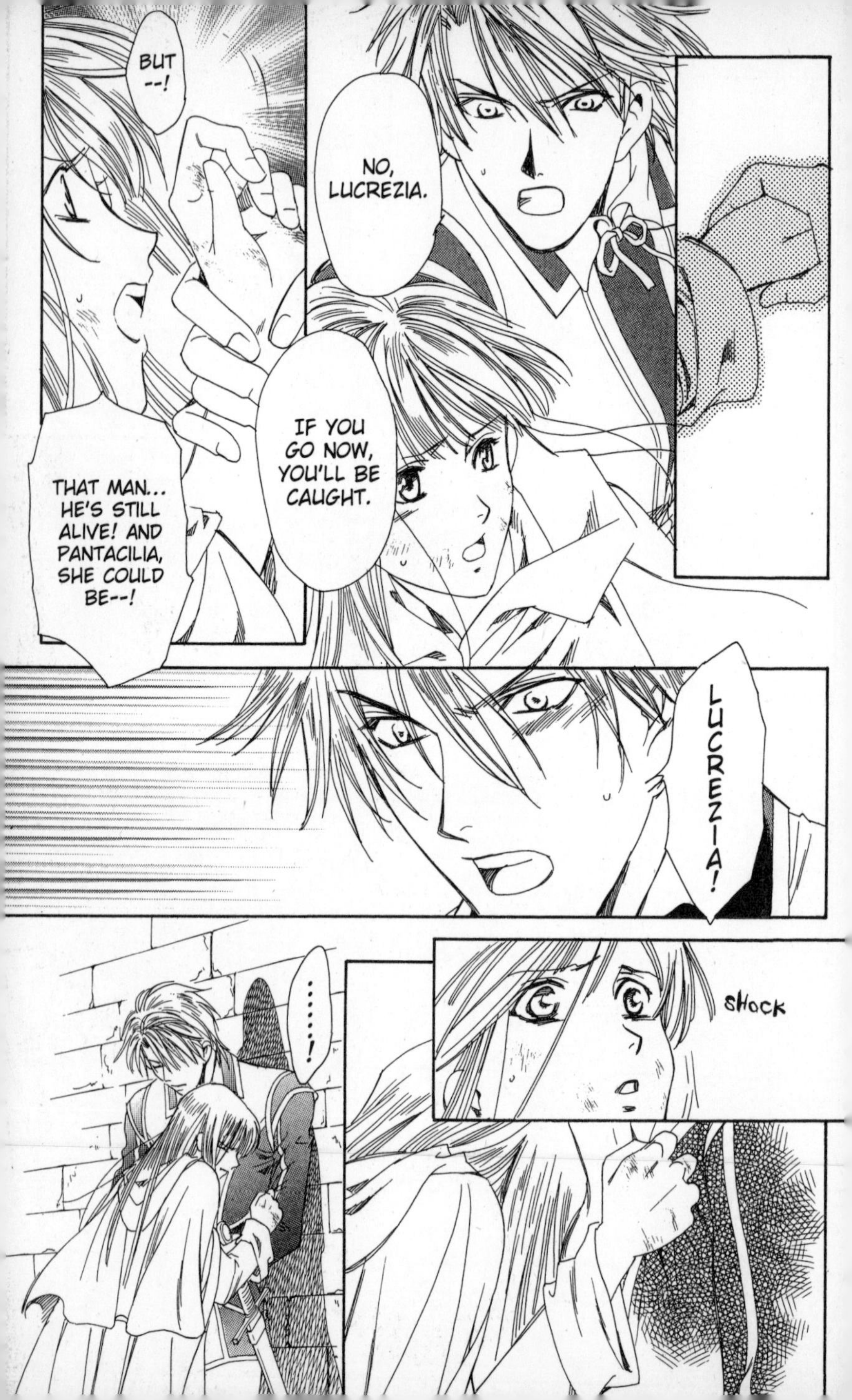
NO, LUCREZIA.
IF YOU GO NOW, YOU'LL BE CAUGHT.
BUT --!
THAT MAN... HE'S STILL ALIVE! AND PANTACILIA, SHE COULD BE--!
LUCREZIA!
SHOCK
......!

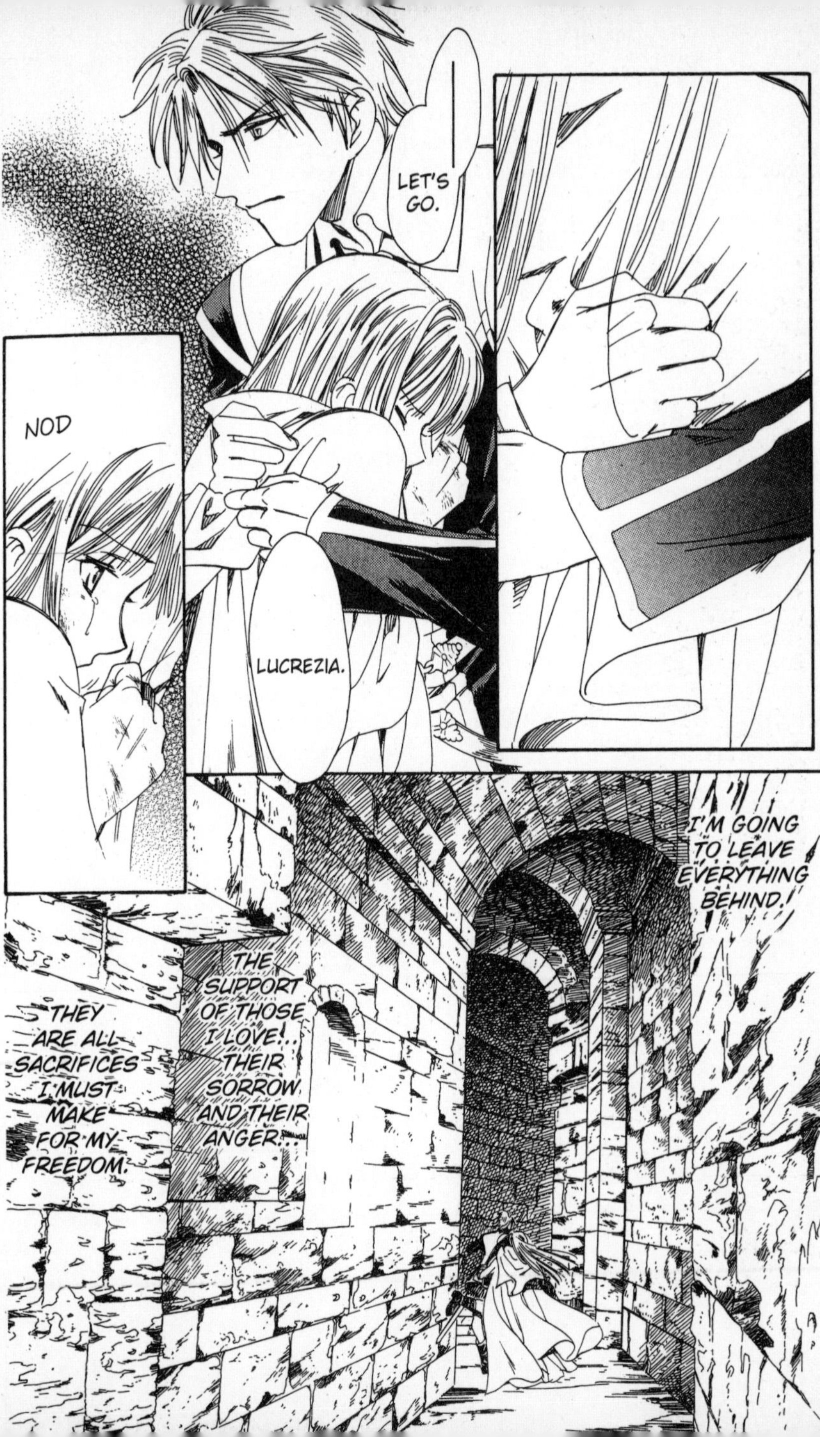
LET'S GO.
LUCREZIA.
NOD
I'M GOING TO LEAVE EVERYTHING BEHIND.
THE SUPPORT OF THOSE I LOVE... THEIR SORROW AND THEIR ANGER...
THEY ARE ALL SACRIFICES I MUST MAKE FOR MY FREEDOM.

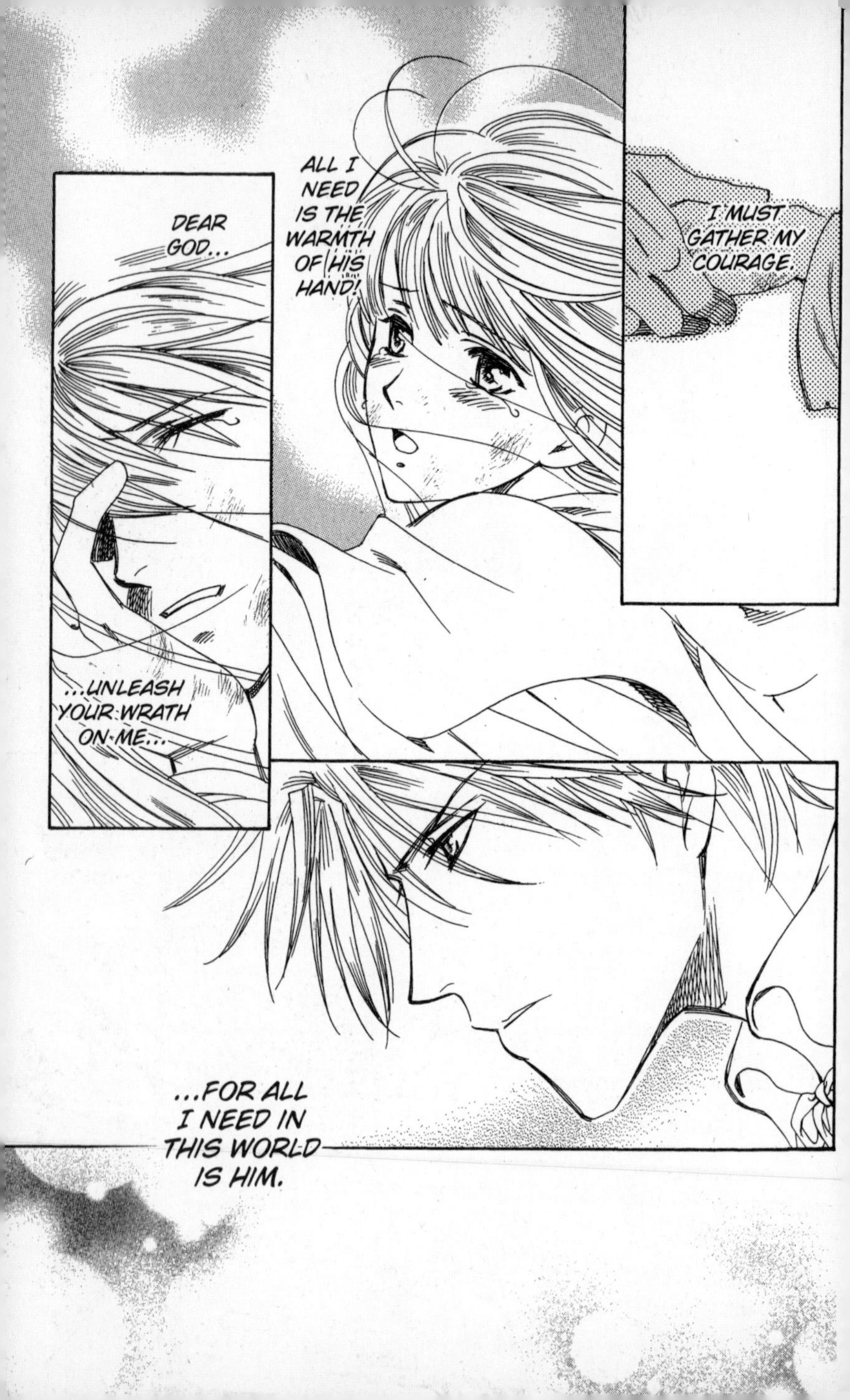
I MUST GATHER MY COURAGE.
ALL I NEED IS THE WARMTH OF HIS HAND!
DEAR GOD...
...UNLEASH YOUR WRATH ON ME...
...FOR ALL I NEED IN THIS WORLD IS HIM.

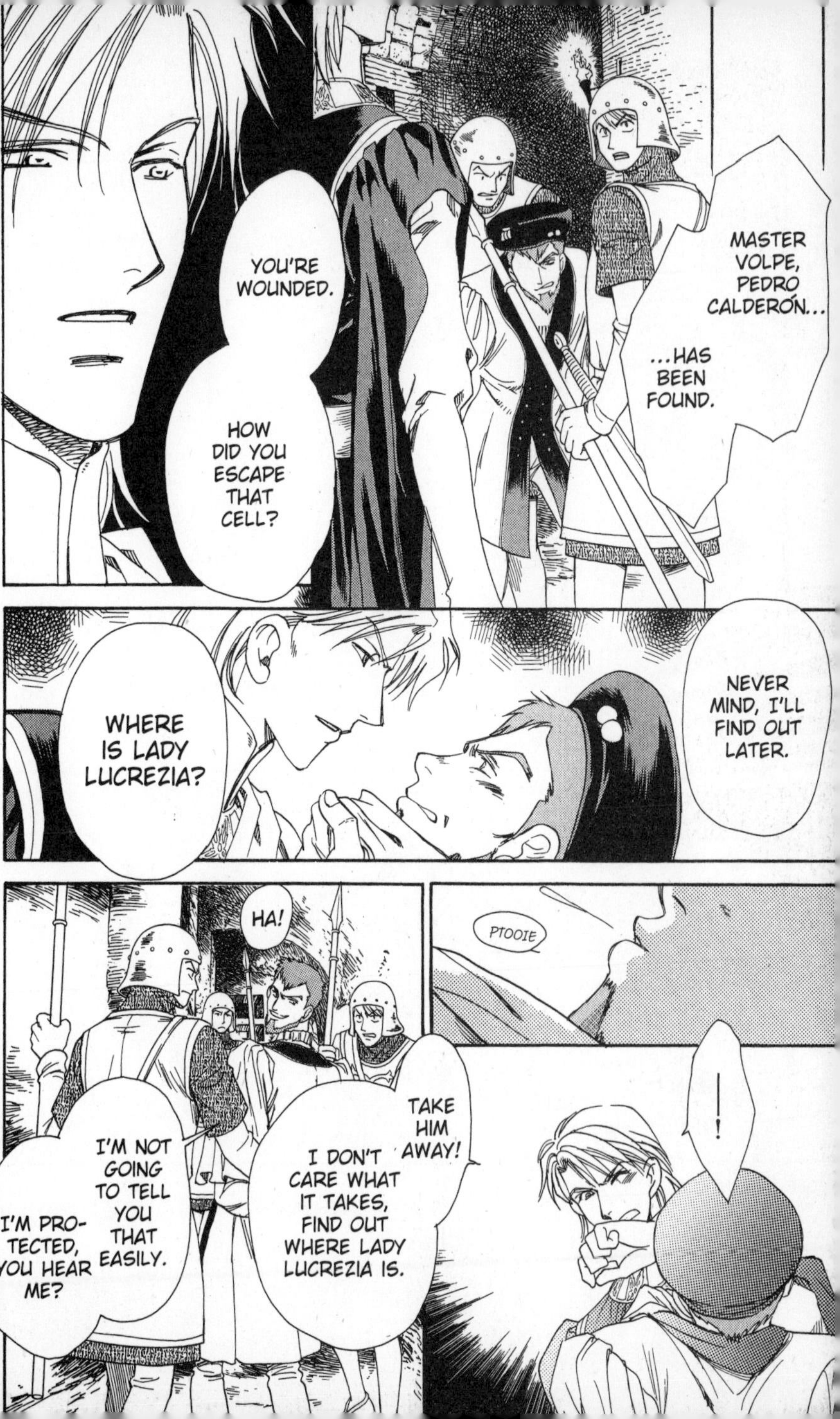
MASTER VOLPE, PEDRO CALDERÓN...
...HAS BEEN FOUND.
YOU'RE WOUNDED.
HOW DID YOU ESCAPE THAT CELL?
NEVER MIND, I'LL FIND OUT LATER.
WHERE IS LADY LUCREZIA?
PTOOIE
!
HA!
TAKE HIM AWAY!
I DON'T CARE WHAT IT TAKES, FIND OUT WHERE LADY LUCREZIA IS.
I'M NOT GOING TO TELL YOU THAT EASILY.
I'M PRO-TECTED, YOU HEAR ME?

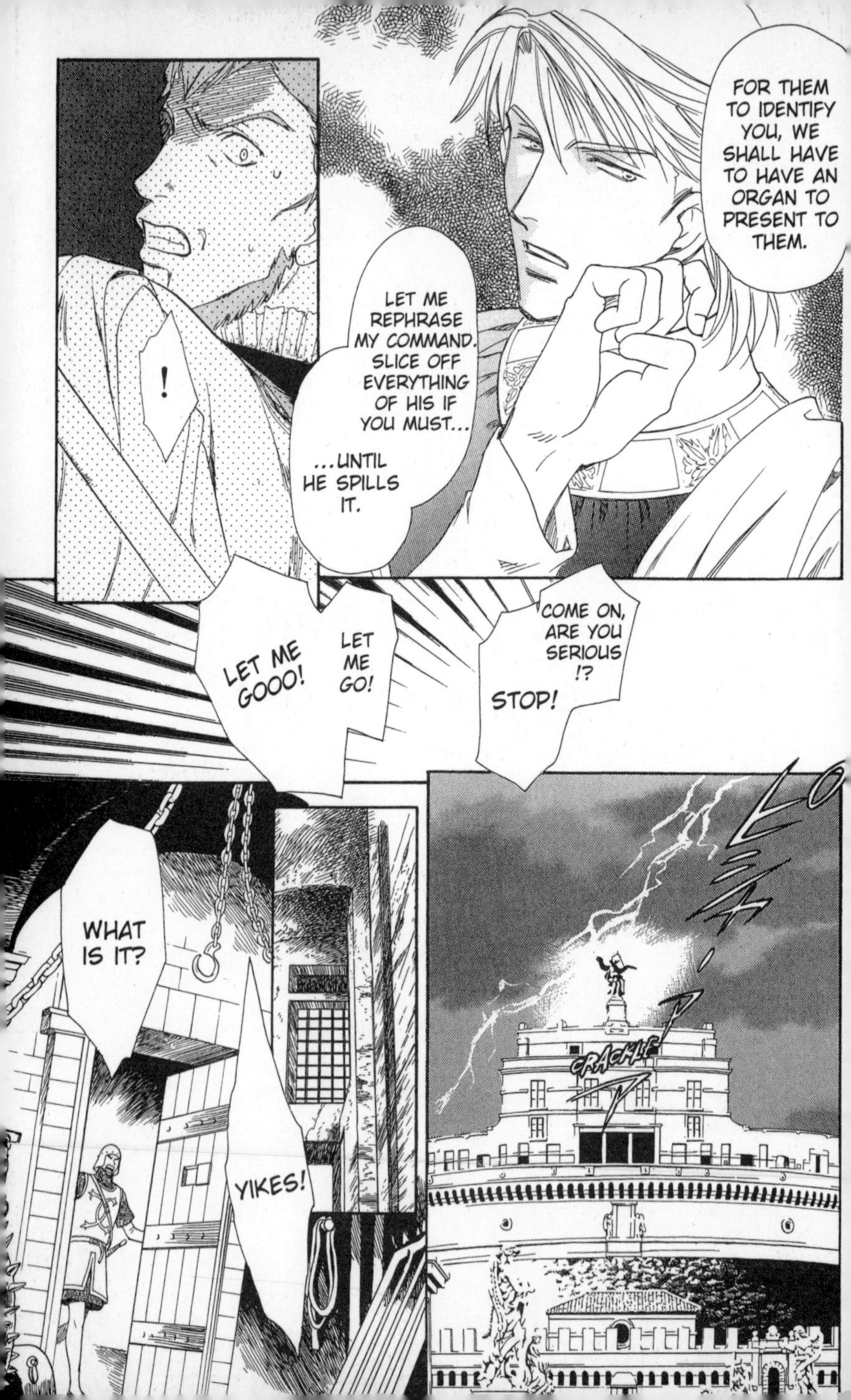
FOR THEM TO IDENTIFY YOU, WE SHALL HAVE TO HAVE AN ORGAN TO PRESENT TO THEM.
LET ME REPHRASE MY COMMAND. SLICE OFF EVERYTHING OF HIS IF YOU MUST...
...UNTIL HE SPILLS IT.
!
COME ON, ARE YOU SERIOUS !?
STOP!
LET ME GO!
LET ME GOOO!
CRACKLE
YIKES!
WHAT IS IT?

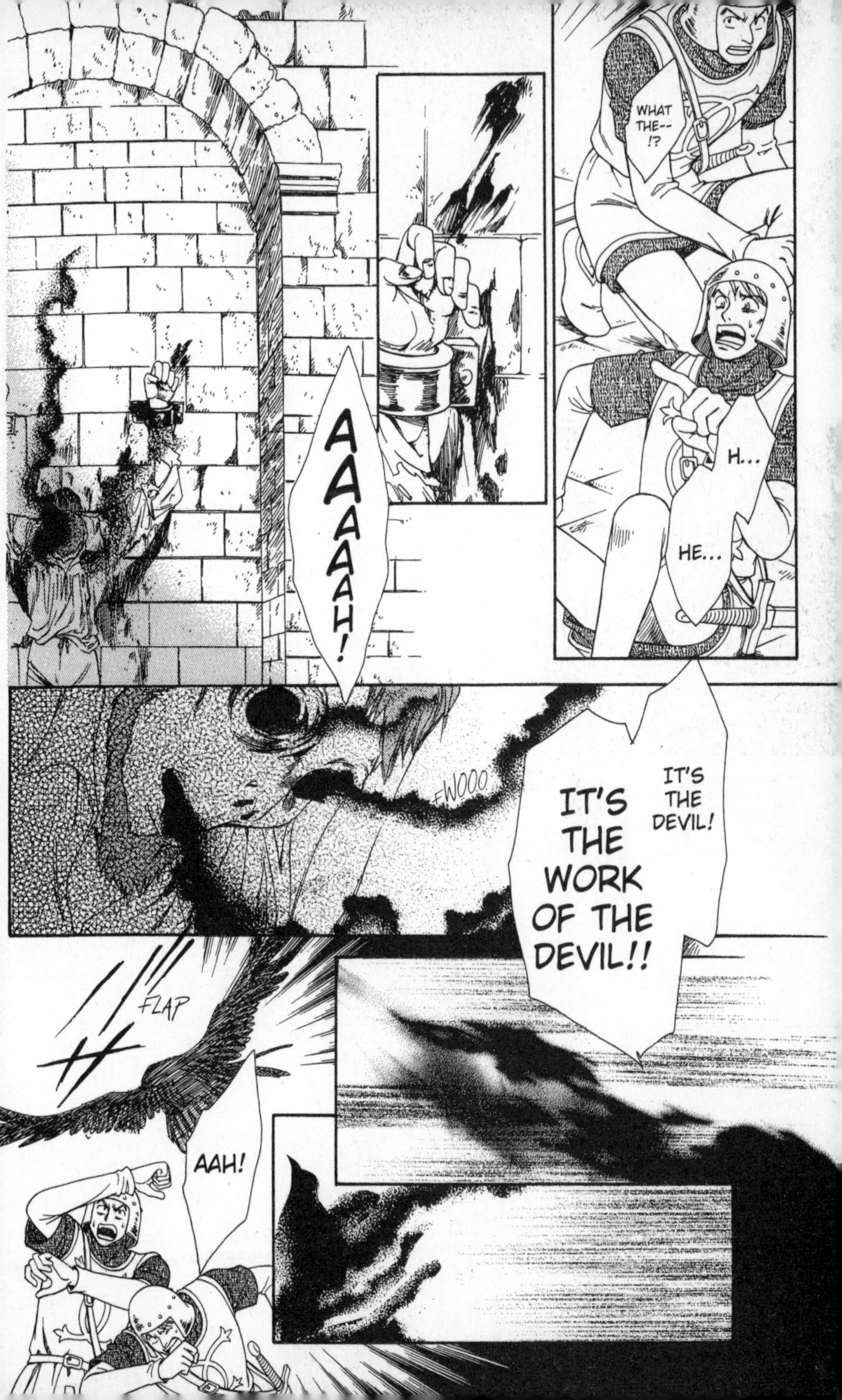
WHAT THE--!?
H...
HE...
AAAAAAH!
IT'S THE DEVIL!
IT'S THE WORK OF THE DEVIL!!
FWOOO
FLAP
AAH!

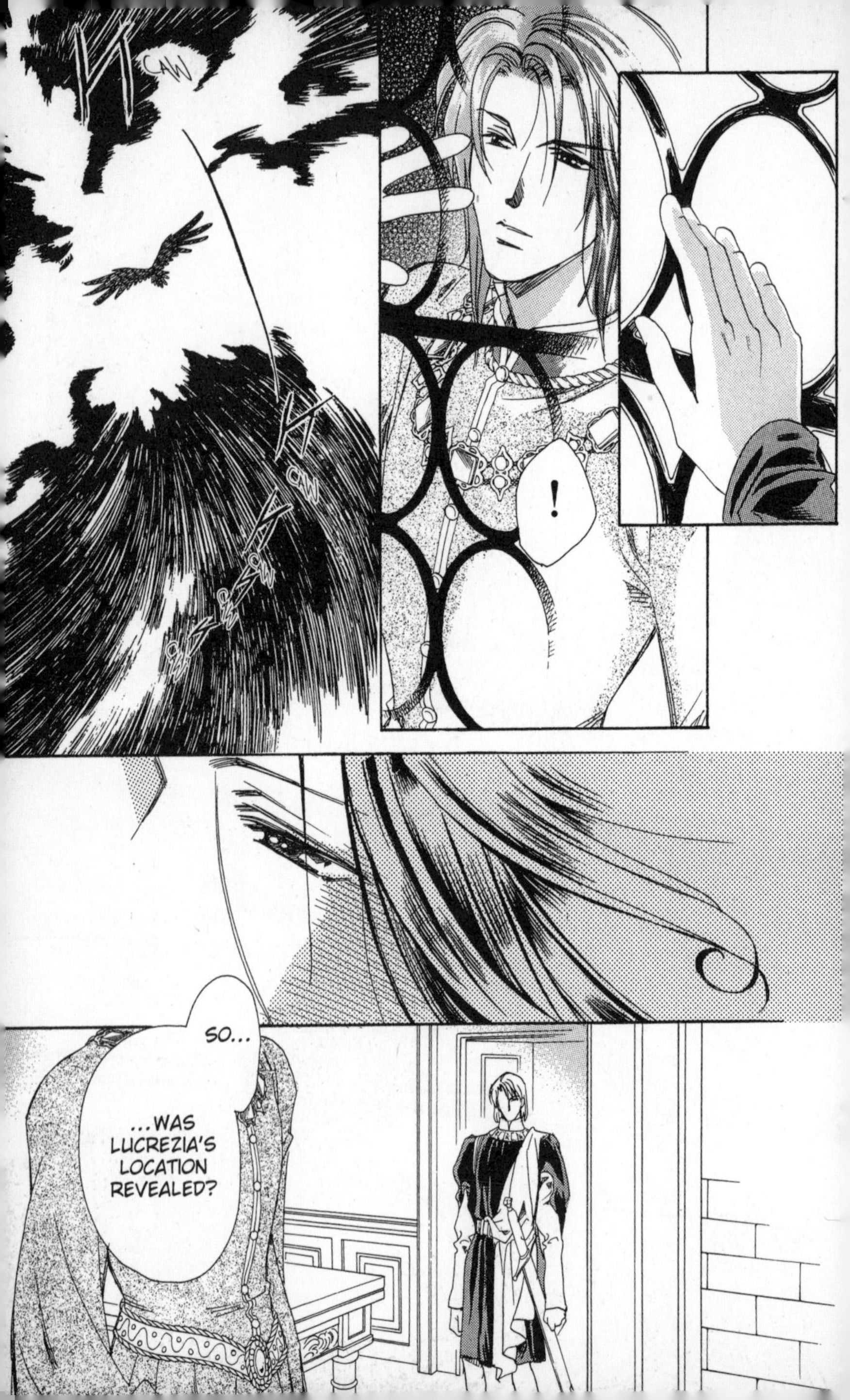
!
CAW
CAW
CAW
CAW
SO...
...WAS LUCREZIA'S LOCATION REVEALED?

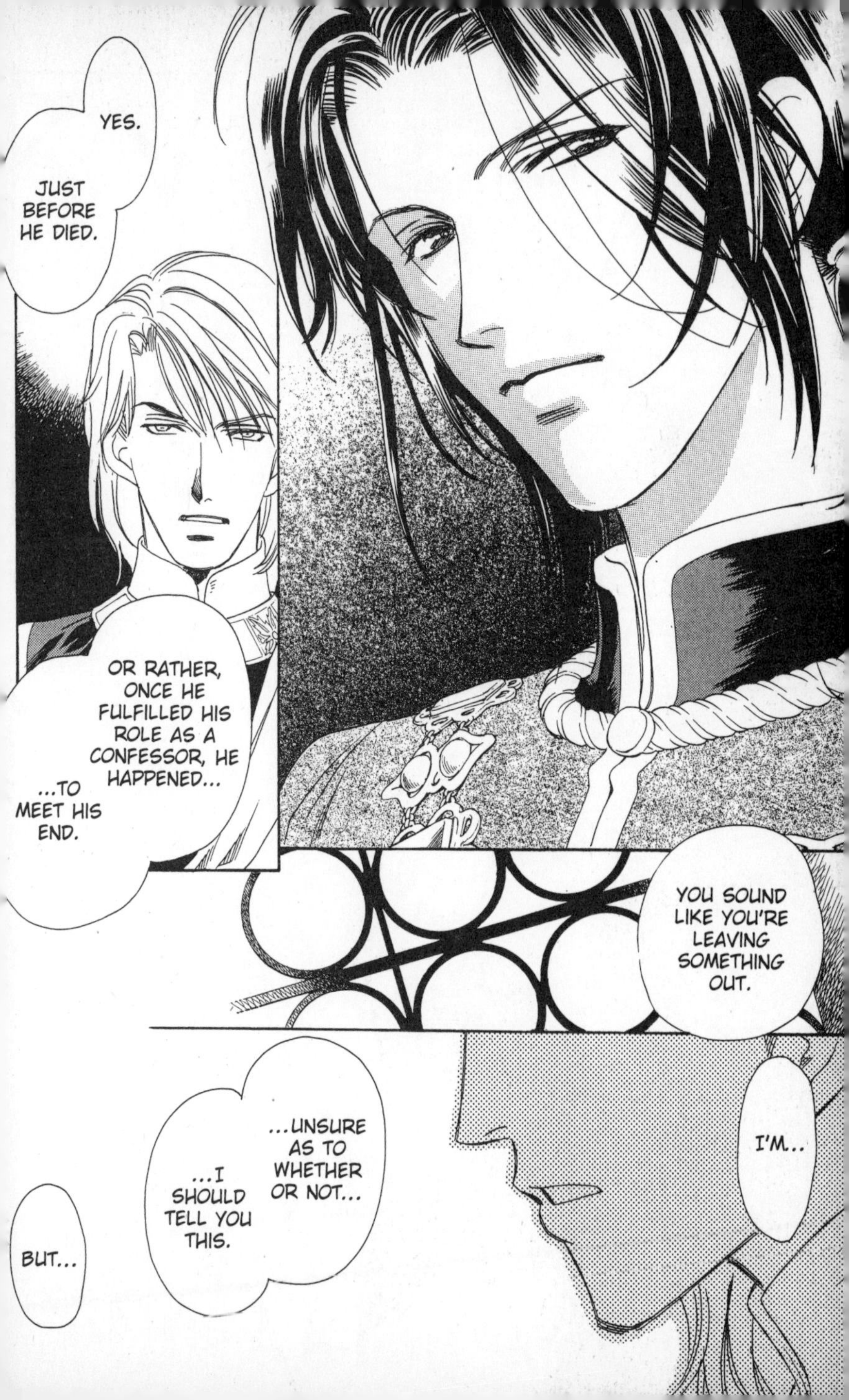
YES.
JUST BEFORE HE DIED.
OR RATHER, ONCE HE FULFILLED HIS ROLE AS A CONFESSOR, HE HAPPENED... ...TO MEET HIS END.
YOU SOUND LIKE YOU'RE LEAVING SOMETHING OUT.
I'M...
...UNSURE AS TO WHETHER OR NOT... ...I SHOULD TELL YOU THIS.
BUT...

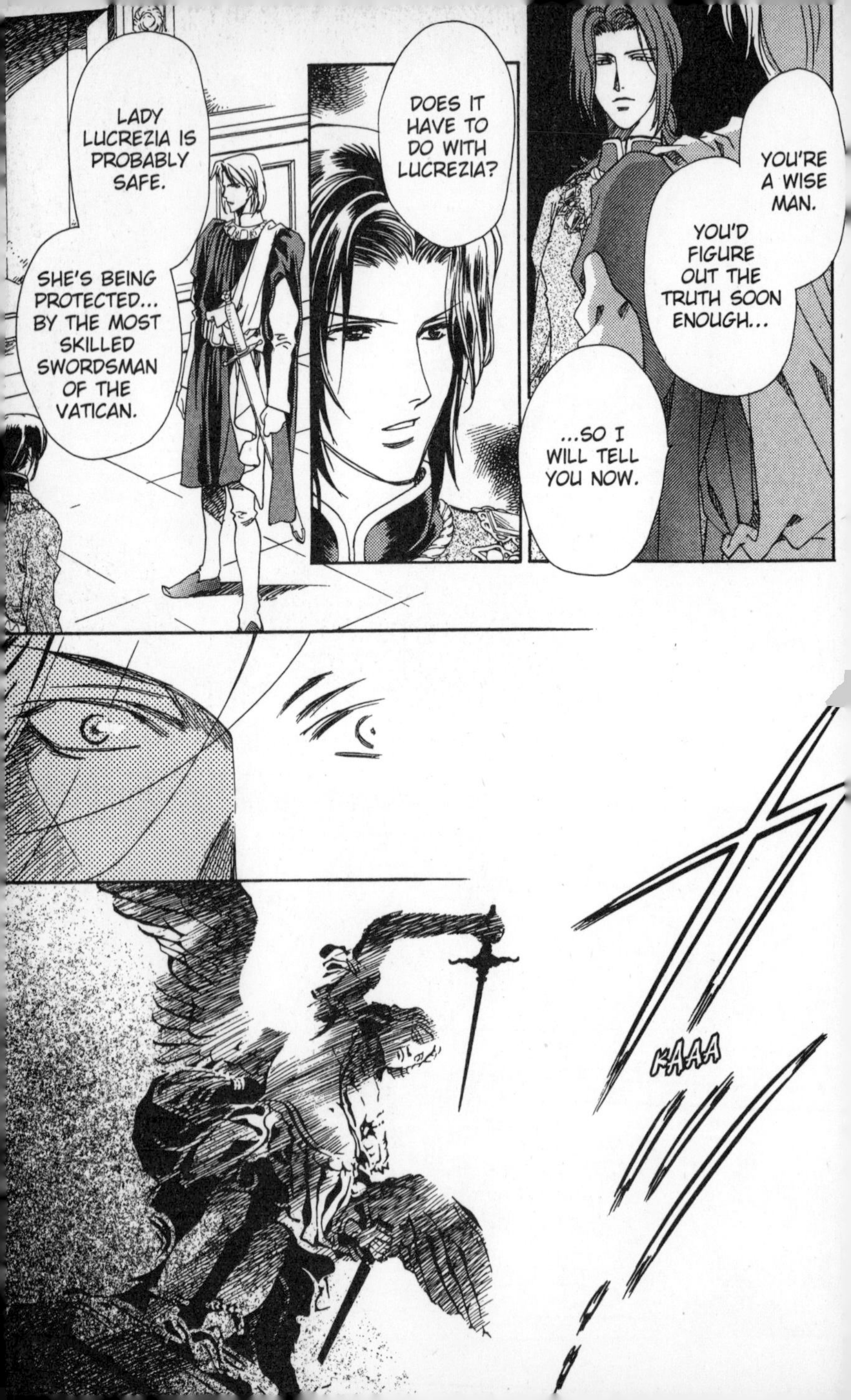
YOU'RE A WISE MAN.
YOU'D FIGURE OUT THE TRUTH SOON ENOUGH...
...SO I WILL TELL YOU NOW.
DOES IT HAVE TO DO WITH LUCREZIA?
LADY LUCREZIA IS PROBABLY SAFE.
SHE'S BEING PROTECTED... BY THE MOST SKILLED SWORDSMAN OF THE VATICAN.
KAAA

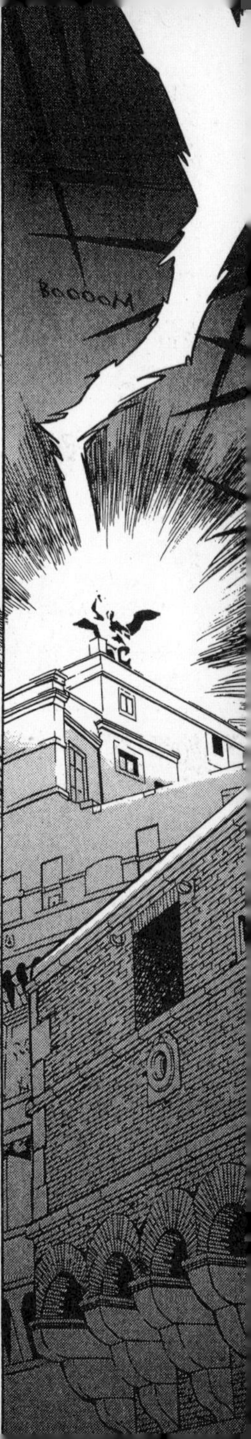
BOOOOM
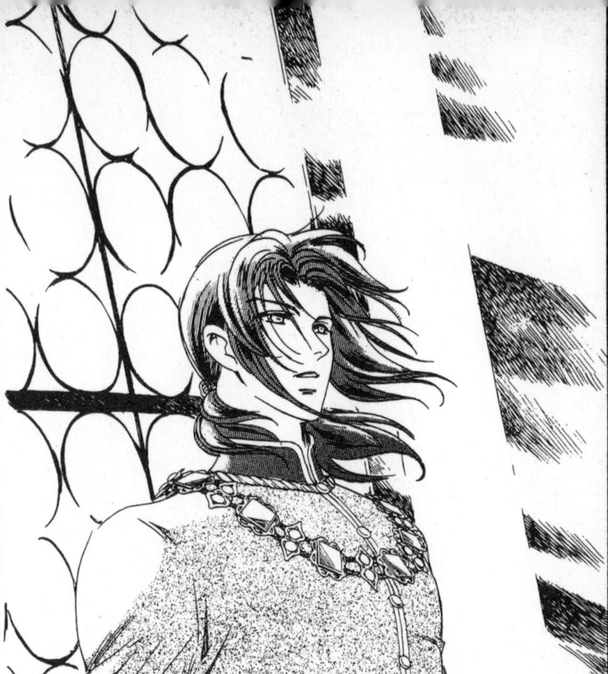
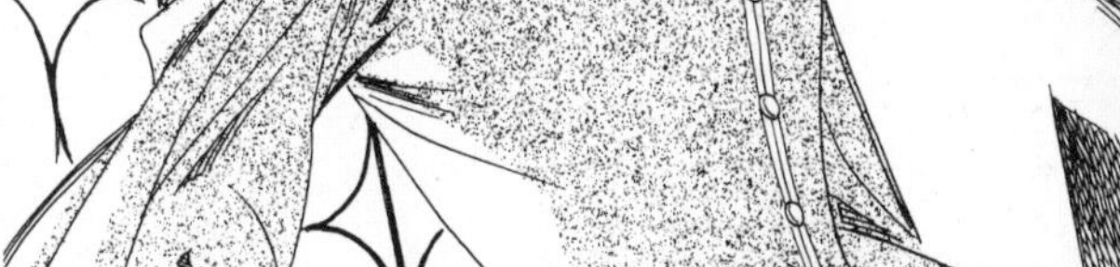
TUMBLE

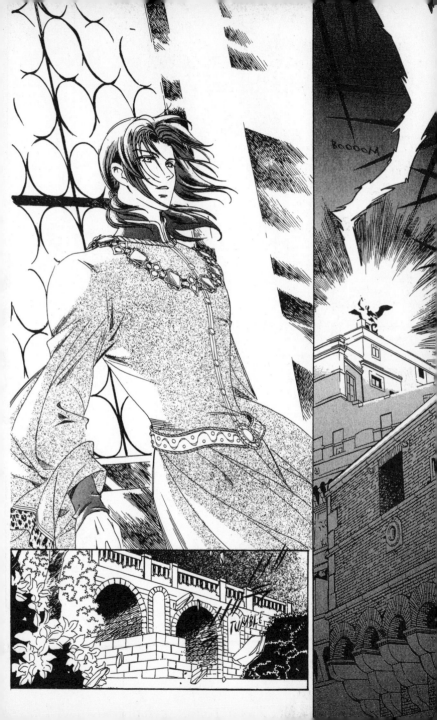

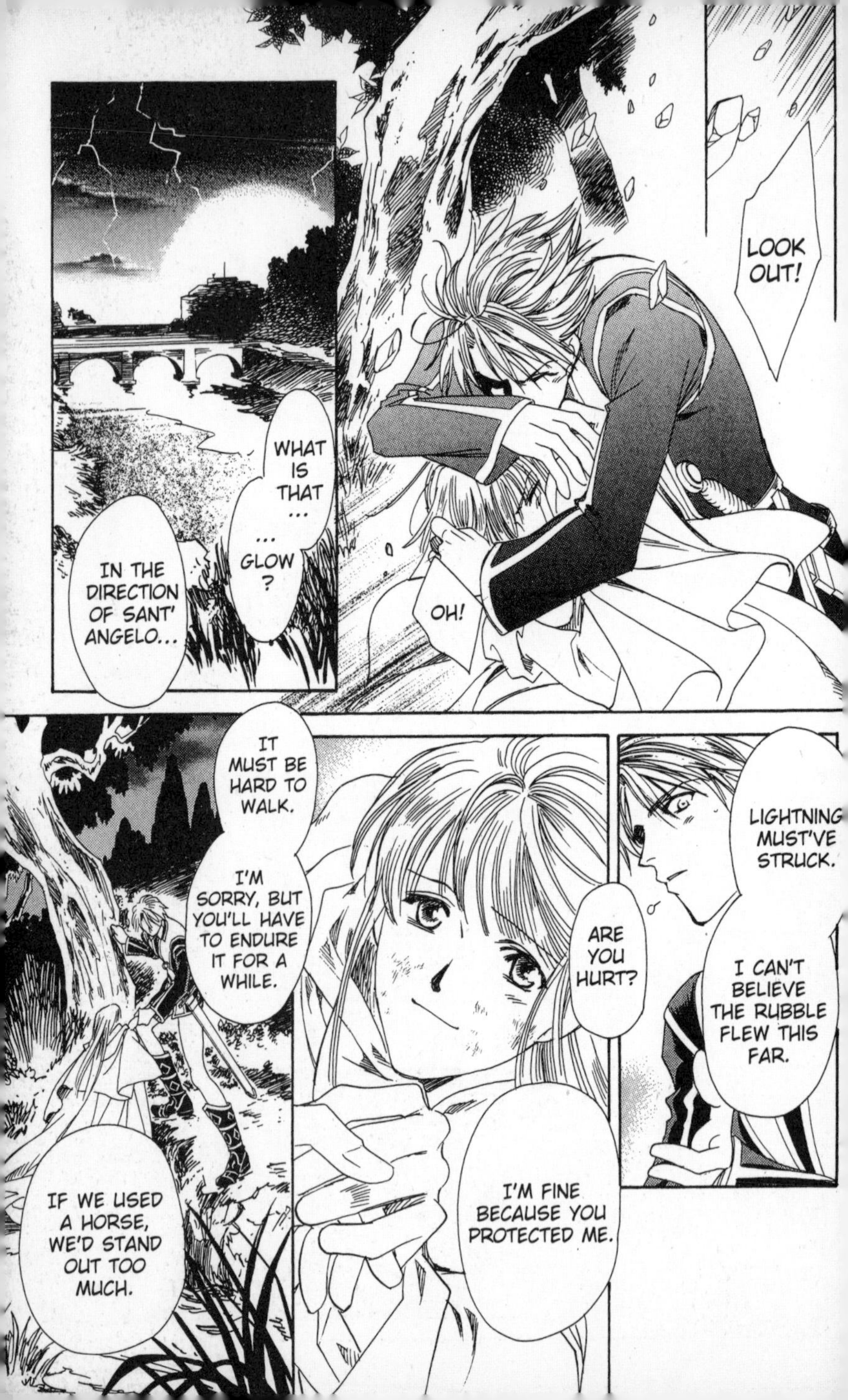
LOOK OUT!
OH!
WHAT IS THAT ... ... GLOW?
IN THE DIRECTION OF SANT' ANGELO...
LIGHTNING MUST'VE STRUCK.
I CAN'T BELIEVE THE RUBBLE FLEW THIS FAR.
ARE YOU HURT?
I'M FINE BECAUSE YOU PROTECTED ME.
IT MUST BE HARD TO WALK.
I'M SORRY, BUT YOU'LL HAVE TO ENDURE IT FOR A WHILE.
IF WE USED A HORSE, WE'D STAND OUT TOO MUCH.

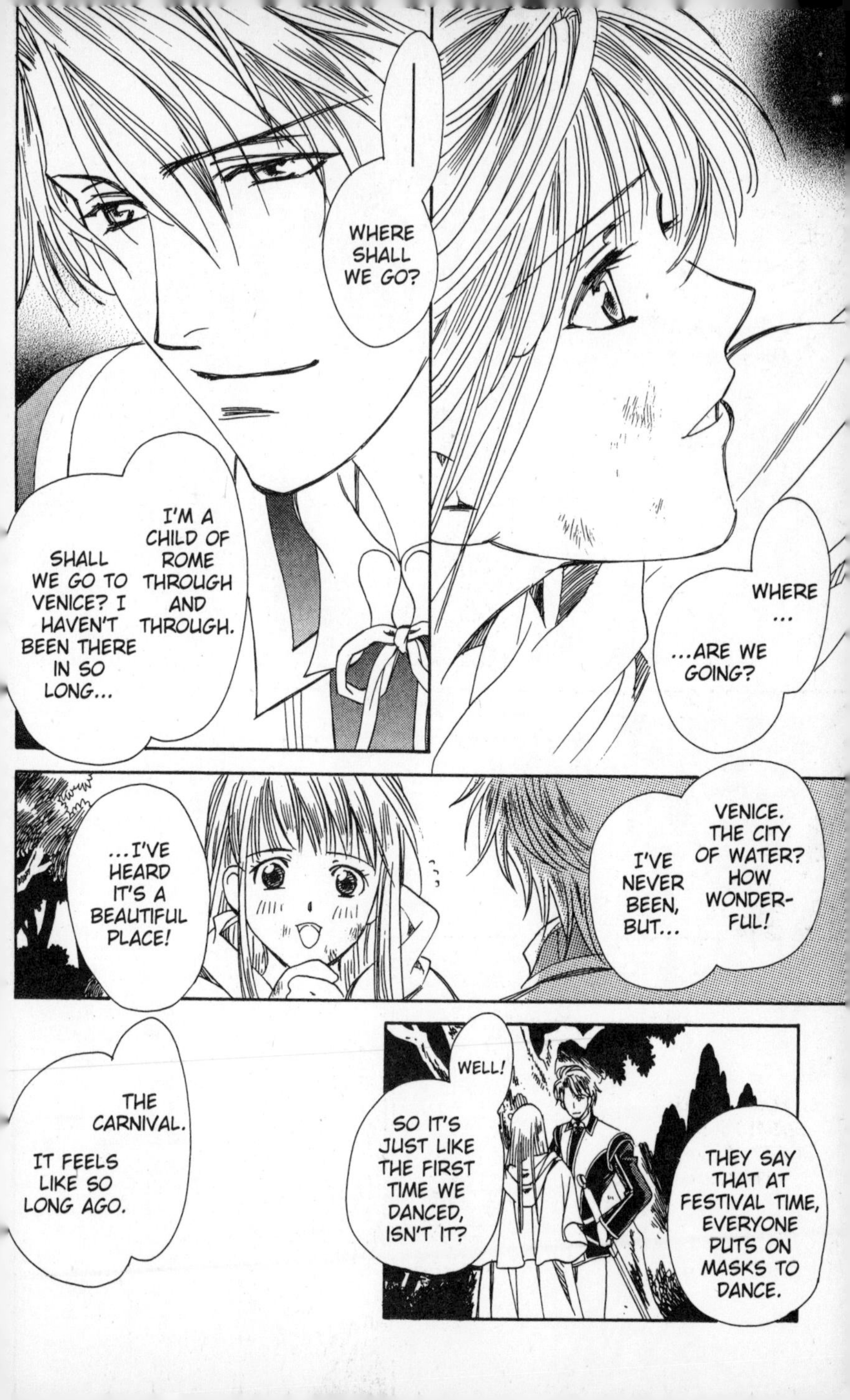
WHERE ... ...ARE WE GOING?
WHERE SHALL WE GO?
I'M A CHILD OF ROME THROUGH AND THROUGH.
SHALL WE GO TO VENICE? I HAVEN'T BEEN THERE IN SO LONG...
VENICE. THE CITY OF WATER? HOW WONDER-FUL!
I'VE NEVER BEEN, BUT...
...I'VE HEARD IT'S A BEAUTIFUL PLACE!
THEY SAY THAT AT FESTIVAL TIME, EVERYONE PUTS ON MASKS TO DANCE.
WELL!
SO IT'S JUST LIKE THE FIRST TIME WE DANCED, ISN'T IT?
THE CARNIVAL.
IT FEELS LIKE SO LONG AGO.

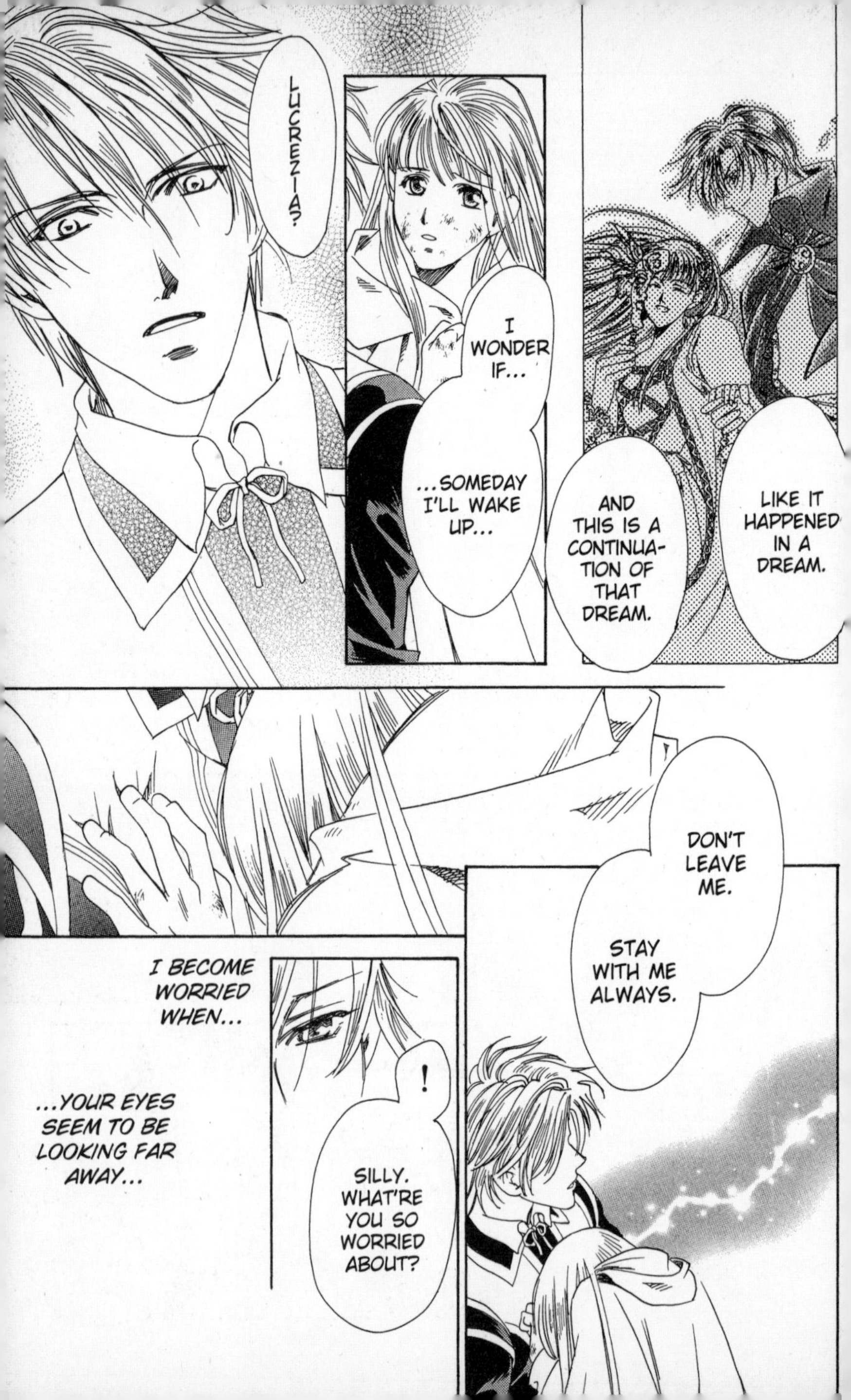
LIKE IT HAPPENED IN A DREAM.
AND THIS IS A CONTINUATION OF THAT DREAM.
I WONDER IF...
...SOMEDAY I'LL WAKE UP...
LUCREZIA?
DON'T LEAVE ME.
STAY WITH ME ALWAYS.
SILLY. WHAT'RE YOU SO WORRIED ABOUT?
!
I BECOME WORRIED WHEN...
...YOUR EYES SEEM TO BE LOOKING FAR AWAY...

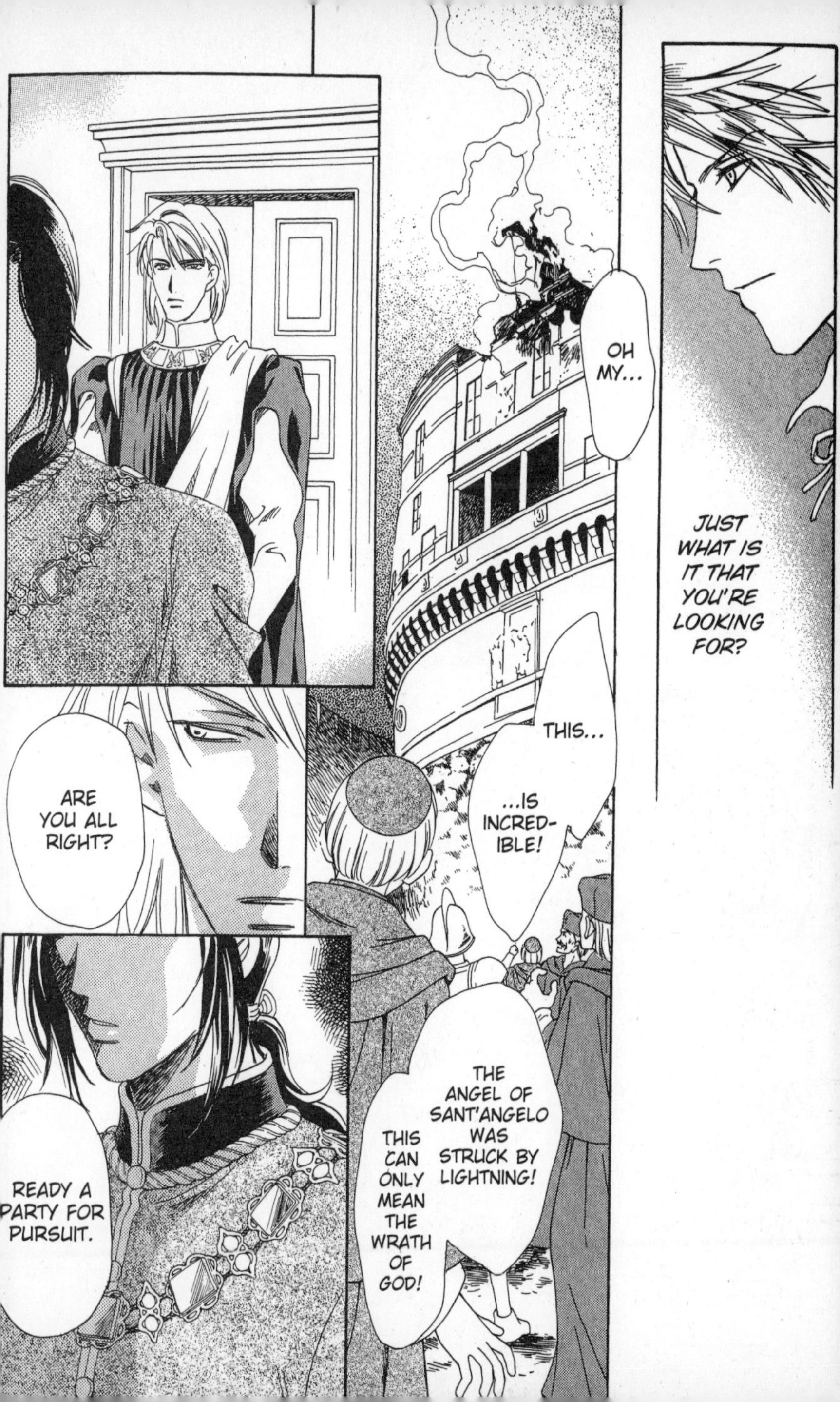
JUST WHAT IS IT THAT YOU'RE LOOKING FOR?
OH MY...
THIS...
...IS INCREDIBLE!
THE ANGEL OF SANT'ANGELO WAS STRUCK BY LIGHTNING!
THIS CAN ONLY MEAN THE WRATH OF GOD!
ARE YOU ALL RIGHT?
READY A PARTY FOR PURSUIT.

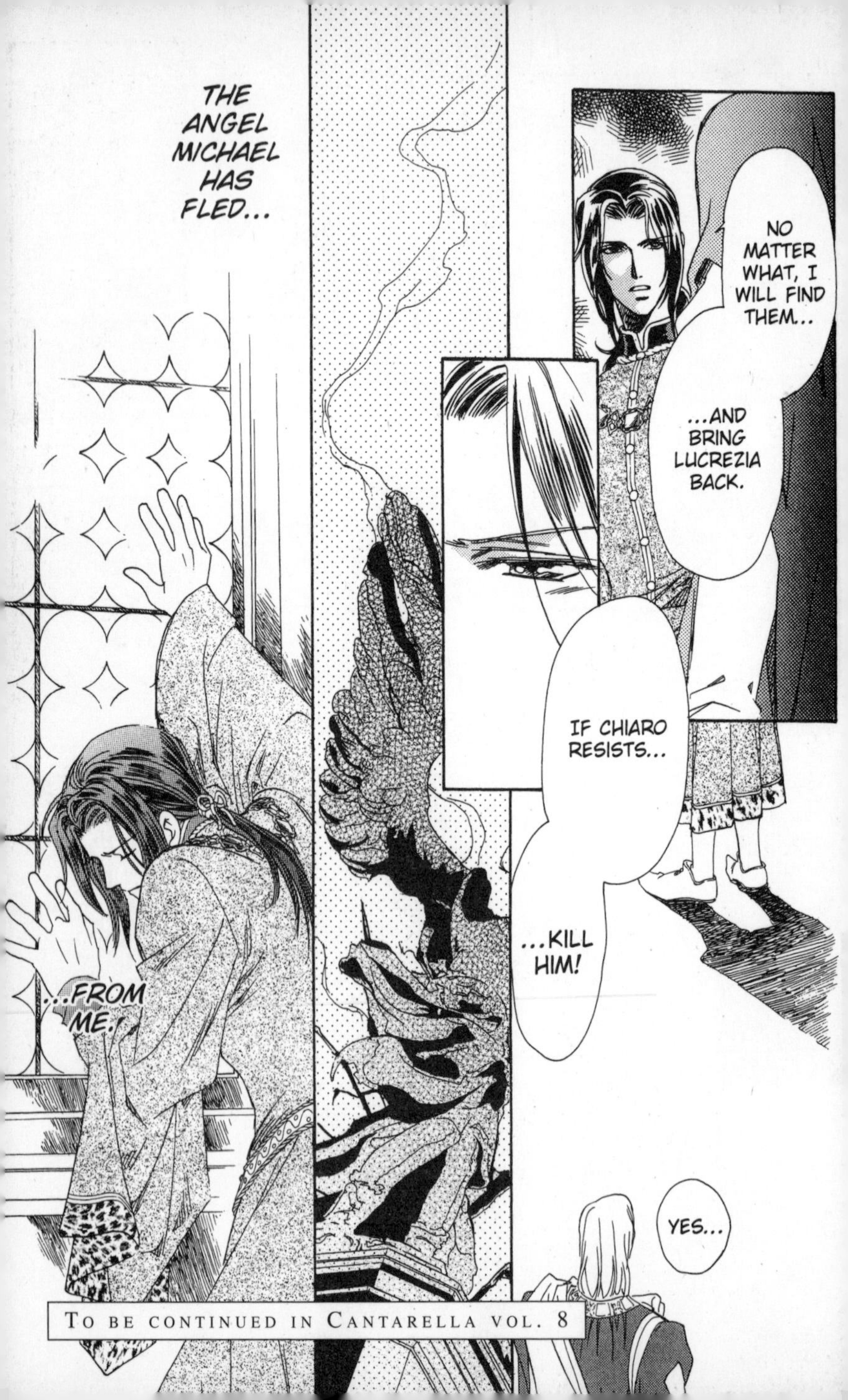
NO MATTER WHAT, I WILL FIND THEM..
...AND BRING LUCREZIA BACK.
IF CHIARO RESISTS...
...KILL HIM!
YES...
THE ANGEL MICHAEL HAS FLED...
...FROM ME.

To be continued in Cantarella vol. 8

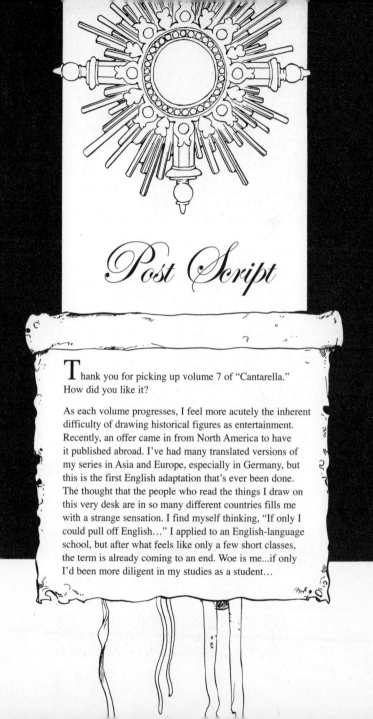

Post Script

Thank you for picking up volume 7 of "Cantarella." How did you like it?

As each volume progresses, I feel more acutely the inherent difficulty of drawing historical figures as entertainment. Recently, an offer came in from North America to have it published abroad. I've had many translated versions of my series in Asia and Europe, especially in Germany, but this is the first English adaptation that's ever been done. The thought that the people who read the things I draw on this very desk are in so many different countries fills me with a strange sensation. I find myself thinking, "If only I could pull off English..." I applied to an English-language school, but after what feels like only a few short classes, the term is already coming to an end. Woe is me...if only I'd been more diligent in my studies as a student...

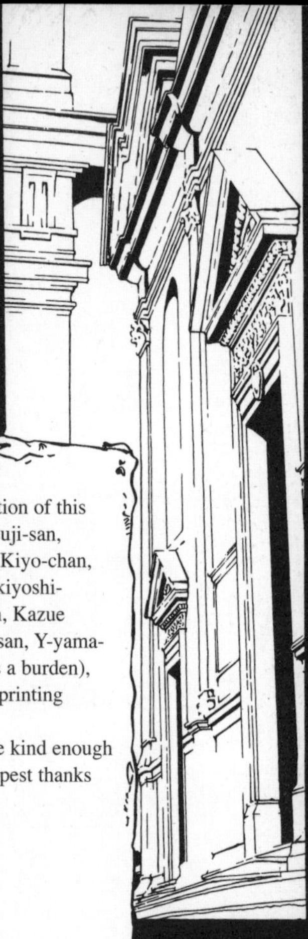

To those who cooperated in the creation of this manga: Izumi Hijiri-san, Naoko Nakatsuji-san, Chiiko In-san, Wakusa Miyakoshi-san, Kiyo-chan, Kana Kitahara-san, Koh Ozawa-san, Akiyoshi-san, Aya Kuriuta-san, Akiko Tahara-san, Kazue Shimazawa-san, my Chief Ryoka Oda-san, Y-yama-san (my manager to whom I am always a burden), all my editors, and to the people at the printing company…thank you very much.
And to all my readers out there who are kind enough to pick up this book and buy it, my deepest thanks from the bottom of my heart.

My best regards for the next volume.
Address for letters ♥:

You Higuri
c/o Audry Taylor
Go! Media Entertainment, LLC
5737 Kanan Rd. #591
Agoura Hills CA 91301

Or visit her official website in English at:
http://www.youhiguri.com

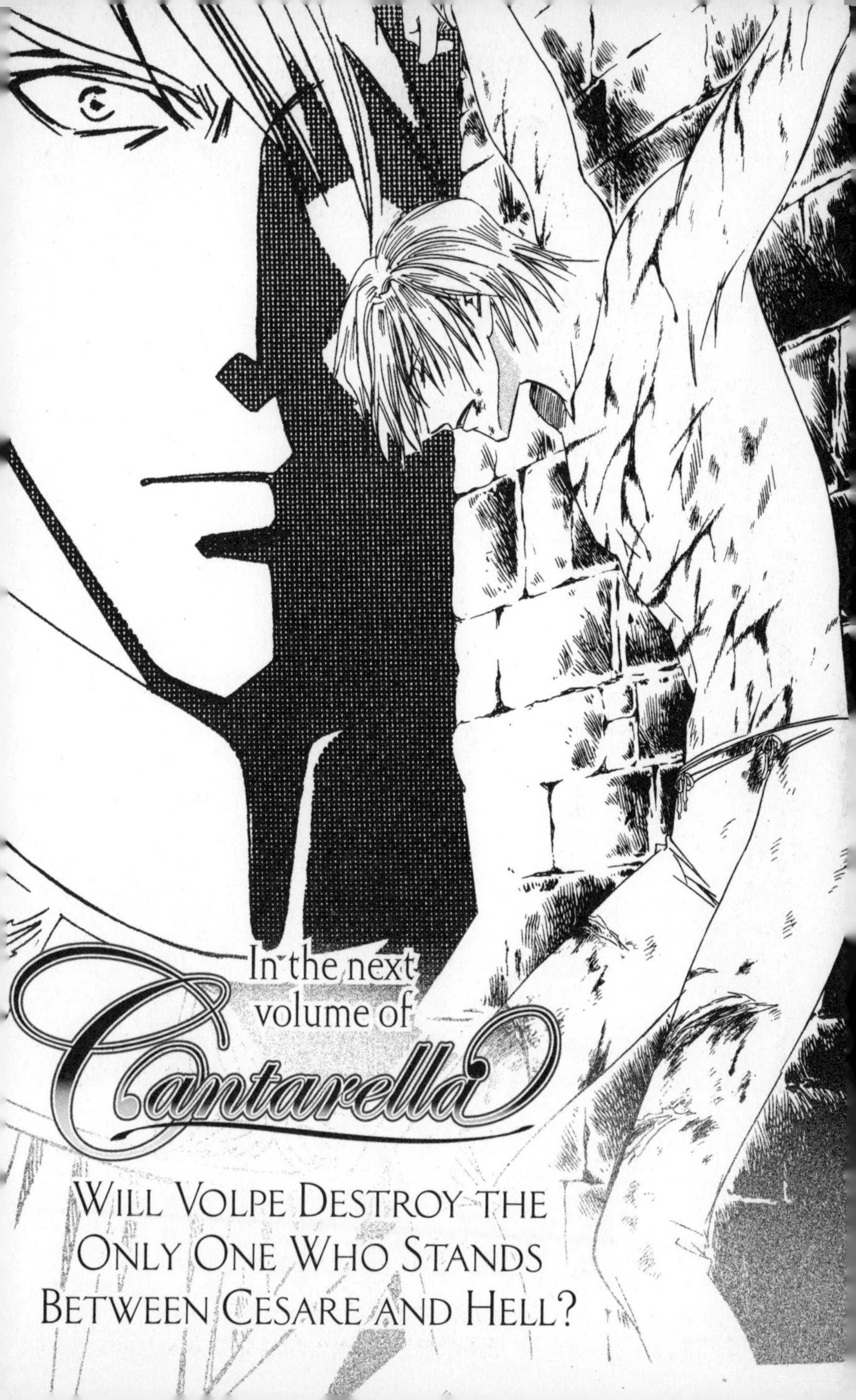
In the next volume of
Cantarella
WILL VOLPE DESTROY THE ONLY ONE WHO STANDS BETWEEN CESARE AND HELL?

Cantarella FAN ART

JIM C.
PLYMOUTH MEETING, PA

JADE W.
RAPID FALLS, SD

Claire Leslie

CLAIRE L.
HATFIELD, PA

Cantarella FAN ART

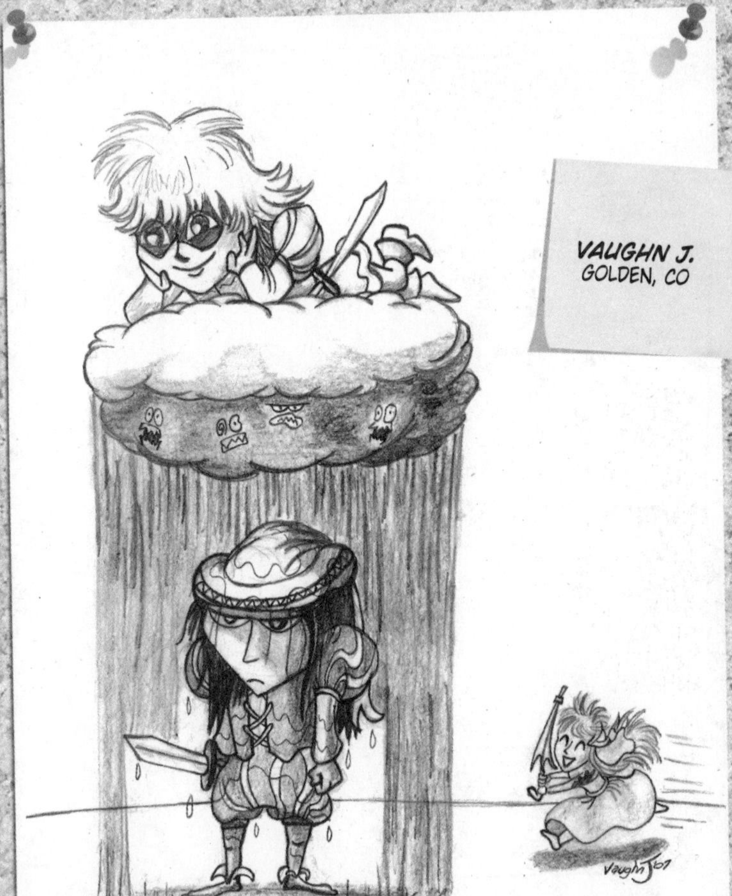

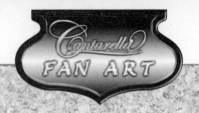

VAUGHN J.
GOLDEN, CO

Cantarella

FAN ART

YOU REMEMBER WE TALKED ABOUT USING THEM FOR TRIFLES?
Cesare
zing!
zang!
BUT.
DON'T YA THINK THIS IS A WEE BIT UN-NECESSARY?
I'll take this one too!
AND I KNOW IT'S YOUR SISTER'S BIRTH DAY.
tra la la...
NONSENSE! I COULD NEVER CARRY ALL THESE ALONE!

SARA H.
SIMI VALLEY, CA

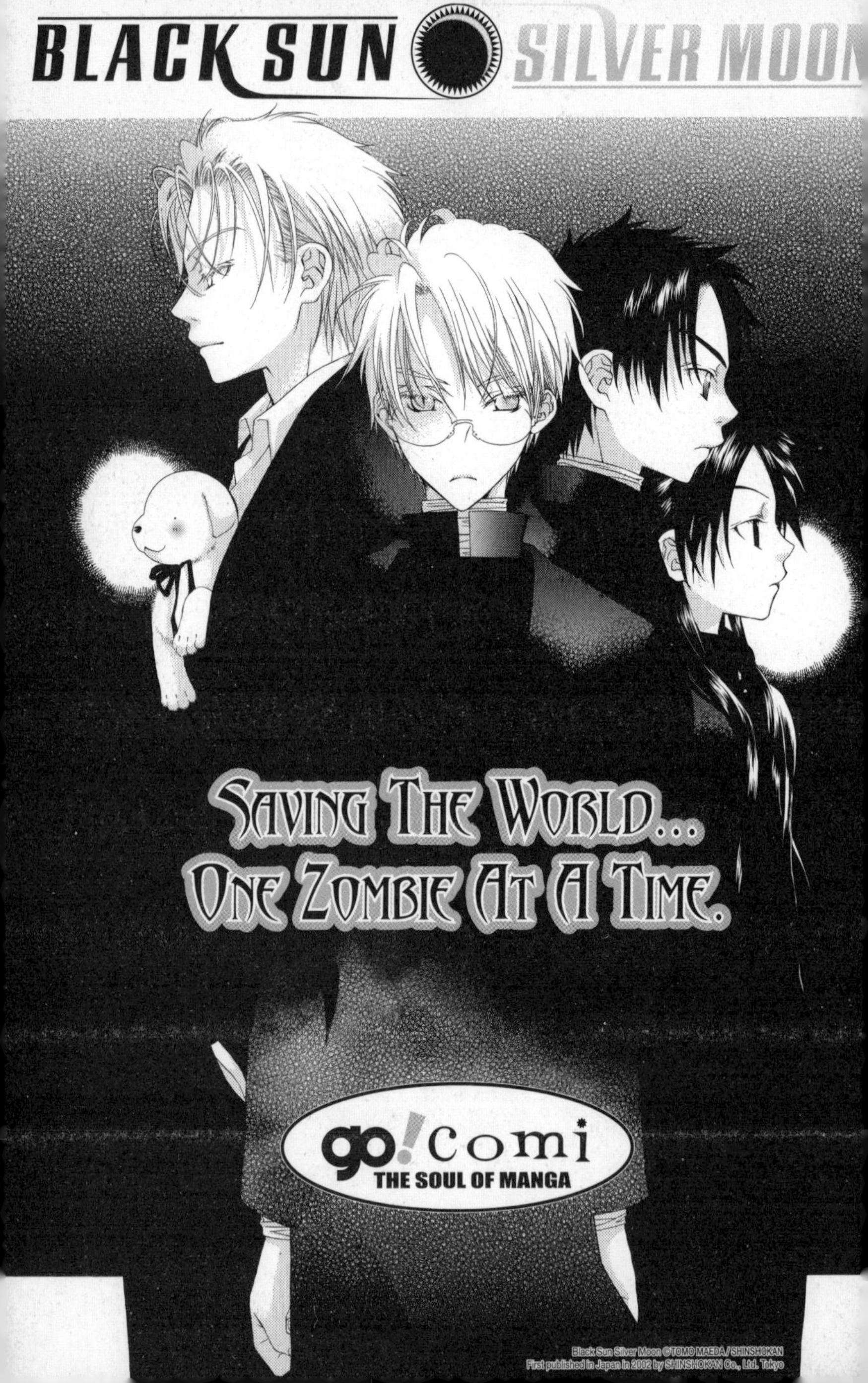

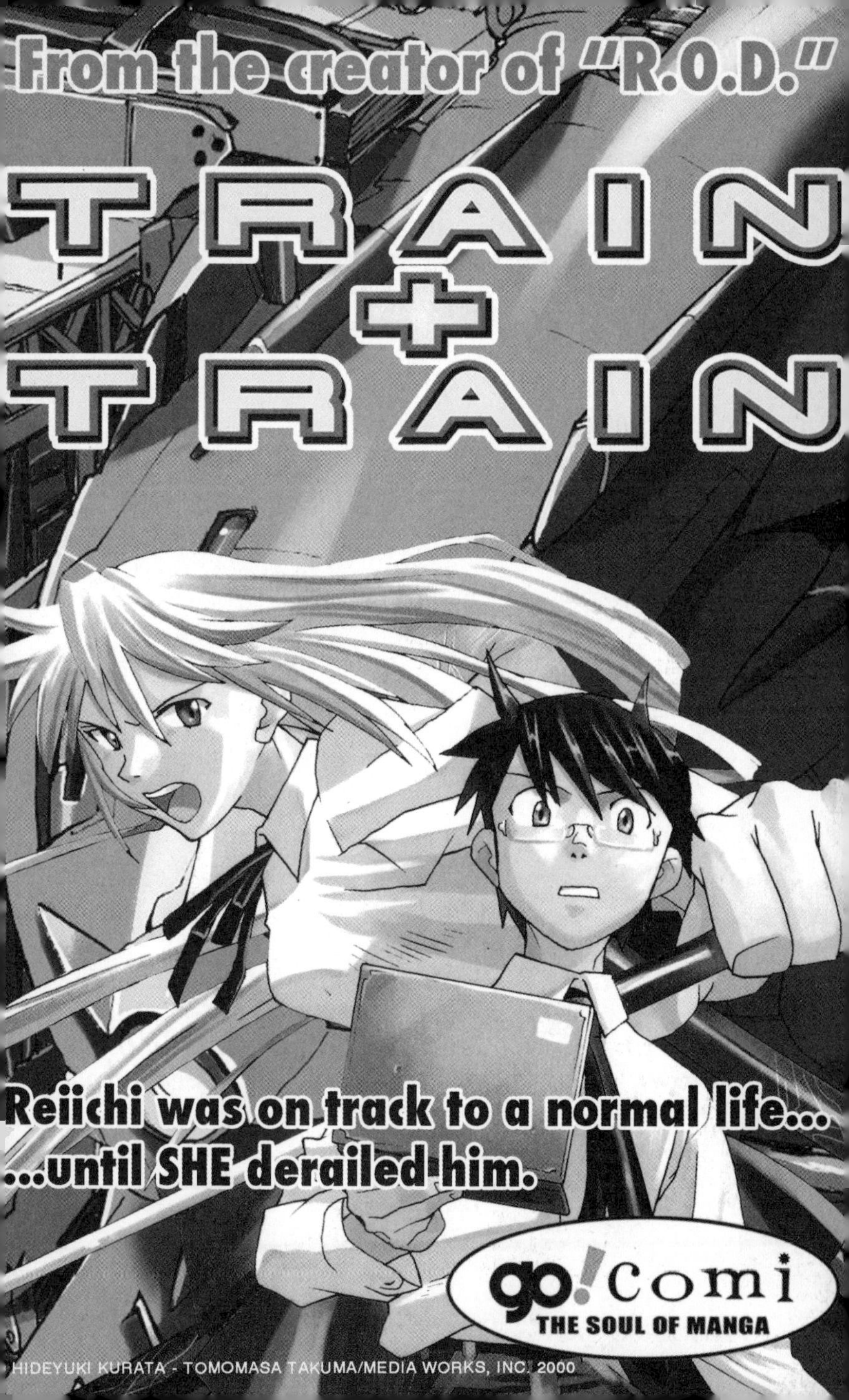
From the creator of "R.O.D."
TRAIN + TRAIN
Reiichi was on track to a normal life...
...until SHE derailed him.
go!comi
THE SOUL OF MANGA
HIDEYUKI KURATA - TOMOMASA TAKUMA/MEDIA WORKS, INC. 2000

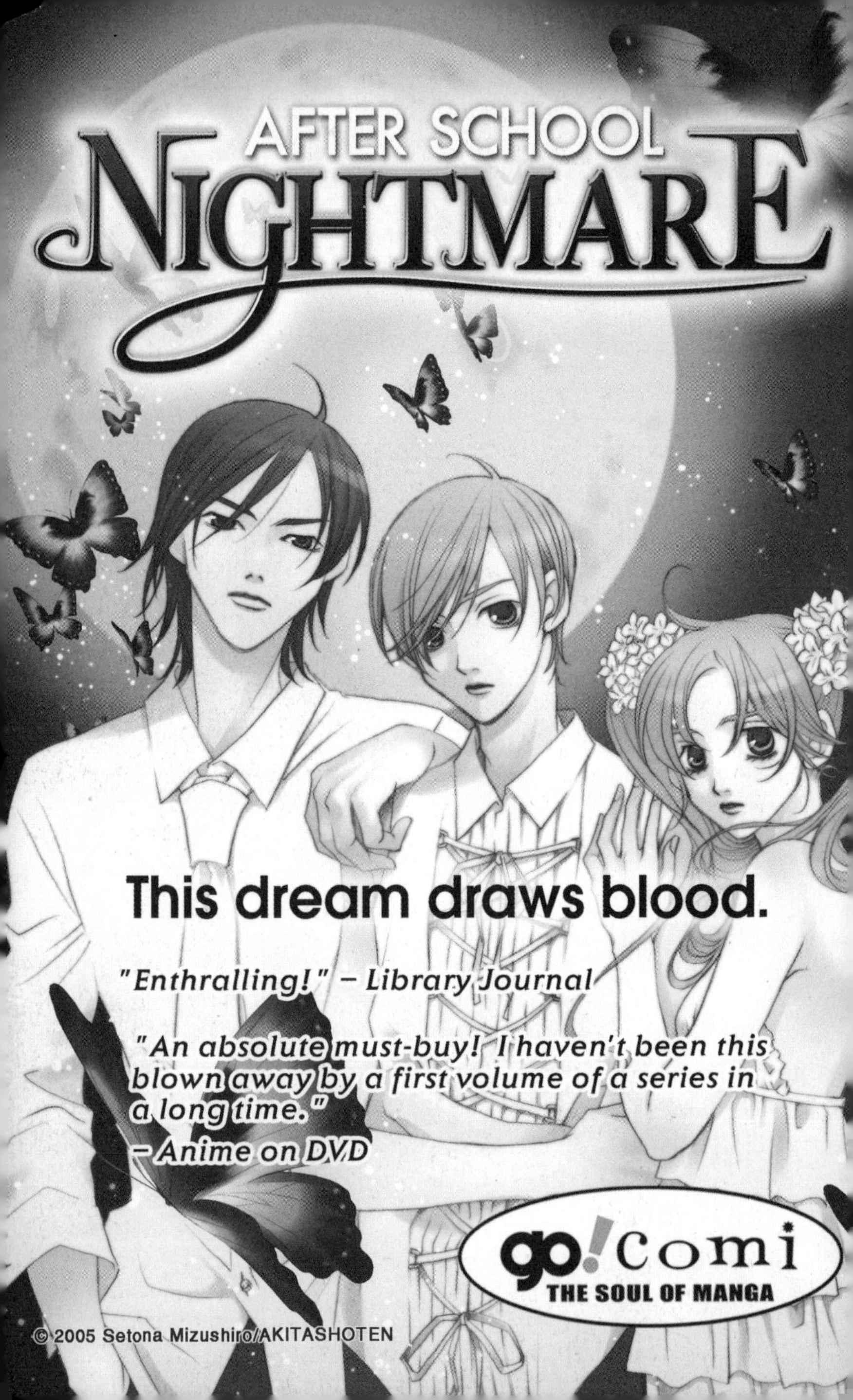
AFTER SCHOOL
NIGHTMARE
This dream draws blood.
"Enthralling!" – Library Journal
"An absolute must-buy! I haven't been this blown away by a first volume of a series in a long time."
– Anime on DVD
go!comi
THE SOUL OF MANGA
© 2005 Setona Mizushiro/AKITASHOTEN

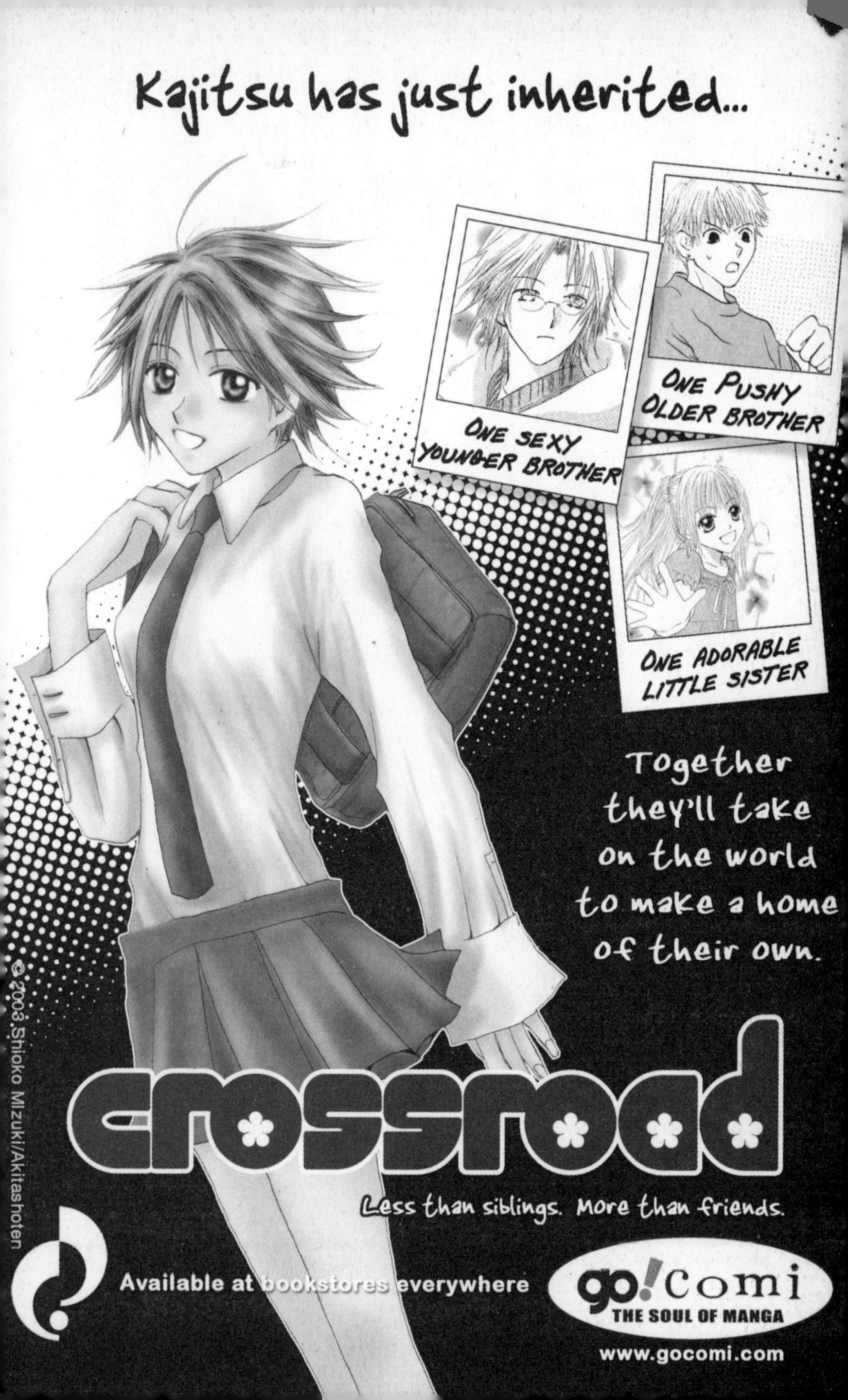
Kajitsu has just inherited...
ONE SEXY YOUNGER BROTHER
ONE PUSHY OLDER BROTHER
ONE ADORABLE LITTLE SISTER
Together they'll take on the world to make a home of their own.
© 2003 Shioko Mizuki/Akitashoten
crossroad
Less than siblings. More than friends.
Available at bookstores everywhere
go!comi
THE SOUL OF MANGA
www.gocomi.com

The Nation's Largest Anime/Manga Convention
June 29-July 2, 2007
Long Beach Convention Center

www.anime-expo.org

Huge Exhibit Hall
Concerts
Film & Video Programming
Masquerade
Cosplay Events
Special Guests
Panels
Autograph Sessions
Summer Festival
Karaoke
Game Shows
Anime Music Video Contest
Art Show
Art Exhibition
Console & Tabletop Gaming
Dances
Charity Auction
& much more!

illustrated by Zelda C. Wang

AUTHOR'S NOTE

I've recently become obsessed with shochu.*
It's fun that there are so many different flavors,
like rice, barley, potato, and black sugar. I like
wine, too, but since my accident (see "Higuri's
Italian Gadget" in volume 5), I haven't been able
to open a bottle of the stuff by myself...

*Editor's Note: Shochu is a nickname for the
Korean equivalent of Japanese sake.

Visit You Higuri online at
www.youhiguri.com